Brilliant
Microsoft®
Office 2007

Tips and
Tricks

Paul McFedries

PEARSON
Prentice
Hall

Harlow, England • London • New York • Boston • San Francisco • Toronto
Sydney • Tokyo • Singapore • Hong Kong • Seoul • Taipei • New Delhi
Cape Town • Madrid • Mexico City • Amsterdam • Munich • Paris • Milan

Contents at

Pearson Education Limited
Edinburgh Gate
Harlow
Essex CM20 2JE
England

and Associated Companies throughout the world

Visit us on the World Wide Web at:
www.pearsoned.co.uk

Original edition, TRICKS OF THE MICROSOFT OFFICE GURUS, 1st edition,
9780789736666 by PAUL MCFEDRIES., published by Pearson Education, Inc,
publishing as Que/Sams, Copyright © 2007 Que Publishing.

This UK edition published by PEARSON EDUCATION LTD, Copyright © 2008

This edition is manufactured in the UK and available for sale only in the United
Kingdom, Europe, the Middle East and Africa

The right of Paul McFedries to be identified as author of this work has been asserted
by him in accordance with the Copyright, Designs and Patents Act 1988.

ISBN: 978-0-273-71576-4

British Library Cataloguing-in-Publication Data
A catalogue record for this book is available from the British Library

10 9 8 7 6 5 4 3 2 1
12 11 10 09 08

Printed and bound by Ashford Colour Press, Gosport, Hants.

The publisher's policy is to use paper manufactured from sustainable forests.

Table of Contents

II MICROSOFT EXCEL TRICKS

IV MICROSOFT OUTLOOK TRICKS

APPENDICES

About the Author

Paul McFedries is the president of Logophilia Limited, a technical writing company. Now primarily a writer, Paul has worked as a programmer, consultant, spreadsheet developer, and Web site developer. He has written more than 50 books that have sold more than three million copies worldwide. These books include *Brilliant Microsoft Access 2007 Forms, Reports, and Queries* (Prentice Hall, 2008), *Brilliant Microsoft Excel 2007 Formulas and Functions* (Prentice Hall, 2008), *Brilliant VBA for Microsoft Office 2007* (Prentice Hall, 2008), and *Windows Vista Unleashed* (Sams, 2006).

Dedication

To Karen and Gypsy.

Acknowledgments

Being an author is the most wonderful vocation (I don't think of it as a job) I can imagine. I get to play with words, I get to talk about things I'm intensely interested in, and I get some big-time warm, fuzzy feelings when people write to me to tell me that, in some small way, something I've written has helped them.

However, just because my name is the only one that appears on the cover, don't think that this book is solely my creation. Any book is the result of the efforts of many hard-working people. The Que editorial staff, in particular, never fails to impress me with its dedication, work ethic, and commitment to quality. There are a few I'd like to thank personally: acquisitions editor Loretta Yates, development editor Todd Brakke, project editor San Dee Phillips, copy editor Ginny Munroe, and technical editor Greg Perry.

INTRODUCTION

It has been estimated that although Microsoft Office 2007 contains more than 10,000 features, the average user is familiar with only about 150 of them. That means that most people have left a whopping 98.5 percent of Office territory unexplored. In practical terms, it also means that most people aren't taking advantage of the power of the Office suite. It means that most people work inefficiently by trying to make the techniques they know serve a wide range of situations, and it means that most people work ineffectively because they aren't aware of techniques that could solve their problems and add sophistication to their documents.

You'll no doubt be happy to hear that the goal of this book is *not* to give you a tour of the 98.5 percent (or whatever) of Office features that you may be unfamiliar with now. I don't know anyone who wants to learn *all* of Office. Instead, the purpose here is to share with you the tips, shortcuts, and little-known techniques—in short, the *tricks*—that I've amassed in my nearly 20 years of wrestling with the Office programs. You'll also no doubt be happy to hear that this book shuns what I call "stunt tricks," which are those arcane and useless tips that have no purpose in the real world and serve only to show off the knowledge and smarts of the writers. A pox on their houses! This book is grounded firmly in the real world of business and other practical concerns, and the tricks I offer are designed to help you work better, faster, safer, and smarter.

What's in the Book?

This book isn't meant to be read from cover to cover, although you're certainly free to do just that if the mood strikes you. Instead, most of the chapters are set up as self-contained units that you can dip into at will to extract whatever nuggets of information you need. The book is divided into five main parts, each of which covers a major Office application. To give you the big picture before diving in, here's a summary of what you'll find in each part:

- Part 1, "Microsoft Word Tricks"—The chapters in Part 1 offer up a collection of tricks for Word in four categories: "Text Tricks" (Chapter 1), "Formatting Tricks" (Chapter 2), "Document Tricks" (Chapter 3), and "Page Layout Tricks" (Chapter 4).

- Part 2, "Microsoft Excel Tricks"—The chapters in Part 2 focus on Excel, and I've gathered up my favorite spreadsheet tricks in four categories: "Formula and Functions Tricks" (Chapter 5), "Workbook and Worksheet Tricks" (Chapter 6), "Data Analysis Tricks" (Chapter 7), and "Chart Tricks" (Chapter 8).

- Part 3, "Microsoft PowerPoint Tricks"—This part presents three chapters that help you take your PowerPoint presentations to the next level. You learn "Slide and Presentation Tricks" (Chapter 9), "Animation Tricks" (Chapter 10), and "Slide Show Tricks" (Chapter 11).

- Part 4, "Microsoft Outlook Tricks"—The chapters in Part 4 concentrate on Outlook and present a large collection of tricks in two categories: "Email Tricks" (Chapter 12) and "Calendar and Contacts Tricks" (Chapter 13).

- Part 5, "Microsoft Access Tricks"—The book closes with a look at a program we can also use some help with: Microsoft Access. You learn "Table and Query Tricks" (Chapter 14) and "Form and Report Tricks" (Chapter 15).

This Book's Special Features

Brilliant Microsoft Office 2007 Tips and Tricks is designed to give you the information you need without making you wade through ponderous explanations and interminable technicalities. To make your life easier, this book includes various features and conventions that help you get the most out of the book and from Excel. These include the following:

- Steps—Throughout the book, each Office task is summarized in step-by-step procedures.

- Things you type—Whenever I suggest that you type something, what you type appears in a **bold** font.

- Commands—I use the following style for menu commands: <u>F</u>ile, <u>O</u>pen. This means that you pull down the File menu and select the Open command.

- Code-continuation character (➥)—When a line of code is too long to fit on a single line of this book, it's broken at a convenient place, and the code-continuation character displays at the beginning of the next line.

This book also uses the following boxes to draw your attention to important (or merely interesting) information.

The Note box presents asides that give you more information about the topic under discussion. These tidbits provide extra insights that give you a better understanding of the task at hand.

NOTE

The Tip box tells you about Office methods that are easier, faster, or more efficient than the standard methods.

TIP

The all-important Caution box tells you about potential accidents waiting to happen. There are always ways to mess things up when you're working with computers. These boxes help you avoid

CAUTION

at least some of the pitfalls.

→ These cross-reference elements point you to related material elsewhere in the book.

Microsoft Word Tricks

Text Tricks

1

Microsoft Word just might be the most used productivity program in the world. Its user base is measured in the hundreds of millions (only Excel boasts comparable numbers), and if you work in an Office shop, chances are that you use Word at least some of the time (and probably a lot of the time). Unfortunately, using Word and getting the most out of Word are often different things. Part of the problem is the sheer size of the program, which comes with hundreds of separate commands, many of which redefine the word *obscure*. However, another part of the problem is that Word is chock full of truly useful commands and features that can make your life easier and your work more efficient. This book's Word chapters are designed to introduce you to these great features and to show you how to incorporate them into your working life.

This chapter gets you started by showing you more than 20 tricks that help you tame text in Word. You learn how to make tables easier to read by keeping the headings in view; how to perform useful table calculations; how to quickly enter boilerplate and dummy text; how to take advantage of hyperlinks; how to analyze your documents by displaying sentence word counts and the longest sentence; how to create a custom spelling check dictionary, and much more.

Keeping Table Headings in View

Word's tables are a great way to neatly and efficiently display row and column data. In addition, with the new table styles in Word 2007, you can make great looking tables with just a mouse click or two. However, multi-page tables suffer from a glaring drawback: The table's header row appears only on the first page, so when you navigate to any other page, the header row disappears, and your data becomes much harder to read.

One way to solve this problem is to split the document window into two panes: You keep the table's header row visible in the top pane and use the bottom pane to navigate the rest of the table. To split the document window, you have two choices:

■ Choose View, Split to display the split bar. Use your mouse or keyboard (the Up and Down arrows) to move the split bar to the bottom edge of the header row and then click (or press Enter).

■ Click and drag the Split button that displays at the top of the vertical scroll bar (above the View Ruler button) and then drop it on the bottom edge of the header row.

Figure 1.1 shows a document window split with the top pane showing the header row and the bottom pane showing the rest of the table. To return to the regular document view, either choose View, Remove Split or double-click the split bar.

Figure 1.1
Split the document window into two panes to keep table headings in view.

Split Bar   Top Pane

Bottom Pane

Another solution to the problem is to configure the table to repeat its header row on each page. This isn't quite as nice as splitting the window because the header row still scrolls off the top of screen if your current settings don't allow you to see at least one full page of data at a time. However, it does make your document easier to navigate, and the header row also displays at the top of each page if you print the document.

NOTE How do you see at least one full page of a document at all times? There are two ways to get this "big picture." In Word, adjust the Zoom setting down until you see the entire page. The easiest way to do this is to hold down Ctrl and then rotate the wheel button on your mouse (forward to increase the zoom; backward to decrease the zoom). You can also choose View, Zoom (or click the Zoom Level value in the status bar), click the Whole Page option, and click OK. Alternatively, increase Windows' screen resolution. In Vista, right-click the desktop, click Personalize, click Display Settings, and then drag the Resolution slider toward High. In Windows XP, right-click the desktop, click Properties, display the Settings tab, and then drag the Screen Resolution slider towards More.

To display the header row at the top of each page, click inside the table to activate the Table Tools tab, and then choose Layout, Repeat Header Rows. Figure 1.2 shows a two-page view (choose View, Two Pages) in which you can see the header row at the top of both pages.

Figure 1.2
Activate the Repeat Header Rows command to see your table's header row at the top of each page.

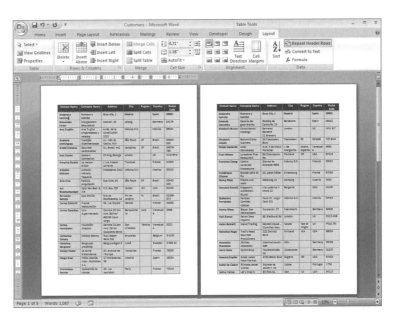

Summing a Column in a Table

Word tables are useful for organizing text into rows and columns and for providing an attractive layout option for lists and other data. However, tables get especially powerful and dynamic when you apply formulas to the numeric data contained within a table's rows or columns. For example, if you have a table of sales for various departments, you can display the total sales in a cell at the bottom of the table. Similarly, if your table contains an invoice with a column showing the subtotals for each item, you can display the invoice total in a cell.

The trick to using formulas within tables is to reference the table cells correctly. The easiest way to do this is to use *relative referencing*, which is built into Word tables:

Relative Reference	Refers To
ABOVE	All the cells above the formula cell in the same column.
BELOW	All the cells below the formula cell in the same column.
LEFT	All the cells to the left of the formula cell in the same row.
RIGHT	All the cells to the right of the formula cell in the same row.

To display the sum of the values that display in the column above a cell, you place the formula =SUM(ABOVE) in a Word field in that cell:

1. Click inside the cell.
2. Press Ctrl+F9 to create a new Word field.
3. Type =SUM(ABOVE).
4. Press F9. Word updates the cell to display the sum of the cells above it.

Figure 1.3 shows an example of this formula field in action in the SUBTOTAL cell (showing the result $82.22). Note that this cell is bookmarked with the name Subtotal so that I can use that name in a formula. (I discuss this in more detail later in this chapter; see "Calculating Tax in an Invoice Document.")

Formula is =SUM(ABOVE)

Figure 1.3
The subtotal in this invoice document is calculated using a field with the formula =SUM(ABOVE).

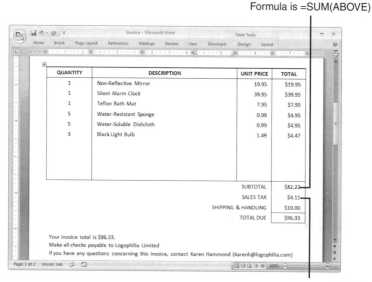

Formula is =Subtotal * .05

This example uses the SUM function, but Word offers several others you can take advantage of; they are listed in Table 1.1.

Function	Returns
Table 1.1	**Word's Formula Field Functions**
ABS(x)	The absolute value of x.
AND(x,y)	1 if both x and y are true; 0 otherwise.
AVERAGE(x,y,z,...)	The average of the list of values given by x,y,z,....
COUNT(x,y,z,...)	The number of items in the list of values given by x,y,z,....
DEFINED(x)	1 if the expression x can be calculated; 0 otherwise.
FALSE	0.
INT(x)	The integer portion of x.
MIN(x,y,z,...)	The smallest value in the list of values given by x,y,z,....
MAX(x,y,z,...)	The largest value in the list of values given by x,y,z,....
MOD(x,y)	The remainder after dividing x by y.
NOT(x)	1 if x is false; 0 if x is true.
OR(x,y)	1 if either or both x and y are true; 0 if both x and y are false.
PRODUCT(x,v,z,....)	The result of multiplying together the items in the list of values given by x,y,z,...
ROUND(x,y)	The value of x rounded to the number of decimal places specified by y.
SIGN(x)	1 if x is positive; –1 if x is negative.
SUM(x,y,z,...)	The sum of the items in the list of values given by x,y,z,....
TRUE	1.

Calculating Tax in an Invoice Document

Another common table calculation is the tax on an invoice based on the subtotal of the items. To perform this calculation, you also use a field, but becuase you need to refer to specific cells in the formula, you should use *absolute referencing*, which is similar to Excel's cell referencing. That is, the table columns are assigned the letters A (for the first column), B (for the second column), and so on; the table rows are assigned the numbers 1 (for the first row), 2 (for the second row), and so on. Following are some examples:

Absolute Reference	Refers To
A1	The cell in the first row and first column.
D5	The cell in the fifth row and fourth column.
A1,D5	The cells A1 and D5.
A1:D5	The rectangular range of cells created by A1 in the top-left corner and D5 in the bottom-right corner.
B:B	All the cells in the second column.
3:3	All the cells in the third row.

In the invoice shown in Figure 1.3, for example, the total for the Non-Reflective Mirror item is derived using the following formula field:

```
{ =A2 * C2 }
```

> **CAUTION**
>
> If you want to use an absolute reference for an entire column (such as A:A) or an entire row (such as 1:1), make sure you place your formula in a different row or column. For example, consider the following formula field:
>
> ```
> { =SUM(A:A) }
> ```
>
> This sums all the cell values in the first column. However, if you insert the field into a cell in column A, the field result will be included in the sum the next time you update the field. In Excel, this is flagged as a circular reference. In Word, you just get the wrong answer.

Finally, you can also use bookmarks to create formulas that have "named" operands. For example, if you select a cell and insert a bookmark named GrossMargin, you can refer to that cell using the bookmark name, as in this example:

```
{ =B3 * GrossMargin }
```

In the invoice document shown in Figure 1.3, I assigned a bookmark named Subtotal to the subtotal cell. To calculate the sales tax value (assuming 5 percent sales tax), I used the following formula field:

```
{ = Subtotal * .05 }
```

> **NOTE**
>
> To create a bookmark, select the text and then choose Insert, Bookmark to open the Bookmark dialog box. Type a name in the Bookmark Name text box and then click Add.

Figure 1.4 shows all the formulas used in the invoice. (Note that each formula field also includes \# $0.00. This tells Word to display the result as a dollar value.)

T I P To toggle a field between showing its result and its code, click the field and then press Shift+F9. If you change the data, you can update a field by clicking it and pressing F9.

→ To learn how you can use a macro to update all your fields at once, **see** "Updating All Fields Automatically," see Chapter 3, "Document Tricks," **p. 86**

Figure 1.4
The field formulas used to calculate the values shown in the invoice document in Figure 1.3.

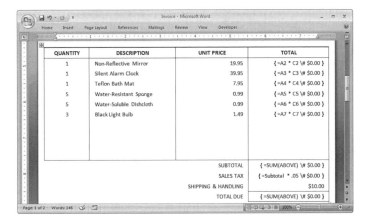

Highlighting All Instances of a Word or Phrase

If you've used the Google toolbar when browsing the web, you may have tried one of its most useful research features: the Highlight button. After you perform a search and navigate to a matching page, clicking this button adds a yellow highlight to all the instances of the search text that appear in the page. It's a great way to see exactly where the information you want resides within a page, how often it appears, and so on.

A similar feature is now part of Word 2007. It's called Reading Highlight, and it's part of the Find feature. Here's how you use it:

1. Choose Home, Find to display the Find tab of the Find and Replace dialog box.
2. Type the text you want to highlight in the Fi<u>n</u>d What text box.
3. Click <u>R</u>eading Highlight and then click <u>H</u>ighlight All. Word applies a highlight to every instance of the text in the document and tells you the number of items it highlighted, as shown in Figure 1.5.
4. To clear the highlights, click <u>R</u>eading Highlight and then click <u>C</u>lear Highlighting.

T I P To control the color of the highlight, choose the Home tab and then click a color in the Text Highlight Color palette.

Figure 1.5
Use Word's new Reading Highlight feature to apply a highlight to each instance of the text in the Find What box.

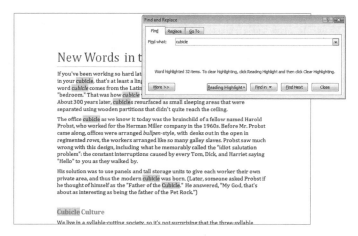

Using AutoCorrect to Insert Your Signature

Not many people know about one of AutoCorrect's most powerful features: Its replacement "text" can also include (or consist of) an image. For example, you can set up an AutoCorrect entry where the word logo is associated with your company logo. Type **logo** and press Enter (you can also press spacebar, tab, or any nonalphanumeric character); Word replaces the text with the image.

This makes it easy to insert any image that you use frequently. A prime example is a scanned version of your signature. This enables you to "sign" any document that you plan on distributing via email or fax.

The first thing you need to do is scan your signature and save it as a graphic file. Sign a piece of paper, insert the paper into your scanner, and then launch your scanning software. If you want to use the Office Document Imaging program, select Start, All Programs, Microsoft Office, Microsoft Office Tools, Microsoft Office Document Scanning. Click the Scan button and then click Close when the scan is complete. In the Office Document Imaging program, choose File, Save, select a name and location for the image, and then click Save.

Now follow these steps to create an AutoCorrect entry for your signature:

1. In Word, choose Insert, Picture, and then click the signature image file. Then click Insert.

2. Select the scanned signature.

3. If there is a lot of white space around the signature, choose Format, Crop, then click and drag the cropping markers so that only your signature remains and then click outside the cropping markers.

4. Select the signature.

5. Select Office, Word Options, click Proofing, and then click <u>A</u>utoCorrect Options to display the AutoCorrect dialog box.

6. Select the AutoCorrect tab.

7. Click <u>F</u>ormatted Text.

8. In the <u>R</u>eplace text box, type an abbreviation or code for the signature (such as **sig**).

9. Click <u>A</u>dd.

10. Click OK and then click OK again in the Word Options dialog box.

Using AutoCorrect to Enter Boilerplate Text

Do you have a phrase, a sentence, or even multiple paragraphs that you use regularly? Typing these bits of boilerplate text can be tedious, and it's certainly time-consuming. To stop throwing away those precious seconds and minutes, you can convince Word to store the boilerplate and then recall it with a few keystrokes. Here's how to store and use boilerplate text with Word's AutoCorrect feature:

1. Select the boilerplate text.

2. Select Office, Word Options, and then click Proofing. Click <u>A</u>utoCorrect Options to display the AutoCorrect dialog box.

3. Select the AutoCorrect tab. Your boilerplate text appears in the <u>W</u>ith text box.

4. If the boilerplate includes formatting, and you want to include that formatting each time you insert the boilerplate, click the <u>F</u>ormatted Text option; otherwise, click the <u>P</u>lain Text option.

> **CAUTION**
>
> The AutoCorrect feature is available in all the major Office applications. However, the formatted AutoCorrect replacements are available only in Word. This can lead to problems if you have a formatted entry defined in Word and a plain text entry from another program that uses the same original text. For example, you might have a formatted entry for *addr* in Word and a plain text entry for *addr* that was defined in Access. If you insert the *addr* entry in Word, you always get the formatted correction. To avoid this confusion, never use the same original text for two different entries.

5. In the <u>R</u>eplace text box, type a short abbreviation or code. For example, if the boilerplate consists of your contact information, you might type **addr**, as shown in Figure 1.6.

6. Click <u>A</u>dd.

7. Click OK and then click OK again in the Word Options dialog box.

Figure 1.6
Use the AutoCorrect tab to enter an abbreviation that "corrects" to display boilerplate text you use often.

To use the boilerplate, type the abbreviation you entered in step 5 and then type a space or punctuation mark or press Tab or Enter.

Saving Boilerplate as an AutoText Building Block

Saving boilerplate text as an AutoCorrect entry is perfect for chunks of text that you insert frequently. However, if you have boilerplate that you need only occasionally, creating an AutoCorrect entry for it is probably overkill. A better solution is to save the text using Word 2007's new Building Blocks feature. Building blocks are bits of text, graphics, and formatting that you store in the Building Blocks Organizer, from which you can insert any item with just a few mouse clicks. Word 2007 comes with dozens of built-in building blocks for cover pages, headers, footers, page numbers, tables, text boxes, watermarks, and more. You save boilerplate text as an AutoText building block.

> **NOTE** In previous versions of Word, you could insert an AutoText entry by typing the first few characters of the entry and pressing Enter. This feature no longer works in Word 2007. To insert an AutoText entry, you must use the Building Blocks Organizer.

Here's how to store and use boilerplate text with Word's AutoText feature:

1. Select the boilerplate text.

TIP Another compelling feature of AutoText is its capability to preserve the formatting of the boilerplate text. To ensure that this happens, when you select the boilerplate text, you must include the paragraph mark at the end of the text. To make this easier, display paragraph marks by activating the Home, Show/Hide ¶ toggle button.

2. Choose Insert, Quick Parts, <u>S</u>ave Selection to Quick Part Gallery. The Create New Building Block dialog box displays, as shown in Figure 1.7.

Figure 1.7
Use the Create New Building Block dialog box to define an AutoText entry for boilerplate text.

3. Type a <u>N</u>ame for the building block.
4. In the <u>G</u>allery list, click AutoText.
5. (Optional) Use the <u>D</u>escription text box to describe the boilerplate.
6. In the <u>O</u>ptions list, click one of the following:
   - Insert Content Only—Click this option to insert the boilerplate text at the cursor's position. The boilerplate picks up the formatting of the surrounding text. (Note that this doesn't work if you included the final paragraph mark in your selection. In that case, Word always inserts the boilerplate in a separate paragraph.)
   - Insert Content In Its Own Paragraph—Click this option to insert the text following a paragraph mark.
   - Insert Content In Its Own Page—Click this option to insert the text on a separate page.
7. Click OK.

To use the boilerplate text, select Insert, Quick Parts, Building Blocks Organizer, click the AutoText entry in the Building Blocks list (see Figure 1.8), and click Insert.

NOTE To get a hard-copy listing of all Word's Building Blocks entries, choose Office, Print to display the Print dialog box. In the Print What list, click Building Blocks Entries.

Figure 1.8
Use the Building Blocks Organizer to insert an AutoText entry.

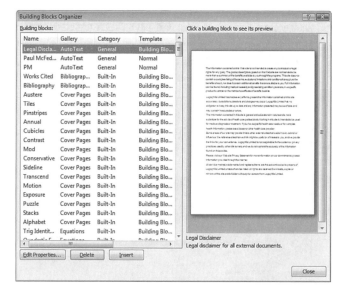

Creating a "Click-and-Type" Text Placeholder

It's often useful to create "click-and-type" text placeholders. The idea is that you click the placeholder, and then you type the required text. Figure 1.9 shows some examples of what I mean. I created this document using Word's Professional theme fax template. As you can see, the document has placeholders, such as [Company Name] and [Street Address].

Figure 1.9
Word's Professional theme fax template includes "click-and-type" text placeholders.

These placeholders are actually fields. Interestingly, in Figure 1.10, look what happens when you expose the field codes for these placeholders.

> **TIP**
> To display the code for a single placeholder field, click the placeholder and then press Shift+F9. To display the code for all the fields in the document, press Alt+F9.

Figure 1.10
The placeholders are really just *MacroButton* fields that reference a nonexistent macro.

{MACROBUTTON DoFieldClick [Street Address]}
{MACROBUTTON DoFieldClick [City, ST Zip Code]}
{MACROBUTTON DoFieldClick [phone]}
{MACROBUTTON DoFieldClick [fax]}
{MACROBUTTON DoFieldClick [Web address]}

{MACROBUTTON DoFieldClick [Company Name]}

Fax

As you can see, each placeholder is actually a MacroButton field:

```
{ MACROBUTTON DoFieldClick [Company Name] }
```

You normally use a MacroButton field to run an existing macro:

```
{ MACROBUTTON MacroName DisplayText }
```

Here, *MacroName* is the name of the macro you want to run, including the project name and module name; *DisplayText* is the text the user double-clicks to launch the macro. (You can also launch the macro by clicking the field and then pressing Alt+Shift+F9.) For example, the following code creates a MacroButton field that displays Update Editing Time and runs the Chapter01.Module1.UpdateEditTime macro:

```
{ MACROBUTTON Chapter01.Module1.UpdateEditTime Update Editing Time }
```

In the placeholder example, the DoFieldClick parameter refers to a nonexistent macro. When you click within the field and begin to type, the field is replaced by the text.

> **CAUTION**
>
> Make sure the fake macro name you use for the placeholder MacroButton field is not the same as a built-in or custom macro that you create. This ensures that the user won't accidentally run the macro.

Asking a User for Text Input

With many templates, the user is required to fill in certain document properties, such as the title, subject, author, or keywords. Ensuring that these values are entered can be a crucial part of a document management system. One way to do this is to use a Fill-in field, which displays a dialog box that prompts the user for data. The entered data is then displayed as the field result:

```
{ FILLIN Prompt }
```

Prompt is the text that appears as a prompt in the dialog box. Here's an example:

```
{ FILLIN "Please enter the document title:" }
```

If you insert this field in a template, Figure 1.11 shows the dialog box that appears when the user creates a new document based on the template.

Figure 1.11
When you update a
Fill-in field, Word
displays a dialog box similar to this one.

Although it may occasionally be useful to store user input in the document (this often happens in mail merges, for example), what if what you really want to do is change the actual document properties? Because each document property has its own field type, you can change many properties by specifying the Fill-in result as the new property value. For example, the following code prompts the user for a document title and then stores the result in the Title property using the Title field:

```
{ TITLE { FILLIN "Please enter a document title:" } }
```

> **TIP**
> Unfortunately, the result of the Title field displays in the document text. To avoid this, you can hide the result by placing everything inside a Seq field. You normally use this field to create a sequential numbering system, but it comes with a \h switch that hides the field. Here's the hidden form of the Fill-in field:
>
> ```
> { SEQ \h { TITLE { FILLIN "Please enter a document title:" } } }
> ```

> **TIP**
> If you're not sure of the field name to use for a particular property, you can display a list of the various document property fields. Choose Insert, Quick Parts, Field to open the Field dialog box. In the Categories list, click Document Information. The Field Names list shows all the document property fields.

> **NOTE**
> Word also comes with an Ask field type. This works the same as Fill-in, except that the result is stored in a bookmark:
>
> ```
> { ASK Bookmark Prompt }
> ```

Creating a Dynamic AutoCorrect Entry

AutoCorrect entries are usually static. That is, you specify the error and its correction, and then whenever Word comes across the error, it replaces it with the correct text. However, there may be times when you want the correct text to be more dynamic. For example, it's easy to set up an AutoCorrect entry that replaces your initials with your name. But what if you want to set up an AutoCorrect entry that inserts the name of the author of the current document? You can do that by inserting the `Author` field and then setting up an AutoCorrect entry for that field. Here are the steps to follow for the document author example:

1. Select where you want the field to appear in the document.
2. Choose Insert, Quick Parts, <u>F</u>ield to display the Field dialog box.
3. In the <u>C</u>ategories list, click (All).
4. In the <u>F</u>ield Names list, click Author.
5. Click OK. Word inserts the field.
6. Select the entire field.
7. Choose Office, Word Op<u>t</u>ions, click Proofing, and then click <u>A</u>utoCorrect Options to display the AutoCorrect dialog box.
8. Select the AutoCorrect tab. Your field result displays in the <u>W</u>ith text box.
9. In the <u>R</u>eplace text box, type a short abbreviation or code (for example, `author`).
10. Click <u>A</u>dd.
11. Click OK and then click OK again in the Word Options dialog box.

You use similar steps to set up dynamic AutoCorrect entries that include the current date (insert a `Date` field), any document property (insert a `DocProperty` field and specify the property you want), the file name (a `FileName` field), the file size (a `FileSize` field), and the current time (a `Time` field), to name a few. For the ultimate dynamic AutoCorrect entry, include a `Fill-in` field (see the previous section) as part of the correction text. In this case, when Word goes to insert the AutoCorrect text, it displays the `Fill-in` field dialog box to prompt for whatever input you request.

Adding Dummy Text to a Document

In business settings, it's common to have one person (or group) designing a document and another person (or group) composing the document text. This is often an efficient way to work, but it often raises a problem: How can the designers work on the document if they don't have the text? The usual solution is to fill the document with *dummy text*, which is placeholder text that temporarily substitutes for the real document text, thus enabling the design process to proceed. Ideally, the dummy text should at least resemble real-world text: a variety of word lengths, sentence lengths, and so on. Word gives you two methods for generating this text: the RAND function and the Repeat command.

Using the RAND **Function**

Word's RAND function enables you to insert dummy text automatically:

```
=RAND(paragraphs, sentences)
```

Here, the *paragraphs* value specifies the number of paragraphs of dummy text that Word will generate, and *sentences* specifies the number of sentences per paragraph. You can specify up to 200 paragraphs of up to 99 sentences each, or up to 99 paragraphs with up to 200 sentences in each.

For example, to generate five paragraphs with six sentences in each, you type the following formula at the spot in the document where you want the dummy text to display and then press Enter:

```
=RAND(5,6)
```

In all cases, Word generates the text from the following nine sentences:

> On the Insert tab, the galleries include items that are designed to coordinate with the overall look of your document. You can use these galleries to insert tables, headers, footers, lists, cover pages, and other document building blocks. When you create pictures, charts, or diagrams, they also coordinate with your current document look. You can easily change the formatting of selected text in the document text by choosing a look for the selected text from the Quick Styles gallery on the Home tab. You can also format text directly by using the other controls on the Home tab. Most controls offer a choice of using the look from the current theme or using a format that you specify directly. To change the overall look of your document, use the Page Layout tab's Themes gallery. To change the looks available in the Quick Style gallery, use the Change Current Quick Style Set command. Both the Themes gallery and the Quick Styles gallery provide reset commands so that you can always restore the look of your document to the original contained in your current template.

If you specify fewer than nine sentences using RAND, then Word inserts a subset of this text. If you specify more than nine sentences, Word repeats the text as necessary.

Using the Repeat Command

If you have a bit of the document text ready, you can take advantage of Word's Repeat feature, which is found on the Quick Access toolbar. As you might expect, the Repeat command repeats your most recent action in Word. For example, if you format text as bold, select different text, and then click Repeat (or use one of the faster keyboard shortcuts—F4 or Ctrl+Y), Word applies bold formatting to the new text.

Similarly, if you type some text and then run the Repeat command, Word "repeats" the typing by inserting the typed text again at the current cursor position. This means that you can quickly insert dummy text by selecting Repeat several times. Alternatively, copy some text, paste it, and then run Repeat as often as you need.

Even better, use that old document designer standby, the semi-Latin text snippet:

> Lorem ipsum dolor sit amet, consectetuer adipiscing elit, sed diam nonummy nibh euismod tincidunt ut laoreet dolore magna aliquam erat volutpat. Ut wisi enim ad minim veniam, quis nostrud exerci tation ullamcorper suscipit lobortis nisl ut aliquip ex ea commodo consequat.

Duis autem vel eum iriure dolor in hendrerit in vulputate velit esse molestie conse-
quat, vel illum dolore eu feugiat nulla facilisis at vero eros et accumsan et iusto odio
dignissim qui blandit praesent luptatum zzril delenit augue duis dolore te feugait
nulla facilisi. Nam liber tempor cum soluta nobis eleifend option congue nihil
imperdiet doming id quod mazim placerat facer possim assum.

I've pasted this text into the `Chapter01.doc` example file.

> **NOTE** You'll find the examples used in this book on my website at `www.mcfedries.com/` `Office2007Gurus`.

Inserting a Hyperlink in a Document

Although it has been around for a while, one of the most interesting innovations in Office
is still the capability to create hyperlinks in any kind of Office document: Word documents, Excel worksheets, Access databases, PowerPoint presentations, and even Outlook
email messages. This section shows you the various techniques available for inserting
hyperlinks into Word documents.

Word accepts hyperlinks within the body of a document. This lets you create "active" documents that enable the reader to click special text sections and "surf" to another document,
which may be on the web, your corporate intranet, or your hard drive.

For example, consider the Word document shown in Figure 1.12. As you can see, the
phrase "amortization schedule" is displayed underlined and in a different color (blue). This
formatting indicates that this phrase is a hyperlink. Hovering the mouse pointer over the
hyperlink displays a ScreenTip with the linked address and the message `CTRL+click to`
`follow link`. Holding down Ctrl and clicking this link displays the linked Excel worksheet.

> **TIP** Yes, you Ctrl+click a Word hyperlink instead of just clicking as you would in a web browser. That's
> because you may need to position the cursor inside the link text, and to do that with a mouse, you
> need to be able to click the text. If that's not a concern for you, you can turn off the Ctrl+click
> method. Choose Office, Word Options, click Advanced, deactivate the Use CTRL+Click to Follow
> Hyperlink check box, and then click OK. You can now click a Word hyperlink to follow it.

Word gives you three methods for constructing a hyperlink:

- Using Word's AutoCorrect feature to create links automatically
- Entering the appropriate information by hand
- Pasting information from another document

Figure 1.12
A Word document containing a hyperlink.

The following sections discuss each method.

Word gives you a fourth method for creating a hyperlink: drag and drop. Right-click and drag a file from a folder window, a link from a web page, or an address displayed in the Internet Explorer Address bar (actually, you right-drag the page icon that displays on the left side of the Address bar). Drop the object inside a Word document and, in the shortcut menu that displays, click Create Hyperlink Here. If you see an Internet Explorer Security dialog box, click Allow.

Creating a Hyperlink Using AutoCorrect

The easiest way to create a hyperlink in Word is to type the address into your document. As long as the address is a network path or an Internet URL, Word will convert the text into a hyperlink, no questions asked.

If this doesn't work for you, you need to turn on this feature by following these steps:

1. Select Office, Word Options to open the Word Options dialog box.
2. Click Proofing and then click AutoCorrect Options to display the AutoCorrect dialog box.
3. Click the AutoFormat as You Type tab.
4. Activate the Internet and Network Paths with Hyperlinks check box.
5. Click OK, and then click OK again in the Word Options dialog box.

Creating a Hyperlink from Scratch

For more control over your hyperlinks, you need to use Word's Hyperlink command, which lets you specify not only linked documents, but named locations within documents (such as a named range within an Excel worksheet). Here are the steps to follow:

1. Either select the text that you want to use for the hyperlink or select the position in the document in which you want the link to display. Note that if you don't select any text beforehand, the link text will be the hyperlink address.

2. Choose Insert, Hyperlink (or press Ctrl+K). Word displays the Insert Hyperlink dialog box, as shown in Figure 1.13.

Figure 1.13
Use the Insert Hyperlink dialog box to create your hyperlinks from scratch.

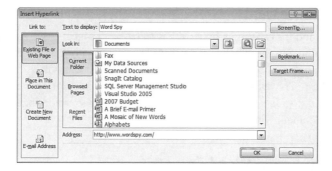

3. Use the Text to Display box to edit the link text, if necessary.

4. To set the ScreenTip text, click ScreenTip, type the ScreenTip text, and click OK. Note that this replaces the address that Word displays in the ScreenTip by default. Word still displays the CTRL+click to follow link message in the ScreenTip.

5. Use the Address text box to specify the name of the file or web page that the users jump to when they Ctrl+click the link. You can enter any of the following:

   • A path to another Word document

   • A path to a document from a different application on your hard drive

   • A path to a multimedia file (such as a sound or video file)

   • A network (UNC) path to a document on your company's intranet

   • A URL on the World Wide Web

6. If you want to link to a specific part of the file, you can do this in Word by linking to a bookmark. Click Bookmark, select the bookmark you want to link to, and click OK.

7. Click OK to insert the hyperlink.

> **NOTE**
>
> If you right-click a hyperlink, the shortcut menu that displays contains the following commands:
>
> - Edit Hyperlink—Displays the Edit Hyperlink dialog box, which is identical to the Add Hyperlink dialog box.
> - Select Hyperlink—Selects the hyperlink text.
> - Open Hyperlink—Opens the linked document.
> - Copy Hyperlink—Copies the hyperlink to the Clipboard.
> - Remove Hyperlink—Deletes the hyperlink but not the hyperlink text.

Pasting a Hyperlink in Word

The final method for creating a hyperlink is to paste an object from the Clipboard. That is, you copy an object to the Clipboard—it could be a section of text, an Excel range, some records from a table—position the cursor where you want the link to display, and then select Edit, Paste Hyperlink. When you click this hyperlink, not only does Word load the application and document from which you copied the information, but it also moves to the spot in the document where the information resides.

Displaying Sentence Word Counts

When you grammar check a document, you can elect to display the document's readability statistics. (Select Office, Word Options, click Proofing, and activate the Show Readability Statistics check box.) Among other values, the Readability Statistics dialog box offers the average number of words per sentence. This is useful because you don't want your average sentence to be too long or too short. However, writing gurus also stress that you should have a variety of sentence lengths in your prose, with some shorter and longer sentences thrown in for reading variety. Unfortunately, the Readability Statistics dialog box doesn't tell you the lengths of your sentences, but it's easy enough to get a VBA macro to do it for you, as shown in Listing 1.1.

→   To learn how to use the Visual Basic Editor and incorporate macros into your documents, **see** "Working with VBA Macros," **p. 429**

Listing 1.1   A Macro That Displays the Lengths of Sentences in the Active Document

```
Sub DisplaySentenceLengths()
    Dim s As Range
    Dim maxWords As Integer
    Dim i As Integer
    Dim sentenceLengths() As Integer
    Dim str As String

    With ActiveDocument
        '
        ' Run through all the sentences to find the longest
        '
```

```
        maxWords = 0
        For Each s In .Sentences
            If s.Words.Count > maxWords Then
                maxWords = s.Words.Count
            End If
        Next 's
        '
        ' Redimension the array of sentence lengths
        '
        ReDim sentenceLengths(maxWords)
        '
        ' Run through the sentences again to count
        ' the number of sentences for each length
        '
        For Each s In .Sentences
            sentenceLengths(s.Words.Count - 1) = sentenceLengths(s.Words
➡.Count - 1) + 1
        Next 's
        '
        ' Construct the string that displays the sentence lengths
        ' and their frequencies
        '
        str = "Sentence Length:" & vbTab & "Frequency:" & vbCrLf & vbCrLf
        '
        ' The UBound() function tells you the upper bound of an array.
        ' In this case, it tells us the largest value in sentenceLengths.
        '
        For i = 0 To UBound(sentenceLengths) - 1
            '
            ' Build the string
            '
            str = str & IIf(i + 1 < 10, "  ", "") & i + 1 & _
                IIf(i = 0, " word:  ", " words: ") & _
                vbTab & vbTab & sentenceLengths(i) & vbCrLf
        Next 'i
        '
        ' Display the string
        '
        MsgBox str
    End With
End Sub
```

Using the `ActiveDocument` object, the macro makes a first pass through all the sentences to find the one with the most words. The macro then uses this maximum word count to redimension the `sentenceLengths` array, which is used to hold the number of occurrences of each sentence length within the document. To calculate these frequencies, the macro then runs through all the sentences again and increments the array values for each length. The macro finishes by constructing and then displaying a string that holds the sentence lengths and frequencies. Figure 1.14 shows an example.

Figure 1.14
The *Display-SentenceLengths* macro displays a message box such as this to show you the document's sentence lengths and the frequency with which each length occurs.

Microsoft Word

Sentence Length:	Frequency:
1 word:	0
2 words:	0
3 words:	0
4 words:	0
5 words:	0
6 words:	7
7 words:	6
8 words:	6
9 words:	5
10 words:	6
11 words:	11
12 words:	7
13 words:	6
14 words:	0
15 words:	4
16 words:	5
17 words:	2
18 words:	6
19 words:	6

OK

> **TIP** If you're also interested in displaying data for each paragraph, replace .Sentences in Listing 1.1 with .Paragraphs. Because the variable s is a Range object, you can work with either the words in each paragraph—s.Words.Count—or the sentences in each paragraph— s.Sentences.Count.

Finding the Longest Sentence in a Document

One of the hallmarks of good business writing is that it's succinct and to the point: no digressions, minimal adjectives and adverbs, and no run-on sentences. If you use the code in Listing 1.1 to study the sentence lengths of your document, you may find one sentence that's quite a bit longer than the others. For example, all your sentences may be fewer than 25 words, but there may be one that's 50 words. That one sentence is obviously far too long, and the problem may be mistaken punctuation (such as a comma instead of a period) or a sentence that needs to be broken up into two or three smaller sentences. Either way, you need to find the problem sentence, and the code in Listing 1.2 does just that.

Listing 1.2   Finding the Longest Sentence in a Document

```
Sub FindLongestSentence()
    Dim s As Range
    Dim maxWords As Integer
    Dim longestSentence As String

    With ActiveDocument
```

```
        ' Run through all the sentences to find the longest
        '
        maxWords = 0
        For Each s In .Sentences
            If s.Words.Count > maxWords Then
                maxWords = s.Words.Count
                longestSentence = s.Text
            End If
        Next 's
        '
        ' Move to the top of the document
        '
        Selection.HomeKey Unit:=wdStory
        '
        ' Set up the Find object
        '
        With Selection.Find
            '
            ' Clear Find object formatting
            '
            .ClearFormatting
            '
            ' Check the length of the sentence
            '
            If Len(longestSentence) <= 256 Then
                '
                ' The length of the sentence is okay,
                ' so go ahead and find the text.
                '
                .Text = longestSentence
                .Execute
            Else
                ' The sentence is too long for the Text
                ' property, so find just the first 256 characters
                '
                .Text = Left(longestSentence, 256)
                .Execute
                '
                ' Extend the selection to the entire sentence
                '
                Selection.MoveEnd Unit:=wdSentence
            End If
        End With
        '
        ' Display a message
        '
        MsgBox "The selected sentence is the longest in the document " & _
                "at " & maxWords & " words."
    End With
End Sub
```

As in Listing 1.1, the FindLongestSentence macro runs through the active document's sentences to find the longest one. In this case, however, the macro stores not only the length of the longest sentence, but its text as well. The macro then uses this text to locate the sentence using the Find object. Note, however, that the Find object's Text property can accept only up to 256 characters. Because a long sentence can easily have more characters than that, the macro checks the length of the sentence: If it's too long, the Find object is set up to look for only the first 256 characters in the sentence.

Toggling Hidden Codes and Text

When you choose Home, Show/Hide, Word displays symbols that represent hidden "characters," such as tabs, spaces, paragraph marks, and optional hyphens, as well as any text formatted as hidden. This is handy for looking "under the hood" of the document. However, a thorough check of a document's inner workings should also include other normally hidden items: bookmarks, comments, revisions, and field codes. You can toggle all of these by hand individually, but if you need to do this often, the procedure in Listing 1.3 is much easier.

Listing 1.3   Toggling Hidden Codes and Text

```
Public Sub ShowAll()
    Dim currentState As Boolean
    With ActiveWindow.View
        currentState = .ShowBookmarks
        .ShowBookmarks = Not currentState
        .ShowComments = Not currentState
        .ShowFieldCodes = Not currentState
        .ShowHiddenText = Not currentState
        .ShowHyphens = Not currentState
        .ShowOptionalBreaks = Not currentState
        .ShowParagraphs = Not currentState
        .ShowRevisionsAndComments = Not currentState
        .ShowSpaces = Not currentState
        .ShowTabs = Not currentState
        .Type = wdNormalView
    End With
End Sub
```

The procedure is named ShowAll, which is the internal name of the command that Word runs when you click the Show/Hide button. Therefore, clicking Show/Hide will now run the ShowAll procedure. Using the active window's View object, the program first checks the current state of the ShowBookmarks property and stores the state in the currentState variable. Then each of the View properties is set to the opposite value. Figure 1.15 and 1.16 show the two states produced by the procedure.

Figure 1.15
The document view with the hidden codes and text turned off.

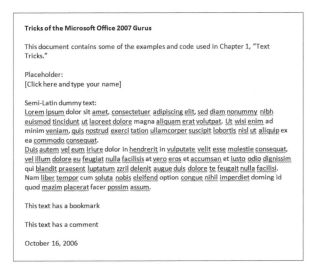

Figure 1.16
The document view with the hidden codes and text turned on.

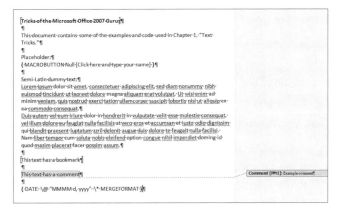

Creating a Custom Spell Check Dictionary

The Office spell checker is great for catching those typos and other errors that AutoCorrect misses. Good business writing must be clear and readable, and the spell checker ensures that spelling mistakes don't mar your prose. (This is particularly crucial for documents you send outside of the company—say, to clients and potential customers—because spelling gaffes can quickly tarnish your or your company's reputation.)

However, the spell checker is only as useful as it is accurate. The built-in dictionary is massive with hundreds of thousands of words, Fortune 1000 company names, ethnic names, somewhat new coinages (such as *outsourcing*), computer terms, country names, and more. However, you probably still see that squiggly red line under a lot of words that you use every day. Your goal should be to minimize or even eliminate these "false positives" so that the spell checker flags only actual misspellings.

One way to do that is to add words to the spell checker's default custom dictionary, which is a text file called CUSTOM.DIC, located in the following folder:

```
%UserProfile%\AppData\Roaming\Microsoft\UProof
```

You add words to the dictionary by right-clicking a word flagged by the spell checker and then clicking Add to Dictionary. The spell checker then inserts the unknown word into this dictionary. That works, but what if you have many words that you want to add?

> **TIP**   If you accidentally add a misspelled word to CUSTOM.DIC, you can delete it. Choose Office, Word Options, click Proofing, and then click Custom Dictionaries. Click CUSTOM.DIC, and then click Edit Word List. When Word displays the CUSTOM.DIC dialog box, click the word you want to remove and then click Delete. Click OK in all open dialog boxes.

To handle a large list of new words, you need to create your own custom dictionary. This involves two main steps: creating the dictionary and telling the spell checker about it.

Here are the steps to follow to create the custom dictionary:

1. Launch a text editor such as Notepad (choose Start, All Programs, Accessories, Notepad).
2. Choose File, Save, and then save the text file as follows:
   - Be sure to save the file in the UProof folder mentioned earlier.
   - Give the filename the .dic extension.

> **TIP**   To ensure that Windows accepts the .dic extension (instead of the default .txt extension for text files), surround the file name with quotation marks. For example, if you want to name your custom dictionary jargon.dic, type the name as "**jargon.dic**".

3. For each word you want to include in the custom dictionary, type the word and then press Enter.
4. Save your work and close the text editor.

Now follow these steps to tell the spell checker about your custom dictionary:

1. Choose Office, Word Options and then click Proofing.
2. Click Custom Dictionaries to open the Custom Dictionaries dialog box.
3. Click Add to open the Add Custom Dictionary dialog box.
4. Click the text file you created and then click Open.
5. Click OK and then click OK again in the Word Options dialog box.

> **TIP** The default custom dictionary is the one that the spell checker adds words to when you click the Add to Dictionary command. If you want your custom dictionary to be the default, display the Custom Dictionaries dialog box, click your dictionary, and then click Change Default.

1

From Here

- To learn lots of useful techniques for formatting your text, **see** Chapter 2, "Formatting Tricks," **p. 35**.
- For tips related to Word documents, **see** Chapter 3, "Document Tricks," **p. 61**.
- To ensure your text is laid out exactly the way you want, **see** Chapter 4, "Page Layout Tricks," **p. 89**.
- To learn how to build a PowerPoint presentation from a Word outline, **see** "Converting a Word Outline into a PowerPoint Presentation," in Chapter 9, "Slide and Presentation Tricks," **p. 222**.
- You can also use Word to format PowerPoint handouts; **see** "Using Word to Custom Format Handouts," in Chapter 9, "Slide and Presentation Tricks," **p. 246**.
- To learn how to use the Visual Basic Editor and incorporate macros into your documents, **see** "Working with VBA Macros," **p. 429**.

Formatting Tricks

2

Every experienced Word user knows that content rules the desktop. Before you even consider bolding a word, justifying a paragraph, or adjusting the margins of a document, you need to make sure that the content you're working with is up-to-date, accurate, relevant, and error-free. This doesn't, however, mean that you should ignore document formatting. Today's business readers have a keen eye for design and appreciate a document that has been made easier to read by a judicious use of fonts, styles, lists, and other formatting effects. No one's going to refuse to read an unformatted document, of course. But if you want your content to get the best reception possible, you need to dress it up a bit.

When it comes to document formatting, Word users tend to fall into two camps: minimalists and fritterers. The minimalists think formatting is a waste of time, so they just apply a few token Heading styles, and maybe some italics here and there. The minimalists need a few tricks that make applying formatting faster. The fritterers do just the opposite: They spend endless amounts of time tweaking fonts, type sizes, effects, borders, colors, and more to try and get exactly the right effect. The fritterers need a few tricks that streamline formatting chores to make them more efficient. This chapter appeals to both camps by offering a number of tricks that make formatting quicker and easier.

Quickly Modifying the Normal Style

You use the Normal style for standard document text, so it's the style that you use most often. The Normal style uses the Body font specified in the current theme, applies a little extra space between each line in a paragraph (1.15 spacing instead of straight single spacing), and creates space after each paragraph (10 points). If some or all of these default formats don't suit your needs, you can easily modify the Normal style. (In the Home tab, right-click Normal in the Quick Style Gallery and then click Modify.)

However, what if you already have a word or paragraph that has the exact formatting you'd prefer to use for the Normal style? Instead of modifying Normal to match the existing text, you can do the opposite: Click inside the word or paragraph, choose the Home tab, right-click Normal in the Quick Style Gallery, and then click Update Normal to Match Selection. Word applies the current formatting to the Normal style and updates all instances of Normal in the current document.

> **NOTE**   You can use existing text to update the formatting of any style, not just Normal. Click inside the existing text, chose the Home tab, right-click the style you want to modify in the Quick Style Gallery, and then click Update *Style* to Match Selection, where *Style* is the name of the style you right-clicked.

> **NOTE**   Normal is Word's default paragraph style, but you can set up any style as the default. Choose Office, Word Options, click Advanced, and then use the Default Paragraph Style list to click the style you want to use.

Setting Up the Quick Style Gallery to Suit the Way You Work

 Word 2007's new Quick Style Gallery on the Home tab is a welcome innovation because it lets you apply some common styles with just one or two mouse clicks. If you have Live Preview turned on, you can see the effects of the style on the current text selection by hovering the mouse pointer over the style.

> **NOTE**   To turn Live Preview on, choose Office, Word Options, click Popular, and then click to activate the Enable Live Preview check box.

If the Quick Style Gallery has a down side, it's that only a dozen so-called "recommended" styles appear, and some of them are obscure (for example, the Subtle Reference and Intense Reference styles). When you apply a style that's not in the Quick Style Gallery, in most cases, Word adds it to the Quick Style Gallery, which makes it easy to reapply. You can customize the makeup of the Quick Style Gallery using two methods:

- To remove an existing style, right-click it in the Quick Style Gallery and then click Remove from Quick Style Gallery.

■ To return a previously removed style to the gallery, click the Styles dialog box launcher (or press Ctrl+Alt+Shift+S) to open the Styles pane, right-click the style you want to return, and then click Add to Quick Style Gallery.

How does Word decide which styles appear in the Quick Style Gallery? It applies one of three settings to every style:

Show—The style always appears in the Quick Style Gallery. These are the "recommended" styles, and they comprise the dozen styles you see by default in the Quick Styles Gallery.

Hide Until Used—The style doesn't appear in the Quick Styles Gallery until you apply it at least once in your document.

Always Hidden—The style never appears in the Quick Style Gallery.

If you have a style you use frequently, you should ensure that it always appears in the Quick Style Gallery by changing its recommended setting to show. You can modify a style's recommended setting and the order that style appears in the Quick Styles Gallery by following these steps:

1. In the Home tab, click the Styles dialog box launcher (or press Ctrl+Alt+Shift+S) to open the Styles pane.

2. Click the Manage Styles button. Word opens the Manage Styles dialog box.

3. Click the Recommend tab, shown in Figure 2.1.

Figure 2.1
Use the Recommend tab to customize the styles that appear in the Quick Styles Gallery.

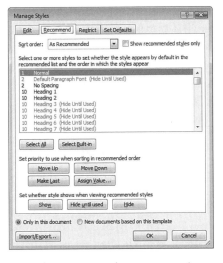

4. Click the style with which you want to work.

5. Set the recommended setting by clicking one of the following buttons: Show, Hide Until Used, or Hide.

6. Modify the position of the style by clicking one of the following buttons: <u>M</u>ove Up, Move <u>D</u>own, Make <u>L</u>ast, or Assign <u>V</u>alue. (The last of these displays the Assign Value dialog box, which you use to assign a relative priority for the style.)

7. Repeat steps 4–7 to modify other styles.

8. If you want these settings to apply to all documents that you create using the current template, activate the New Documents Based On This Template option. (Otherwise, the custom Quick Styles Gallery applies only to the current document.)

9. Click OK.

You can also tweak the Quick Style Gallery by adding your own custom styles. Here are the steps to follow:

1. Set up text or a paragraph with the custom formatting that you want to save as a Quick Style.

2. Right-click the text or paragraph and then choose S<u>t</u>yles, Save Selection as a New Quick Style. The Create New Style from Formatting dialog box displays.

3. Type a <u>N</u>ame for the style.

4. Click OK. Word adds the style to the beginning of the Quick Styles Gallery. (You may want to run through the previous steps to change the custom style's priority.)

> **NOTE**
>
> After you create a style, you might want to use it in another document. One easy way to do this is to select text that uses the style, copy it, and then paste it in the other document. If you have multiple custom styles that you want to use in the other document, use the Organizer. Press Ctrl+Alt+Shift+S to open the Styles pane, click Manage Styles, and then click Import/E<u>x</u>port to open the Organizer dialog box. On the left side of the dialog box, use the Styles A<u>v</u>ailable In list to select the document or template that contains the styles you want to copy; on the right side of the dialog box, use the Styles Availa<u>b</u>le In list to select the document or template to which you want to copy the styles. For each style, click it in the left list, and then click <u>C</u>opy.

Changing the Document Map Formatting

If you often create or work with long documents, you've probably discovered one of Word's most useful document navigation features: the *document map*. This is an aspect of the Navigation Window, a pane that appears on the left side of the Word window. When you display it by activating the View, Document Map check box, Word populates the Navigation Window with all your document's Heading styles, as shown in Figure 2.2. You can jump to any section of your document just by clicking its heading in the document map.

Figure 2.2
You can navigate a long document quickly by using the Document Map.

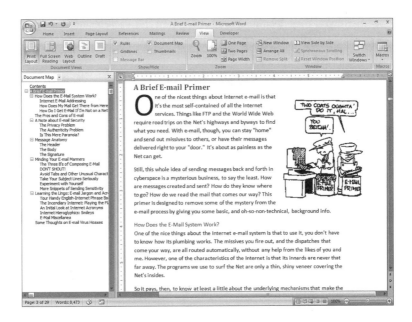

You have a bit of control over what appears in the document map. Right-click the Navigation Window, and then click the highest Heading level you want to show. Unfortunately, the shortcut menu that appears gives you no option for formatting the document map. This is a real problem if you find the document map too small to read (the default font is 8-point Tahoma) or if (as sometimes happens) the document map font becomes spontaneously large. (Actually, the latter is a bug in Word 2003. So far, I haven't seen this bug appear in Word 2007.) Fortunately, Word has a Document Map style that controls the look of the document map text. Follow these steps to modify this style:

1. In the Home tab, click the Styles dialog box launcher (or press Ctrl+Alt+Shift+S) to open the Styles pane.

2. Click the Manage Styles button. Word opens the Manage Styles dialog box.

3. Click the Edit tab.

4. In the Select a Style to Edit list, click Document Map.

5. Click Modify to open the Modify Style dialog box.

6. Make your changes to the formatting, and then click OK.

7. Click OK.

Selecting Text with Similar Formatting

One task that can really slow you down is having to change a particular set of formatting options in many different places in a document. For example, if you've applied a bold, underlined, Times New Roman font to every instance of a book title throughout a document, you may decide later that you'd prefer each instance to use an italic, Verdana font, instead. Reformatting two or three instances of the text isn't so bad, but tweaking a dozen or two is nobody's idea of fun.

To make this kind of chore easier, Word enables you to select every instance of a particular kind of formatting—it can be a style or a combination of font or paragraph formatting—within a document. With every instance selected, you can then apply new formatting, and Word will update the selected instances.

To select similar formatting throughout a document, you have two choices:

- For a style, right-click the style in either the Quick Style Gallery or the Styles pane (click the Styles dialog launcher or press Ctrl+Alt+Shift+S) and then click Select All X Instance(s) (where X is the number of times you've applied the style in the document).

> **NOTE** If you want to remove all instances of a particular style in your document, right-click the style in either the Quick Style Gallery or the Styles pane, and then click Clear Formatting of X Instance(s) (where X is the number of times the style appears in the document).

- For font or paragraph formatting, right-click any instance of the formatting and then choose Styles, Select Text With Similar Formatting.

Copying Formatting from One Section to Another

It's common in Word to take the formatting that you have in one text selection and apply it to another selection. This is most easily accomplished using the Format Painter tool:

1. Select the text that has the formatting you want to copy.
2. Choose Home, Format Painter (or press Ctrl+Shift+C).
3. Click inside the text to which you want to apply the formatting. Word copies the formatting from the first selection to the second.

> **TIP** If you want to copy the formatting to multiple selections, double-click the Format Painter tool. Click inside each selection to which you want to apply the formatting, and then click the Format Painter tool to turn it off.

Comparing the Formatting of Two Text Selections

Copying formatting with the Format Painter tool (as described in the previous section) works well, but you might not always want to apply *all* of a selection's formatting. For example, you might want to apply just the font, the character spacing, the line spacing, or some combination of these. In that case, you need to tweak the formatting of the other selection by hand. However, one of the most frustrating experiences in Word occurs when you adjust the second selection's formatting, but you just can't make it look like the original selection.

You can eliminate this frustration by taking advantage of Word's little-used Reveal Formatting pane. As the name implies, this pane displays all the font, paragraph, and section formatting that has been applied to the current selection. This is quite useful on its own, but the Reveal Formatting pane has another trick: You can compare the formatting for two different selections. This will show you exactly where the two selections differ, which then makes it easy for you to adjust the formatting as needed.

Here are the steps to follow to compare the formatting of two text selections:

1. Select the first bit of text you want to compare.

2. Press Shift+F1 to display the Reveal Formatting pane.

3. Activate the Compare to Another Selection check box.

4. Select the second bit of text you want to compare. Word displays the formatting differences in the Reveal Formatting pane, as shown in Figure 2.3. The differences are separated by the -> symbol, with the original text formatting on the left and the second text formatting on the right.

5. When you're done, press Shift+F1 to close the Reveal Formatting pane.

Figure 2.3
You can use the Reveal Formatting pane to compare the formatting in two different text selections.

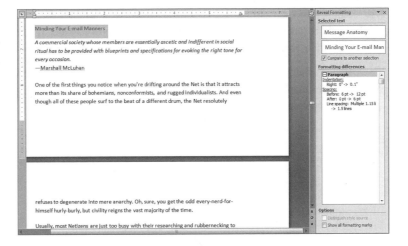

Removing Formatting with Precision

Ask anyone who uses Word extensively for a list of pet peeves, and one that will come up on almost every list is Word's annoying habit of wiping out existing formatting when you apply a style to a text selection. For example, let's say you apply the Emphasis character style to a text selection, and then you make the selection bold. If later you decide to change the character style to Default Paragraph Font, Word also removes the bold formatting that you applied. If you walk by someone's office and you hear a growling sound, it's probably because the occupant has just had Word blow away a bunch of carefully applied formatting.

 Such frustrations may become obsolete in Word 2007, thanks to Word's new Style Inspector. This is a pane that's similar to Reveal Formatting, but has a simpler display. In fact, the Style Inspector shows just four things for the currently selected text:

- The paragraph style applied to the text
- Extra paragraph formatting applied to the text
- The character style applied to the text
- Extra character formatting applied to the text

This is useful information, but the real beauty of the Style Inspector is that each of the previous four formatting displays also comes with a Clear button that enables you to remove just that formatting:

> **Reset to Normal Paragraph Style**—Resets the paragraph style to Normal.
>
> **Clear Paragraph Formatting**—Removes the extra paragraph formatting.
>
> **Clear Character Style**—Resets the character style to Default Paragraph Font.
>
> **Clear Character Formatting**—Removes all the extra character formatting.

These buttons enable you to be much more precise about what formatting you clear from a text selection. In the example I used earlier, where you applied the Emphasis character style and bold character formatting, you could have retained the bold by clicking the Clear Character Style button.

To work with the Style Inspector, press Ctrl+Alt+Shift+S to open the Styles pane and then click the Style Inspector button. Figure 2.4 shows the Style Inspector pane and points out the buttons you can use.

Figure 2.4
Use the new Style Inspector to remove certain types of formatting from a text selection.

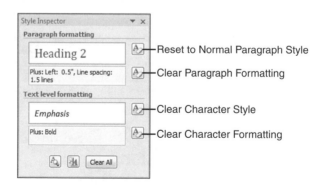

Replacing One Style with Another

One task that comes up regularly with people who use Word often is the need to replace a style throughout a document. For example, you may need to change all Heading 2 styles to Heading 3 or all Quote styles to Normal. Your day won't be ruined if you have just one or two text selections to change, but it can be if you have dozens.

Fortunately, Word makes it easy to replace one style with another. Begin by selecting all instances of the style you want to replace (see "Selecting Text with Similar Formatting," earlier in this chapter). Then click the style you want to use as the replacement. (Either choose Home and then click the style in the Quick Style Gallery, or press Ctrl+Alt+Shift+S and then click the style in the Styles pane.)

A slightly trickier situation is when you want to replace only *some* of the instances of a particular style. In this case, you need to use Word's Replace feature:

1. Choose Home, Replace (or press Ctrl+H). Word opens the Find and Replace dialog box with the Replace tab displayed.
2. Click More to expand the dialog box.
3. Click inside the Find What text box.
4. Click Format, Style to open the Find Style dialog box, click the style you want to replace, and then click OK.
5. Click inside the Replace With text box.
6. Click Format, Style to open the Find Style dialog box, click the style you want to use as a replacement, and then click OK. You should now see Style values below the Find What and Replace With text boxes, as shown in Figure 2.5.

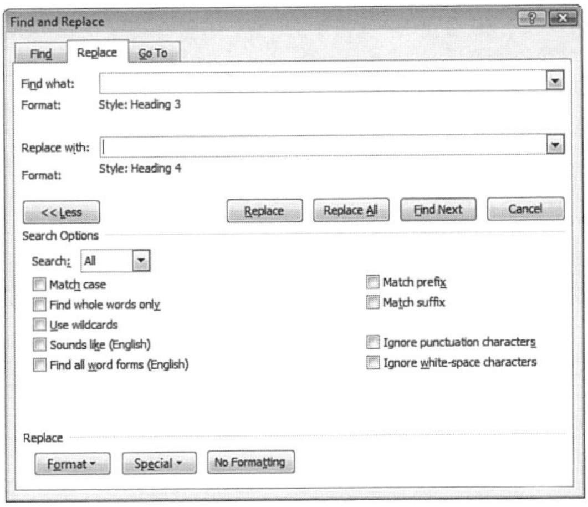

Figure 2.5
You can use the Replace tab to replace one or more instances of one style with another.

7. Click Find Next. Word selects the next instance of the style.
8. If this is an instance that you want to replace, click Replace.

9. Repeat steps 7 and 8 until you have finished replacing the style.

10. Click Cancel.

> **TIP** You can also use the Replace tab on the Find and Replace dialog box to replace specific formatting options, such as replacing underlining with italics or replacing double-spacing with single-spacing. Click inside the Find What text box, click the Format button, and then click the type of formatting you want (Font, Paragraph, and so on). Do the same thing for the Replace With text box and then run the Find and Replace.

> **TIP** In the Find and Replace tabs, you can use shortcut keys to specify formatting options in the Find What and Replace With text boxes. Click inside the text box and then press the formatting shortcut key (such as Ctrl+U for underlining; see the next section). For font formatting, keep pressing the shortcut key to get more options. For example, when you press Ctrl+U the first time, the Format value changes to Underline; press Ctrl+U a second time and the Format value changes to No Underline; press Ctrl+U a third time, and no underline setting appears.

Applying Formatting from the Keyboard

Most Word users think of formatting as a mouse-driven exercise, with the exception of a few well-known keyboard shortcuts (such as Ctrl+B for Bold). That's always seemed strange to me because Word is perhaps the most keyboard-intensive of the Office applications. Why reach over to the mouse to apply a format or two when there's a good chance that you can apply the same formatting with a keystroke or two? Think Word only has a few keyboard shortcuts for formatting? Think again: Word actually has more than 40 of them!

When you have a ton of typing to get through, the last thing you want to do is switch over to the mouse to get your formatting chores accomplished. Fortunately, you may not have to bother much with the mouse because Word offers a huge number of formatting shortcuts via the keyboard. Table 2.1 offers the complete list.

Table 2.1   Word's Keyboard Shortcuts for Formatting

Press	To apply
Ctrl+B	Bold
Ctrl+I	Italics
Ctrl+U	Underline
Ctrl+Shift+D	Double underline
Ctrl+Shift+W	Underline each word in the selection

Press	To apply
Ctrl+D or Ctrl+Shift+F	Display the Font dialog box with Font selected
Ctrl+Shift+P	Display the Font dialog box with Size selected
Ctrl+Shift+A	Uppercase
Shift+F3	Cycle case
Ctrl+Shift+K	Small caps
Ctrl+=	Subscript
Ctrl++	Superscript
Ctrl+Shift+Q	Symbol font
Ctrl+>	Grow font
Ctrl+]	Grow font size by one point
Ctrl+<	Shrink font
Ctrl+[	Shrink font size by one point
Ctrl+Shift+N	Normal style
Ctrl+Alt+1	Heading 1 style
Ctrl+Alt+2	Heading 2 style
Ctrl+Alt+3	Heading 3 style
Ctrl+Shift+S	Display the Apply Styles pane
Ctrl+Alt+Shift+S	Display the Styles pane
Shift+F1	Display the Reveal Formatting pane
Ctrl+L	Align left
Ctrl+E	Center
Ctrl+R	Align right
Ctrl+J	Justify
Ctrl+T	Increase hanging indent
Ctrl+Shift+T	Decrease hanging indent
Ctrl+M	Increase indent
Ctrl+Shift+M	Decrease indent
Ctrl+Shift+L	Bullet
Ctrl+1	Set paragraph line spacing to 1
Ctrl+5	Set paragraph line spacing to 1.5
Ctrl+2	Set paragraph line spacing to 2
Ctrl+*	Show/Hide (formatting symbols)

continues

2

Table 2.1   Continued

Press	To apply
Ctrl+Shift+C	Copy formatting from selection
Ctrl+Shift+V	Paste formatting to selection
Ctrl+Space or Ctrl+Shift+Z	Clear character formatting
Ctrl+Q	Clear paragraph formatting

If you want to display a border between two paragraphs, one way to do it (as shown in Figure 2.6) is to drop down the Home tab's Border tool and then click either the Top Border button (if the cursor is in the second of the two paragraphs) or the Bottom Border button (if the cursor is in the first paragraph).

Figure 2.6
Use the Border list to add a border between paragraphs.

There's nothing onerous about using Word's Border tool, but if you're a dedicated keyboardist, you should know that you can avoid the mouse clicking entirely and insert the same line by pressing hyphen (-) three or more times on a line by itself, and then pressing Enter.

Either technique works nicely, as long as you want the default border, which is a thin, straight line. If you want a different style—for example, a thicker line or a wavy line—you need to choose Home, pull down the Border list, choose Borders and Shading, and then select your border options in the Borders and Shading dialog box.

Or do you? Interestingly, the —-+Enter keyboard shortcut has five cousins that produce different line styles:

Character	Key Combo	Resulting Line Style
_ (underscore)	___+Enter	Thick
= (equal sign)	===+Enter	Double
# (pound)	###+Enter	Triple (two thin, one thick)
~ (tilde)	~~~+Enter	Wavy
* (asterisk)	***+Enter	Dotted

Figure 2.7 shows the resulting lines.

Figure 2.7
Examples of borders you can create on-the-fly using your keyboard.

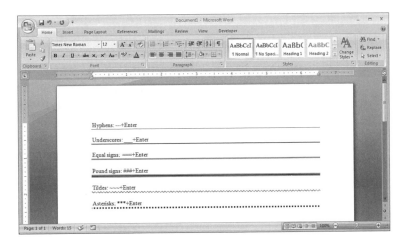

> **NOTE** These keyboard-based borders are part of Word's AutoFormat feature, so you can turn them off. If you've just created such a border, you'll see the AutoCorrect Options smart tag nearby. Click the smart tag, and then click Stop Automatically Creating Border Lines. Otherwise, choose Office, Word Options, click Proofing and then click AutoCorrect Options. In the AutoCorrect dialog box, click the AutoFormat as You Type tab and deactivate the Border Lines check box.

Specifying a Custom Bullet Image

When you need a bulleted list, the usual route is to click the Home tab's Bullets button or pull down the Bullets list and click the type of bullet you want to use. However, to add a bit of visual interest to your lists, Word gives you a couple of methods for using special symbols and even custom images as bullets.

The first method uses AutoCorrect, which enables you to create bulleted lists on-the-fly. The easiest way to go about this is to first type any of the following characters:

```
*
o
—   (em dash)
-
--
>
->
=>
```

Then press Tab or the spacebar, enter the first bullet text, and press Enter. (If you use the lowercase *o* as the starting character, you must press Tab to create the bulleted list.) Word converts the paragraph into a bulleted list and starts a second bullet. Figure 2.8 shows the various bullet styles created by each character in the left column.

> **NOTE**
> Keyboard-based bullets are an AutoFormat feature, so you can turn them off. If you've just created such a bullet, you'll see the AutoCorrect Options smart tag. Click the smart tag and then click Stop Automatically Creating Bulleted Lists. Otherwise, choose Office, Word Options, click Proofing, and then click AutoCorrect Options. In the AutoCorrect dialog box, click the AutoFormat as You Type tab and deactivate the Automatic Bulleted Lists check box.

Figure 2.8
Examples of bullets you can create on-the-fly using your keyboard.

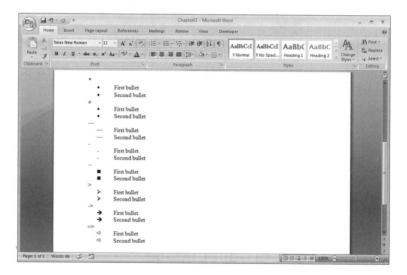

This trick also works with characters from a symbol typeface such as Symbol, Webdings, or Wingdings. Here's how:

1. Choose Insert, Symbol, More Symbols to open the Symbol dialog box.

2. Use the Font list to choose the typeface you want to use.

3. Click the symbol you want to use as the bullet.

4. Click Insert.

5. Click Close.

6. Press Tab.

7. Type the first bullet text and press Enter. Word adds a second bullet using the symbol you chose.

This also works if you want to use a picture as the bullet. Choose Insert, Picture and use the Insert Picture dialog box to select the image you want to use. Note that the following folder contains a number of images suitable for bullets:

```
%ProgramFiles%\Microsoft Office\Media\Office12\Bullets
```

> **CAUTION**
>
> To use an image as a bullet, the image should be no taller than about 15 pixels. To ensure that you don't choose a larger image, in the Insert Picture dialog box, pull down the Views menu and select Details. In the Details view, right-click any column header and then click Dimensions to add the Dimensions column, which tells you the width and height of each image.

Click Insert to add the picture to the document and then click beside the picture to deselect it. Press Tab or the spacebar, type the bullet text, and then press Enter to convert the text into a list with the picture as the bullet.

The second method uses the Define New Bullet dialog box. Choose Home, pull down the Bullets list, and choose Define New Bullet. Click the Symbol button to open the Symbol dialog box and choose a symbol to use as a bullet or click the Picture button to open the Picture Bullet dialog box and choose a picture to use as a bullet.

Creating an Inline Numbered List

You can create a numbered list of items by choosing the Home tab and then by either clicking the Numbering button or pulling down the Numbering list and clicking the style you prefer. However, what if you prefer to have an *inline* numbered list where the list of items appears in a single paragraph? Here's an example:

> **prosumer** *n.* A consumer who is an amateur in a particular field, but who is knowledgeable enough to require equipment that has some professional features (*professional* + *consumer*). A person who helps to design or customize the products they purchase (*producer* + *consumer*). A person who creates goods for their own use and also possibly to sell (*producing* + *consumer*). A person who takes steps to correct difficulties with consumer companies or markets and to anticipate future problems (*proactive* + *consumer*).

You could just insert the numbers by hand, but if the list is dynamic—either because you regularly add new items or move existing items around—it can be a pain to constantly renumber the items. You can get Word to handle the numbering for you by inserting `ListNum` fields at each spot where you want a number to appear. Here are the steps to follow:

1. Position the cursor where you want the number to appear.
2. Choose Insert, Quick Parts, Field to open the Field dialog box.
3. In the Categories list, click (All), and in the Field Names list, click ListNum.
4. In the List Name list, click NumberDefault. (You can also click OutlineDefault or LegalDefault for different list formats; see the table after step 5.)
5. Activate the Level in the List check box and then type a level number on the text box. Here are the default formats used by each list name:

Level	NumberDefault	OutlineDefault	LegalDefault
1	1)	**I.**	1.
2	a)	**A.**	1.1.
3	i)	**1.**	1.1.1.
4	(1)	a)	1.1.1.1.
5	(a)	(1)	1.1.1.1.1.
6	(i)	(a)	1.1.1.1.1.1.
7	**1.**	(i)	1.1.1.1.1.1.1.
8	**a.**	(a)	1.1.1.1.1.1.1.1.
9	**i.**	(i)	1.1.1.1.1.1.1.1.1.

6. If you want the field to start at a particular value, activate the Start-at Value check box and then type the number in the text box.
7. Click OK.
8. Repeat steps 1–7 for other numbers you want to add to the paragraph.

TIP Rather than trudging through all seven steps to insert each number, there's a shortcut method you can use. Insert the first number, but don't specify a start-at value (the default is 1). In the document, select the number field and then press Ctrl+C to copy it. Move the insertion point to where you want the next number to appear in the list and then press Ctrl+V to paste the field. Word inserts the new number and increments it.

Each time you add a number, Word inserts a `ListNum` field with the following syntax:

```
{ LISTNUM Name \l level \s start }
```

Here, *Name* is the list name (such as `NumberDefault`), *level* is the level number, and *start* is the starting number (if any). Figure 2.9 shows two paragraphs with inline numbering—the first uses level 1, and the second uses level 7. I copied the paragraphs below and displayed the field codes (by selecting the text and pressing Shift+F9).

Figure 2.9
Examples of inline numbered lists—the bottom paragraphs show the field codes used in the top paragraphs.

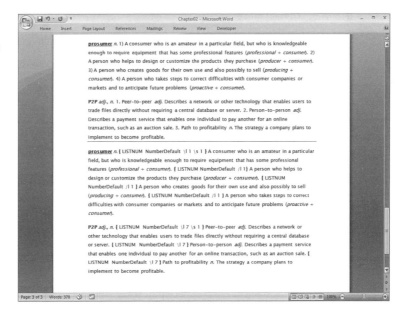

Converting Uppercase Words to Another Case

A common Word dilemma is downloading or receiving data where some of the text is in uppercase letters. This often happens with reports from mainframe computers, for example. If the entire document is uppercase, you select all the text (press Ctrl+A) and then apply the case you want, which is probably Capitalize Each Word (in the Home tab, pull down the Change Case menu and click <u>C</u>apitalize Each Word). You can also press Shift+F3 to cycle through the cases.

If some of the text is uppercase, then the problem becomes much harder. Listing 2.1 solves the problem with a VBA macro.

> **NOTE** You'll find the examples used in this book on my website at `www.mcfedries.com/Office2007Gurus`.

Listing 2.1   A VBA Macro That Converts All Uppercase Text to a Specifed Case

```
Public Sub ConvertUppercase()
    Dim intCase As Variant
    Dim strPrompt As String
    Dim i As Long
    Dim j As Long
    Dim intWords As Long
    Dim rngWord As Range
    '
    ' Get the desired case
    '
    strPrompt = "Enter the case you want UPPERCASE words converted to:" & _
                vbCrLf & vbCrLf & _
                "0 = lowercase" & vbCrLf & _
                "2 = Capitalize Each Word" & vbCrLf & _
                "4 = Sentence case"
    intCase = InputBox(strPrompt, , 0)
    '
    ' Bail if we didn't get the right number
    '
    If intCase <> 0 And intCase <> 2 And intCase <> 4 Then Exit Sub
    '
    ' Get the total number of words
    '
    intWords = ActiveDocument.Words.Count
    '
    ' Run through all the words
    '
    i = 1
    j = 0
    For Each rngWord In ActiveDocument.Words
        Application.StatusBar = "Checking word " & i & " of " & intWords
        If rngWord.Case = wdUpperCase Then
            rngWord.Case = intCase
            j = j + 1
        End If
        i = i + 1
    Next 'rngWord
    Application.StatusBar = j & " words converted."
End Sub
```

This macro begins by prompting you for the case to which you want to convert the upper-case words. Figure 2.10 shows the dialog box that displays. You enter 0 for a lowercase conversion, 2 for Capitalize Each Word, and 4 for sentence case. The macro then runs through every word in the document. Each time it finds an uppercase word, it converts it to the case you specified. The macro shows the progress of the conversion in the status bar, and at the end, it displays the number of words that it converted.

Figure 2.10
Examples of inline num-
bered lists—the bottom
paragraphs show the
field codes used in the
top paragraphs.

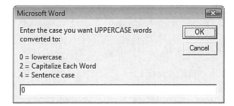

Converting Smart Quotes to Straight Quotes

The quotation marks available via the keyboard—the single quote (') and the double quote
(")—are fine in most cases, but they're decidedly plain. For more formal documents, you
might prefer to use the curly quote variations where ' and ' replace the single quote and "
and " replace the double quote. You can enter these quotation marks using your keyboard.
Here are the codes:

Press	To Get
Alt+0145	'
Alt+0146	'
Alt+0147	"
Alt+0148	"

In each case, be sure to use your keyboard's numeric keypad to type the numbers.

You can also set up Word to convert straight quotes (' and ") into "smart" quotes (such as
' and ") automatically. This is part of the AutoCorrect's AutoFormat As You Type feature
and is turned on by default in most Word installations. To make sure, choose Office, Word
Options, click Proofing, click AutoCorrect Options, and then display the AutoFormat As
You Type tab. Make sure the Straight Quotes with Smart Quotes check box is activated and
then click OK in all open dialog boxes.

The opposite situation is when you have a document that contains smart quotes and you
want to convert them all to straight quotes. This is a common scenario when you want to
send the document to a page layout program, commercial printer, web page, and email
message. In most cases, the destination program won't recognize the smart quotes and will
substitute garbage characters for them. To avoid this, you need to convert each smart quote
into its equivalent straight quote. Unfortunately, a typical document might contain dozens
of quotation marks, and Word offers no feature for converting quotation marks. You might
think a find-and-replace operation would do the trick, but that doesn't work because Word
reconverts the regular quotes back to smart quotes. Fortunately, you can work around this
limitation by using the VBA macro shown in Listing 2.2.

Listing 2.2   A VBA macro that converts smart quotes into straight quotes

```vba
Sub ConvertQuotes()
    Dim blnAutoFormatQuotes As Boolean
    '
    ' Save the current Replace Quotes setting
    '
    blnAutoFormatQuotes = Options.AutoFormatAsYouTypeReplaceQuotes
    '
    ' Turn off automatic replacement of straight quotes
    '
    Options.AutoFormatAsYouTypeReplaceQuotes = False
    '
    ' Perform the conversions
    '
    With ActiveDocument.Range.Find
        '
        ' Clear any formatting
        '
        .ClearFormatting
        .Replacement.ClearFormatting
        '
        ' Convert ' to '
        '
        .Text = Chr(145)
        .Replacement.Text = Chr(39)
        .Execute Replace:=wdReplaceAll
        '
        ' Convert ' to '
        '
        .Text = Chr(146)
        .Replacement.Text = Chr(39)
        .Execute Replace:=wdReplaceAll
        '
        ' Convert " to "
        '
        .Text = Chr(147)
        .Replacement.Text = Chr(34)
        .Execute Replace:=wdReplaceAll, Format:=False
        '
        ' Convert " to "
        '
        .Text = Chr(148)
        .Replacement.Text = Chr(34)
        .Execute Replace:=wdReplaceAll
    End With
    '
    ' Restore the Replace Quotes setting
    '
    Options.AutoFormatAsYouTypeReplaceQuotes = blnAutoFormatQuotes
End Sub
```

For this macro to work, the "Straight Quotes" with "Smart Quotes" check box must be temporarily deactivated. So the macro begins by taking the current value of this setting (as given by the AutoFormatAsYouTypeReplaceQuotes property) and storing it in the `blnAutoFormatQuotes` Boolean variable. Then the macro turns off the features (by setting the `AutoFormatAsYouTypeReplaceQuotes` property to `False`). The macro then runs four separate `Replace` operations, one for each type of smart quote. Finally, the macro restores the value of the `AutoFormatAsYouTypeReplaceQuotes` property.

Formatting a Single Column in Tab-Separated Text

If you have data that you want to display in a row-and-column format within a Word document, the quickest way to set this up is to enter the data with a tab that separates each item in a row. You can then adjust your tab stops to ensure that all the columns line up neatly. This works great, except when you later decide that you need to format one of the columns. For example, if the items in the first column are headings, you might want to make them bold or a different color. Unfortunately, if you try any of Word's regular text-selection techniques, you'll find it impossible to select a single column because Word is set up to select only regular text horizontally.

One solution is to convert the text to a table, which enables you to select any column by clicking the top edge of the column. This works, but it may not be an ideal solution for you. For example, many page layout programs don't understand Word's tables, so in such a case you'd need to convert your table back to regular text.

You can avoid table conversion altogether by employing a useful trick that enables Word to select text vertically. Follow these steps:

1. Press and hold the Alt key.
2. Move the mouse pointer slightly to the left of the topmost item in the column you want to select.
3. Click and drag the mouse down and to the right. As you drag, Word selects text vertically.
4. When you've selected the text you want, release the mouse button and release Alt.

Figure 2.11 shows some tab-separated text where the first column has been selected using this method.

Figure 2.11
Hold down Alt and click-and-drag the mouse to select a column in tab-separated text.

| Inflation Rates by Month 1995-2005 | | | | | | | | | | | | | |
YEAR	JAN	FEB	MAR	APR	MAY	JUN	JUL	AUG	SEP	OCT	NOV	DEC	AVE
2005	2.97%	3.01%	3.15%	3.51%	2.80%	2.53%	3.17%	3.64%	4.69%	4.35%	3.46%	3.42%	3.39%
2004	1.93%	1.69%	1.74%	2.29%	3.05%	3.27%	2.99%	2.65%	2.54%	3.19%	3.52%	3.26%	2.68%
2003	2.60%	2.98%	3.02%	2.22%	2.06%	2.11%	2.11%	2.16%	2.32%	2.04%	1.77%	1.88%	2.27%
2002	1.14%	1.14%	1.48%	1.64%	1.18%	1.07%	1.46%	1.80%	1.51%	2.03%	2.20%	2.38%	1.59%
2001	3.73%	3.53%	2.92%	3.27%	3.62%	3.25%	2.72%	2.72%	2.65%	2.13%	1.90%	1.55%	2.83%
2000	2.74%	3.22%	3.76%	3.07%	3.19%	3.73%	3.66%	3.41%	3.45%	3.45%	3.45%	3.39%	3.38%
1999	1.67%	1.61%	1.73%	2.28%	2.09%	1.96%	2.14%	2.26%	2.63%	2.56%	2.62%	2.68%	2.19%
1998	1.57%	1.44%	1.37%	1.44%	1.69%	1.68%	1.68%	1.62%	1.49%	1.49%	1.55%	1.61%	1.55%
1997	3.04%	3.03%	2.76%	2.50%	2.23%	2.30%	2.23%	2.23%	2.15%	2.08%	1.83%	1.70%	2.34%
1996	2.73%	2.65%	2.84%	2.90%	2.89%	2.75%	2.95%	2.88%	3.00%	2.99%	3.26%	3.32%	2.93%
1995	2.80%	2.86%	2.85%	3.05%	3.19%	3.04%	2.76%	2.62%	2.54%	2.81%	2.61%	2.54%	2.81%
Source: http://inflationdata.com/													

Ensuring Consistent Document Formatting

One of the hallmarks of professional Word documents is that they are formatted in a consistent manner. For example, a professional document applies bold formatting either by applying the Strong style or by applying the formatting directly with the Bold command, but it never mixes the two methods. (In fact, most professional documents always use character styles instead of direct formatting because you can automatically make changes to character styles, and Word updates every instance.) Similarly, any two adjacent paragraphs of regular text will use the same paragraph formatting.

Of course, *wanting* your document formatting to be consistent and actually *making sure* of this are two different things. You can get Word to help you by asking it to look for formatting inconsistencies. Follow these steps to turn on this feature:

1. Choose Office, Word Options to open the Word Options dialog box.
2. Click the Advanced tab.
3. Activate the Mark Formatting Inconsistencies check box. (If this check box is disabled, activate the Keep Track of Formatting check box.)
4. Click OK.

When Word spots a formatting inconsistency, it displays a wavy blue line under the offending text. Right-click the text to see Word's suggested solution. In Figure 2.12, for example, Word has found adjacent paragraphs with inconsistent formatting. Click the suggestion to implement it. You can also click Ignore Once to skip this instance, or Ignore Rule to tell Word to stop flagging this particular inconsistency.

Figure 2.12
Activate the Mark Formatting Inconsistencies setting to have Word look for inconsistent formatting in your documents.

Wrapping Text Around an Image

You can add a great deal of visual pizzazz to a document by inserting an image. This can be a picture that illustrates a concept, a digital photo of a person, an event described in your text, a chart, your company logo, or simply a striking or fun bit of clip art. Whatever the image, it will look better and your document will read more smoothly if the text wraps around the image.

Unfortunately, Word's default wrapping behavior doesn't provide the best results for most images. The default wrapping is called In Line With Text, and it means that Word moves the image along with the text as you insert and delete text before the image. Unfortunately, the text lines up with the bottom edge of the image, so for all but the smallest images, this creates a huge and unsightly gap in the document. Follow these steps to fix this:

1. Click the image.
2. Click the Format tab.
3. For a drawing or SmartArt graphic, click Arrange.
4. To set the position of the image within the page, click Position, and then click one of the preset position options, shown in Figure 2.13. Note that the options in the With Text Wrapping section automatically apply Square text wrapping (see step 5 for the details).

Figure 2.13
Use the Position gallery to set the image's position with Square text wrapping.

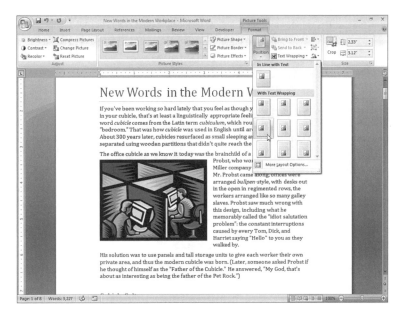

5. To set the text wrapping, click Text Wrapping and then click one of the following options:

In Line With Text—Moves the image along with the text as you insert and delete text before the image.

Square—Wraps the text around the image's frame.

Tight—Wraps the text along the edges of the image itself.

Behind Text—Moves the image behind the text layer.

In Front of Text—Moves the image in front of the text layer.

Top and Bottom—Stops the text above the image and resumes the text on a new line below the object.

Through—This is the same as the tight text wrapping, except Word also wraps the text into any open space within the image.

Edit Wrap Points—This option (which is only available if you select the Tight text wrapping) enables you to specify exactly where Word wraps text around the image. This can be useful if the image is an unusual shape because the text may wrap in a strange way when you use the Tight text wrapping. When you click Edit Wrap Points, Word displays a series of edit handles around the image. Click and drag the edit handles to define the edges around which Word wraps the surrounding text in a Tight text wrap.

More Layout Options—Displays the Advanced Layout dialog box, which enables you to set precise values for position and wrapping.

> **TIP**
>
> To set one of these text-wrapping options as Word's default wrapping behavior, choose Office, Word Options. In the Word Options dialog box, click Advanced and then use the Insert/Paste Pictures As list to click the wrapping you prefer.

Adding a Drop Cap

You can add visual interest to your documents by adding one or more *drop caps*. A drop cap refers to an initial letter in a paragraph that has been formatted with large font size. Word also places the letter inside its own frame, which enables the letter to display either in the top left corner of the paragraph or in the margin. Most documents that use a drop cap use it only in the first paragraph, although it's not unusual to also see drop caps in the first paragraph of each section of a document.

Follow these steps to create a drop cap:

1. Click inside the paragraph where you want the drop cap to display.
2. Choose Insert, Drop Cap. Word displays a gallery of drop cap styles.
3. For a quick drop cap, click either Dropped or In Margin and skip the rest of these steps. Otherwise, click Drop Cap Options to open the Drop Cap dialog box.
4. Click Dropped or In Margin.
5. Click the Font you want to use.
6. Use the Lines to Drop spin box to set the size of the drop cap frame.
7. Use the Distance from Text spin box to set the amount of space, in inches, that Word adds to the right of the drop cap frame to separate it from the text.

8. Click OK. Word creates a frame around the first letter of the paragraph, positions the frame according to the drop cap style you chose, and formats the font size of the letter. Figure 2.14 shows an example.

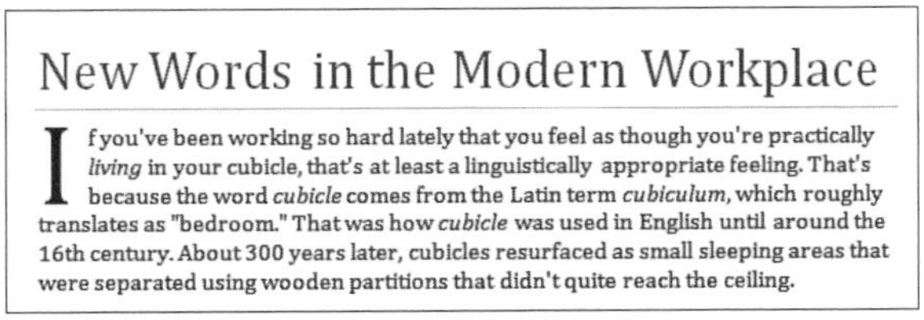

Figure 2.14
A drop cap often adds a nice touch to a document's opening paragraph.

New Words in the Modern Workplace

If you've been working so hard lately that you feel as though you're practically *living* in your cubicle, that's at least a linguistically appropriate feeling. That's because the word *cubicle* comes from the Latin term *cubiculum*, which roughly translates as "bedroom." That was how *cubicle* was used in English until around the 16th century. About 300 years later, cubicles resurfaced as small sleeping areas that were separated using wooden partitions that didn't quite reach the ceiling.

From Here

- To learn how to prevent other users from messing with your formatting, **see** "Locking Document Formatting, **p. 77.**

- To ensure you can see the formatting changes made by others, **see**, "Preventing Untracked Changes," **p. 79.**

- To learn how to compare two different parts of a document, **see** "Viewing Two Documents Side by Side," **p. 85.**

- To add a custom watermark to a document, **see** "Creating a Custom Watermark," **p. 93.**

- To learn how to use the Visual Basic Editor and incorporate macros into your documents, **see** "Working with VBA Macros," **p. 429.**

Document Tricks

3

If you're a regular Word user, then you probably work with many different Word documents during an average work day, and you've probably got hundreds or even thousands of Word documents stored on your hard drive. The document is the basic Word container, and knowing how to work with documents is a fundamental Word skill. However, working with documents doesn't just mean using the commands on the Office menu (Open, Save, Close, and so on). Word is chock full of tricks, shortcuts, and settings that can make working with documents faster, easier, more powerful, and more efficient. This chapter introduces you to many of the techniques that cover everything, from easier ways to save and protect your documents to scripts that calculate editing time and billable time.

Recovering More of Your Work with a Shorter AutoRecover Interval

No one who has used Word for any length of time needs to be convinced of the importance of saving a document regularly. We've all experienced that moment of horror (sometimes called the *ohnosecond*) when we realize that Word has locked solid and we haven't saved for awhile, so all our recent work is toast. Most of us have become friendly with the Ctrl+S shortcut for the Save command and use it as often as possible. However, it's easy to forget to save when you're busy and a deadline looms large. As a safety net, Word has an AutoRecover feature that automatically stores information about the changes you've made to your document since the last save. If Word goes down for the count, it can use the AutoRecover data to help you recover some or all of your work.

AutoRecover has saved me on a number of occasions, so I'm a big fan of this feature. If it has a downside, however, it's that the default interval that Word uses to save the AutoRecover data is too long: 10 minutes. You can lose a lot of work in 10 minutes, so it's a good idea to shorten the interval:

■ If you work with only small- or medium-sized documents, shorten the interval to 1 minute.

■ If you're working with a large document (several dozen pages or more), the AutoRecover process can take quite awhile. Therefore, if you occasionally work with large documents, shorten the interval to 3 or 4 minutes.

■ If you work with large documents only, you might not want Word to use AutoRecover. In this case, you can turn off the AutoRecover feature.

To work with AutoRecover, choose Office, Word Options to open the Word Option dialog box, click Save, and then use the Save AutoRecover Information Every *X* Minutes spin box to set the interval you prefer. If you want to turn off AutoRecover, deactivate the Save AutoRecover Information check box. Click OK to put the new setting into effect.

Automatically Saving Your Work Frequently

Setting the AutoRecover interval to 1 minute, as described in the previous section, is probably good enough for most people. However, a fast typist can easily write dozens of words in a minute, so you can still lose a fair amount of work even when using the shortest AutoRecover interval.

To get an even faster save interval, you can use VBA, specifically, Word's OnTime method, which runs a procedure at a specified time. The OnTime method uses the following syntax:

```
Application.OnTime(When, Name [, Tolerance])
```

When	The time (and date, if needed) you want the procedure to run.
Name	The name of the procedure to run when the time given by *When* arrives.
Tolerance	If Word isn't ready to run the procedure at *When*, it will keep trying for the number of seconds specified by *Tolerance*. If you omit *Tolerance*, VBA waits until Word is ready.

You must enter the *When* argument as a date/time serial number. The easiest way to do this is to use the TimeValue function:

```
TimeValue(Time)
```

Time	A string representing the time you want to use (such as "8:00 PM" or "20:00").

For example, the following code runs a procedure called `MakeBackup` at 8:00 PM:

```
Application.OnTime _
    When:=TimeValue("8:00 PM"), _
    Name:="MakeBackup"
```

What we really want to do here is run a macro that saves the current document, and we want to run that macro at a specified time interval (for example, every 30 seconds). If you want the `OnTime` method to run after a specified time interval, use the expression `Now + TimeValue(Time)` for `When` (where `Time` is the interval you want to use). For example, if you want to save your work every 30 seconds, use the following expression for `When`:

```
Now + TimeValue("00:00:30"),
```

Listing 3.1 shows a macro that does this.

> **NOTE** You'll find the Word and Excel files used as examples in this chapter on my website at www.mcfedries.com/Office2007Gurus.

Listing 3.1   A Macro That Saves the Active Document Every 20 Seconds

```
Public Sub FileSave()
    ActiveDocument.Save
    DoEvents
    Application.OnTime _
        When:=Now + TimeValue("00:00:20"), _
        name:="FileSave"
    Application.StatusBar = "Saved: " & ActiveDocument.Name
End Sub
```

The `FileSave` macro begins by saving the current document using the `ActiveDocument` object's `Save` method. The `DoEvents` method processes any keystrokes that occurred during the save, and then the `OnTime` method sets up the `FileSave` procedure to run again in 20 seconds. The macro ends by displaying a status bar message to let you know the document was saved.

> **TIP** It's important that the macro in Listing 3.1 is named `FileSave` because this is also the internal name of Word's Save command (the one you run when you choose Office, Save). By giving your procedure the same name (and preceding the `Sub` keyword with `Public` to make it available to all documents), you intercept any calls to the Save command and replace Word's internal procedure with your own. This isn't strictly necessary, but it's handy because it means that your procedure will run as soon as the Office, Save command is chosen.

To find out the internal names of Word's commands, choose Office, Word Options, click Customize, and then click the Customize button to display the Customize Keyboard dialog box. Select an item in the Categories list and then look up the internal command name in the Commands list. Alternatively, hold down Ctrl and Alt, press the + key on your numeric keypad, and then click the Ribbon command associated with the command you want to use. Word displays the Customize Keyboard dialog box with only the selected command displayed.

Closing a Document Without Saving

It's occasionally convenient to close a document without saving your changes. For example, you might create a new document to use as a scratch pad or to test out a new feature. Similarly, you might open an existing document, make some temporary changes, and then close the document without saving those changes. In each case, when you choose Office, Close, Word asks if you want to save the document. This not only slows you down by requiring an extra step that you don't need, but there's also the real danger that you might click Yes by accident.

To work around these problems, I use a macro that automatically closes a document without saving any changes and without prompting to save changes. Listing 3.2 shows the macro.

Listing 3.2   A Macro That Closes a Document Without Saving Changes

```
Sub CloseWithoutSaving()
    ActiveDocument.Close SaveChanges:=wdDoNotSaveChanges
End Sub
```

As you can see, this is a simple procedure that runs only the ActiveDocument object's Close method with the SaveChanges argument set to the constant value wdDoNotSaveChanges.

A more involved example is shown in Listing 3.3.

Listing 3.3   A Macro That Closes a Document Without Saving Changes and Then Reopens the Document

```
Sub CloseAndReopen()
    Dim currDoc As String, nState As Integer
    Dim nLeft As Integer, nTop As Integer
    Dim nWidth As Integer, nHeight As Integer
    '
    ' Preserve the window position and dimensions
    '
    With ActiveWindow
        nState = .WindowState
        nLeft = .Left
        nTop = .Top
```

```
        nWidth = .Width
        nHeight = .Height
    End With
    '
    ' Close it without saving changes
    '
    With ActiveDocument
        currDoc = .FullName
        .Close SaveChanges:=wdDoNotSaveChanges
    End With
    '
    ' Reopen the document
    '
    Documents.Open currDoc
    '
    ' Restore the window
    '
    With ActiveWindow
        .WindowState = nState
        If Not .WindowState = wdWindowStateMaximize Then
            .Left = nLeft
            .Top = nTop
            .Width = nWidth
            .Height = nHeight
        End If
    End With
End Sub
```

This macro first uses various properties of the ActiveWindow object to save the document's current window state, position, and dimensions. Then the code saves the document's full path name (as given by the FullName property), and the document is closed without saving changes. The Open method reopens the document, and then the window is restored to its former state, position, and dimensions.

> ___ C A U T I O N _____
>
> Be sure to move the CloseAndReopen macro to a document other than the one that you'll be closing and reopening. (For example, you could store it in the Normal template.) Otherwise, when the document is closed, the code module is closed along with it, so the document can't reopen.

Closing All Your Open Documents

Later in this chapter, you learn how to create *workspaces*—collections of Word documents that you open as a unit. Before you open a workspace, it's a good idea to close all your open documents. You might also want to close all your open documents to get a fresh start with Word. In previous versions of Word, you can do this by holding down the Shift key, pulling down the File menu, and then selecting the Close All command. Unfortunately, that trick does not work in Word 2007. The other alternative is to shut down and restart Word, but that's often time-consuming. A faster method is to use the macro in Listing 3.4.

→ To learn how to create Word workspaces, **see** "Creating and Opening Document Workspaces," **p. 70**

> **TIP** The Close All command still exists in Word, but it's not part of the Ribbon. To add it to the Quick Access Toolbar, pull down the Customize Quick Access toolbar list and click More Commands. In the Choose Commands From list, click All Commands, scroll down the list of commands, and click Close All. Click Add and then click OK.

Listing 3.4   A Macro That Closes All Open Documents

```
Sub CloseAllOpenDocuments()
    Dim doc As Document
    For Each doc In Documents
        doc.Close
    Next 'doc
End Sub
```

This macro runs through the Document objects that are in the Documents collection, which holds all the documents that are currently open in Word. For each document, the macro runs the Close method without any arguments, which means that Word will prompt you to save changes.

Making Backups as You Work

Even if you're using the macros earlier in the chapter to save your work frequently, you can still lose data if your hard drive crashes. So we've all learned from hard experience not only to save our work regularly, but also to make periodic backup copies. The macro I use most often in Word is one that does both in a single procedure! That is, the macro not only saves your work, but it also makes a backup copy on another drive, such as a removable disk, a second hard drive, or a network folder. Listing 3.5 shows the code.

Listing 3.5   A Procedure That Creates a Backup Copy of the Active Document on Another Drive

```
Sub MakeBackup()
    Dim currFile As String
    Dim backupFile As String
    Const BACKUP_FOLDER = "G:\Backups\"
    With ActiveDocument
        '
        ' Don't bother if the document is unchanged or new
        '
        If .Saved Or .Path = "" Then Exit Sub
        '
        ' Mark current position in document
        '
        .Bookmarks.Add Name:="LastPosition"
        '
        ' Turn off screen updating
        '
```

```
        Application.ScreenUpdating = False
        '
        ' Save the file
        '
        .Save
        '
        ' Store the current file path, construct the path for the
        ' backup file, and then save it to the backup drive
        '
        currFile = .FullName
        backupFile = BACKUP_FOLDER + .Name
        .SaveAs FileName:=backupFile
    End With
    '
    ' Close the backup copy (which is now active)
    '
    ActiveDocument.Close
    '
    ' Reopen the current file
    '
    Documents.Open FileName:=currFile
    '
    ' Return to the pre-backup position
    '
    Selection.GoTo What:=wdGoToBookmark, Name:="LastPosition"
End Sub
```

The backupFile and currFile variables are strings that store the full pathnames for the active document and the backup version of the document. Use the BACKUP_FOLDER constant to specify the folder in which you want the backup stored.

The procedures first check to see if the backup operation is necessary. In other words, if the document has no unsaved changes (the Saved property returns True) or if it's a new, unsaved document (the Path property returns ""), bail out of the procedure (by running Exit Sub).

Otherwise, a new Bookmark object is created to save the current position in the document, screen updating is turned off, and the file is saved.

We're now ready to perform the backup. First, the currFile variable is used to store the full pathname of the document, and the pathname of the backup file is built with the following statement:

```
backupFile = BACKUP_FOLDER + .Name
```

This is used to save the file to the specified folder. The actual backup takes place via the SaveAs method, which saves the document to the path given by backupFile. From there, the procedure closes the backup file, reopens the original file, and uses the GoTo method to return to the original position within the document.

> **TIP**
>
> Using a `Bookmark` object to reset the insertion point is useful because it takes you back to the exact point in the document where you were before the backup started. However, you may be interested only in returning to the last position within the document where an edit occurred. If that's the case, use the following statement in place of the `Selection.GoTo` statement:
>
>   Application.GoBack
>
> Note, however, that there's a bug in the `GoBack` method, whereby Word doesn't save the last edit position (technically, it's a hidden bookmark named `\PrevSel1`) in some cases. Specifically, when you exit Word, if you elect to save changes in the last document that gets closed, Word doesn't save the last edit position in that document.

Showing More Items on the Recent Documents List

When you pull down the Office menu in Word, you see the various "File" commands on the left and a list of your most recently used documents on the right. This list is called the Recent Documents list, and most Word installations display up to 17 documents on this list. If you regularly deal with many different Word documents, you might want to see even more files on this list. Follow these steps to increase the size of the Recent Document list:

1. Choose Office, Word Options to open the Word Options dialog box.
2. Click Advanced.
3. In the Display section, use the Show This Number of Recent Documents spin box to set the number of documents you want to see.

> **NOTE**
>
> The maximum number of recent documents you can display is 50. If you specify more than your screen height can handle, Word just displays as many as it can.

4. Click OK.

Opening the Most Recently Used Document at Startup

Word's `RecentFiles` object represents the collection of most recently used files displayed in the Recent Documents list. Each item on this list is a `RecentFile` object. You specify a `RecentFile` object by using `RecentFiles(Index)`, where *Index* is an integer that specifies the file you want to work with. The most recently used file is 1, the second most recently used file is 2, and so on.

When you close a Word session, the document you last made changes to becomes the most recently used document. There's a good chance that you'll want to continue working on that document the next time you start Word. Therefore, it would be handy to have Word open the most recently used file each time you start the program.

If you want Word to run some code each time it's started, open the Visual Basic Editor (either by choosing Developer, Visual Basic or by pressing Alt+F11), click the Normal project in the Visual Basic Editor's Project Explorer, and then create a new module (by choosing Insert, Module) named AutoExec. In this module, create a Sub procedure named Main and enter your code in that procedure. Listing 3.6 shows such a procedure:

> **NOTE** If you don't see the Developer tab in Word's Ribbon, choose Office, Word Options, click Popular, click to activate the Show Developer Tab in the Ribbon check box, and then click OK.

Listing 3.6   A Procedure That Opens the Most Recently Used Document

```
Sub Main()
    Application.RecentFiles(1).Open
End Sub
```

Clearing the Recent Documents List

The Recent Documents list is great for quickly reopening files you've worked with recently, particularly because you can increase the size of the list, as described earlier. It's not so great if other people have access to your computer because then they can easily see what you've been working on, and if you've been working on documents that contain sensitive data, the Recent Document list just makes life a bit *too* easy for a snoop. To increase security, you should remove sensitive items from the Recent Documents list. You can do this either by removing specific documents or by clearing the entire list.

To remove a single item from the Recent Documents list, follow these steps:

1. Press Ctrl+Alt+-. (Use the dash on the upper row of the keyboard, not the one on the numeric keypad.) The mouse pointer changes to a horizontal line.

2. Click the Office button.

3. In the Recent Documents list, click the document you want to clear.

For maximum privacy and security, you might prefer to clear the entire Recent Documents list (say, at the end of the day when you're done working or when you are leaving your desk for an extended time). You can do this by running the procedure shown in Listing 3.7.

Listing 3.7   A Procedure That Removes All Items From the Recent Documents List

```
Sub ClearRecentFiles()
    Dim rf As RecentFile
    For Each rf In Application.RecentFiles
        rf.Delete
    Next 'rf
End Sub
```

TIP If you don't want Word to store *any* items on the Recent Documents list, you can disable it. Choose Office, Word Options, click Advanced, and then set the Show This Number of Recent Documents spin box to 0.

Creating and Opening Document Workspaces

When I work in Word (which I do pretty much all day long), I usually work with distinct groups of documents:

- If I'm working on a book, I open the current chapter, the outline, a notes document, a document to record screen shots, and so on.
- If I'm working on an article, I open the article, the proposal, my research notes, and so on.
- If I'm working on a blog post, I open the post and perhaps a few supporting documents.

It's not unusual for me to work on two, three, or even four such projects during the day. I like the variety, but it's a major pain to close all the documents for one project and then open all the documents I need for the next project. Perhaps that's why the Word macros I'm going to show you in this chapter are my favorites. Their purpose, as you'll see, is to create *workspaces* for Word projects that you can easily and quickly open.

→ Excel has a built-in command for creating workspaces; **see** "Creating a Workspace of Workbooks," **p. 153**

A workspace is just a collection of related documents. Unfortunately, Word doesn't come with this functionality, but you can use VBA to create your own workspaces, as shown in Listing 3.8.

Listing 3.8   Procedures That Create and Open a Workspace of Files

```
' CreateWorkspace()
' Saves the path and filename data of all the
' open files to the Windows Registry. Before
' running this procedure, make sure only the
' files you want in the workspace are open.
'
Sub CreateWorkspace(strWorkspaceName As String)
    Dim total As Integer
    Dim doc As Document
    Dim i As Integer
    '
    ' Delete the old workspace Registry settings
    ' First, get the total number of files
    '
    total = GetSetting("Word", strWorkspaceName, "TotalFiles", 0)
    For i = 1 To total
        '
        ' Delete each Registry setting
        '
```

```
            DeleteSetting "Word", strWorkspaceName, "Document" & i
    Next 'i
    '
    ' Create the new workspace
    '
    i = 0
    For Each doc In Documents
        '
        ' Make sure it's not a new, unsaved file
        '
        If doc.Path <> "" then
            '
            ' Use i to create unique Registry setting names
            '
            i = i + 1
            '
            ' Save the FullName (path and filename) to the Registry
            '
            SaveSetting "Word", strWorkspaceName, "Document" & i, doc.FullName
        End If
    Next 'doc
    '
    ' Save the total number of files to the Registry
    '
    SaveSetting "Word", strWorkspaceName, "TotalFiles", i
    Application.StatusBar = i & " documents saved to workspace."
End Sub
'
' OpenWorkspace()
' Accesses the Registry's workspace settings
' and then opens each workspace file.
'
Sub OpenWorkspace(strWorkspaceName As String)
    Dim total As Integer
    Dim i As Integer
    Dim filePath As String
    Dim doc As Document
    Dim fileAlreadyOpen As Boolean
    '
    ' See if we should first close all the open documents
    '
    If MsgBox("Close all the open documents first?", vbYesNo) = vbYes Then
        CloseAllOpenDocuments
    End If
    '
    ' Get the total number of files from the Registry
    '
    total = GetSetting("Word", strWorkspaceName, "TotalFiles", 0)
    For i = 1 To total
        '
        ' Get the path and filename
        '
        filePath = GetSetting("Word", strWorkspaceName, "Document" & i)
        '
        ' Make sure the file isn't already open
```

continues

Listing 3.8   Continued

```
        fileAlreadyOpen = False
        For Each doc In Documents
            If filePath = doc.FullName Then
                fileAlreadyOpen = True
                Exit For
            End If
        Next 'doc
        '
        ' Open it
        '
        If Not fileAlreadyOpen Then
            Documents.Open filePath
        End If
    Next 'i
End Sub
```

Listing 3.8 shows two procedures that create the workspace functionality for Word:

- CreateWorkspace—This procedure uses the Windows Registry to store a list of open documents. Before running this procedure, make sure that only those files you want to include in the workspace are currently open.

- OpenWorkspace—This procedure first asks if you want to close all the open documents. (If you click Yes, the procedure runs the CloseAllOpenDocuments macro from Listing 3.4.) The procedure then accesses the Registry and runs through the list of saved files. For each setting, the procedure checks to see if the file is already open. If it's not, the procedure runs the Documents.Open method to open the file.

Notice that both procedures take strWorkspaceName as an argument. This is a string value that specifies the name of the workspace you want to create or open. This enables you to create as many different workspaces as you need. Here are two simple procedures that demonstrate how you'd use the macros in Listing 3.8 to create and open a workspace:

```
Sub CreateWorkspaceTest()
    CreateWorkspace "My Project"
End Sub

Sub OpenWorkspaceTest()
    OpenWorkspace "My Project"
End Sub
```

Automatically Prompting for Document Properties

One of the interesting innovations in Windows Vista is the placement of document meta-data—properties such as the document author, subject, and status, as well as one or more tags that describe the document—at the heart of the operating system. In Vista, you can use metadata to sort documents, organize documents in to groups, filter documents, and search for documents. This is great in theory, but in practice the utility of metadata depends entirely on how much of it there is. Some metadata is generated automatically by the program you use to create a document: the last modified date, the size of the file, and so on. However, most metadata is user-generated, so to get the most out of metadata, you need to remember to enter the data when you create new documents.

Older versions of Word had a setting that, when activated, configured Word to display the Properties dialog box each time you saved a new document for the first time. This was a great way to remember to enter metadata, but Word 2007 goes one better: It will also prompt you for metadata (by displaying the Document Information Panel) each time you open a document. Here's how to enable this setting in Word 2007:

1. Choose Developer, Document Panel to open the Document Information Panel dialog box.

2. Click to activate the Always <u>S</u>how Document Information panel On Document Open and Initial Save check box.

3. Click OK.

If you want an easier way to toggle this setting on and off, use the simple macro shown in Listing 3.9.

Listing 3.9   A Macro That Toggles the Automatic Display of the Document Information Panel

```
Sub ToggleDocumentPanel()
    With Application
        .DisplayDocumentInformationPanel = Not .DisplayDocumentInformationPanel
    End With
End Sub
```

Then put on Quick menu a button

> **TIP**
>
> If you want Word to display the Properties dialog box instead of the Document Information Panel, use the following statement to activate this setting:
>
> ```
> Application.Options.SavePropertiesPrompt = True
> ```
>
> If you created an `AutoExec` module earlier (see "Opening the Most Recently Used Document at Startup"), insert the `Application.Options.SavePropertiesPrompt` statement into the `Main` procedure so that it runs each time you start Word.

Creating a Trusted Location for Documents

Macro security is quite stringent in Office 2007, which shouldn't come as a surprise given the number of nasty VBA-based viruses and other malware that have spawned in the past few years. For a macro to work in Office 2007, the macro must come with a digital signature that is both valid and current, and the macro developer must be set up on your computer as a trusted publisher. To set up a developer as a trusted publisher, click Options when you see the Security Warning information bar, click to activate the Trust All Documents From This Publisher option, and then click OK.

What if you just want to run your own macros? In that case, you need to sign your own projects and then set yourself up as a trusted publisher.

> **NOTE** To digitally sign your own VBA projects, choose Start, All Programs, Microsoft Office, Microsoft Office Tools, Digital Certificate for VBA Projects. In the Create Digital Certificate dialog box, type a name (such as your own name) in the Your Certificate's Name text box and then click OK. When the SelfCert Success dialog box appears, click OK. Now open the Visual Basic Editor, select your project, and then choose Tools, Digital Signature. Click Choose, click your certificate, and then click OK.

If that all sounds like too much work, but you don't want to enable all macros, Word gives you a third choice: Store your macro-enabled documents in a trusted location. A *trusted location* is a folder that Word assumes contains only trustworthy documents, so it automatically enables any macros contained in those documents. By default, Word comes with three trusted locations:

%ProgramFiles%\Microsoft Office\Templates—This folder holds the application templates for all of Office.

%UserProfile%\Application Data\Microsoft\Templates—This folder holds the Office templates you create yourself.

%UserProfile%\Application Data\Microsoft\Word\Startup—This folder holds the global templates that you have created yourself and that are loaded into Word automatically at startup.

None of these locations are particularly convenient, but it's possible to set up a more suitable folder as a trusted location. Here are the steps to follow:

1. Choose Office, Word Options to open the Word Option dialog box.
2. Click Trust Center.
3. Click Trust Center Settings. The Trust Center dialog box displays.
4. Click Trusted Locations.

> **NOTE** While you're in the Trust Center, you might want to adjust your macro security setting. Click Macro Settings and then click the security option you prefer. If you're going to put all your macro-enabled documents in the trusted location that you're creating in these steps, you can click either Disable All Macros With Notification or Disable All Macros Without Notification.

5. If the trusted location is on your network, click to activate the Allow Trusted Locations On My Network check box.
6. Click Add New Location. The Microsoft Office Trusted Location dialog box displays, as shown in Figure 3.1.

Figure 3.1
Use the Trusted Locations page to set up new trusted locations in Word.

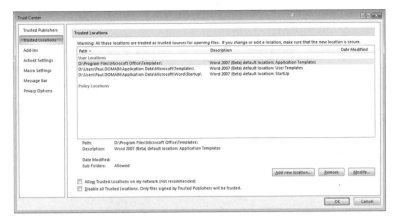

7. Use the Path text box to type the path of the trusted location.

8. If you want Word to also trust this location's subfolders, click to activate the <u>S</u>ubfolders of This Location Are Also Trusted check box.

9. Click OK.

10. Click OK to return to the Word Options dialog box.

11. Click OK.

Viewing Total Editing Time Updated in Real-Time

The total amount of time that a document has been edited is useful for freelancers, lawyers, consultants, and other professionals who bill for their time. Knowing how long you have spent working on a document enables you to provide a more accurate accounting of your time.

If you have a time budget that you're trying to stick to, you may find yourself constantly checking the document's Properties dialog box to view the Total editing time value. Rather than wasting time performing that chore, add the EditTime field to your document. Word's EditTime field displays the total time, in minutes, that the document has had the system focus (and, presumably, has been edited) since the time at which the document was created. This is the same as the Total editing time value displayed in the Statistics tab of the document's Properties dialog box.

> **NOTE**
> To display the Properties dialog box for the current document, choose Developer, Document Panel and click OK (or choose Office, Pr<u>e</u>pare, <u>P</u>roperties). Pull down the Document Properties list and then click Advanced Properties.

Follow these steps to add some code that displays the total editing time with the word `min-utes` added for clarity:

1. Type some descriptive text (such as **Total Editing Time:**).
2. Press Ctrl+F9 to start a new Word field (signified by the { and } braces).
3. Between the field braces, type the following:

```
EDITTIME \# "0 minutes" \* mergeformat
```

4. Press F9 to complete and update the field.

Now all you have to do is update the field to check the total editing time.

If even that sounds like a hassle, you can add a relatively simple macro to the document that will update the `EditTime` field in real-time. Open the Visual Basic Editor and insert a module in the document's project. Add the code in Listing 3.10 to the module.

Listing 3.10   Updating the `EditTime` Field in Real-Time

```
Public Sub UpdateEditTime()
    Dim f As Field
    For Each f In ThisDocument.Fields
        If f.Type = wdFieldEditTime Then
            f.Update
        End If
    Next 'f
    Application.OnTime Now + TimeValue("00:01:00"), "UpdateEditTime"
End Sub
```

This procedure runs through all the fields in the document looking for one where the `Type` property is `wdFieldEditTime`, which corresponds to the `EditTime` field. When the property is found, the `Update` method refreshes the field. The key to the real-time updating is the `Application.OnTime` statement, which sets up the `UpdateEditTime` procedure to run again in one minute. Note that you'll probably need to adjust the project name ("Chapter03") and the module name ("Chapter3") to match the name of your project and module.

> **TIP**
> To constantly monitor the `EditTime` field as it's updated in real-time, you can place the field at the top or bottom of the document and then split the window (choose View, Split), so that the field remains visible in one pane. If that's not convenient, you can display the latest `EditTime` result in the status bar. In Listing 3.10, insert the following statement after the `f.Update` method:
>
> ```
> Application.StatusBar = f.Result
> ```
>
> The Field object's `Result` property returns the current result of the specified field.

Calculating Billable Time Charges

You saw in the previous section that you use the EditTime field to return the total editing time for a document. If you bill by the hour based on the amount of time you have worked on a document, you might want to keep track of how much money you've earned so far. If you earn, for instance, $40 per hour, the following formula displays your current billable earnings:

```
{ = { EDITTIME } / 60 * 40 }
```

The EditTime result is given in minutes, so you have to divide by 60 to get the number of hours. You then multiply that result by 40 to get the earnings.

To ensure accurate billing, you may want to use the ROUND function to round the result to the nearest dollar:

```
{ = ROUND( { EDITTIME } / 60 * 40, 0) \#$0.00 }
```

This formula field also uses a numeric format to display the result with a dollar sign and two decimal places, as shown in Figure 3.2.

Figure 3.2
A formatted formula field that calculates the billable charge based on the current *EditTime* result.

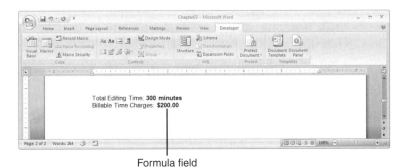

Formula field

Locking Document Formatting

Like most modern word processors, Word fits into the category of *fritterware*—programs with so many formatting bells and whistles that you can end up frittering away hours and hours by tweaking fonts, colors, alignments, and so on. Whether you think of such activity as "frittering" depends on your point of view, but we all agree that a well-formatted document makes a better impression than a plain or sloppy-looking one. So no matter how much time you've devoted to getting your document just so, the last thing you want is another person running roughshod over your careful look and layout.

Fortunately, Word offers the capability to lock your document's formatting, which prevents others from changing the formatting unless they know the password. Here are the steps to follow:

1. Choose Review, Protect Document (or choose Developer, Protect Document) and then click Restrict Formatting and Editing. Word displays the Restrict Formatting and Editing task pane.

2. Click to activate the Limit Formatting to a Selection of Styles check box.

3. Click Settings to display the Formatting Restrictions dialog box, shown in Figure 3.3.

Figure 3.3
Use the Formatting Restrictions dialog box to restrict the formatting another user can apply to a document.

4. In the Checked Styles Are Currently Allowed list, deactivate the check box next to each style that you want to disallow. Alternatively, use the following buttons to set the check boxes:

   - All—Click this button to activate all the check boxes and thus enable unauthorized users to apply formatting using only the existing styles; these users cannot modify the existing styles or create new styles.

   - Recommended Minimum—Click this button to activate the check boxes for only those styles that Word determines are necessary for the document.

   - None—Click this button to deactivate all the check boxes and thus prevent unauthorized users from changing any document formatting.

5. Choose your formatting options:

   - Allow AutoFormat to Override Formatting Restrictions—Click to activate this check box if you want any AutoFormats that the user applies to affect restricted styles.

   - Block Theme or Scheme Switching—Click to activate this check box to prevent the user from changing formatting by applying a formatting theme or scheme.

   - Block Quick Style Set Switching—Click to activate this check box to prevent the user from changing formatting by applying a Quick Style.

6. Click OK.

7. If Word warns you that the document contains disallowed styles, click Yes to remove them or click No to keep them.

8. In the Restrict Formatting and Editing task pane, click Yes, Start Enforcing Protection. The Start Enforcing Protection dialog box displays.

9. Type the password twice and then click OK. Word disables all the formatting commands on the Ribbon.

If you or another authorized user need to change the document formatting, choose Review, Protect Document (or choose Developer, Protect Document), click Restrict Formatting and Editing, and then click Stop Protection. Type the password, click OK, and then deactivate the Limit Formatting to a Selection of Styles check box.

Preventing Untracked Changes

QMS - might be important

When you share a Word document, it's common to turn on the Track Changes feature (choose Review, Track Changes) so that you can see all the edits made by the other person. Unfortunately, it's easy to turn off Track Changes (either accidentally or on purpose) so you can never be sure whether your document contains any untracked changes.

If it's important that you track all edits, it's possible to set up Word to prevent untracked changes and even to enforce this option with a password. Here are the steps to follow:

1. Choose Review, Protect Document (or choose Developer, Protect Document) and then click Restrict Formatting and Editing. Word displays the Restrict Formatting and Editing task pane.

2. Click to activate the Allow Only This Type of Editing in the Document check box.

3. In the Editing Restrictions list, click Tracked Changes.

4. Click Yes, Start Enforcing Protection. The Start Enforcing Protection dialog box displays.

5. Type the password twice and then click OK.

TIP If you're using Word in a Windows domain or an Exchange shop, you can set up portions of a document as read-only, and you can make exceptions for certain users. In the Restrict Formatting and Editing task pane, use the Editing Restrictions list to select No Changes (Read-only). If you want users to edit only a portion of the document, select that portion. In the Exceptions group, click More Users and then type the usernames or email addresses (separated by semicolons) of the users you want to be able to freely edit the selected portion. In the Individuals list, activate the check box next to each user.

If you or another authorized user need to freely edit the document text, choose Review, Protect Document (or choose Developer, Protect Document), and then Restrict Formatting and Editing to display the Restrict Formatting and Editing task pane. Click Stop Protection, type the password, click OK, and then deactivate the Allow Only This Type of Editing in the Document check box.

Setting Up a Document for Structured Editing

 A common business scenario involves creating an overall design for a document, filling in some standard text, and then leaving a few sections blank for other users to fill in. In a company report, for example, the design and most of the content might be fixed, but it might also have sections in which different departments can enter results, mission statements, goals, and so on. In these situations, it's crucial that the other users who add their content to the document do not also change the document design or any of the other content.

The previous two sections showed you how to lock document formatting and prevent untracked changes. You can also designate a document to be read-only (choose Office, Prepare, Mark as Final) so that no changes can be made. However, none of these techniques solve the problem of preventing users from editing or deleting parts of a document, while also allowing them the ability to add specific types of content. This is called *structured editing*, and Word 2007 offers a number of other tools that make it possible.

The first part of structured editing involves setting up regions of the document so that other people can't edit them or delete them. In Word 2007, you do that by forming those regions into a *group*. By default, a group cannot be edited or formatted, and you can also configure a group so that it cannot be deleted.

To convert text into a group, select the text and then choose Developer, Group, Group. Word locks the group, although you don't see anything on screen to tell you this. (This is by design: Your document looks exactly as it did before, so the quality and design of the document is not changed by creating a group.) If you also want to prevent users from deleting all or part of the group, follow these steps:

1. Click inside the group.
2. Choose Developer, Properties to open the Group Properties dialog box shown in Figure 3.4.
3. Click to activate the Content Control Cannot Be Deleted check box.
4. Click OK.

 TIP   In most cases, you probably don't want users to insert any content to the document, except in the sections that you designate (more on this later in this section). To ensure this, select the entire document and then run the Group command. This locks the whole document against editing.

Figure 3.4
Use the Group Properties dialog box to prevent the grouped text from being deleted.

If you need to work with the grouped content or if you just want to remind yourself of the extent of the group, choose Developer, Design Mode. As you can see in Figure 3.5, Word adds "Group" icons at the beginning and end of the grouped content and also displays a box around the content when you click inside the group.

Figure 3.5
Choose Developer, Design Mode to see the Group icons.

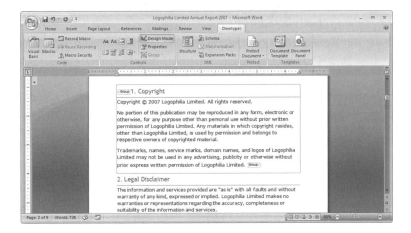

> **NOTE**
> To remove the group, switch to Design Mode, select the entire group, and then close Developer, Group, Ungroup. If the Ungroup command is disabled, choose Developer, Properties, click to deactivate the Content Control Cannot Be Deleted check box, click OK, and then try again.

The second part of structured editing involves allowing users to add content to the document, although you don't allow just any content to be added anywhere inside the document. Instead, the editing is "structured" because you place one or more of the following restrictions on content additions:

- You designate a precise location within the location for the content.
- You designate the type of content that the user can add (such as a date or a table).
- You assist the user by offering some kind of user interface feature that leads the user to enter exactly the type of data you want.

You can set up any of these restrictions by using Word 2007's new *content controls*, which are dialog box-like controls that you can draw directly inside your document. The idea is that you draw each control exactly where you want it, and the control dictates the type of data the user can enter and often comes with some sort of user interface that helps the user enter the data.

In the Developer tab's Controls group, Word 2007 offers seven content controls (see Figure 3.6):

Rich Text—Use this control for formatted text that consists of one or more paragraphs.

Text—Use this control for plain text that consists of no more than one paragraph. (If you need plain text for multiple paragraphs, click the control, choose Developer, Properties, and then click to activate the Allow Carriage Returns [Multiple Paragraphs] check box.)

Picture—Use this control to enable the user to insert a picture into the document. The user clicks the picture icon and then uses the Insert Picture dialog box to select the image.

Combo Box—Use this control to enable the user to enter text or select an item from a drop-down list. To add items to the list, click the control, choose Developer, Properties, and then click Add. In the Add Choice dialog box, type a Display Name and a Value, and then click OK. Repeat to add other list items. Figure 3.6 shows an example combo box control.

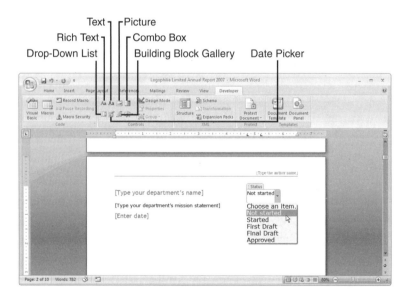

Figure 3.6
Use a Combo Box content control to enable the user to type text or select an item from a list.

Drop-Down List—Use this control to enable the user to select an item from a drop-down list. You add items to the list using the same method as I described for the Combo Box control.

Date Picker—Use this control to enable the user to enter a date by clicking the date from a calendar, as shown in Figure 3.7. To specify the date format, click the control, choose Developer, Properties, and then click the format in the Display the Date Like This list.

Figure 3.7
Use a Date Picker content control to enable the user to specify a date by clicking it in a calendar.

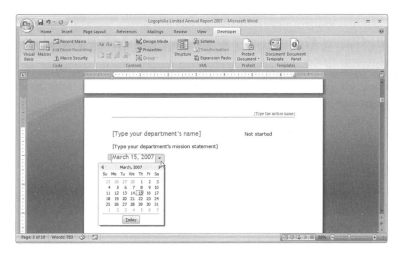

Building Block Gallery—Use this control to enable the user to select an item from the Building Blocks Gallery. If you want the user to have a choice of a specific type of building block only, click the control, choose Developer, Properties, and then use the Gallery list to click the building block type (AutoText, Quick Parts, Tables, and so on).

Here are the general steps to follow to insert a content control into a document:

1. Position the insertion point where you want the content control to display.
2. Choose the Developer tab, and then click the content control you want. Word inserts the control.
3. Choose Developer, Properties to open the Content Control Properties dialog box.
4. Type a Title for the content control. (This text displays above the control when the user clicks it.)
5. (Optional) Type a Tag for the content control. (This text displays on either side of the control when you switch to Design Mode.)
6. If you want to apply a style to the control contents, click to activate the Use a Style to Format Contents check box and then use either Style or New Style to specify the style you want to use.
7. To prevent the user from deleting the control, click to activate the Content Control Cannot Be Deleted check box.

8. After the control has been edited, you can prevent anyone else from making changes to it by clicking to activate the Contents Cannot Be Edited check box.

9. Configure any control-specific settings, as described earlier.

10. Click OK.

Inspecting a Document for Personal Information

 Earlier in this chapter, I showed you how to get Word to automatically prompt you for document properties because saving metadata is a good idea for most documents. However, it's not such a good idea if you are sharing a document with other people, particularly people outside of your organization. That's because the metadata might contain private or sensitive data that you probably don't want outsiders to see. This also applies to other document data, such as reviewers' comments and annotations.

Removing this kind of data by hand is not only time-consuming, but it's also easy to miss a thing or two. To help out, Word (and the other main Office 2007 programs) comes with a Document Inspector that can search for potentially private data and remove it from the document automatically. The Document Inspector can remove the following document data:

- Document properties
- Headers, footers, watermarks, and hidden text
- Personal information, such as your username and your personal summary information
- Document versions
- Reviewer comments and annotations
- Custom XML data

Follow these steps to use the Document Inspector:

1. Save the document. If you want to keep an internal version that maintains the personal information, choose Office, Save As and save a copy of the document that you can then share.

2. Choose Office, Prepare, Inspect Document. Word opens the Document Inspector.

3. Click to deactivate the check box next to any content types you don't want to check.

4. Click Inspect. The Document Inspector checks the document, and then it displays the results of the inspection, as shown in Figure 3.8.

5. For each type of data you want to delete from the document, click the Remove All button.

6. When you're done, click Close.

Figure 3.8
Use the Document
Inspector to look for
potentially private or
sensitive data before
sharing a document.

Viewing Two Documents Side by Side

When you share a document with another person, you usually turn on revision marks, so that you can see the changes the other person makes. Unfortunately, it often happens that the other person accidentally turns off revision marks before or in the middle of editing so that you can no longer easily see the changes he made. In the past, this meant opening the two versions and then switching from one window to another or trying to arrange the documents, so that you could see both at once.

Word 2007 helps you avoid this extra work by offering a new View Side By Side feature, which arranges the document windows so that you can easily compare the two files. Here's how it works:

1. Open the two documents you want to compare and make one of them the active document.
2. Choose View, View Side By Side. Word displays the Compare Side By Side dialog box.
3. Click the other document you want to use and then click OK. Word arranges the two windows side by side, as shown in Figure 3.9.

> **NOTE**
> The View Side By Side feature includes *synchronous scrolling*, which means that as you scroll up or down (or even side to side) in one document, Word scrolls in the same direction and by the same amount in the other document. If you find this distracting, you can turn it off by choosing View, Window, Synchronous Scrolling.

4. When you're done, choose View, Window, Compare Side By Side.

Figure 3.9
Activate the View Side
By Side command to
compare two documents
side by side.

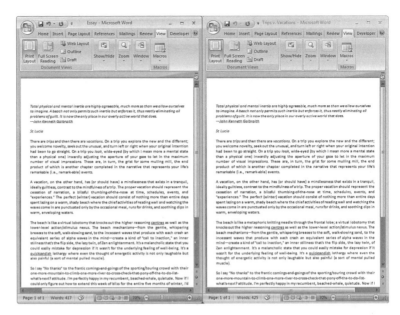

> **TIP**
>
> You can get Word to help you compare the two documents. Choose Review, Compare, Compare to open the Compare Documents dialog box. Use the Original Document list to specify the original document and use the Revised Document list to select the document with changes. If you want to specify what changes to look for, click More and use the check boxes to modify the Comparison Settings. Click OK, and Word opens a Compare Result window, which includes the Original Document pane, the Revised Document pane, the Reviewing Pane with a list of the changes, and a Compared Document pane that combines the changes into a single document.

Updating All Fields Automatically

When you're working with fields, it's common to need to update all of a document's fields at one time. One way to do this is to select the entire document and press F9. This works, but it's a hassle because not only must you perform the extra step of selecting the entire document, but that extra step also means that you lose your current cursor position.

To avoid this problem, use the VBA macro in Listing 3.11 to update all the document's fields.

Listing 3.11   A Macro to Update All the Fields in the Active Document

```
Sub UpdateAllFields()
    ActiveDocument.Fields.Update
End Sub
```

Add this macro to a Quick Access toolbar button or assign it a keyboard shortcut (I use Ctrl+Alt+Shift+F9).

It's also often useful to update all of a document's fields when the document is opened. Word doesn't do that by default, but you can create a macro that does.

Launch the Visual Basic Editor and open the project that corresponds to your document. In the project's Microsoft Word Objects branch, double-click the `ThisDocument` object. In the code window that displays, select Document in the object list and select Open in the event list. Add the following statement to the `Document_Open()` stub that displays:

```
ThisDocument.Fields.Update
```

Figure 3.10 shows the completed code.

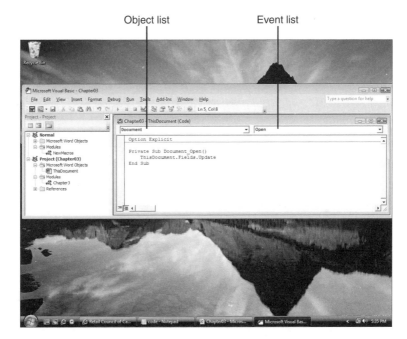

Figure 3.10
Add this code to your document's Open event to update all fields each time the document is opened.

From Here

- To learn how to add a custom watermark to a document, **see** "Creating a Custom Watermark," **p. 93**.

- To learn how to protect Excel worksheets, **see** "Preventing Users from Changing Parts of a Worksheet," **p. 148**.

- Excel has a built-in command for creating workspaces; **see** "Creating a Workspace of Workbooks," **p. 153**.

- To learn how to use the Visual Basic Editor and incorporate macros into your documents, **see** "Working with VBA Macros," **p. 429**.

Page Layout Tricks

When you create Word documents in a business environment, many of those documents are plain affairs that don't need much in the way of formatting or design. That's fine because no one expects a memo for the troops or a report for the boss to be inordinately fancy. Content rules this simple, workday communication.

However, there's a large body of Word work that *does* require more than plain documents. Annual reports, client communications, newsletters, brochures, invoices, and catalogs are just a few of the document types that you'll want to spend some time tweaking the overall look so that these documents reflect well on you and your company. The formatting tricks I covered in Chapter 3, "Document Tricks," are a good start, but you also need to give some thought to the bigger picture of page layout, which governs the composition of elements on each page and the overall look of a document. This chapter can help by presenting several useful page layout tricks, including linked text boxes, jump text, custom page backgrounds, line numbers, custom headers and footers, and custom outline levels.

Displaying Text in Multiple, Linked Text Boxes

When you read a newspaper, magazine, or newsletter, you often come across an article that starts on one page and then continues on a different page later in the publication. In some cases, you may have to make several "jumps" from one page to another to complete the article. This is a useful technique because it enables the publisher to place

4

several articles on the front page of the publication, which helps create interest. It also helps on the inner pages of the publication because it gives the publisher more flexibility to lay out the articles (whether they're continuations from the front page or new articles).

If you're creating a multi-page publication in Word, how can you break up articles so that they appear on different pages? The most obvious way is to insert the first part of each article on the front page and then copy the rest to an inner page. That might work if all your text is complete and no longer requires editing. However, you may still have trouble fitting the text properly on the pages, so it may require quite a bit of cutting and pasting to get a suitable layout. And, certainly, this type of setup is a nightmare waiting to happen if your text or formatting still needs to be revised.

The problem with cutting and pasting to get this effect is that the different parts of any one article aren't connected in any way, so there's no flow. In Word, you usually create flowing text by converting that text into two or more columns: The text flows from one column to the next and from the last column on one page to the first column on the next. Even better, each time you add, format, move, or delete text in one column, Word automatically adjusts the position of the text in the other columns to compensate. Unfortunately, you must keep columns together; you can't start an article in columns on one page and then continue it in columns on a different page.

The solution that gives you both flowing text *and* the ability to jump from one part of the publication to another is the concept of *linked text boxes*. This refers to two or more text boxes configured so that the text in one box flows into the next box, even if that box is located elsewhere in the document.

Assuming you've created two text boxes (choose Insert, Text Box), you create a link between them by clicking inside the first text box, choosing Format, Create Link (the mouse pointer changes to a pitcher), and then clicking inside the second text box.

> **CAUTION**
>
> If you have existing text that you want to include in the text boxes, resist the temptation to cut and paste the text into the boxes for now. For linking to work, the text boxes (particularly the second one) should be empty.

Now add all your text to the first text box. When the text reaches the end of the first text box, it flows into the second text box.

What if you want to use more than two text boxes? That's not a problem because Word enables you to link up to 32 text boxes. Begin by creating all the text boxes. Then link one text box to the next using the Create Link command. (That is, link the first to the second, then link the second to the third, and so on.) When that's done, add all your text to the first text box.

Whether you use 2 or 32 linked text boxes, you need to know how to navigate from one to the other. Word gives you the following techniques:

- **To move to the next text box**—Move the cursor to the end of the current text box and then press the right arrow key. Alternatively, right-click any border of the current text box and then click Next Text Box.

- **To move to the previous text box**—Move the cursor to the beginning of the current text box and then press the left arrow key. Alternatively, right-click any border of the current text box and then click Previous Text Box.

> **NOTE** Unfortunately, Word doesn't give you any way to reorder linked text boxes. If you need to change the order of the links, you must break them and then recreate them in the new order.

Creating Jump Text

Using linked text boxes is a great way to get control over your layout while still maintaining text flow. However, as convenient as it is for you, it may not be all that convenient for your readers, who might find it difficult to follow the story from one text box to the next.

One solution would be to include an instruction below the first text box that tells the reader where to go to continue reading the article (for example, `Continued on page 4`). Make sure you put this instruction outside of the text box, or you'll interrupt the flow between the text boxes.

In the publishing world, such an instruction to the reader is called *jump text*. In the Word world, however, it does suffer from a fairly major problem: In most cases, you can only be sure of the page number after you've completed the entire document. This means that after your document is finished, you need to run through the whole thing and insert the correct page numbers into all the jump text. That is inefficient and labor-intensive.

A much better solution—and one that takes advantage of one of the inherent strengths of electronic documents—is to set up the jump text as a link to the next text box. This enables you to use a more generic instruction—such as `Ctrl+click here to continue this article`—and it makes life much easier for the reader by creating true "jump" text.

The first task here is to create a bookmark for the spot in the document to which you want to jump. Your initial thought might be to create a bookmark for the next text box. However, that's not a great idea because when you jump to a text box, Word selects the entire text box, which isn't something you want your readers handling. Your second thought might be to jump to the top left corner of the text box (that is, the position to the left of the first character). That's better because Word doesn't select anything, but that position may change if you edit or format the text. The ideal jump spot is an empty line just above the text box. Click that line, choose Insert, Bookmark to display the Bookmark dialog box, type a Bookmark Name, and then click Add.

4

Now you can set up the jump text by following these steps:

1. Click below the text box from which you want to jump.
2. Choose Insert, Hyperlink to display the Insert Hyperlink dialog box.
3. Use the <u>T</u>ext to Display box to type the jump text you want the reader to click.

> **TIP**
>
> When the reader hovers the mouse pointer over a hyperlink, Word displays a ScreenTip that shows the path name of the document and the bookmark name, which is not friendly. I prefer to use the article name, which helps to reinforce to the reader that the link continues the article (see Figure 4.1). To change the ScreenTip text that the reader sees, click ScreenTip, type the text that you want to display, and then click OK.

4. Click Pl<u>a</u>ce in This Document.
5. In the Select a Pla<u>c</u>e in This Document list, click the bookmark for the next text box.
6. Click OK.

Figure 4.1 shows a document with a couple of linked text boxes, each of which has jump text below it.

Figure 4.1
You can add jump text to enable the reader to quickly navigate to the next linked text box.

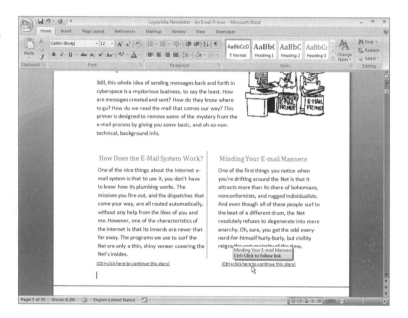

Creating a Custom Watermark

A *watermark* is a bit of text (or sometimes an image) that displays "behind" the text on each page and is visible both onscreen and in the printed version of the document. The purpose of a watermark is to display a broad message to the reader about an aspect of the document. For example, a watermark consisting of the word "DRAFT" tells the reader that this is not the final version of the document. Similarly, the watermark "ASAP" tells the reader you want the document handled as soon as possible.

Word offers a number of built-in watermarks. In the Watermarks gallery (choose Page Your, Watermark), for example, you can select from watermarks that use the following text: CONFIDENTIAL, DO NOT COPY, DRAFT, SAMPLE, ASAP, or URGENT, each of which you can display diagonally or horizontally across the page.

If none of these predefined watermarks is quite right for your needs, you can build a custom watermark that consists of the text you want to display and the font, size, color, and layout you prefer. Here are the steps to follow:

1. Choose Page Layout, Watermark, Custom Watermark. Word displays the Printed Watermark dialog box.
2. Click Text Watermark.
3. Use the Text combo box to either select existing watermark text or to type a custom message.
4. Use the Font list to select the watermark font.
5. Use the Size list to choose a size for the watermark.
6. Use the Color palette to choose the watermark text color.
7. Click either Diagonal or Horizontal.
8. Click OK. Word adds the custom watermark to your document.

4

> **NOTE** If you want to use an image as a watermark instead of text, choose Page Layout, Watermark, Custom Watermark, click the Picture Watermark option, click Select Picture, use the Insert Picture dialog box to click the picture you want to use, and then click OK.

Giving a Document a Parchment Paper Background

The vast majority of documents look best when formatted with dark text on a light background—especially a white background. However, there may be times when you need something a little more interesting. For example, light text on a dark background is a great way to make text box text and table headers stand out. For the document as a whole, you want to avoid busy backgrounds because they almost always render the document text unreadable. An occasionally useful exception is to use a background that resembles some kind of specialty paper. This can add a sense of realism to the document, which can be effective (if used sparingly, of course).

One of the nicest of these specialty paper backgrounds is parchment paper, which can give documents a classy, slightly old-time feel. Follow these steps to apply a parchment paper background:

1. Choose Page Layout, Page Color, Fill Effects. Word opens the Fill Effects dialog box.
2. Click the Texture tab.
3. In the Texture list, click the Parchment swatch.

> **NOTE** The Texture list also comes with the following paper textures: Papyrus, Paper Bag, Newsprint, Recycled Paper, Stationery, Blue Tissue Paper, and Pink Tissue Paper.

4. Click OK. Word applies the texture to the background

Displaying a Document with a Random Texture Background

One of my goals in this book is to present you with tricks that are practical in the sense that you can use them right away to be more productive or more efficient. I also try to focus on reducing drudgery, mostly by automating tedious or routine tasks with macros. This section's trick isn't even remotely practical, but I think it falls somewhat into the "reducing drudgery" category, as you'll see (I hope!).

We all have certain documents that we use almost every day. A good example is a to-do list that is checked constantly throughout the day and that is added to or deleted from as necessary. Any document that you look at many times a day gets boring awfully fast. To add some visual interest, Listing 4.1 presents a macro that applies a random background texture to a specified document.

Listing 4.1   A Macro That Applies a Random Background Texture to a Specified Document

```
Public Sub ApplyRandomTexture(doc As Document)
    Dim i As Integer
    '
    ' Initialize the random number generator
    '
    Randomize
    '
    ' Generate a random number between 1 and 24
    '
    i = Int(24 * Rnd + 1)
    '
    ' Apply the random number as a background texture constant
    '
    doc.Background.Fill.PresetTextured i
End Sub
```

Word has 24 predefined textures, and these are given the numbers 1 through 24 in the Office object model (these are `msoTexture` constants). This macro uses the `Rnd` function to generate a random number between 1 and 24 and then uses the `PresetTextured` property to apply the random texture. Note that the macro takes a `Document` variable named `doc` as its argument. To run this macro each time you open a document, display the Visual Basic Editor, click the document's project, and then double-click the `ThisDocument` object. In the Object list, select Document and in the Event list select Open. In the `Document_Open()` stub that displays, add the `ApplyRandomTexture ThisDocument` statement, as shown in the following:

```
Private Sub Document_Open()
    ApplyRandomTexture ThisDocument
End Sub
```

Displaying Text with Line Numbers

One problem that crops up in certain special circumstances is a difficulty in specifying what part of a document you're talking about. For example, if someone asks for feedback on a document, you often have to say something such as, "On page two, in the third paragraph, second sentence, change affect to effect." As cumbersome as it is, there are other examples for which you can't be as specific. If a document consists of a series of lines with paragraphs—for example, programming code or a poem—then you have to say something such as, "page four, twelfth line" or "page 1, sixth line from the bottom."

None of these solutions are easy to use, and each one can lead to problems if the reader misinterprets your instructions. If you want to effortlessly and accurately pinpoint a part of a document, then you need to add line numbers. These appear off to the side and are for display purposes only (that is, they don't become part of the document itself). You can add line numbers to some or all of the document, and you can even restart the numbers by section or by page.

To get started, first position the insertion point as follows:

- If your document has only one section and you want to display line numbers for the entire document, position the insertion point anywhere in the document.

- If your document has more than one section and you want to display line numbers for just one of those sections, position the insertion point anywhere in that section.

- If your document has more than one section and you want to display line numbers for the entire document, select the entire document.

With that done, choose Page Layout, Line Numbers, and then choose one of the following commands:

- **None**—Hides existing line numbers.

- **Continuous**—Displays line numbers for the section or document. The line numbers don't restart at any point in the section or document.

- **Restart Each Page**—Displays line numbers and resets the numbering to 1 at the start of each page.

4

- **Restart Each Section**—Displays line numbers and resets the numbering to 1 at the start of each section.

- **Suppress for Current Section**—Hides line numbers for the current section. The line numbers in subsequent sections don't change.

- **Line Numbering Options**—Displays the Layout tab of the Page Setup dialog box. Click Line <u>N</u>umbers to display the Line Numbers dialog box, shown in Figure 4.2. Click to activate the Add Line Numbering check box and then set the following options (click OK when you're done):

  Start <u>A</u>t—The starting line number.

  From <u>T</u>ext—The distance, in inches, between the line numbers and the text.

  Count <u>B</u>y—The value by which to increase each line number.

  Numbering—The type of line numbering you want to use.

Figure 4.2
Use the Line Numbers dialog box to specify advanced line numbering options.

Figure 4.3 shows a document with some programming code and line numbers displayed.

Figure 4.3
A document with line numbers.

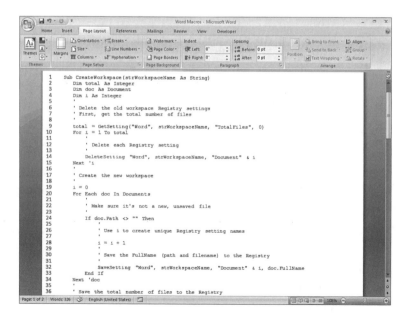

Using Continuous Numbers in Two Separate Numbered Lists

Numbered lists (choose Home, Numbering) are a great way to present a sequential series of items—steps in a procedure, rankings, Top Ten lists, and so on. When you create one numbered list, press Enter twice after the last item and then start a second numbered list, (Word starts the second list at 1). That's usually the behavior you want, but there may be times when you have to insert text between two steps. In this case, you want to make sure that Word continues the numbering when the list continues after the inserted text.

Word gives you a couple of ways to do this, and the method you choose depends on when you want to insert the text: while you're creating the numbered list or after you've finished the numbered list.

The easiest method is to insert the text after you have completed the numbered list:

1. Navigate to the end of the step before which you want to insert the non-numbered text.
2. Press Enter. Word inserts a new step.
3. Choose Home, Numbering to deactivate the Numbering button. Word converts the new step into a regular paragraph.
4. Insert your text.

To insert the text while you're creating the numbered list, follow these steps:

1. Enter the step before which you want to insert the non-numbered text.
2. Press Enter twice. Word creates a regular paragraph.
3. Insert your text and press Enter to start a new paragraph.
4. Choose Home, Numbering. Word starts a new numbered list and displays a smart tag to the left of the first number.
5. Click the smart tag and then click Continue Numbering, as shown in Figure 4.4. Word resumes the numbering sequence of the previous numbered list.

4

Figure 4.4
When you resume the numbered list, click the smart tag and then click Continue Numbering.

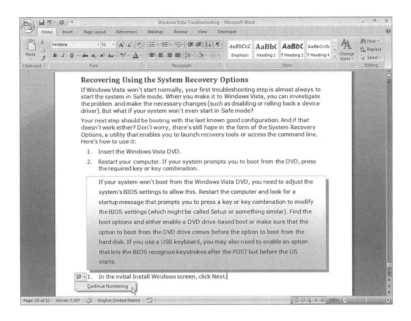

Using Multiple Page Number Formats in the Same Document

You've probably seen or read books where the introductory material displays page numbers using lower-case Roman numerals (i, ii, iii, and so on), whereas the rest of the book displays page numbers using Arabic numerals (1, 2, 3, and so on). Using multiple page number formats in this way is an easy method for differentiating two different sections of a book, and it's a technique you can apply to your own Word documents.

The trick here is to create a section break between the parts of the document where you want to use the different page numbers. A *section* is a document part that stores page layout options such margins, page size, page orientation, columns, line numbering, and footnotes and endnotes. The transition from one section to another is called a *section break*. Sections also include headers and footers, and we'll use that fact to set up our different numbering schemes.

The first step is to create the section break, which you do by following these steps:

1. Position the cursor at the point where you want the new section to start.
2. Choose Page Layout, Breaks. Word displays a menu of break options.
3. In the Section Breaks group, click the type of section break you want:
   - **Next Page**—Starts a new section on a new page.
   - **Continuous**—Starts a new section at the cursor. (Note that this command doesn't create a page break, so you probably won't use it in this context.)
   - **Even Page**—Starts a new section on the next even-numbered page.
   - **Odd Page**—Starts a new section on the next odd-numbered page.

> **TIP**
>
> To show the current section number in the status bar, right-click the status bar, and then click to activate the Section item.

You're now ready to add your two different page number formats—one for each of the two sections in your document. The idea here is to add page numbers to the document and then break the link between the second section header and the first section header. This enables you to set up different page numbering schemes in each section. Follow these steps:

1. With the cursor in the same position as when you created the section page, choose Insert, Page Number, Top of Page (or another position, if you prefer, such as Bottom of Page) and then click a page number format. Word adds a header to the document and displays the page number.

2. Under Header & Footer Tools, choose Design, Link to Previous to deactivate the command. This tells Word that the header in section 2 should not be the same as the header in section 1.

3. Choose Insert, Page Number, Format Page Numbers. Word displays the Page Number Format dialog box.

4. Use the Number Format list to click the page number format you want to use in section 2 (such as 1, 2, 3...).

5. Click the Start At option and use the associated spin box to set the starting page number for section 2. In most cases, you'll want to start the new section's page numbers at 1, as shown in Figure 4.5.

Figure 4.5
In the second section, you'll most likely want to start the numbering over again at 1.

6. Click OK.

7. Under Header & Footer Tools, choose Design, Previous Section. Word displays the header and page numbers for the first section.

8. Choose Insert, Page Number, Format Page Numbers to open the Page Number Format dialog box.

9. Use the Number Format list to click the page number format you want to use in section 1 (such as i, ii, iii…).

10. Click OK.

11. Under Header & Footer Tools, choose Design, Close Header and Footer.

Making the First Page Header and Footer Unique

Word assumes that you want to make all your documents' headers and footers the same, and that will likely be the case most of the time. However, you saw in the previous section that it's sometimes useful to have two (or more) different page number formats. Another common scenario is having a unique header and/or footer on the first page of the document or the first page of a section.

As an example, examine this book. As you can see, each page has a header that displays the page number and other data, such as the chapter number and name. However, if you turn to the first page of any chapter, you see that the header doesn't appear. This is a common setup in all forms of publishing.

As another example, you might have a document that includes instructions on how to use the document or notes explaining other document data. It makes sense to place this text in the first page header or footer, but it's wasteful to repeat it on every page.

Whatever your needs, you can configure the document to use a first page header and footer that's different from the headers and footers in the rest of the document or section:

1. Position the cursor in the section with which you want to work. (If your document has only one section, you can place the cursor anywhere you like.)

2. Choose Insert and then choose either Header, Edit Header or Footer, Edit Footer.

3. Under Header & Footer Tools, click to activate the Design, Different First Page check box.

You can now configure a unique header or footer for the first page of the document or section.

Using Different Odd and Even Page Headers

Even if you set up a unique first page header or footer, as described in the previous section, you still might not want the rest of the document or section headers and footers to be the same. Again, this book provides a good example. If you examine the header of each even page, you see that it contains the current page number on the left, followed by the current chapter number and chapter name. However, if you examine the headers for the odd pages (except the first page of every chapter), you see the name of the current main section and then the current page number on the right.

Using different odd and even page headers or footers is common and useful because it essentially enables you to display twice as much information without overwhelming the reader. Follow these steps to configure a document or section to use different odd and even headers and footers:

1. Position the cursor in the section with which you want to work. (If your document has only one section, you can place the cursor anywhere you like.)

2. Choose Insert and then choose either Header, Edit Header or Footer, Edit Footer.

3. Under Header & Footer Tools, click to activate the Design, Different Odd & Even Pages check box.

You can now configure separate header and footers for the odd and even pages of the document or section.

Adding a Gutter for a Bound Document

When you print a document, you often have to "bind" the document in some way. This can be a simple as inserting the pages in a two- or three-ring binder or adding vertical stables down the side of the document stack, or a more professional binding job where the pages are glued together at the edges. Whatever type of binding you require, you end up using a fair amount of space on the inner edge of each page to accommodate the binding. This can create a problem if you use standard margins because the binding might use up all or most of the inner margin, and this can make the text difficult to read.

The solution to this problem is to designate a *gutter*, which is extra space outside of the margin that is set aside to handle the binding. In most cases, the gutter appears to the left of the document's left margin (that is, the gutter extends from the leftmost edge of the page to the beginning of the left margin).

Follow these steps to add a gutter to your document:

1. Choose Page Layout, Margins, Custom Margins. Word displays the Margins tab of the Page Setup dialog box.

2. Use the Gutter spin box to set the size of the gutter, in inches.

3. Use the Gutter Position list to click Left or Top.

4. (Optional) If your document will be printed on both sides of the paper, then you need a gutter on the left side of the odd-numbered pages and on the right side of the even-numbered pages. The easiest way to set this up is to use *mirrored* margins, which means that the margins (and also the gutter) used on odd pages are the mirror opposite of the margins (and gutter) used on even pages. In the Multiple Page list, click Mirror Margins. The Preview section shows the position of the gutter or gutters (see Figure 4.6)

5. In the Apply To list, make sure that Whole Document is selected.

6. Click OK. Word applies the gutter to the document.

4

Figure 4.6
In the Margins tab, the Preview section shows the position of the gutter or gutters in the document.

Gutters

Creating Custom Outline Levels

Word's Outline view (choose View, Outline or click the Outline button in the status bar) is a useful tool for building and working with complex documents. You can collapse entire sections and even entire levels so that you can easily see the big picture for a document with many different headings and levels.

Word generates the Outline view by using the document's Heading styles—Heading 1 through Heading 9. Paragraphs formatted as Heading 1 go to the top of the outline hierarchy as Level 1. Subsequent Heading styles are given corresponding outline levels: Heading 2 becomes Level 2, Heading 3 becomes Level 3, and so on.

All this works well if your document uses the built-in Heading styles. However, it's not unusual for documents to use other styles for designating headings inside a document. For example, many corporations have style guidelines that require custom styles for document titles, subtitles, section heads, text headings, subheadings, and more. Fortunately, you can still use these custom styles to generate a document outline that you can display in Outline view. The trick is to assign each custom style a corresponding outline level, as shown in the following steps:

1. Choose Home and then click the Styles dialog box launcher (or press Ctrl+Alt+Shift+S) to open the Styles pane.

2. Right-click the style you want to work with and then click Modify. Word opens the Modify Style dialog box.

3. Choose F<u>o</u>rmat, <u>P</u>aragraph. Word opens the Paragraph dialog box.

4. In the <u>O</u>utline Level list, click the outline level you want to associate with the style.

5. Click OK to return to the Modify Style dialog box.

6. Click OK.

7. Repeat steps 2 through 6 for each of the other Heading styles you want to assign an outline level.

From Here

- To learn how to create a numbered list within a single paragraph, **see** "Creating an Inline Numbered List," **p. 49**.

- You can turn a Word outline into a PowerPoint presentation; **see** "Converting a Word Outline into a PowerPoint Presentation," **p. 222**.

- To learn how to use the Visual Basic Editor and incorporate macros into your documents, **see** "Working with VBA Macros," **p. 429**.

4

Microsoft Excel Tricks

II

Formula and Function Tricks

5

Although you can use Excel worksheets just to store data, it's more likely that the vast majority of your sheets will actually do something to the data they contain. And in Excel, doing something to data means building formulas that process the data in some way and return results. Creating formulas is really the essence of Excel, and you can make the program do some amazing things with just a few formula basics. However, if you really want to make Excel sing, then you need to go beyond the basics and learn more advanced techniques that take advantage of Excel's formula-building prowess and its vast collection of worksheet functions. Excel gurus have an extensive bag of formula tricks they can call upon to make any worksheet give up its secrets. As you'll see in this chapter, these tricks aren't difficult to master, and they can be handy tools to have around for any business user.

Allowing Only Certain Values in a Cell

Data entry errors are the bane of any Excel user who wants accurate results. Even if your formulas are perfect, if the data they process contains errors, then the results generated by those formulas are worthless. (Programming types have a saying for this phenomenon: "garbage in, garbage out"—often shortened to GIGO.) If you create spreadsheets for other people to use or if you share your workbooks with other users, how do you reduce (or even eliminate) the risk of bad data wrecking an otherwise good model? The best way to do this is to use Excel's data validation feature. This involves creating one or more rules that dictate the type of data or range of values that a user can enter into a cell. If the user tries to enter something that breaks a rule, you can configure Excel to display an error message and reject the entry.

Follow these steps to configure a data validation rule that allows only certain values in a cell:

1. Select the cell to which you want to apply the data validation rule.

2. Choose Data, Data Validation. Excel displays the Data Validation dialog box, shown in Figure 5.1.

3. In the Settings tab, open the Allow list and then select List.

4. In the Source box, you have two choices:

   ■ If the list of allowable values exists in a worksheet, specify either the range or a range name that contains the list. (Precede the range or range name with an equals sign.)

   ■ Type the allowable values directly into the Source box, separated by commas, as shown in Figure 5.1.

Figure 5.1
Use the Data Validation dialog box to set up a data validation rule that allows only certain values in a cell or range.

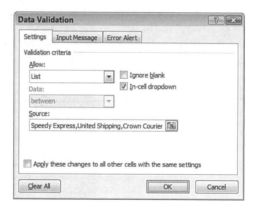

5. If you want the user to be able to select from the allowable values using a drop-down list, leave the In-Cell drop down check box activated.

6. To prevent blank entries, click to deactivate the Ignore Blank check box.

7. Click the Input Message tab.

8. If you want a pop-up box to display when the user selects the restricted cell or any cell within the restricted range, leave the Show Input Message When Cell Is Selected check box activated. Use the Title and Input Message boxes to specify the message that displays. For example, you can use the message to tell the user that a value for the cell must be chosen from the drop-down list.

9. Click OK to apply the data validation rule.

In Figure 5.2, I've applied the data validation rule shown in Figure 5.1 to the Ship Via cell, and you can see the drop-down list that displays.

> **NOTE** You can find the workbook containing the examples used in this chapter on my Web site at www.mcfedries.com/Office2007Gurus.

→ Another way to allow only certain cell values is to use the Worksheet dialog box controls; **see** "Using Dialog Box Controls to Input Data," **p. 160**

Figure 5.2
When you set up a list-based validation rule, Excel displays a list of the possible choices for the cell.

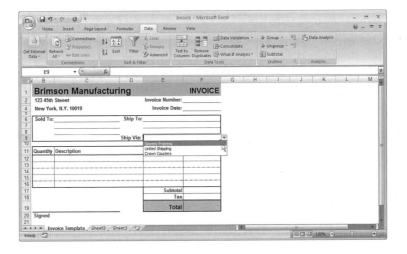

Looking Up a Value in a Discount Rate Schedule

When one business supplies a product that another business intends to sell, the purchase price is never the same as the list price of the product. The retail business has to make money, of course, and for the most part it does that by buying products from the supplier at a cost below the list price and then selling to the likes of you and me at or near the list price. The gross profit is the difference between what it paid to the supplier and what it received from its customers.

The supplier's purchase price is usually a percentage off the list price, and this percentage is called the *discount*. For example, most publishers sell books to bookstores at a discount off the suggested list prices. However, the discount isn't usually a fixed percentage. Rather, it depends (usually) on the quantity of books purchased. For example, ordering 1–5 copies might result in a 20 percent discount, ordering 6–25 copies might result in a 40 percent discount, and so on.

If you're setting up a worksheet model for such transactions (either as a supplier or as a retailer), you need to handle the varying discount. In Excel, you do that by using a *lookup function* that takes a *lookup value* (such as the number of copies purchased) and checks a *lookup table* (such as a table of discounts) for the corresponding item.

Most people use the VLOOKUP() function for this type of work. VLOOKUP() operates by looking in the first column of a table for the value you specify. (The *V* in VLOOKUP() stands for *vertical.* A similar function is HLOOKUP(), which looks in the first row of a table you specify; the *H* in HLOOKUP() stands for *horizontal*.) It then looks across the appropriate number of columns (which you specify) and returns whatever value it finds there. Here's the full syntax for VLOOKUP():

VLOOKUP(*lookup_value, table_array, col_index_num*[, *range_lookup*])

lookup_value	This is the value you want to find in the first column of *table_array*. You can enter a number, a string, or a reference.
table_array	This is the table to use for the lookup. You can use a range reference or a name.
col_index_num	If VLOOKUP() finds a match, *col_index_num* is the column number in the table that contains the data you want returned (the first column—that is, the lookup column—is 1, the second column is 2, and so on).
range_lookup	This is a Boolean value that determines how Excel searches for *lookup_value* in the first column:

TRUE—VLOOKUP() searches for the first exact match for *lookup_value*. If no exact match is found, the function looks for the largest value that is less than *lookup_value* (this is the default).

FALSE—VLOOKUP() searches only for the first exact match for *lookup_value*.

CAUTION

If *range_lookup* is TRUE or omitted, you must sort the values in the first column in ascending order.

Figure 5.3 shows a worksheet that uses VLOOKUP() to determine the discount a customer gets on an order that is based on the number of units purchased.

Figure 5.3
A worksheet that uses VLOOKUP() to look up a customer's discount in a discount schedule.

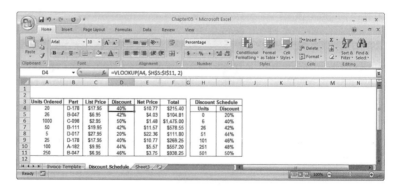

For example, cell D4 uses the following formula:

```
=VLOOKUP(A4, $H$5:$I$11, 2)
```

The *range_lookup* argument is omitted, which means VLOOKUP() searches for the largest value that is less than or equal to the lookup value; in this case, this is the value in cell A4. Cell A4 contains the number of units purchased (20, in this case), and the range $H$5:$I$11 is the discount schedule table. VLOOKUP() searches down the first column (H5:H11) for the largest value that is less than or equal to 20. The first such cell is H6 (because the value in H7—24—is larger than 20). VLOOKUP() therefore moves to the second column (because we specified *col_num* to be 2) of the table (cell I6) and grabs the value there (40%).

Looking Up a Customer Account Number

The discount schedule lookup table in the previous section is an example of a *range lookup* where you check to see if the lookup value falls within a range of values, such as 1–5 or 6–25. However, you often come across situations in which you need to match specific values instead of ranges. For example, you might need to look up an employee ID, a part code, or a book's ISBN number. These are examples of *discrete value lookups* where your formula needs to match some value exactly.

A table of customer names and account numbers is a good example of a lookup table that contains discrete lookup values. In this case, you want to use the VLOOKUP() function (or, less likely, the HLOOKUP() function) to find an exact match for a customer name you specify, and then return the corresponding account number. Figure 5.4 shows a simple data-entry screen that automatically adds a customer account number in column E after the user selects the customer name from a drop-down list in column D.

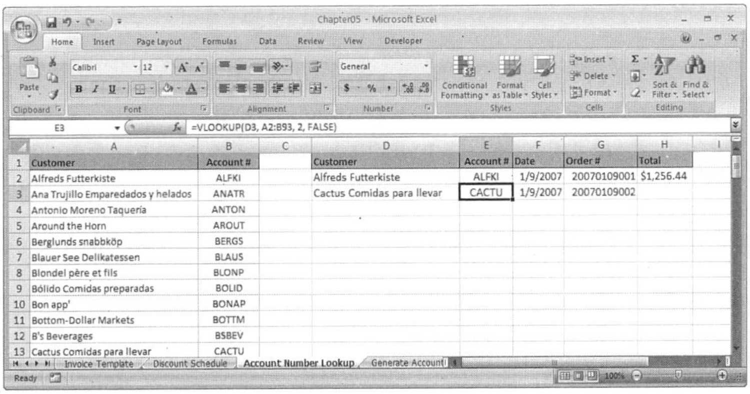

Figure 5.4
A simple data-entry worksheet that uses the exact-match version of VLOOKUP() to look up a customer's account number based on the selected account name.

An example of a function that accomplishes this is in cell E3:

```
=VLOOKUP(D3, A2:B93, 2, FALSE)
```

The value in D3 is looked up in list of customer names in column A, and because the *range_lookup* argument is set to FALSE, VLOOKUP() searches for an exact match. If it finds one, it returns the corresponding account number from column B.

TIP

If you start with the formula in cell E4 and fill it down column E, you'll get #N/A errors in all the new columns. VLOOKUP() generates this error if no match is found in the lookup range, which will be the case while the value in column D is blank. It is better to have Excel display the null string ("") instead. To do that, use the IFERROR() function to test whether the lookup will fail, as shown here:

```
=IFERROR(VLOOKUP(D3, A2:B93, 2, FALSE), "")
```

The IFERROR() function first calculates the VLOOKUP() result. If the result isn't an error, IFERROR() displays the result normally; if the result is an error, IFERROR() displays the null string.

Generating Account Numbers

It's often handy to generate account numbers for your customers. If you have many customers, you probably don't want to do this by hand, however. One simple way to generate an account number is to simply take the first *n* characters in the customer's name and convert them to uppercase letters. For example, if you have a customer name in cell A2, the following formula generates a five-character account number:

```
=UPPER(LEFT(A2, 5))
```

Here, the LEFT() function extracts characters from the left of the value in A2, and the UPPER() function converts them to uppercase.

That's fine, but what if you have customer names that share the first five characters? Or, even trickier, what if you have customer names where the first five characters include one or more spaces, periods, dashes, or foreign characters? In other words, what you really want to do is generate a unique account number that includes only the characters a through z and A through Z. To do this, we need to turn to VBA. The function shown in Listing 5.1 generates such an account number.

Listing 5.1   A VBA Function That Generates an Eight-Character Account Number Based on the Customer Name

```
Function GenerateAccountNumber(strName As String) As String
    Dim nPos As Integer      ' The current character position within strName
    Dim strChar As String    ' The current character within strName
    Dim strTemp As String    ' The temporary account number
    Application.Volatile False  ' Don't recalculate
    '
    ' Initialize the variables
    '
```

```
      nPos = 1
      strTemp = ""
      '
      ' Run through the characters in the customer name
      '
      Do While nPos <= Len(strName)
          '
          ' Get the character in the position given by nPos
          '
          strChar = Mid(strName, nPos, 1)
          '
          ' Check the character value
          '
          Select Case Asc(strChar)
              '
              ' Between A and Z
              '
              Case 65 To 90
                  strTemp = strTemp & strChar
              '
              ' Between a and z
              '
              Case 97 To 122
                  strTemp = strTemp & UCase(strChar)
          End Select
          '
          ' If the text part of the account number is
          ' 5 characters long, exit the loop
          '
          If Len(strTemp) = 5 Then Exit Do
          nPos = nPos + 1
      Loop
      '
      ' Check for failure
      '
      If strTemp <> "" Then
          '
          ' If the account is good so far, add a random 3-digit number
          '
          Randomize
          GenerateAccountNumber = strTemp & Format(Rnd * 999, "000")
      Else
          '
          ' Otherwise, generate an error
          '
          GenerateAccountNumber = "No account number generated!"
      End If
  End Function
```

The function takes the customer name as an argument in the strName variable. The main Do loop then runs through the characters in strName one letter at a time. Inside the loop, the next character is stored in the strChar variable, and then a Select Case structure checks the value of Asc(strChar), where Asc is a function that returns the character code of the specified character. The function then checks to see whether the Asc result is between 65 and 90 (which means the character is a letter between A and Z) or between 97 and 122 (which means the character is a letter between a and z). If either one is true, the character is appended to the strTemp variable. When strTemp is five characters long (or we hit the end of the customer name), the loop exits. Finally, if strTemp isn't null, the function uses Randomize and Rnd to generate a random three-digit number that's added to strTemp., which is then returned as the function result. Figure 5.5 shows the function in used in a worksheet.

> **TIP**
>
> After you generate your account numbers, you want them to remain static. Unfortunately, each time you apply the function to a new cell, Excel reruns the function on all the existing cells! This generates new account numbers for each customer, which is not what you want. The solution is to add the following statement near the top of the function (as shown in Listing 5.1):
>
>   Application.Volatile False
>
> This tells VBA not to recalculate the function, so your account numbers remain static.

Figure 5.5
Account numbers created by the GenerateAccountNumber function in Listing 5.1.

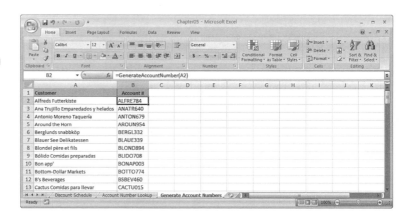

Generating Random Numbers to Test Worksheet Models

When you're building a worksheet model that analyzes or manipulates data or sets up a simulation, you may not have access to the data right away. That's not a major problem because you can always just use some realistic dummy data to test your model. Most people just make up the dummy data as they go along, but that's not always a good idea. Your model may require truly random data, and trying to randomize data by hand is extremely difficult: You'll almost always skew the data unconsciously. Similarly, your model might require data that fits a particular type of distribution—such as a normal distribution—and there's simply no way to do that by hand.

Excel offers several tools for generating random numbers automatically. The most basic of these tools is the RAND() function, which returns a random number that is greater than or equal to 0 and less than 1. This is very useful for generating random percentages or random time values, both of which require values between 0 and 1. However, most real-world scenarios require values in some other range.

For example, random hour values require numbers between 0 and 23, while random cent values require numbers between 0 and 100. When you need to generate random numbers greater than or equal to 0 and less than *n*, use the following expression:

```
INT(RAND() * n)
```

The INT() function rounds a number down to then nearest integer. (I'm assuming here that you need integers for your worksheet. If not, leave the INT() function out of the expression.) For example, the following formula generates a random number greater than or equal to 0 and less than 24:

```
=INT(RAND() * 24)
```

Of course, not all ranges of random numbers begin at 0. The more general scenario is when you want random numbers greater than or equal to some number *m* and less than some number *n*. Here's the expression to use for this case:

```
INT(RAND() * (n - m)) + m
```

For example, the following formula produces random test scores greater than or equal to 40 and less than 101:

```
=INT(RAND() * (101 - 40)) + 40
```

Rather than messing around with such a formula, Excel offers a much easier way to generate random numbers between two values: The RANDBETWEEN() function. RANDBETWEEN() lets you specify a lower bound and an upper bound and then returns a random integer between them:

```
RANDBETWEEN(bottom, top)
```

bottom	The smallest possible random integer. (That is, Excel generates a random number that is greater than or equal to *bottom*.)
top	The largest possible random integer. (That is, Excel generates a random number that is less than or equal to *top*.)

For example, the following formula returns a random integer between 0 and 59:

```
=RANDBETWEEN(0, 59)
```

CAUTION

RAND() and RANDBETWEEN() are *volatile* functions, which means that their value changes each time you recalculate or reopen the worksheet or edit any cell on the worksheet. To enter a static random number in a cell, type **=RAND()** or **=RANDBETWEEN(bottom, top)**, press F9 to evaluate the function and return a random number, and then press Enter to place the random number into the cell as a numeric literal.

If you need your random numbers distributed in a particular way, the Analysis ToolPak's Random Number Generation tool can produce static random numbers in any range and in one of several different distributions, depending on the application. Table 5.1 summarizes the seven available distribution types.

> **NOTE** You may need to install the Analysis ToolPak. Choose Office, Excel Options to open the Excel Options dialog box and then click Add-Ins. In the Manage list, select Excel Add-ins and then click Go to open the Add-Ins dialog box. Click to activate the Analysis ToolPak check box and then click OK. When Excel asks if you want to install the add-in, click Yes.

Table 5.1   The Distributions Available with the Random Number Generation Tool

Distribution	Description
Uniform	Generates numbers with equal probability from the range of values you provide. Using the range 0 to 1 produces the same distribution as the RAND() function.
Normal	Produces numbers in a bell curve (normal) distribution based on the mean and standard deviation you enter. This is good for generating samples of things such as test scores and population heights.
Bernoulli	Generates a random series of 1s and 0s based on the probability of success on a single trial. A common example of a Bernoulli distribution is a coin toss (in which the probability of success is 50%; in this case, as in all Bernoulli distributions, you would have to assign either heads or tails to be 1 or 0).
Binomial	Generates random numbers characterized by the probability of success over a number of trials. For example, you could use this type of distribution to model the number of responses received for a direct-mail campaign. The probability of success would be the average (or projected) response rate, and the number of trials would be the number of mailings in the campaign.
Poisson	Generates random numbers based on the probability of a designated number of events occurring in a time frame. The distribution is governed by a value, Lambda, that represents the mean number of events known to occur over the time frame.
Patterned	Generates random numbers according to a pattern that's characterized by a lower and upper bound, a step value, and a repetition rate for each number and the entire sequence.
Discrete	Generates random numbers from a series of values and probabilities for these values (in which the sum of the probabilities equals 1). You could use this distribution to simulate the rolling of dice (where the values would be 1 through 6, each with a probability of 1/6; see the following example).

5

Follow these steps to use the Random Number Generation tool:

> **NOTE**
> If you'll be using a Discrete distribution, be sure to enter the appropriate values and probabilities before starting the Random Number Generation tool.

1. Choose Data, Data Analysis to display the Data Analysis dialog box.

2. In the Analysis Tools list, click Random Number Generation and then click OK. The Random Number Generation dialog box appears, as shown in Figure 5.6.

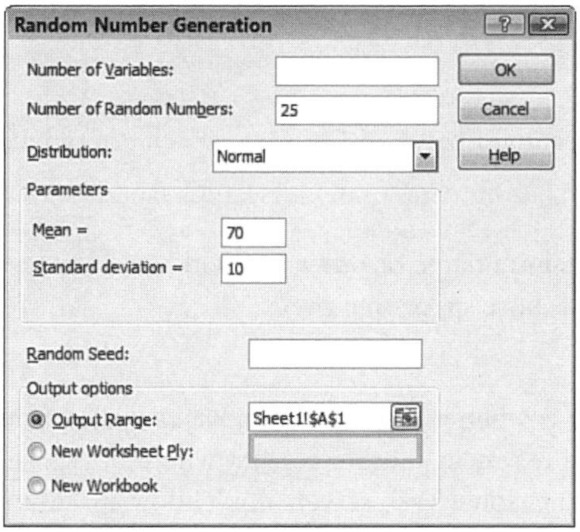

Figure 5.6
Use the Random Number Generation dialog box to set up the options for your random numbers.

3. If you want to generate more than one set of random numbers, enter the number of sets (or variables) you need in the Number of Variables box. Excel enters each set in a separate column. If you leave this box blank, Excel uses the number of columns in the Output Range.

4. Use the Number of Random Numbers text box to enter how many random numbers you need. Excel enters each number in a separate row. If you leave this box blank, Excel fills the Output Range.

5. Use the Distribution drop-down list to click the distribution you want to use.

6. In the Parameters group, enter the parameters for the distribution you selected. (The options you see depend on the selected distribution.)

7. The Random Seed number is the value Excel uses to generate the random numbers. If you leave this box blank, Excel generates a different set each time. If you enter a value (which must be an integer between 1 and 32,767), you can reuse the value later to reproduce the same set of numbers.

8. Use the Output Options group to select a location for the output.

9. Click OK. Excel calculates the random numbers and displays them in the worksheet.

Removing Excess Spaces from a Cell

The data you use in Excel occasionally comes from an external data source, such as a mainframe database, a Web page, or a text file. Unfortunately, the data from external sources such as these often comes with unwanted characters, the most common of which are extra spaces. Fortunately, Excel comes with a function called TRIM() that deletes extra spaces in a cell. Here's the simple syntax:

```
TRIM(text)
```

> text   The string from which you want the excess spaces removed.

So what exactly does the TRIM() function trim from the *text* string? Three things:

- All spaces before *text*.
- All spaces after *text*.
- Any two or more consecutive spaces within *text*, which are reduced in each case to a single space.

For example, if cell A1 contains a name or other text with excess spaces, the following formula returns the string with those spaces removed:

```
=TRIM(A1)
```

A slightly different scenario is when you want to remove *all* spaces from a cell. For example, you might want to use the text in another context where the spaces would be illegal (such as a Web page file name; some Web servers don't allow spaces in file names). In that case, you can use the SUBSTITUTE() function:

```
SUBSTITUTE(text, old_text, new_text [,instance_num])
```

> text   The original string that contains the substring you want to replace.
>
> old_text   The substring you want to replace.
>
> new_text   The substring you want to use as the replacement.
>
> instance_num   The number of replacements to make within the string (the default is all instances).

If you want to use SUBSTITUTE() to remove spaces from a cell, use a space as the *old_text* argument and the null string as the *new_text* argument. Here's an example formula that removes all the spaces from the string in cell A1:

```
=SUBSTITUTE(A1, " ", "")
```

> **TIP**
>
> You can use a similar technique to remove *any* character from a cell. Here's a generic formula that does this:
>
>   =SUBSTITUTE(text, character, "")
>
> Here, replace *text* with the original string and *character* with the character you want to remove.

When you apply this formula to data imported from a Web page, you may find that it doesn't remove some spaces. That's because many Web pages use the *nonbreaking space* character to ensure that the Web browser renders the space. To get rid of nonbreaking space characters, take advantage of the fact that the character's ANSI code is 160. This means you can remove it with the following formula:

    =SUBSTITUTE(A1, CHAR(160), "")

Finally, here's a formula that removes both regular spaces and nonbreaking spaces from a cell:

    =SUBSTITUTE(SUBSTITUTE(A1, CHAR(160), ""), " ", "")

Here, the nested SUBSTITUTE() function serves as the *text* argument for the main SUBSTITUTE() function.

Removing Unprintable Characters from a Cell

Another problem with data imported from an external source is that it might contain so-called *unprintable* characters. These are the first 32 characters in the ASCII character set — codes 0 to 31; see Table 5.2—and they include many characters that don't display properly in Excel and in most cases won't print properly, either.

Table 5.2   The First 32 Nonprintable Characters in the ASCII Character Set

Value	Character	Description	Value	Character	Description
0	NUL	Null	16	DLE	Data Link Escape
1	SOH	Start of Header	17	DC1	Device Control 1 (usually XON)
2	STX	Start of Text	18	DC2	Device Control 2
3	ETX	End of Text	19	DC3	Device Control 3 (usually XOFF)
4	EOT	End of Transmission	20	DC4	Device Control 4
5	ENQ	Enquiry	21	NAK	Negative Acknowledgment

continues

Table 5.2   Continued

Value	Character	Description	Value	Character	Description
6	ACK	Acknowledgment	22	SYN	Synchronous Idle
7	BEL	Bell	23	ETB	End of Transmission Block
8	BS	Backspace	24	CAN	Cancel
9	HT	Horizontal Tab	25	EM	End of Medium
10	LF	Line Feed	26	SUB	Substitute
11	VT	Vertical Tab	27	ESC	Escape
12	FF	Form Feed	28	FS	File Separator
13	CR	Carriage Return	29	GS	Group Separator
14	SO	Shift Out	30	RS	Request to Send
15	SI	Shift In	31	US	Unit Separator

If you have data that includes any of these characters, you can use the CLEAN() function to remove them:

CLEAN(*text*)

> *text*   The string from which you want the nonprintable characters removed.

Figure 5.7 shows an example.

Figure 5.7
Use the CLEAN() function to remove nonprintable characters from a cell.

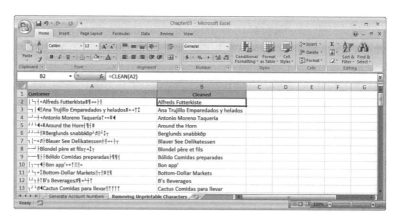

> **CAUTION**
>
> If you have a multiline cell entry, it means the entry includes a Line Feed character (ASCII code 10) at the end of each line. Applying CLEAN() to the cell removes the Line Feed characters, but in the result, the end of one line is followed immediately by the start of the next. Ideally, you want a space between any two lines. You can do that using the following formula, which substitutes a space for each Line Feed and then performs the clean:
>
> ```
> =CLEAN(SUBSTITUTE(A1, CHAR(10), " "))
> ```

> **TIP**
>
> After you use the CLEAN() function, you may still see unprintable characters in a cell. The likely cause is that these are from the Unicode character set, which includes six unprintable characters: codes 127, 129, 141, 143, 144, and 157. To remove these characters, first use SUBSTITUTE() to convert them to an ASCII characters with a value between 0 and 31 and then use the CLEAN() function to remove those characters.
>
> For example, the following formula converts Unicode character 127 to ASCII code 1 and then removes ASCII code 1:
>
> ```
> =CLEAN(SUBSTITUTE(A1, CHAR(127), CHAR(1)))
> ```

Extracting a Person's First Name or Last Name

Your worksheet might contain a column with people's full names. If you're preparing the data for export to a database or for a mail merge, you might want to extract the first and last name into separate columns. Similarly, if you want to sort the data on last name, you'd need to extract the last name into its own column.

The method for extracting the first names or last names requires two steps. The first step is to locate the space that separates the first and last names. You can do that using the FIND() function:

FIND(*find_text*, *within_text* [,*start_num*])

find_text	The substring you want to look for (such as a space).
within_text	The string in which you want to look (such as the person's full name).
start_num	The character position at which you want to start looking (the default is 1).

FIND() returns the character position of the first character of *find_text*. If you have a person's full name in A2, then the following expression returns the character position of the space separating the first and last name:

FIND(" ", A2)

The next step is to then use either the LEFT() function to extract the first name or the RIGHT() function to extract the last name. Here is the syntax for the LEFT() and RIGHT() functions, which return a specified number of characters starting from the left or right of a string:

```
LEFT(text [,num_chars])
RIGHT(text [,num_chars])
```

text	The string from which you want to extract the substring.
num_chars	The number of characters you want to extract from the right (the default value is 1).

For the first name, use the following formula (assuming that the full name is in cell A2):

```
=LEFT(A2, FIND(" ", A2) - 1)
```

Notice how the formula subtracts 1 from the FIND(" ", A2) result to avoid including the space in the extracted substring. You can use this formula in more general circumstances to extract the first word of any multiword string.

For the last name, you need to build a similar formula using the RIGHT() function:

```
=RIGHT(A2, LEN(A2) - FIND(" ", A2))
```

To extract the correct number of letters, the formula takes the length of the original string and subtracts the position of the space. You can use this formula in more general circumstances to extract the second word in any two-word string.

Figure 5.8 shows a worksheet that uses both formulas.

Figure 5.8
Use the LEFT() and FIND() function to extract the first name; use the RIGHT() and FIND() functions to extract the last name.

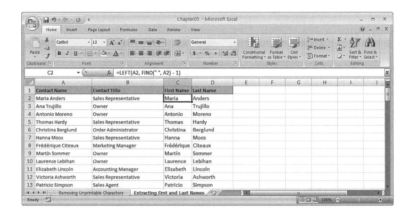

CAUTION

These formulas cause an error in any string that contains only a single word. To allow for this, use the IFERROR() function:

```
=IFERROR(LEFT(A2, FIND(" ", A2) - 1), A2)
```

If the cell doesn't contain a space, the FIND() function returns an error, so IFERROR() returns just the cell text, instead.

TIP How do you extract the last name if the person has three names? You need to run a FIND() function where the *start_num* value comes *after* the first space. FIND() will then locate the *next* space, which is the one that separates the middle name and last name. To do this, set the *start_num* argument to the location of the first space, plus 1:

```
FIND(" ", A2) + 1
```

You then plug this into another FIND() function:

```
=FIND(" ", A2, FIND(" ", A2) + 1)
```

Finally, you can then apply this result within the RIGHT() function to extract the last name:

```
=RIGHT(A2, LEN(A2) - FIND(" ", A2, FIND(" ", A2) + 1))
```

Building an Accounts Receivable Aging Worksheet

If you use Excel to store accounts receivable data, it's a good idea to set up an aging worksheet that shows past-due invoices, calculates the number of days past due, and groups the invoices into past-due categories (1–30 days, 31–60 days, and so on).

Figure 5.9 shows a simple implementation of an accounts receivable database. For each invoice, the due date (column D) is calculated by adding 30 to the invoice date (column C). Column E subtracts the due date (column D) from the current date (in cell B1) to calculate the number of days each invoice is past due.

Figure 5.9
A simple accounts
receivable database.

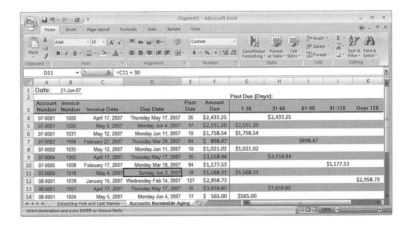

You might have noticed a problem with the due dates in Figure 5.9. The date in cell D11 falls on a weekend. The problem here is that the due date calculation just adds 30 to the invoice date. To avoid weekend due dates, you need to test whether the invoice date plus

30 falls on a Saturday or Sunday. The WEEKDAY() function helps because it returns 7 if the date is a Saturday, and 1 if the date is a Sunday:

```
WEEKDAY(serial_number[,return_type])
```

serial_number   The date for which you want to calculate the day of the week.

return_type   An integer value that determines how Excel calculates the days of the week:

return_type	Days of the Week
1	1 (Sunday) through 7 (Saturday); this is the default value.
2	1 (Monday) through 7 (Sunday)
3	0 (Monday) through 6 (Sunday)

So, to check for a Saturday, you use the following formula:

```
=IF(WEEKDAY(C4 + 30) = 7, C4 + 32, C4 + 30)
```

Here, I'm assuming that the invoice date resides in cell C4. If WEEKDAY(C4 + 30) returns 7, the date is a Saturday, so you add 32 to C4 instead (this makes the due date the following Monday). Otherwise, you just add 30 days as usual.

Checking for a Sunday is similar:

```
=IF(WEEKDAY(C4 + 30) = 1, C4 + 31, C4 + 30)
```

The problem, though, is that you need to combine these two tests into a single formula. To do that, you can nest one IF() function inside another. Here's how it works:

```
=IF(WEEKDAY(C4+30) = 7, C4+32, IF(WEEKDAY(C4+30) = 1, C4+31, C4+30))
```

The main IF() checks to see if the date is a Saturday. If it is, you add 32 days to C4; otherwise, the formula runs the second IF(), which checks for Sunday.

For cash-flow purposes, you also need to correlate the invoice amounts with the number of days past due. Ideally, you'd like to see a list of invoice amounts that are between and 1 and 30 days past due, between 31 and 60 days past due, and so on. Figure 5.10 shows one way to set up accounts receivable aging.

For the invoice amounts shown in column G (1–30 days), the sheet uses the following formula (this is the formula that displays in G4):

```
=IF(E4 <= 30, F4, "")
```

If the number of days the invoice is past due (cell E4) is less than or equal to 30, the formula displays the amount (cell F4); otherwise, it displays a blank.

The amounts in column H (31–60 days) are a little trickier. Here, you need to check if the number of days past due is greater than or equal to 31 days *and* less than or equal to 60 days. To accomplish this, you can press the AND() function into service:

```
=IF(AND(E4 >= 31, E4 <= 60), F4, "")
```

Figure 5.10
Using IF() and AND() to categorize past-due invoices for aging purposes.

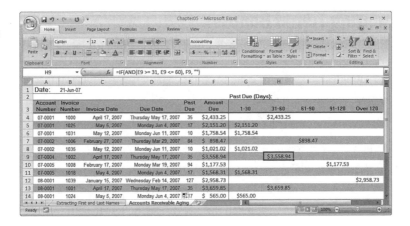

The AND() function checks two logical expressions: E4> = 31 and E4 <= 60. If both are true, AND() returns TRUE, and the IF() function displays the invoice amount. If one of the logical expressions isn't true (or if they both are not true), AND() returns FALSE, and the IF() function displays a blank. Similar formulas display in column I (61–90 days) and column J (91–120 days). Column K (over 120) looks for past-due values that are greater than 120.

Converting Mainframe Dates to Excel Dates

If you import mainframe or server data into your worksheets or if you import online service data such as stock market quotes, you often end up with date formats that Excel cannot handle. One common example is the YYYYMMDD format (for example, 20070823).

To convert this value into a date that Excel can work with, first use the LEFT(), MID(), and RIGHT() functions to extract the separate date parts:

- LEFT(A1, 4) extracts the year (assuming the unrecognized date is in cell A1).
- MID(A1, 3, 2) extracts the month. Note that the syntax here is MID(*text, start_num, num_chars*), where *start_num* is the number of the first character to extract from *text*, and *num_chars* is the number of characters you want to extract.
- RIGHT(A1, 2) extracts the day.

Given these three date components—the year, the month, and the day—you can generate a proper date from them by using Excel's DATE() function:

DATE(*year, month, day*)

year	The year component of the date (a number between 1900 and 9999).
month	The month component of the date.
day	The day component of the date.

Plugging the date components into a DATE() function gives Excel a date it can handle:

```
=DATE(LEFT(A1, 4), MID(A1, 3, 2), RIGHT(A1, 2))
```

Calculating Tiered Bonuses

If you manage salespeople or other employees eligible for bonuses, calculating the bonus is often quite simple. For example, suppose employees get a bonus for sales over $100,000. If the employee sales are in column A, then you'd use formulas similar to the following:

```
=IF(A2 > 100000, "Bonus", "")
```

The formula returns the string Bonus if the sales figure goes over $100,000.

A slightly more complex case is when you want to calculate tiered bonuses for a sales team. Here's an example:

- If the salesperson did not meet the sales target, no bonus is given.

- If the salesperson exceeded the sales target by less than 10 percent, a bonus of $1,000 is awarded.

- If the salesperson exceeded the sales target by 10 percent or more, a bonus of $10,000 is awarded.

Assuming the percentage over or under the sales target is in column D, here's a formula that handles these rules:

```
=IF(D2 < 0, "", IF(D2 < 0.1, 1000, 10000))
```

If the value in D2 is negative, nothing is returned; if the value in D2 is less than 10 percent, the formula returns 1000; if the value in D2 is greater than or equal to 10 percent, the formula returns 10000. Figure 5.11 shows this formula in action.

Figure 5.11
This worksheet uses nested IF ( ) functions to calculate a tiered bonus payment.

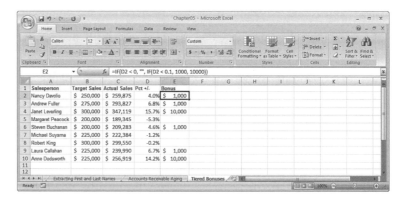

Calculating the Number of Weekdays Between Two Dates

Calculating the difference between two dates is useful in many business scenarios, including receivables aging, interest calculations, benefits payments, and more. If all you need is the number of days between two dates, you can just subtract one date from another:

```
=Date1 - Date2
```

Here, replace *Date1* and *Date2* with date values (not date strings). Excel returns a positive number if *Date1* is larger than *Date2*; it returns a negative number if *Date1* is less than *Date2*.

Besides the basic date-difference formula, you can use the date functions from earlier in this chapter to perform date-difference calculations. Also, Excel boasts a number of worksheet functions that enable you to perform more sophisticated operations to determine the difference between two dates. The rest of this section runs through a number of these date-difference formulas and functions.

In many business situations, you need to know the number of *workdays* between two dates. For example, when calculating the number of days an invoice is past due, it's often best to exclude weekends and holidays. This is easily done using the NETWORKDAYS() function (read the name as "net workdays"), which returns the number of working days between two dates:

NETWORKDAYS(*start_date*, *end_date*[, *holidays*])

> *start_date* The starting date (or a string representation of the date).
>
> *end_date* The ending date (or a string representation of the date).
>
> *holidays* A list of dates to exclude from the calculation. This can be a range of dates or an array constant (that is, a series of date serial numbers or date strings, separated by commas and surrounded by braces, {}).

For example, here's an expression that returns the number of workdays between December 1, 2007, and January 10, 2008, excluding December 25, 2007 and January 1, 2008:

=NETWORKDAYS("12/1/2007", "1/10/2008", {"12/25/2007","1/1/2008"})

Figure 5.12 shows an update to the accounts receivable worksheet that uses NETWORKDAYS() to calculate the number of workdays that each invoice is past due.

5

Figure 5.12
This worksheet calculates the number of workdays that each invoice is past due by using the NETWORK-DAYS() function.

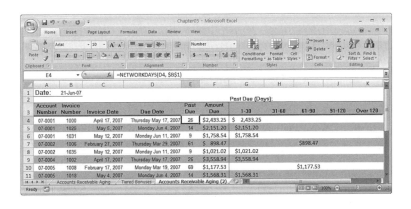

Determining the Fiscal Quarter in Which a Date Falls

If you work with budget model or financial worksheets, it's often handy to know the fiscal quarter in which a date falls. For example, if you're applying a percentage increase to various budget numbers, you might want to use a different percentage depending on the quarter.

If your fiscal year corresponds with the calendar year, you can calculate the fiscal quarter of any date by using a formula that includes the CEILING() function. First, here's the CEILING() syntax:

```
CEILING(number, significance)
```

number	The number you want to round.
significance	The multiple to which you want number rounded.

CEILING() rounds the value given by number to a multiple of the value given by significance. In particular, CEILING() rounds away from 0. For example, CEILING(1.56, 0.1) returns 1.6, and CEILING(-2.33, -0.5) returns -2.5.

To calculate the fiscal quarter in a calendar year for a given Date, divide the month value of Date by 3 and then use CEILING() to round the result up:

```
=CEILING(MONTH(Date) / 3, 1)
```

Here are two examples:

```
=CEILING(MONTH(DATEVALUE("3/31/2007")) / 3, 1)  — Returns 1
=CEILING(MONTH(DATEVALUE("4/1/2007")) / 3, 1)   — Returns 2
```

Most companies use a fiscal year that doesn't correspond with the calendar year. In this case, you need to calculate the number of months that a given date falls after the start of the fiscal year. The easiest way to do that is to use the DATEDIF() function, which returns the difference between two specified dates based on a specified unit:

```
DATEDIF(start_date, end_date[, unit])
```

start_date	The starting date.
end date	The ending date.
unit	The date unit used in the result:

unit	What It Returns
y	The number of years between start_date and end_date.
m	The number of months between start_date and end_date.
d	The number of days between start_date and end_date.
md	The difference in the day components between start_date and end_date (that is, the years and months are not included in the calculation).

ym The difference in the month components between *start_date* and *end_date* (that is, the years and days are not included in the calculation).

yd The number of days between *start_date* and *end_date*, with the year components excluded from the calculation.

For our fiscal quarter calculation, you use the m unit:

```
DATEDIF(FiscalStart, Date, "m") + 1
```

Here, *FiscalStart* is the date on which your fiscal year begins, and *Date* is the date for which you want to calculate the fiscal quarter. Note that you need to add 1 to the result because DATEDIF() doesn't include the current month in the calculation. (For example, if *Date* falls within the first fiscal month, DATEDIF() returns 0.)

You can now divide the DATEDIF() result by 3 and apply the CEILING() function as before:

```
=CEILING((DATEDIF(FiscalStart, MyDate, "m") + 1) / 3, 1)
```

Here are two examples that assume the beginning of the fiscal year is August 1 and that the opening date of the fiscal year resides in cell A1:

```
=CEILING(DATEDIF(A1, DATEVALUE("10/31/2007"), "m") + 1 / 3, 1)  — Returns 1
=CEILING(DATEDIF(A1, DATEVALUE("11/1/2007"), "m") + 1 / 3, 1)   — Returns 2
```

Setting a Product Price Point

One common worksheet task is to calculate a list price for a product based on the result of a formula that factors in production costs and profit margin. If the product is sold at retail, you likely need the decimal (cents) portion of the price to be .95 or .99 or some other standard value. You can use the INT() function to help with this "rounding," as shown in the following:

```
INT(number)
```

number The number you want to round.

For example, INT(6.75) returns 6. (Note, too, that for negative values, INT() returns the next number away from 0. For example, INT(-3.42) returns -4)._

To calculate a price point, the simplest case is to always round up the decimal part to .95. Here's a formula that does this:

```
=INT(RawPrice) + 0.95
```

Assuming that *RawPrice* is the result of the formula that factors in costs and profit margin, the formula simply adds 0.95 to the integer portion. (Note, too, that if the decimal portion of *RawPrice* is greater than .95, the formula rounds down to .95.)

Another case is to round up to .50 for decimal portions less than or equal to 0.5 and to round up to .95 for decimal portions greater than 0.5. Here's a formula that handles this scenario:

`=VALUE(INT(RawPrice) & IF(RawPrice - INT(RawPrice) <= 0.5, ".50", ".95"))`

Again, the integer portion is stripped from the *RawPrice*. Also, the `IF()` function checks to see if the decimal portion is less than or equal to 0.5. If so, the string `.50` is returned; otherwise, the string `.95` is returned. This result is concatenated to the integer portion, and the `VALUE()` function ensures that a numeric result is returned, as shown in Figure 5.13.

Figure 5.13
A worksheet that uses INT() and IF() to calculate the retail price point of several books given the Raw Price calculated from the costs and desired margin.

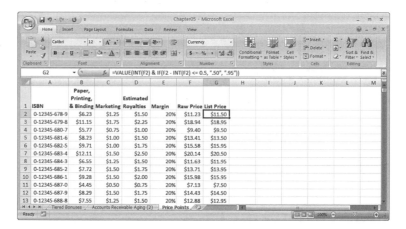

Calculating the Principal and Interest for a Loan

Any loan payment has two components: principal repayment and interest charged. Interest charges are almost always *front-loaded*, which means that the interest component is highest at the beginning of the loan and gradually decreases with each payment. This means, conversely, that the principal component increases gradually with each payment. How can you tell what the principal and interest components are for any given period of a loan? You can use the `PPMT()` and `IPMT()` functions, respectively:

`PPMT(rate, per, nper, pv[, fv][, type])`

`IPMT(rate, per, nper, pv[, fv][, type])`

rate	The fixed rate of interest over the term of the loan.
per	The number of the payment period (where the first payment is 1 and the last payment is the same as *nper*).
nper	The number of payments over the term of the loan.
pv	The loan principal.
fv	The future value of the loan (the default is 0).
type	The type of payment. Use 0 (the default) for end-of-period payments; use 1 for beginning-of-period payments.

Figure 5.14 shows a worksheet that applies these functions to a loan. The data table shows the principal (column E) and interest (column F) components of the loan for the first ten periods and for the final period. Note that with each period, the principal portion increases, and the interest portion decreases. However, the total remains the same (as confirmed by the Total column), which is as it should be because the payment remains constant through the life of the loan.

> **NOTE**
>
> When working with loan and investment formulas, always remember that amounts you pay out—such as loan payments and deposits to investments—are negative values, and amounts you receive—such as loan principal amounts and investment payouts—are positive values.

> **CAUTION**
>
> To ensure that your loan and investment models return accurate results, be sure to use consistent units when dealing with the interest and term. For example, if you have an annual interest rate and a term expressed in years and you want to calculate the monthly principal and interest, you need divide the interest rate by 12 and multiply the term by 12, as shown in Figure 5.14.

Figure 5.14
This worksheet uses the PPMT( ) and IPMT( ) functions to break out the principal and interest components of a loan payment.

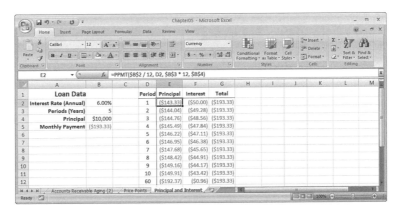

When deciding whether to take out a mortgage, car loan, or other form of debt, it's a good idea to know how much interest you'll pay over the term of the loan. The easiest way to calculate this is to multiply the monthly payment by the number of payments to get the total cost of the loan and then subtract the principal:

`=(Monthly Payment * Total Payments) - Principal`

To calculate the loan payment, use the PMT() function:

PMT(*rate*, *nper*, *pv*[, *fv*][, *type*])

rate	The fixed rate of interest over the term of the loan.
nper	The number of payments over the term of the loan.
pv	The loan principal.
fv	The future value of the loan.
type	The type of payment. Use 0 (the default) for end-of-period payments; use 1 for beginning-of-period payments.

In Figure 5.14, for example, given the annual interest rate (cell B2), the period in years (B3), and the loan principal (B4), here's the formula in cell B5 that calculates the monthly payment:

=PMT(B2 / 12, B3 * 12, B4)

In Figure 5.15, I've added a Total Interest cell (B6) that uses the payment, period, and principal to calculate the total interest costs over the life of the loan.

Figure 5.15
Given the payment, period, and principal, you can calculate the total interest paid out during a loan.

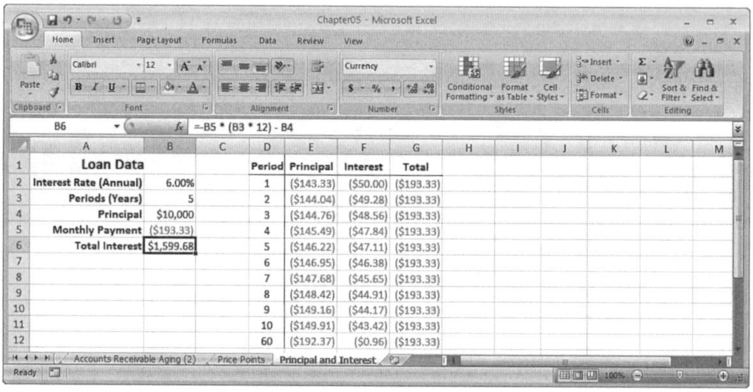

There are many business scenarios where you need to know not only the principal and interest you pay each period and the total interest over the loan term, but also how much principal or interest you've paid up to a given period. For example, if you sign up for a mortgage with a five-year term, how much principal will you have paid off by the end of the term? Similarly, a business might need to know the total interest payments a loan requires in the first year so that it can factor the result into its expense budgeting.

You can solve these kinds of problems by using a couple of functions:

```
CUMPRINC(rate, nper, pv, start_period, end_period, type)
CUMIPMT(rate, nper, pv, start_period, end_period, type)
```

`rate`	The fixed rate of interest over the term of the loan.
`nper`	The number of payments over the term of the loan.
`pv`	The loan principal.
`start_period`	The first period to include in the calculation.
`end_period`	The last period to include in the calculation.
`type`	The type of payment. Use 0 for end-of-period payments; use 1 for beginning-of-period payments.

> **CAUTION**
>
> In both CUMPRINC() and CUMIPMT(), *all* of the arguments are required. If you omit the *type* argument (which is optional in most other financial functions), Excel returns the #N/A error.

The main difference between CUMPRINC() and CUMIPMT() and PPMT() and IPMT() is the *start_period* and *end_period* arguments. For example, to find the cumulative principal or interest in the first year of a loan, you set *start_period* to 1 and *end_period* to 12; for the second year, you set *start_period* to 13 and *end_period* to 24. Here are a couple of formulas that calculate these values for any year, assuming that the year value (1, 2, and so on) is in cell D2:

```
start_period: (D2 - 1) * 12 + 1
end_period: D2 * 12
```

In Figure 15.6, I've updated the loan model to include columns for the Cumulative Principal and Cumulative Interest.

Figure 5.16
This worksheet uses the CUMPRINC() and CUMIPMT() functions to return the cumulative principal and interest for several periods of a loan.

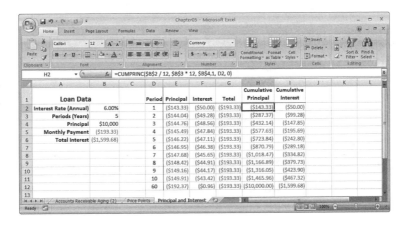

> **NOTE** Note that the CUMIPMT() function gives you an easier way to calculate the total interest costs for a loan. Set the *start_period* to 1 and the *end_period* to the number of periods (the value of *nper*), as shown in cell I12 in Figure 5.16. Note that this value is the same as the Total Interest calculation (cell B6).

Determining How Much You Can Borrow

If you know the current interest rate that your bank offers for loans, when you want to have the loan paid off, and how much you can afford each month for the payments, you might then wonder what the maximum amount is that you can borrow under those terms. To figure this out, you need to solve for the principal—that is, present value. You do that in Excel by using the PV() function:

PV(*rate*, *nper*, *pmt*[, *fv*][, *type*])

rate	The fixed rate of interest over the term of the loan.
nper	The number of payments over the term of the loan.
pmt	The periodic payment.
fv	The future value of the loan (the default is 0).
type	The type of payment. Use 0 (the default) for end-of-period payments; use 1 for beginning-of-period payments.

For example, suppose that the current loan rate is 6 percent, you want the loan paid off in 5 years, and you can afford payments of $500 per month. Figure 5.17 shows a worksheet that calculates the maximum amount that you can borrow—$25,862.78—using the following formula:

=PV(B2 / 12, B3 * 12, B4)

Figure 5.17
You can use the PV() function to calculate the maximum principal that you can borrow, given a fixed interest rate, term, and monthly payment.

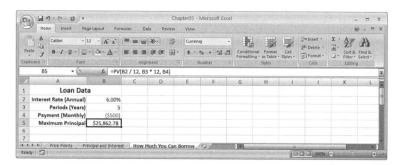

Calculating the Future Value of an Investment

Just as the payment is usually the most important value for a loan calculation, the future value is usually the most important value for an investment calculation. After all, the purpose of an investment is to place a sum of money (the present value) in an instrument for a time, after which you end up with a new (and, hopefully, greater) amount: the future value.

To calculate the future value of an investment, use the FV() function:

FV(*rate*, *nper*[, *pmt*][, *pv*][, *type*])

rate	The fixed rate of interest over the term of the investment.
nper	The number of periods in the term of the investment.
pmt	The amount deposited in the investment each period (the default is 0).
pv	The initial deposit (the default is 0).
type	The type of deposit. Use 0 (the default) for end-of-period deposits; use 1 for beginning-of-period deposits.

> **NOTE** Because both the amount deposited per period (the *pmt* argument) and the initial deposit (the *pv* argument) are sums that you pay out, you must enter these as negative values in the FV() function.

In the simplest future value scenario, you invest a lump sum and let it grow according to the specified interest rate and term, without adding any deposits along the way. In this case, you use the FV() function with the *pmt* argument set to 0:

FV(*rate*, *nper*, 0, *pv*, *type*)

For example, Figure 5.18 shows the future value of $10,000 invested at 5 percent over 10 years.

Figure 5.18
When calculating the future value of an initial lump sum deposit, set the FV() function's *pmt* argument to 0.

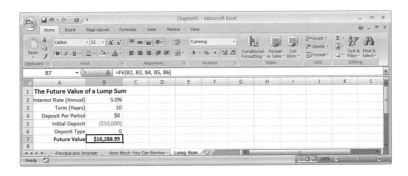

Another common investment scenario is to make a series of deposits over the term of the investment, without depositing an initial sum. In this case, you use the FV() function with the *pv* argument set to 0:

FV(*rate*, *nper*, *pmt*, 0, *type*)

For example, Figure 5.19 shows the future value of $100 invested each month at 5 percent over 10 years. Notice that the interest rate and term are both converted to monthly amounts because the deposit occurs monthly.

Figure 5.19
When calculating the future value of a series of deposits, set the FV() function's *pv* argument to 0.

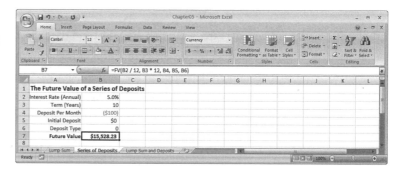

For best investment results, you should invest an initial amount and then add to it with regular deposits. In this scenario, you need to specify all the FV() function arguments (except *type*). For example, Figure 5.20 shows the future value of an investment with a $10,000 initial deposit and $100 in monthly deposits at 5 percent over 10 years.

Figure 5.20
This worksheet uses the full FV() function syntax to calculate the future value of a lump sum plus a series of deposits.

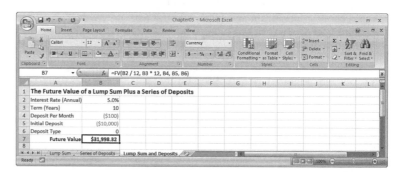

Deciding Whether to Buy or Lease

Another common business conundrum is whether to purchase equipment outright or to lease it. To make such a decision, you figure the present value of both options and then compare the results, with the preferable option being the one that provides the lower present value. (I'm going to ignore complicating factors such as depreciation and taxes.)

Assume (for now) that the purchased equipment has no market value at the end of the term and that the leased equipment has no residual value at the end of the lease. In this case, the present value of the purchase option is simply the purchase price. For the lease option, you determine the present value using the following form of the PV() function:

```
=PV(discount rate, lease term, lease payment)
```

For the *discount rate*, you plug in a value that represents either a current investment rate or a current loan rate. For example, if you could invest the lease payment and get, say, 6 percent per year, you would plug 6 percent into the function as the *rate* argument.

For example, suppose that you can either purchase a piece of equipment for $5,000 now or lease the equipment for $240 a month over 2 years. Assuming a discount rate of 6 percent, what's the present value of the leasing option? Figure 5.21 shows a worksheet that calculates the answer: $5,415.09. This means that purchasing the equipment is the less costly choice.

Figure 5.21
Using the PV() function to compare buying versus leasing equipment.

What if the equipment has a future market value (on the purchase side) or a residual value (on the lease side)? This won't make much difference in terms of which option is better because the future value of the equipment raises the two present values by about the same amount. However, note how you calculate the present value for the purchase option:

=*purchase price* + PV(*discount rate*, *term*, 0, *future value*)

That is, the present value of the purchase option is the price plus the present value of the equipment's future market value. (For the lease option, include the residual value as the PV() function's *fv* argument.) Figure 5.22 shows the worksheet with a future value added.

Figure 5.22
Using the PV() function to compare buying versus leasing equipment that has a future market or residual value.

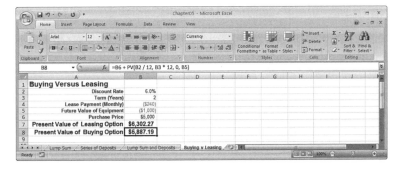

5

From Here

- If you want to prevent other people from modifying your formulas, **see** "Preventing Users from Changing Parts of a Worksheet," **p. 148**.

- Another way to allow only certain cell values is to use the worksheet dialog box controls; **see** "Using Dialog Box Controls to Input Data," **p. 160**.

- When analyzing loans and investments, a data table can help; **see** "Calculating Multiple Solutions to a Formula," **p. 167**.

- If you want to see the effect of different input values on a formula, use scenarios; **see** "Plugging Multiple Input Values into a Formula," **p. 171**.

- To learn how to use the Visual Basic Editor and incorporate macros into your documents, **see** "Working with VBA Macros," **p. 429**.

5

Workbook and Worksheet Tricks

Formulas and functions are the meat and potatoes of any spreadsheet model, but you don't use them in isolation. Rather, your formulas and functions must reside within worksheets, and those worksheets reside within workbooks. So in the same way that a beautiful painting on the wall of a house is diminished if the wall is cracked or dirty or if the house as a whole is untidy and needs repair, so too will your formulas be less effective if you don't maintain your worksheets and workbooks.

This chapter helps you do just that by showing you a number of tricks that operate at the worksheet and workbook levels. For example, you learn how to apply text and formatting to multiple sheets, techniques for collaborating with other people on a workbook, using dialog box controls to insert data, creating workbook workspaces, saving all your open workbooks, and much more.

Applying Text or Formatting to Multiple Worksheets

Many workbooks consist of multiple worksheets that use a similar structure and formatting. For example, a budget workbook might have separate sheets for each division, but each sheet uses the same labels (for sales and expenses), which are formatted the same way for consistency and readability.

If you have just a few worksheets like this, you can copy the labels and formatting from the first sheet and then paste them into the other sheets. However, this isn't efficient or practical if you're dealing with a dozen sheets or more. A better solution when you're dealing with more than a few worksheets is to enter the common text and apply

6

the common formatting to all the worksheets at the same time. To do that, you first need to group the worksheets with which you want to work. To form a group from multiple sheets, use any of the following techniques:

- To select adjacent sheets, click the tab of the first sheet, hold down the Shift key, and click the tab of the last sheet.

- To select nonadjacent sheets, hold down the Ctrl key and click the tab of each sheet you want to include in the group.

- To select all the sheets in a workbook, right-click any sheet tab and click the Select All Sheets command.

When you've selected your sheets, each tab is highlighted and [Group] appears in the workbook title bar.

> **NOTE** To ungroup the sheets, click a tab that isn't in the group. Alternatively, you can right-click one of the group's tabs and select the Ungroup Sheets command from the shortcut menu.

With the sheets now grouped, you can use any of the following techniques:

- To enter text into all the grouped worksheets, activate any grouped worksheet (by clicking its tab), select the cell you want to work with, and then type the text. When you press Enter, Excel adds the text to the same cell in all the grouped sheets.

- To format a cell in all the grouped worksheets, activate any grouped sheet, select the cell you want to format, and then apply the formatting. Excel applies the formatting to the same cell in all the grouped sheets.

- To create a *3D range*—the same range selected on multiple worksheets—activate any of the grouped sheets and then select a range. Excel selects the same cells in all the other sheets in the group.

Annotating a Worksheet with Comments

When building a spreadsheet model, it's often useful to get feedback from other people. Feedback might include verification of some content, confirmation that a formula works as it should, suggestions for improving the layout, a critique of the overall model, or just general notes about the worksheet. If someone sends you a workbook and requests your feedback, you can place that feedback in a separate document such as an email message or a Word document. However, this means your feedback will lack context. You can work around this by specifying the cell or range you're talking about, but it still means the owner of the workbook has to go back and forth between the documents.

A better way to provide worksheet feedback is to add that feedback directly to the worksheet itself. By this I don't mean typing text into a worksheet cell. Instead, you can add a *comment*, which is text that Excel associates with an individual cell but keeps separate from the worksheet itself.

To add a comment, follow these steps:

1. Click the cell to which you want to add the comment. (Note that you can't add a comment to a range of cells or if you have multiple worksheets selected.)

2. Choose Review, New Comment (or press Shift+F2). Excel displays comment balloon with your user name at the top.

> **NOTE** To change your user name, choose Office, Excel Options to open the Excel Options dialog box. In the Popular page, use the User Name text box to type the name you prefer and then click OK.

3. Type the comment text.

4. Click outside the comment balloon.

Excel indicates that a cell has an associated comment by placing a small red triangle in the upper-right corner of the cell. To view the comment, hover the mouse pointer over the cell.

> **TIP** After you have examined the comments, you might want to hide the comment indicators. Choose Office, Excel Options to open the Excel Options dialog box. Click Advanced, scroll down to the Display section, and then click to activate the No Comments or Indicators option.

Excel also offers the following techniques for dealing with comments:

- To make changes to the comment in the current cell, choose Review, Edit Comment.
- To move to the previous comment, choose Review, Previous.
- To move to the next comment, choose Review, Next.
- To toggle the comment in the current cell on and off, choose Review, Show/Hide Comment.
- To toggle all the worksheet's comments on and off, choose Review, Show All Comments. (Note that this is the same as choosing Office, Excel Options, clicking Advanced, and then activating the Comments and Indicators option in the Display section.)
- To remove the comment from the current cell, choose Review, Delete.

6

Removing All Comments from a Workbook

If you have a worksheet with many comments, you can delete them by following these steps:

1. Choose Home, Find & Select, Comments to select all the cells with comments.

2. Choose Home, Clear, Clear Comments. Excel removes all the comments.

A larger task is to remove all the comments from an entire workbook. In Excel 2007, you can do this using the new Document Inspector:

1. Choose Office, Prepare, Inspect Document.

2. If Excel tells you the document has unsaved changes, click Yes to save the workbook.

3. In the Document Inspector dialog box, deactivate all the check boxes except Comment and Annotations, as shown in Figure 6.1.

Figure 6.1
In the Document Inspector, leave only the Comments and Annotations check box activated.

4. Click Inspect. The Document Inspector tells you it found comments.

5. Click Remove All. The Document Inspector removes all the comments in the workbook.

6. Click Close.

Rather than going to all that trouble, you can use the VBA procedure shown in Listing 6.1 to delete all the comments in the active workbook.

Listing 6.1   A VBA Procedure That Deletes the Comments from the Active Workbook

```
Sub ClearAllWorkbookComments()
    Dim w As Worksheet
    Dim c As Comment
    '
    ' Run through all the worksheets
    '
    For Each w In ActiveWorkbook.Sheets
        '
        ' Run through all the comments in the current sheet
        '
        For Each c In w.Comments
            '
            ' Delete the comment
            '
            c.Delete
        Next 'c
    Next 'w
End Sub
```

This procedure uses two `For Each...Next` loops. The outer loop runs through all the worksheets in the active workbook, whereas the inner loop runs through all the comments in the current worksheet. For each comment, the procedure runs the `Delete` method to remove it.

Keeping Track of Worksheet Changes

Annotating a worksheet with comments is the most rudimentary form of collaboration. A more truly collaborative approach is when you ask other people not just to comment on your work, but to make changes to the actual worksheet model. This could be as simple as entering data or as complex as fixing errors, moving ranges, and even building new formulas and models. Whatever changes you need, chances are you don't want the other users to run roughshod over your work. That is, you probably want the ability to reject unnecessary or improper changes, while also accepting those changes that you agree to make.

You can reject and accept other users' changes by activating Excel's Track Changes feature. Each user then becomes a *reviewer* of the workbook, and Excel keeps track of most changes made by each reviewer, including the following: cell edits, row and column additions and deletions, range moves, worksheet insertions, and worksheet renames. (Note, however, that Excel does *not* track formatting changes.) You then have the option to reject any changes a reviewer makes and to accept those changes you want to keep.

Follow these steps to set up Track Changes:

1. Choose Review, Track Changes, Highlight Changes. Excel displays the Highlight Changes dialog box.
2. Click to activate the Track Changes While Editing check box. Excel enables the rest of the controls in the dialog box, as shown in Figure 6.2.

6

Figure 6.2
Use the Highlight
Changes dialog box to
activate Excel's Track
Changes feature for the
current workbook.

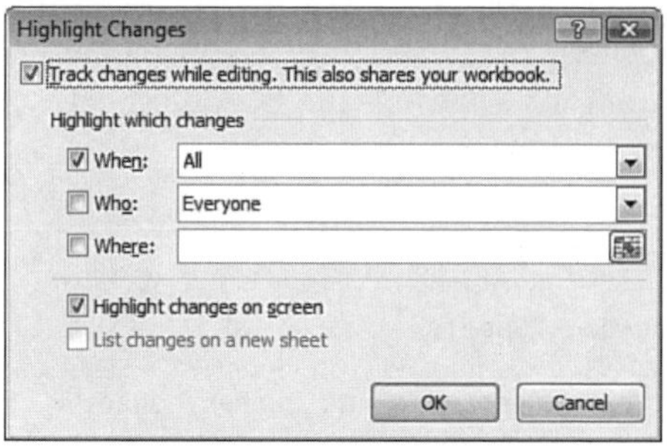

3. Use the following controls to specify the changes that Excel highlights:

When—Filters the highlighted changes by time. You can choose Since I Last Saved or Not Yet Reviewed. To specify a date, click Since Date and then edit the date that displays.

Who—Filters the highlighted changes by reviewer. At first, you can choose Everyone or Everyone but Me. When other users have made changes later on, the list includes the name of each reviewer.

Where—Selects the range in which you want changes highlighted.

4. Click OK. Excel displays a dialog box letting you know that it will save your workbook.

5. Click OK. Excel activates Track Changes and displays [Shared] in the title bar. (See "Sharing a Workbook with Other Users," next, to learn more about workbook sharing.)

When a reviewer makes changes to a workbook cell, Excel displays a triangle in the upper-left corner of the cell and a border around the cell, both of which display in the reviewer's designated color. (If the reviewer deletes a row or column, Excel displays a line in the reviewer's color between the cells where the row or column used to be.) Hover the mouse pointer over the cell to see the change, who made it, and when it was made, as shown in Figure 6.3.

Figure 6.3
After you activate the
Track Changes feature,
you can see the
reviewer's name, the
change date and time,
and the change made by
hovering your mouse
over any cell that shows
the change indicator.

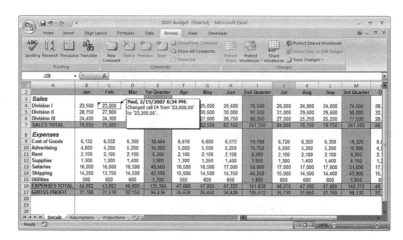

TIP Excel keeps track of the changes made to a workbook for up to 30 days. That should be enough in most cases, but you can specify a higher number if you need more time. Choose Review, Share Workbook, click the Advanced tab, and then adjust the value in the Keep Change History For *X* Days spin box. (The maximum is a whopping 32,767 days, which is just a bit less than 90 years!)

Follow these steps to accept or reject the workbook changes made by the reviewers:

1. Choose Review, Track Changes, Accept or Reject Changes.

2. If Excel tells you it will save the workbook, click OK.

3. In the Select Changes to Accept or Reject dialog box, use the When, Who, and Where controls to filter the changes, as needed.

4. Click OK. Excel displays the Accept or Reject Changes dialog box and displays a change.

5. Perform one of the following actions:

    • If there is no conflict, click Accept to approve the change or Reject to revert the cell to its original value.

    • If the reviewers make two or more changes to a cell, the Accept or Reject Changes dialog box displays the Select a Value for Cell *Cell* list (where *Cell* is the address of the cell). This list shows the original value and the changes. Click the value you want to keep and then click Accept.

    • If you want to approve every change in the workbook, click Accept All.

    • If you want to discard every change in the workbook, click Reject All.

6. Repeat step 5 to review all the changes.

Sharing a Workbook with Other Users

As you saw in the previous section, activating change tracking also activates *workbook sharing*, the Excel feature that enables two or more users to collaborate on a workbook at the same time. This is a powerful tool because it enables you to share the burden of building a workbook. For example, if you coordinate a budget model, you might want to share the workbook and assign a different worksheet to a user in each department.

I should point out here that although turning on change tracking also turns on workbook sharing, the opposite is not the case. That is, you can share a workbook without also tracking changes. Follow these steps to share a workbook:

1. If another person is currently using the workbook, ask that person to close the file.

2. Choose Review, Share Workbook. Excel displays the Share Workbook dialog box.

3. Activate the Allow Changes by More Than One User at the Same Time check box.

6

4. Click OK. Excel tells you it will save the workbook.

5. Click OK.

Excel displays [Shared] in the document title bar to remind you that the workbook is shared. You and your collaborators are now free to work on the file at the same time. Note, however, that Excel doesn't allow the following operations while a workbook is shared:

- Inserting and deleting ranges (although you can insert and delete entire rows and columns)
- Merging cells
- Creating lists
- Creating or modifying PivotTables
- Deleting or moving worksheets
- Applying conditional formatting
- Working with scenarios
- Subtotaling, validating, grouping, and outlining data
- Inserting charts, symbols, pictures, diagrams, objects, and hyperlinks
- Checking for formula errors

To ensure that you always work with the most up-to-date version of the file, save the workbook. This tells Excel to display other reviewers' changes in your view of the workbook. If any changes are added, Excel displays a dialog box to let you know.

To control when Excel updates a shared workbook, follow these steps:

1. Choose Review, Share Workbook to display the Share Workbook dialog box.

2. Click the Advanced tab.

3. In the Update Changes group, click one of the following options:

    When File Is Saved—When you activate this option, Excel updates the workbook automatically when you save the file.

    Automatically Every *X* Minutes—When you activate this option, Excel updates the workbook using the interval you specify (the minimum is 5 minutes; the maximum is 1,440 minutes). You can also elect to have Excel save your changes at the same time or just see the changes made by other users.

4. Click OK.

If you want to know who is currently using the workbook besides yourself, choose Review, Share Workbook. As you can see in Figure 6.4, the Who Has This Workbook Open Now list displays all the current users. If you want to prevent a reviewer from using the workbook, click the user and then click Remove User. Note, however, that you should use this technique only as a last resort because it can easily cause the user to lose unsaved changes. It's safer (and friendlier) to ask the person directly to save his changes and close the workbook.

Figure 6.4
Choose Review, Share Workbook to see a list of the workbook's current reviewers.

What happens if another user changes a cell, saves his changes, and then you change the same cell before updating? This creates a conflict in the workbook versions that must be resolved. To do this, Excel displays the Resolve Conflicts dialog box, shown in Figure 6.5. You have two choices: Click Accept Mine to accept your change or click Accept Other to accept the other user's change.

Figure 6.5
Use the Resolve Conflicts dialog box to choose between a change made by you and one made by another user.

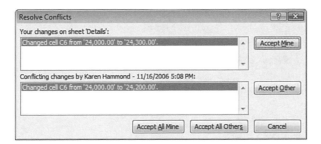

To control how Excel handles conflicts, follow these steps:

1. Choose Review, Share Workbook to display the Share Workbook dialog box.

2. Click the Advanced tab.

3. In the Conflicting Changes Between Users group, click one of the following options:

    Ask Me Which Changes Win—When you activate this option, Excel displays the Resolve Conflicts dialog box.

    The Changes Being Saved Win—When you activate this option, Excel automatically accepts your changes.

6

> **CAUTION**
>
> Collaboration is about cooperation, so it's always good practice to display conflicts in the Resolve Conflicts dialog box so that you can make an intelligent choice about which change to accept. Therefore, activate The Changes Being Saved Win option only as a last resort.

4. Click OK.

Preventing Users from Changing Parts of a Worksheet

When you collaborate with other people on a workbook, you'll often have parts of a worksheet that you don't want altered in any way. You could activate Track Changes and then reject any changes made to those areas, but that's extra work that you shouldn't have to perform. Fortunately, Excel gives you an alternative: *worksheet protection*. With this feature, you can designate worksheet ranges to be *locked*, which means that other people can't change, delete, move, or copy over those ranges.

Here are the steps to follow to set up protection formatting for worksheet cells:

1. Select the cells that you want other people to be able to change. (Skip this step if you want to prevent changes to the entire worksheet.)

2. Choose Home, Format, Lock Cell to deactivate this command.

3. Choose Review, Protect Sheet (or Home, Format, Protect Sheet). Excel displays the Protect Sheet dialog box, shown in Figure 6.6.

Figure 6.6
Use the Protect Sheet dialog box to activate your protection formatting.

4. For added security, enter a password in the Password to Unprotect Sheet text box. This means that no one can turn off the worksheet's protection without first entering the password.

NOTE You might wonder why Excel makes the password for unprotecting the sheet optional. That's because the concern here is worksheet integrity: You don't want a user accidentally modifying or deleting formulas or data. When faced with a protected sheet, most users don't automatically look to unprotect it, so protection without a password is almost always a safe option.

5. Use the check boxes to select the actions unauthorized users are allowed to perform.

6. Click OK.

7. If you entered a password, Excel asks you to confirm it. Reenter the password and then click OK.

To turn off the protection, choose Review, Unprotect Sheet. If you entered a password, Excel displays the Unprotect Sheet dialog box. Type the password into the Password text box and then click OK.

Adding a Live Stock Price Quote to a Worksheet

If you use Excel to track your investments, it can be handy to get the latest quotes for the stocks in your portfolio. Excel comes with a Financial Symbol smart tag that includes an option to insert a "refreshable" stock price for a given stock symbol. Here, "refreshable" means that Excel connects to the MSN Money Web site to gather the latest information about the stock symbol, and it then inserts that information into your worksheet. The stock symbol data includes active links to the Web site for viewing charts, news, and looking up other stock symbols

Before you learn how this works, you first need to ensure that smart tags are turned on in Excel. Follow these steps:

1. Choose Office, Excel Options to display the Excel Options dialog box.

2. Click Proofing.

3. Click AutoCorrect Options to open the AutoCorrect dialog box.

4. Click the Smart Tags tab.

5. Click to activate the Label Data With Smart Tags check box.

6. In the Recognizers list, make sure that the Financial Symbol check box is activated.

7. Click OK.

8. Click OK.

To try out the Financial Symbol smart tag, type a stock symbol into a cell using all upper-case letters and then press Enter. Excel adds a small triangle to the bottom-right corner of the cell. Hover the mouse pointer over the cell to display the smart tag and then click the smart tag. As you can see in Figure 6.7, the Smart Tag Actions list contains several

6

commands related to the stock symbol. Click Insert Refreshable Stock Price to display the Insert Stock Price dialog box, which gives you two choices:

- **On a New Sheet**—Click this option to display the stock quote on a new worksheet that Excel automatically adds to the current workbook.

- **Starting at Cell**—Click this option to display the Stock Quote at the cell address you type in the text box.

Click OK. Excel then gathers the stock quote information from the MSN Money Web site and displays it in the location you specified, as shown in Figure 6.8.

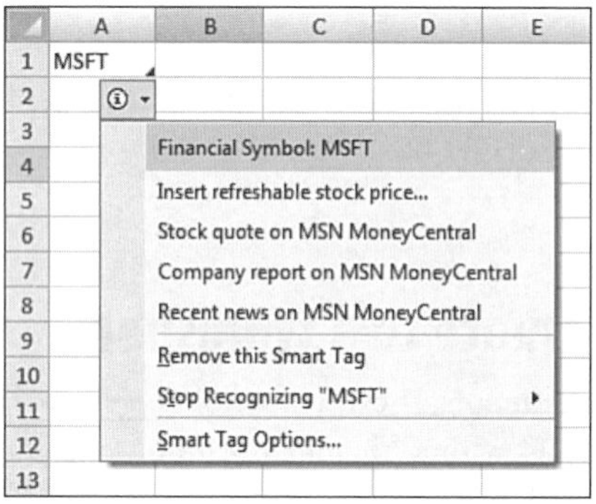

Figure 6.7
When you type a stock symbol, Excel displays a Financial Symbol smart tag that offers the actions shown here.

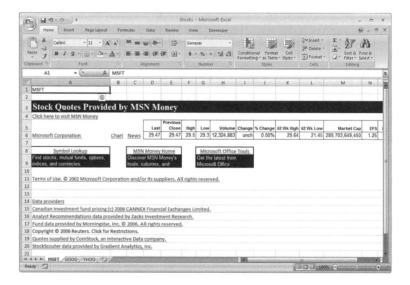

Figure 6.8
Click the Insert Refreshable Stock Price action to insert a stock quote from MSN Money.

Automatically Sorting a Range After Data Entry

If you use Excel to store data, chances are you sort that data in some way. Sorting helps you find items and rank numeric values for analysis. However, sorting is a challenge if you regularly add items to the data because it means you have to resort the range after you enter each item. Sorting is also problematic in ranges where the sort column uses a calculation.

For example, Figure 6.9 shows a products table. The table is sorted on the Gross Margin column (F), the values of which are determined using a formula that requires input from cells in columns D and E. This means that each time a value in column D or E changes, the corresponding Gross Margin value changes, so you need to resort the table.

Figure 6.9
The products table is sorted on the Gross Margin column (F).

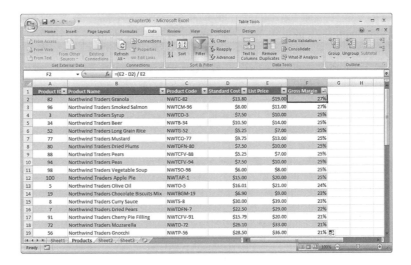

To save time, it is nice if you can keep a range sorted automatically after entering new data or after changing data that affects the sort column. Listing 6.2 shows a couple of VBA procedures that keep a specified range sorted automatically.

Listing 6.2   VBA Procedures That Keep the Products Table Sorted Automatically

```
Sub Auto_Open()
    ThisWorkbook.Worksheets("Products").OnEntry = "SortProducts"
End Sub

Sub SortProducts()
    Dim currCell As Range
    Set currCell = Application.Caller
    If currCell.Column = 4 Or currCell.Column = 5 Then
        Selection.Sort Key1:=Range("F1"), _
                    Order1:=xlDescending, _
                    Header:=xlYes, _
```

continues

6

Listing 6.2 Continued

```
                          OrderCustom:=1, _
                          MatchCase:=False, _
                          Orientation:=xlTopToBottom
        End If
End Sub
```

Auto_Open is a macro that runs automatically when the workbook containing the code is opened. In this case, the statement sets the OnEntry event of the Products worksheet to run the SortProducts macro. The OnEntry event fires whenever data entry occurs in the specified object (in this case, the Products worksheet).

The SortProducts procedure checks the value of the Application object's Caller property, which returns a Range object that indicates which cell invoked the SortProducts macro. In this context, Caller tells us in which cell the data entry occurred, and that cell address is stored in the currCell variable. Next, the macro checks currCell to see if the data entry occurred in either column D or column E. If so, the new value changes the calculated value in the Gross Margin column, so the range needs to be resorted. This is accomplished by running the Sort method, which sorts the range based on the values in column F.

Transposing Range Rows and Columns

When you're building a worksheet model, you often begin by adding some labels or other data in a row or column. After you add some data, however, you may find that it will display better if it's transposed to display in the other direction. That is, row data might look better in a column (the usual case because Excel displays more rows than columns), or column data might look better in a row. Either way, transposing the data by hand is a pain because you need to either click-and-drag or cut-and-paste the cells individually.

Rather than going through that hassle, Excel has a feature that enables you to transpose rows and columns with just a few mouse clicks:

1. Select and copy the source cells.
2. Select the upper-left corner of the destination range.
3. Choose Home, pull down the Paste menu, and choose Transpose.

Automatically Opening a Workbook at Startup

By default, Excel opens a new, blank workbook every time you launch the program. If you use the same workbook every time you open Excel, you can tell the program to automatically open that workbook for you at startup.

To set up a workbook to open automatically, you must store the workbook file in one of the XLSTART folders on your computer. If you selected the default folder setting for storing

Excel on your computer when you installed Office, you can find the XLSTART folder within the following folder:

`%ProgramFiles%\Microsoft Office\Office12\`

There's also an XLSTART folder in your user profile:

`%UserProfile%\AppData\Roaming\Microsoft\Excel\XLSTART`

You can either move your workbook into one of those folders using Windows Explorer, or you can follow these steps to save a copy of your workbook in that folder:

1. Choose Office, Save <u>A</u>s to open the Save As dialog box.
2. In the Address box, type the address of the XLSTART folder you want to use and press Enter.
3. Click Save.

Creating a Workspace of Workbooks

When you work in Excel, you may find that you always use a particular collection of workbooks. In fact, you may spend the first few minutes after launching Excel opening those workbooks. A similar situation occurs when you have separate groups of related workbooks that you use at different times. For example, you might have one collection of budget workbooks, another collection of planning workbooks, and yet another collection for an ongoing project. In these cases, you waste precious time opening the individual files you need.

Excel helps you save most of that time by enabling you to specify *workspaces* of files. A workspace is a collection of workbooks that Excel stores in a special .xlw file. When you open a workspace file, Excel automatically opens all the workbooks that you've associated with it.

NEW Earlier versions of Excel had a Save Workspace command on the File menu. In Excel 2007, you must first add this command to the Quick Access toolbar. Here are the steps to follow:

1. Pull down the Customize Quick Access Toolbar menu and then click <u>M</u>ore Commands. The Excel Options dialog box displays with the Customize page displayed.
2. In the <u>C</u>hoose Command From list, click All Commands.
3. In the list of commands, click Save Workspace.
4. Click <u>A</u>dd.
5. Click OK. Excel adds a button for the Save Workspace command to the Quick Access toolbar.

6

You can now save a workspace of workbooks. Here are the steps to follow:

1. Open the workbooks that you want to include in the workspace. If you have any workbooks open that you don't want in the workspace, close them.

2. In the Quick Access toolbar, click the Save Workspace command. Excel displays the Save Workspace dialog box.

3. Select a location for the workspace file.

4. Type a File Name. (The default name is resume, but you can use any name you like.)

5. Click Save.

6. If any of the open workbooks have unsaved changes, Excel prompts you to save them. In each case, click Yes to save the changes (or click Yes to All).

The next time you run Excel, you can open the workspace by choosing Office, Open and then choosing the workspace file.

Creating a Workbook with a Specified Number of Sheets

Early versions of Excel used to give you 16 worksheets by default in each new workbook. Somebody at Microsoft must have realized this was an absurdly large number, so recent versions of Excel populate new workbooks with just three worksheets. That's a reasonable number because most people probably just use a single worksheet in most of their workbooks. However, it's not uncommon to have workbooks with 10 or 20 sheets, depending on the application. Rather than adding the extra sheets by hand, Listing 6.3 presents a VBA procedure that prompts you for the number of sheets you want and then creates a new workbook populated with that many sheets.

> **TIP**
>
> You can change the number of worksheets that Excel adds by default to new workbooks. Choose Office, Excel Options to display the Excel Options dialog box. Click Popular and then use the Include This Many Sheets spin box to set the number of worksheets you want in each new workbook. Click OK to put the new setting into effect.

Listing 6.3 A VBA Procedure That Prompts You to Specify the Number of Sheets You Want in a New Workbook

```
Sub NewWorkbookWithCustomSheets()
    Dim currentSheets As Integer
    With Application
        '
        ' Save the current value of SheetsInNewWorkbook
        '
        currentSheets = .SheetsInNewWorkbook
        '
```

```
    ' Ask how many sheets to include in the new workbook
    ' and store the result in SheetsInNewWorkbook
    '
    .SheetsInNewWorkbook = InputBox( _
        "How many sheets do you want " & _
        "in the new workbook?", , 3)
    '
    ' Create the new workbook
    '
    Workbooks.Add
    '
    ' Restore the original value of SheetsInNewWorkbook
    '
    .SheetsInNewWorkbook = currentSheets
  End With
End Sub
```

The value of the Include This Many Sheets setting is given by the `Application` object's `SheetsInNewWorkbook` property. The procedure first stores the current `SheetsInNewWorkbook` value in the `currentSheets` variable. Then the macro runs the `InputBox` function to get the number of required sheets (with a default value of 3), and this value is assigned to the `SheetsInNewWorkbook` property. Then the `Workbooks.Add` statement creates a new workbook (which has the specified number of sheets) and the `SheetsInNewWorkbook` property is returned to its original value.

Selecting A1 on All Worksheets

One of Excel's unique features is that it "remembers" where you left off in a workbook when you last closed it, and it then restores that position the next time you open the workbook. For example, if the active cell is D5 in Sheet3 when you close a workbook, the next time you open that file, Excel automatically activates Sheet3 and selects cell D5. Not only that, but Excel also remembers the most recently used cell in *every* worksheet. This also applies to ranges: If you have ranges selected on any worksheet when you close the file, Excel reselects those ranges the next time you open the workbook.

This is useful because in most cases, it enables you to continue working from the spot where you stopped earlier when you closed the file. One situation where this is not great behavior is when you distribute a workbook to other people. When the other users open the file, Excel might take them to a cell or range in a worksheet that's buried deep in the workbook. It's more likely that you'll want the workbook to have no selected ranges and to have the first worksheet activated. A good way to do this is to select cell A1 on each worksheet and to finish by activating the first worksheet. This is reasonable in a workbook with just a few sheets, but it's a hassle in large workbooks. To eliminate that hassle, Listing 6.4 presents a VBA procedure that selects cell A1 in all of a workbook's sheets.

6

Listing 6.4   A VBA Procedure That Selects Cell A1 on All the Sheets in the Active Workbook

```
Sub SelectA1OnAllSheets()
    Dim ws As Worksheet
    '
    ' Run through all the worksheets in the active workbook
    '
    For Each ws In ActiveWorkbook.Worksheets
        '
        ' Activate the worksheet
        '
        ws.Activate
        '
        ' Select cell A1
        '
        ws.[A1].Select
    Next 'ws
    '
    ' Activate the first worksheet
    '
    ActiveWorkbook.Worksheets(1).Activate
End Sub
```

The procedure runs through all the worksheets in the active workbook. In each case, the worksheet is first activated (you must activate a sheet before you can select anything on it) and then the Select method is called to select cell A1. The macro finishes by activating the first worksheet.

Selecting the "Home Cell" on All Worksheets

In the previous section, I showed you a VBA procedure that "reset" a workbook by selecting cell A1 in all worksheets. However, it isn't always the case that cell A1 is the appropriate starting point in a worksheet. For example, if other people work on data in a particular worksheet, it is best to have the first data entry cell selected when they open the file. Similarly, you might want to select a cell that contains a problem or an important result. In these situations, rather than selecting cell A1 on all the worksheets, you might prefer to select each of these "home cells."

An easy way to do this is to first designate each worksheet's home cell by adding a comment to each of those cells. This should be a uniform comment, such as Home Cell or something similar. You can then use the VBA procedure in Listing 6.5 to select each of these home cells.

Listing 6.5   A VBA Procedure That Selects the "Home Cell" on All the Sheets in the Active Workbook

```
Sub SelectHomeCells()
    Dim ws As Worksheet
    Dim c As Comment
```

```
    Dim r As Range
    '
    ' Run through all the worksheets in the active workbook
    '
    For Each ws In ActiveWorkbook.Worksheets
        '
        ' Activate the worksheet
        '
        ws.Activate
        '
        ' Run through the comments
        '
        For Each c In ws.Comments
            '
            ' Look for the "Home Cell" comment
            '
            If InStr(c.Text, "Home Cell") <> 0 Then
                '
                ' Store the cell as a Range
                '
                Set r = c.Parent
                '
                ' Select the cell
                '
                r.Select
            End If
        Next 'c
    Next 'ws
    '
    ' Activate the first worksheet
    '
    ActiveWorkbook.Worksheets(1).Activate
End Sub
```

The SelectHomeCells procedure is similar to the SelectA1OnAllSheets procedure from Listing 6.4. That is, the main loop runs through all the sheets in the active workbook and activates each worksheet in turn. In this case, however, another loop runs through each worksheet's Comments collection. The Text property of each Comment object is checked to see if it includes the phrase Home Cell. If so, the cell containing the comment is stored in the r variable (using the Comment object's Parent property), and then the cell is selected.

Selecting the Named Range that Contains the Active Cell

It's often handy to be able to select the name range that contains the current cell (for example, to change the range formatting). If you know the name of the range, you need only select it from the Name box. However, in a large model or a workbook that you're not familiar with, it may not be obvious which name to choose. Listing 6.6 shows a VBA function and procedure that handles this chore for you.

6

Listing 6.6   A VBA Function and Procedure That Determines and Selects the Named Range Containing the Active Cell

```
Function GetRangeName(r As Range) As String
    Dim n As Name
    Dim rtr As Range
    Dim ir As Range
    '
    ' Run through all the range names in the active workbook
    '
    For Each n In ActiveWorkbook.Names
        '
        ' Get the name's range
        '
        Set rtr = n.RefersToRange
        '
        ' See if the named range and the active cell's range intersect
        '
        Set ir = Application.Intersect(r, rtr)
        If Not ir Is Nothing Then
            '
            ' If they intersect, then the active cell is part of a
            ' named range, so get the name and exit the function
            GetRangeName = n.Name
            Exit Function
        End If
    Next 'n
    '
    ' If we get this far, the active cell is not part of a named range,
    ' so return the null string
    '
    GetRangeName = ""
End Function

Sub SelectCurrentNamedRange()
    Dim r As Range
    Dim strName As String
    '
    ' Store the active cell
    '
    Set r = ActiveCell
    '
    ' Get the name of the range that contains the cell, if any
    '
    strName = GetRangeName(r)
    If strName <> "" Then
        '
        ' If the cell is part of a named range, select the range
        '
        Range(strName).Select
    End If
End Sub
```

The heart of Listing 6.6 is the GetRangeName function, which takes a range as an argument. The purpose of this function is to see if the passed range—r—is part of a named range and if so, to return the name of that range. The function's main loop runs through each item in the active workbook's `Names` collection. For each name, the `RefersToRange` property returns the associated range, which the function stores in the `rtr` variable. The function then uses the `Intersect` method to see if the ranges `r` and `rtr` intersect. If they do, it means that `r` is part of the named range (because, in this case, `r` is just a single cell), so `GetRangeName` returns the range name. If no intersection is found for any name, the function returns the null string ("") instead.

The `SelectCurrentNamedRange` procedure makes use of the `GetRangeName` function. The procedure stores the active cell in the `r` variable and then passes that variable to the `GetRangeName` function. If the return value is not the null string, the procedure selects the returned range name.

Saving All Open Workbooks

If you often work with multiple workbooks at once, you may find yourself moving from one workbook to another, making changes to each one as you go. Unless you remember to save all along, you probably end up with some or all of your open workbooks with unsaved changes. Unfortunately, Excel doesn't tell you which workbooks have unsaved changes, so you have no choice but to trudge through each open workbook and run the Save command.

You can avoid this drudgery by using the `SaveAll` procedure shown in Listing 6.7.

Listing 6.7 A VBA Procedure That Saves All Open Workbooks

```
Sub SaveAll()
    Dim wb As Workbook
    Dim newFilename As Variant
    '
    ' Run through all the open workbooks
    '
    For Each wb In Workbooks
        '
        ' Has the workbook been saved before?
        '
        If wb.Path <> "" Then
            '
            ' If so, save it
            '
            wb.Save
        Else
            '
            ' If not, display the Save As dialog box
            ' to get the workbook's path & filename
            '
            With Application
                newFilename = .GetSaveAsFilename( _
                    FileFilter:="Microsoft Office " & _
                    "Excel Workbook " & _
```

continues

Listing 6.7 Continued

```
                  "(*.xlsx), *.xlsx")
          End With
          '
          ' Did the user click Cancel?
          '
          If newFilename <> False Then
              '
              ' If not, save the workbook using the
              ' specified path and filename
              '
              wb.SaveAs fileName:=newFilename
          End If
      End If
   Next 'wb
End Sub
```

The main loop in the SaveAll macro uses the Workbooks collection and a For Each...Next loop to run through all the open workbooks. For each workbook (given by the wb Workbook variable), the loop first checks the Path property to see if it returns the null string (""). If not, it means the workbook has been saved previously, so the macro runs the Save method to save the file. If Path does return the null string, it means you're saving the workbook for the first time. In this case, the macro runs the GetSaveAsFilename method, which displays the Save As dialog box so that you can select a save location and filename, which are stored in the newFilename variable. If this variable's value is False, it means you clicked Cancel in the Save As dialog box, so the macro skips the file; otherwise, the macro uses the SaveAs method to save the workbook using the specified path and filename.

Using Dialog Box Controls to Input Data

If you are constructing worksheets that other people will use for data entry, ensuring that data is entered as accurately as possible should be your main concern. No matter how solid the rest of the model is, if the data it relies upon is faulty, the results the model generates will be faulty as well. When constructing a worksheet, here are a few notes to bear in mind to help ensure accurate data entry:

- Format the worksheet text in a large, clear, legible font.
- Provide labels that indicate to the user the data type or units a cell requires. For example, if a cell requires a value in months, add the label months in the cell to the right of the input cell.
- Provide instructions that tell the user how to input the data. These instructions can be in a text box at the top of the worksheet or in comments that you insert into each input cell.
- Take advantage of Excel's powerful data validation features to ensure the right types of data get entered.

→ To learn about data validation in Excel, **see** "Allowing Only Certain Values in a Cell," **p. 107**

Another useful technique for ensuring accurate data entry is to add an extra worksheet layer that gives the user an interface for entering the data. This interface takes the form of dialog box controls such as lists, check boxes, and option buttons. You associate certain values with these controls, which then ensure that the user can enter only the values you want.

Before you can work with dialog box controls, you need to display the Ribbon's Developer tab:

1. Choose Office, Excel Options to open the Excel Options dialog box.
2. Click Popular.
3. Click to activate the Show Developer Tab In the Ribbon check box.
4. Click OK.

You add the dialog box controls by choosing Developer, Insert and then selecting tools from the Form Controls list, shown in Figure 6.10. Note that only some of the controls are available for worksheet duty. I discuss the controls in detail a bit later in this section.

Figure 6.10
On the Developer tab, click Insert to see the Form Controls that you can use for data entry on your worksheets.

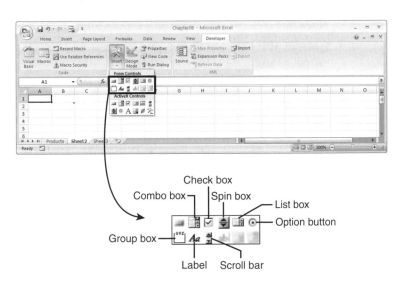

Follow these steps to add any control to a worksheet:

1. Choose Developer, Insert, and then click the form control you want to create. The mouse pointer changes to a crosshair.
2. Move the pointer onto the worksheet at the point where you want the control to display.
3. Click and drag the mouse pointer to create the control.
4. To edit the control caption, right-click the control, choose Edit Text, adjust the text accordingly, and then click outside the control.

5. Right-click the control, and then click <u>F</u>ormat Control to display the Format Control dialog box.

6. Click the Control tab, and then use the Cell <u>L</u>ink box to enter the cell's reference. You can either type the reference or select it directly on the worksheet.

> **NOTE**
> When working with option buttons, you have to enter only the linked cell for one of the buttons in a group. Excel automatically adds the reference to the rest.

Configure other options for the control:

- **<u>C</u>hecked (Check Box and Option Button)**—Click this option to display the control as either checked or activated.

- **<u>U</u>nchecked (Check Box and Option Button)**—Click this option to display the control as either unchecked or deactivated.

- **<u>I</u>nput Range (List Box or Combo Box)**—Enter a reference to the worksheet range that contains the items you want to display in the list.

- **<u>C</u>urrent Value (Scroll Bar or Spin Button)**—The initial value of the scroll bar or spin button.

- **M<u>i</u>nimum Value (Scroll Bar or Spin Button)**—For a scroll bar, the value when the scroll box is at its leftmost position (for a horizontal scroll bar) or its topmost position (for a vertical scroll bar); for spin button, the smallest possible value.

- **Ma<u>x</u>imum Value (Scroll Bar or Spin Button)**—For a scroll bar, the value when the scroll box is at its rightmost position (for a horizontal scroll bar) or its bottommost position (for a vertical scroll bar); for spin button, the largest possible value.

- **I<u>n</u>cremental Change (Scroll Bar or Spin Button)**—For a scroll bar, the amount that the value changes when the user clicks on a scroll arrow; for spin button, the amount the value changes when the user clicks an arrow.

- **<u>P</u>age Change (Scroll Bar)**—The amount that the scroll bar's value changes when the user clicks between the scroll box and a scroll arrow.

7. Choose OK to return to the worksheet.

Figure 6.11 shows a worksheet with a few dialog box controls added.

6

Figure 6.11
You can help ensure
accurate data entry by
using dialog box controls
linked to worksheet
cells.

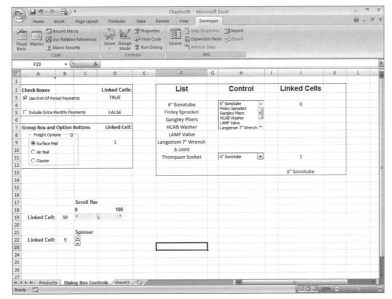

From Here

- You can prevent untracked changes in Word, as well; **see** "Preventing Untracked Changes," **p. 79**.

- Word also supports document controls for data input; **see** "Setting Up a Document for Structured Editing," **p. 80**.

- To learn about data validation in Excel, **see** "Allowing Only Certain Values in a Cell," **p. 107**.

6

Data Analysis Tricks

All data has a story to tell. Whether it's sales, expenses, statistics, inventory, or share prices, the data usually hides something interesting or important that you ought to know. However, even Office gurus understand that although it's relatively easy to enter data into an Excel worksheet, it's much harder to hear what that data is telling you. To put it another way, Office gurus know that to glean meaning from static worksheet data, you have to *animate* the data in some way and turn the data into *information*.

In Excel, animating data really means *analyzing* it. Using Excel's data analysis and business-modeling tools, you can analyze worksheet numbers to make them reveal their secrets. This chapter shows you how to do this by examining a number of Excel's most useful data-analysis techniques and features.

Using a Range Snapshot to Watch a Cell Value

What-if analysis is perhaps the most basic method for understanding worksheet data. With what-if analysis, you first calculate a formula F, based on the input from variables X, Y, and Z. You then say, "What if I change variable X? What if I increase Y? What if I decrease Z? What happens to the result?"

For example, Figure 7.1 shows a worksheet that calculates the monthly payment for a loan or mortgage based on three variables: the interest rate, the term, and the initial principal. Cell C8 shows the result of the PMT() function. Now the questions begin: What if the interest rate is 8 percent? What if the term is 25 years? What if the principal is $125,000? Or $150,000? Answering these questions is a straightforward matter of changing the appropriate variables and watching the effect on the result.

Figure 7.1
The most basic form of
what-if analysis involves
changing worksheet vari-
ables and watching the
result.

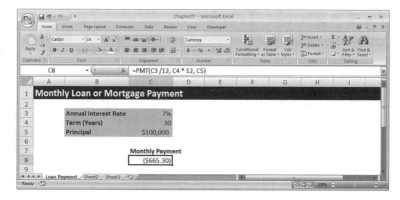

Changing the value of one cell and watching its effect on the values of one or more other
cells is straightforward. However, what if the cells you want to watch reside in another
worksheet or workbook? You can arrange the windows accordingly, but Excel has an easier
method: the Paste Picture Link command. This command takes a copy of a specified range
and turns it into a *snapshot*: a picture of the original range that you can add to any worksheet. The snapshot is "live," however, so any changes that occur in the original range will
also appear automatically in the snapshot. (The snapshot itself is just a Picture object, so
you can't edit the data it displays.)

Follow these steps to use Paste Picture Link to create a range snapshot:

1. Select the range you want to watch.
2. Choose Home, Copy (or press Ctrl+C).
3. Switch to the worksheet and select the cell in which you want the snapshot to display.
4. Choose Home, pull down the Paste menu, and then choose As Picture, Paste Picture
   Link. Excel pastes the snapshot and sets up a link to the original range.

Using a Watch Window to Watch a Cell Value

Using a range snapshot is a useful and nifty trick, but it's only practical if you want to
watch one or two values. However, it's not unusual for a large or complex worksheet model
to have a large number of cells that require watching, particularly when you first build the
model. If you need to keep an eye on a lot of cells, forget the Paste Picture Link command.
Instead, use Excel's more elegant solution: the Watch Window. This window enables you
to keep tabs on both the value and the formula in any cell in any worksheet in any open
workbook. Here's how you set up a watch:

1. Activate the workbook that contains the cell or cells you want to watch.

2. Choose Formulas, Watch Window. Excel displays the Watch Window.

3. Click Add Watch. Excel displays the Add Watch dialog box.

4. Either select the cell you want to watch or type in a reference formula for the cell (for example, =A1). Note that you can select a range to add multiple cells to the Watch Window.

5. Click Add. Excel adds the cell or cells to the Watch Window, as shown in Figure 7.2.

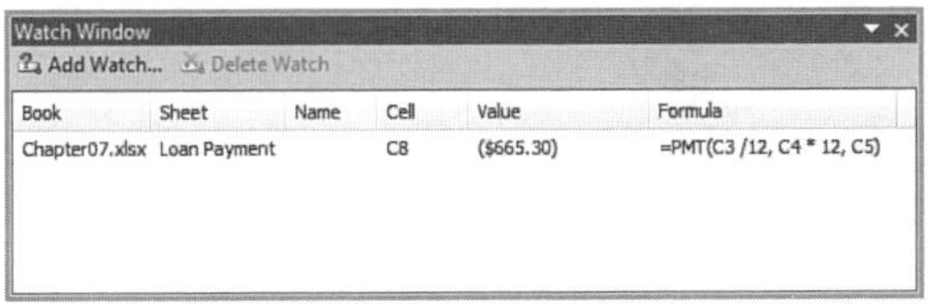

Figure 7.2
Use the Watch Window to keep an eye on the values and formulas of unseen cells that reside in other worksheets or workbooks.

Calculating Multiple Solutions to a Formula

Modifying formula variables suffers from a serious drawback: You see only a single result at one time. If you want to study the effect that a variety of values has on the formula, you need to construct a *data table*. In the loan payment worksheet, for example, suppose that you want to see the payments with the principal varying between $100,000 and $150,000. You can just enter these values into a row or column, and then create the appropriate formulas. Setting up a data table, however, is much easier, as the following procedure shows:

1. Add to the worksheet the values you want to input into the formula. You have two choices for the placement of these values:

   ■ If you want to enter the values in a row, start the row one cell up and one cell to the right of the formula.

   ■ If you want to enter the values in a column start the column one cell down and one cell to the left of the cell containing the formula, as shown in Figure 7.3.

2. Select the range that includes the input values and the formula. (In Figure 7.3, this is B8:C14.)

3. Choose Data, What-If Analysis, Data Table. Excel displays the Data Table dialog box.

4. How you fill in this dialog box depends on how you set up your data table:

   ■ If you entered the input values in a row, use the Row Input Cell text box to enter the cell address of the input cell.

   ■ If the input values are in a column, enter the input cell's address in the Column Input Cell text box. In the future value example, you enter **C5** in the Column Input Cell, as shown in Figure 7.4.

7

Figure 7.3
Enter the values you want to input into the formula.

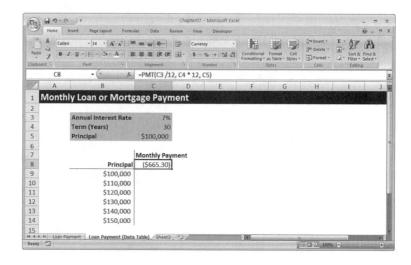

Figure 7.4
In the Data Table dialog box, enter the input cell in which you want Excel to substitute the input values.

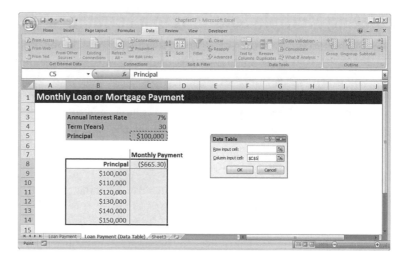

5. Click OK. Excel places each of the input values in the input cell; Excel then displays the results in the data table, as shown in Figure 7.5.

7

Figure 7.5
Excel substitutes each
input value into the input
cell and displays the
results in the data table.

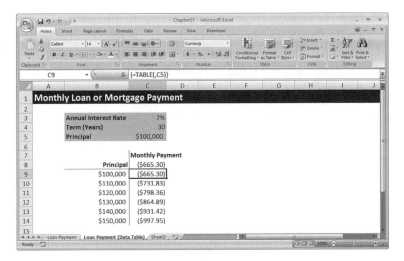

You also can set up data tables that take two input variables. For example, this enables you
to see the effect on a loan payment's value when you enter different values for the principal
and the interest rate. The following steps show you how to set up a two-input data table:

1. Enter one set of values in a column below the formula and the second set of values to
    the right of the formula in the same row, as shown in Figure 7.6.

Figure 7.6
Enter the two sets of values that you want to
input into the formula.

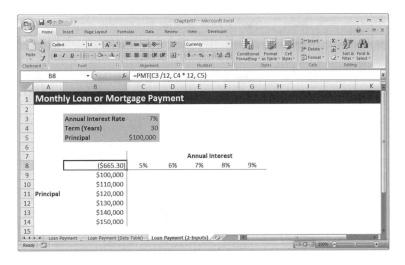

2. Select the range that includes the input values and the formula (B8:G14 in Figure 7.6).
3. Choose Data, What-If Analysis, Data <u>T</u>able to display the Data Table dialog box.
4. In the <u>R</u>ow Input Cell text box, enter the cell address of the input cell that corre-
    sponds to the row values you entered (C3 in Figure 7.6—the Annual Interest variable).

5. In the <u>C</u>olumn Input Cell text box, enter the cell address of the input cell you want to use for the column values (C5 in Figure 7.6—the Principal variable).

6. Click OK. Excel runs through the various input combinations and then displays the results in the data table, as shown in Figure 7.7.

Figure 7.7
Excel substitutes each input value into the input cell and displays the results in the data table.

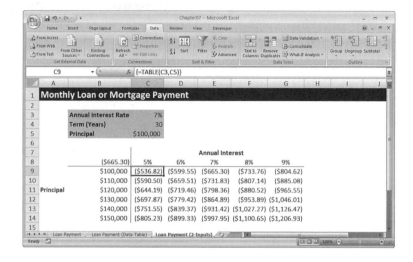

TIP

If you make changes to any of the variables in a table formula, Excel recalculates the entire table. This isn't a problem in small tables, but large ones can take a long time to calculate. If you prefer to control the table recalculation, choose Formulas, Calculation Options, Automatic <u>E</u>xcept Tables. This tells Excel not to include data tables when it recalculates a worksheet. To recalculate all data tables in a workbook, press F9 (or Shift+F9 to recalculate the current worksheet only).

If you want to make changes to the data table, you can edit the formula (or formulas) as well as the input value. However, the data table results are a different matter. When you run the Data Table command, Excel enters an array formula in the interior of the data table. This formula is a `TABLE()` function (a special function available only by using the Data Table command) with the following syntax:

`{=TABLE(row_input_ref, column_input_ref)}`

Here, *row_input_ref* and *column_input_ref* are the cell references you entered in the Table dialog box. The braces ({ }) indicate that this is an array, which means that you can't change or delete individual elements of the array. If you want to change the results, you need to select the entire data table and then run the Data Table command again. If you just want to delete the results, you must first select the entire array and then delete it.

7

Plugging Multiple Input Values into a Formula

In what-if analysis, a particular set of input values that you plug into a model is called a *scenario*. Because most what-if worksheets can take a wide range of input values, you usually end up with a large number of scenarios to examine. Instead of going through the tedious chore of inserting all these values into the appropriate cells, Excel has a Scenario Manager feature that can handle the process for you.

As you've seen in this chapter, Excel has powerful features that enable you to build sophisticated models that can answer complex questions. The problem, though, isn't in *answering* questions, but in *asking* them. For example, Figure 7.8 shows a worksheet model that analyzes a mortgage. You use this model to decide how much of a down payment to make, how long the term should be, and whether to include an extra principal paydown every month. The Results section compares the monthly payment and total paid for the regular mortgage and for the mortgage with a paydown. It also shows the savings and reduced term that result from the paydown.

Figure 7.8
A mortgage analysis
worksheet.

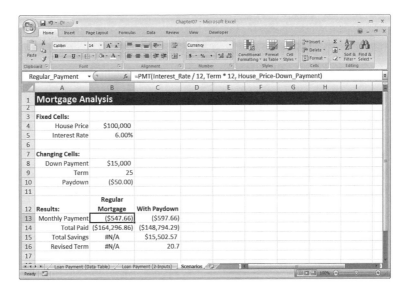

Here are some possible questions to ask in this model:

- How much will I save over the term of the mortgage if I use a shorter term and a larger down payment and include a monthly paydown?

- How much more will I end up paying if I extend the term, reduce the down payment, and forego the paydown?

These are examples of *scenarios* that you can plug into the appropriate cells in the model. Excel's Scenario Manager helps by letting you define a scenario separately from the worksheet. You can save specific values for any or all of the model's input cells, give the scenario a name, and then recall the name (and all the input values it contains) from a list.

Before creating a scenario, you need to decide which cells in your model will be the input cells. These will be the worksheet variables—the cells that, when you change them, change the results of the model. (Not surprisingly, Excel calls these the *changing cells*.) You can have as many as 32 changing cells in a scenario. For best results, follow these guidelines when setting up your worksheet for scenarios:

- The changing cells should be constants. Formulas can be affected by other cells, and that can throw off the entire scenario.

- To make it easier to set up each scenario and to make your worksheet easier to understand, group the changing cells and label them (see Figure 7.8).

- For even greater clarity, assign a range name to each changing cell.

To work with scenarios, use Excel's Scenario Manager tool. This feature enables you to add, edit, display, and delete scenarios, as well as create summary scenario reports.

When your worksheet is set up the way you want it, you can add a scenario to the sheet by following these steps:

1. Choose Data, What-If Analysis, Scenario Manager. Excel displays the Scenario Manager dialog box.

2. Click Add. The Add Scenario dialog box appears. Figure 7.9 shows a completed version of this dialog box.

Figure 7.9
Use the Add Scenario dialog box to define a scenario.

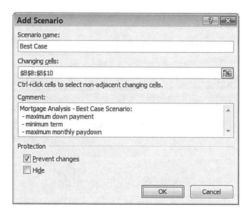

Add Scenario

Scenario name:
Best Case

Changing cells:
$B$8:$B$10

Ctrl+click cells to select non-adjacent changing cells.

Comment:
Mortgage Analysis - Best Case Scenario:
- maximum down payment
- minimum term
- maximum monthly paydown

Protection
☑ Prevent changes
☐ Hide

OK   Cancel

7

3. Use the Scenario <u>N</u>ame text box to enter a name for the scenario.

4. Use the Changing <u>C</u>ells box to enter references to your worksheet's changing cells. You can type in the references (be sure to separate noncontiguous cells with commas) or select the cells directly on the worksheet.

5. Use the C<u>o</u>mment box to enter a description for the scenario. This displays in the Comment section of the Scenario Manager dialog box.

6. Click OK. Excel displays the Scenario Values dialog box, shown in Figure 7.10.

Figure 7.10
Use the Scenario Values dialog box to enter the values you want to use for the scenario's changing cells.

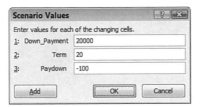

7. Use the text boxes to enter values for the changing cells.

> **NOTE**
> Notice in Figure 7.10 that Excel displays the range name for each changing cell, which makes it easier to enter your numbers correctly. If your changing cells aren't named, Excel just displays the cell addresses instead.

8. To add more scenarios, click <u>A</u>dd to return to the Add Scenario dialog box and repeat steps 3–7. Otherwise, click OK to return to the Scenario Manager dialog box.

9. Click Close to return to the worksheet.

After you define a scenario, you can enter its values into the changing cells by displaying the scenario from the Scenario Manager dialog box. The following steps give you the details:

1. Choose Data, What-If Analysis, S<u>c</u>enario Manager.

2. In the S<u>c</u>enarios list, click the scenario you want to display.

3. Click <u>S</u>how. Excel enters the scenario values into the changing cells. Figure 7.11 shows an example.

4. Repeat steps 2 and 3 to display other scenarios.

5. Click Close to return to the worksheet.

7

Figure 7.11
When you click Show, Excel enters the values for the highlighted scenario into the changing cells.

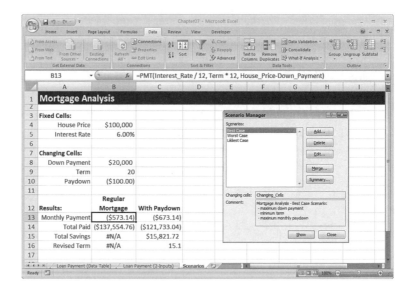

Determining the Break-Even Point

When you're analyzing costs and sales for a new product, perhaps the most basic analysis you can perform is to calculate the *break-even point*. This is the point at which revenue generated by the product equals the costs associated with manufacturing and selling the product. You usually approach a break-even analysis in one (or both) of two ways:

■ If you already know the price you want to charge for the product, then you calculate the number of units you must sell to break even.

■ If you have a target for the number of units you want to sell, then you calculate the price you must charge per unit to break even.

In both cases, you set up a worksheet model that calculates the profits made by the product. Figure 7.12 shows an example of a profit model. Total Revenue (cell C6) is calculated by multiplying the units by the price per unit, and then taking off the average custom discount. Total Costs (C10) is calculated by multiplying the cost per unit by the number of units sold and adding on the fixed costs. Total Profit is just the difference between Total Revenue and Total Costs.

For the initial break-even analysis, let's assume a fixed price of $29.95 for the product. How many units must we sell to get the Total Profit value to 0? The easiest way to figure this out is to use Excel's Goal Seek feature, which uses iterative methods to arrive at the result you're looking for (assuming a solution exists). Here's how it works:

1. Choose Data, What-If Analysis, Goal Seek. Excel displays the Goal Seek dialog box.

2. In the Set Cell range box, type or select the address of the cell that contains the profit formula (cell C12 in Figure 7.12).

3. In the To Value text box, type **0**.

4. In the By Changing Cell range box, type or select the address of the cell that contains the value you want to adjust to seek the break-even point. (In Figure 7.12, that's cell C4, the Units Sold value. Figure 7.13 shows the completed dialog box.)

5. Click OK.

Figure 7.12
A worksheet model that calculates the profit generated by a product.

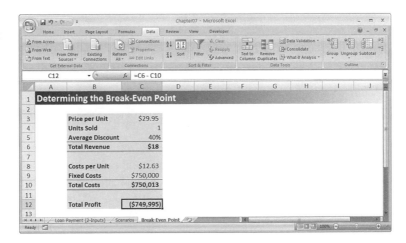

Goal Seek now attempts to find a solution, and you see the Goal Seek Status dialog box as it works. If it finds a solution, you see a dialog box similar to the one shown in Figure 7.14. As you can see, in this example, Goal Seek determined that we must sell 140,449 units to break even. Click OK to keep the solution or click Cancel to discard it.

Figure 7.13
The Goal Seek dialog box ready to calculate the break-even point.

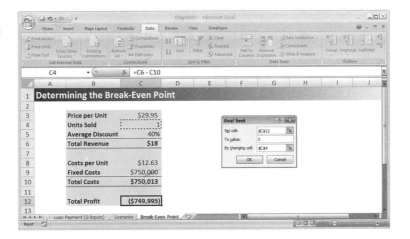

7

Figure 7.14
The break-even solution generated by Goal Seek.

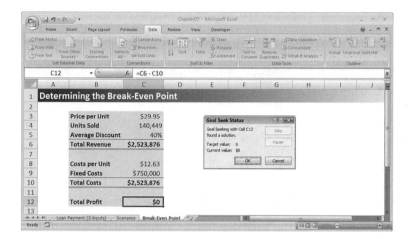

The other break-even model is to predict the number of units sold and then vary the unit price to reach a profit of 0. Figure 7.15 shows Goal Seek set up to perform such an analysis. Notice that in this case, we've assumed unit sales of 200,000, and the changing cell is now C3, the price per unit. Figure 7.16 shows the result: a price of $27.30.

Figure 7.15
The Goal Seek dialog box where the changing cell is now C3, the price per unit.

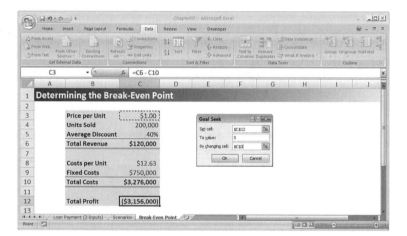

Figure 7.16
The break-even solution
for the price per unit.

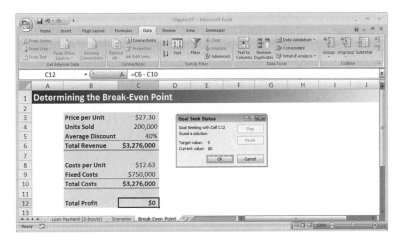

Optimizing Profit and Margin

Breaking even is always nice, but profits are even better, so you might want to use Excel to optimize profits. In this case, I'm using the word *optimize* not in the sense of "maximize," but in the sense of "reach a predetermined level of." For example, in your budgeting for the next fiscal year, you might set a goal of $100,000 in profit for a product or division. If you use a single product model like the one I used in the previous section, then you can optimize profits by using Goal Seek: You set your target cell value (Total Profit) to the profit level you want, and then you set up either the price or the number of units as the changing cell.

This method works for a single product, and you can also apply it to multiple products, where you set up a model for each item and then run Goal Seek on each model. However, in the real world, two (or more) products don't exist in a vacuum. For example, there is cost savings associated with each product because of joint advertising campaigns, combined shipments to customers (larger shipments usually mean better freight rates), and so on. To allow for this, you need to reduce the cost for each product by a factor related to the number of units sold by the other product. In practice, this is difficult to estimate, but to keep things simple, I use the following assumption: Given two products, the costs for each product are reduced by $1 for every unit sold of the other product. For instance, if the product A sells 10,000 units, the costs for product B are reduced by $10,000.

Figure 7.17 shows a worksheet set up with such a model. Note, in particular, the Variable Costs formula. For example, the formula that calculates variable costs for the Finley sprocket (cell C9) becomes the following:

```
=C8 * C5 - D5
```

7

Figure 7.17
A multi-variable model for calculating the profits generated by two products.

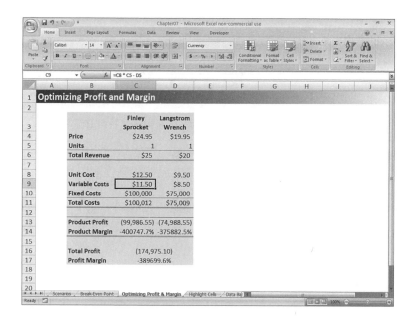

This formula calculates the regular costs (the unit cost multiplied by the number of units sold) and then subtracts the number of units sold by the other product. Similarly, the formula that calculates variable costs for the Langstrom wrench (cell D9) becomes the following:

```
=D8 * D5 - C5
```

By making this change, you move out of Goal Seek's territory. The Variable Costs formulas now have two variables: the units sold for the Finley sprocket and the units sold for the Langstrom wrench. I've changed the problem from one of two single-variable formulas, which Goal Seek can easily handle (individually), to a single formula with two variables, which is the terrain of another Excel data analysis tool: Solver.

Solver is a sophisticated optimization program that enables you to find the solutions to complex problems that would otherwise require high-level mathematical analysis. Solver, like Goal Seek, uses an iterative method to perform its magic. This means that Solver tries a solution, analyzes the results, tries another solution, and so on. However, this cyclic iteration isn't just guesswork on Solver's part. The program looks at how the results change with each new iteration and, through some sophisticated mathematical trickery, can tell (usually) in what direction it should head for the solution. Unlike Goal Seek, however, Solver enables you to specify multiple changing cells (up to 200); it enables you to set up constraints on the adjustable cells; and Solver seeks not only a desired result (the "goal" in Goal Seek), but also the optimal one, which means you can find a solution that is the maximum or minimum possible.

> **NOTE** You may need to install and/or activate the Solver add-in to use it. Choose Office, Excel Options to open the Excel Options dialog box. Click Add-Ins; in the Manage list, click Excel Add-ins, and then click Go. In the Add-Ins dialog box, click to activate the Solve Add-in check box and then click OK.

To see how Solver handles such a problem, follow these steps:

1. Choose Data, Solver. Excel displays the Solver Parameters dialog box.

2. In the Set Target Cell text box, enter a reference to the target cell—that is, the cell with the formula you want to optimize. In the example, you enter **C15** (the Total Profit cell).

3. In the Equal To section, select the appropriate option button: Select Max to maximize the target cell, select Min to minimize it, or select Value Of to solve for a particular value (in which case, you also need to enter the value in the text box provided). In the example, you activate Value Of and enter **100000** in the text box.

4. Use the By Changing Cells box to enter the cells you want Solver to change while it looks for a solution. In the example, you enter **C5,D5**.

5. Click Solve. Solver works on the problem and then displays the Solver Results dialog box, which tells you whether it found a solution.

6. If Solver found a solution that you want to use, click the Keep Solver Solution option and then click OK. If you don't want to accept the new numbers, click Restore Original Values and click OK or just click Cancel. (To learn how to save a solution as a scenario, see the section later in this chapter titled "Saving a Solution as a Scenario.")

Figure 7.18 shows the results for the example. As you can see, Solver has produced a total profit of $100,000 by running the Finley Sprocket with a profit of just under $58,000 and the Langstrom Wrench with a profit of just over $42,000.

In many cases, you want to optimize profit margin, instead. Profit margin is the difference between revenues and costs, divided by revenues. Again, for single-variable models you can use Goal Seek to find the solution, and for multi-variable models, you can use Solver.

Figure 7.18
When Solver finishes its calculations, it displays the Solver Results dialog box and enters the solution (if it found one) into the worksheet cells.

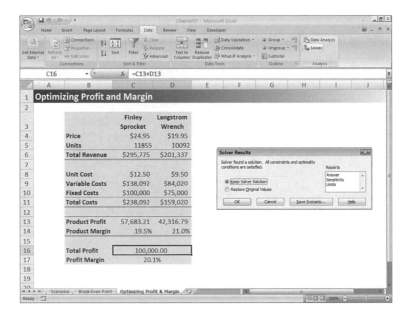

In the two-product example used in this section, assume that you want to find the number of units you need to sell for each product that produces an overall margin of 22 percent. Moreover, you also want a solution where the margins produced by each product are at least 20 percent. In this case, by setting parameters on the type of results you want, you are *constraining* the solution, and such parameters are called *constraints*. Here's how to run Solver with constraints:

1. Choose Data, Solver to open the Solver Parameters dialog box.

2. In the Set Target Cell text box, enter a reference to the target cell—that is, the cell with the formula you want to optimize. In the example, you enter **C17** (the Profit Margin cell).

3. In the Equal To section, select the appropriate option button: Select <u>M</u>ax to maximize the target cell, select Mi<u>n</u> to minimize it, or select <u>V</u>alue Of to solve for a particular value (in which case, you also need to enter the value in the text box provided). In the example, you activate <u>V</u>alue Of and enter **0.22** in the text box.

4. Use the <u>B</u>y Changing Cells box to enter the cells you want Solver to change while it looks for a solution. In the example, you enter **C5,D5**.

5. To add a constraint, click <u>A</u>dd. Excel displays the Add Constraint dialog box.

6. In the Cell Reference box, enter the cell you want to constrain. For the example, you enter cell **C14** (the Product Margin formula for the Finley sprocket).

7. Use the drop-down list in the middle of the dialog box to select the operator you want to use. The list contains several comparison operators for the constraint—less than or equal to (<=), equal to (=), and greater than or equal to (>=)—as well as two other data type operators—integer (int) and binary (bin). For the example, select the greater than or equal to operator (>=).

> **NOTE** Use the int (integer) operator when you need a constraint, such as total employees, to be an integer value instead of a real number. Use the bin (binary) operator when you have a constraint that must be either TRUE or FALSE (or 1 or 0).

8. If you chose a comparison operator in step 4, use the Constraint box to enter the value by which you want to restrict the cell. For the example, enter **0.2**.

9. If you want to enter more constraints, click <u>A</u>dd and repeat steps 6–8. For the example, you also need to constrain cell D14 (the Product Margin formula for the Langstrom wrench) so that it, too, is greater than or equal to 0.2.

10. When you're done, click OK to return to the Solver Parameters dialog box. Excel displays your constraints in the S<u>u</u>bject to the Constraints list box, as shown in Figure 7.19.

11. Click <u>S</u>olve and then either accept or reject the solution, if one was found.

Figure 7.20 shows the results for the example. As you can see, the Profit Margin is 22 percent, and both Product Margin values are at least 20 percent.

Figure 7.19
The Solver Parameters dialog box with constraints added to the model.

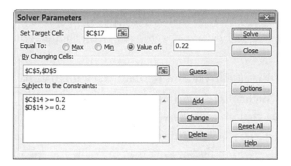

7

Figure 7.20
Solver found a con-
strained solution to the
problem.

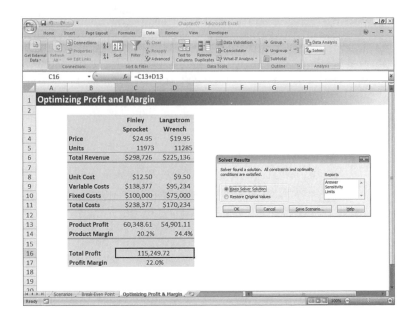

Highlighting Cells Above or Below a Certain Value

If you store a large amount of data in a worksheet, all the numbers tend to look the same after a while, which is a problem if part of your data analysis involves looking for values that are exceptional in some way. For example, suppose you have a worksheet that lists the 2006 and 2007 sales by sales reps and also calculates the percentage increase or decrease, year over year. As part of your analysis, you might be interested to know which reps sold less in 2007 than in 2006. You can just try eyeballing the negative values, or you can sort the list so that the negative values display at the top.

 Excel 2007 gives you another way to analyze thins kind of data: You can highlight with special formatting those cells that have values above or below another value that you specify.
Here's how it works:

1. Select the range that has the values with which you want to work.

2. Choose Home, Conditional Formatting, <u>H</u>ighlight Cells Rules. Excel displays a menu with the following choices:

<u>G</u>reater Than	Choose this command to apply formatting to cells with values greater than the value you specify.
<u>L</u>ess Than	Choose this command to apply formatting to cells with values less than the value you specify.
<u>B</u>etween	Choose this command to apply formatting to cells with values between the two values you specify.
<u>E</u>qual To	Choose this command to apply formatting to cells with values equal to the value you specify.

Text that Contains   Choose this command to apply formatting to cells with text values that contain the text value you specify (which is not case-sensitive).

A Date Occurring   Choose this command to apply formatting to cells with date values that satisfy the condition you choose: Yesterday, Today, Tomorrow, In the Last 7 Days, Next Week, and so on.

Duplicate Values   Choose this command to apply formatting to cells with values that appear more than once in the range.

3. In most cases, you see a dialog box in which you enter your criteria. For example, if you choose Less Than, you see the Less Than dialog box, as shown in Figure 7.21. Type the value (or cell address that contains the value) you want to use as a benchmark and choose a format.

4. Click OK. Excel formats the cells that meet your criteria (see Figure 7.22).

Figure 7.21
If you choose the Less Than command, use the Less Than dialog box to specify the criteria and formatting you want to apply to the range.

Figure 7.22
A range with the negative values highlighted in column D.

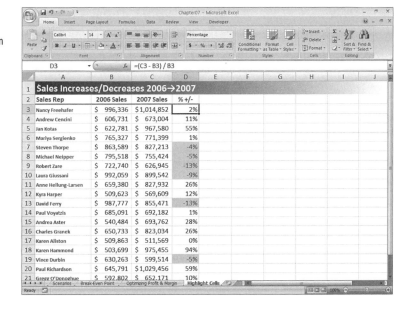

Highlighting Values Below the Median

NEW Another of Excel's new conditional formatting rules is the *top/bottom* rule, which applies a format to cells that rank in the top or bottom (for numerical items, the highest or lowest) values in a range. You can select the top or bottom either as an absolute value (for example, the top 10 items) or as a percentage (for example, the bottom 25 percent). You can also apply formatting to those cells that are above or below the average. To create a top/bottom rule, begin by choosing Home, Conditional Formatting, Top/Bottom Rules. Excel displays six choices:

Top 10 Items	Choose this command to apply formatting to those cells with values that rank in the top X items in the range, where X is the number of items you want to see (the default is 10).
Top 10%	Choose this command to apply formatting to those cells with values that rank in the top X percentage of items in the range, where X is the percentage you want to see (the default is 10).
Bottom 10 Items	Choose this command to apply formatting to those cells with values that rank in the bottom X items in the range, where X is the number of items you want to see (the default is 10).
Bottom 10 %	Choose this command to apply formatting to those cells with values that rank in the bottom X percentage of items in the range, where X is the percentage you want to see (the default is 10).
Above Average	Choose this command to apply formatting to those cells with values that are above the average of all the values in the range.
Below Average	Choose this command to apply formatting to those cells with values that are below the average of all the values in the range.

In each case, you see a dialog box that you use to set up the specifics of the rule. For the Top 10 Items, Top 10%, Bottom 10 Items, and Bottom 10% rules, you use the dialog box to specify the condition and the formatting that you want applied to cells that match the condition. For the Above Average and Below Average rules, you use the dialog box to specify the formatting only.

This all works well and is straightforward to apply. However, none of these top/bottom rules might be quite right for your data analysis needs. For example, suppose your data set includes a few anomalous values that are skewing the average much higher or lower than it should be. In that case, a better measure of the "average" might be the median value, which is the value in a data set that falls in the middle when all the values are sorted in numeric order. That is, half of the values fall below the median, and half fall above it. You calculate the median using the MEDIAN() function:

```
MEDIAN(number1[,number2,...])
```

number1, number2,...	A range, array, or list of values of which you want the median.

For example, to calculate the median of the values in the sales list shown earlier in Figure 7.22, use the following formula:

`=MEDIAN(D3:D21)`

How do you get Excel to highlight cells that are, for example, below the median value? To handle this, Excel 2007 comes with another conditional formatting component that makes this feature even more powerful: You can apply conditional formatting based on the results of a formula. In particular, you set up a logical formula as the conditional formatting criteria. If that formula returns `TRUE`, Excel applies the formatting to the cells; if the formula returns `FALSE`, instead, Excel doesn't apply the formatting. In most cases, you use an `IF()` function, often combined with another logical function such as `AND()` or `OR()`. However, you can also use a simple comparison formula. For example, the following formula compares the value in cell D3 with the median of the value in the range D3:D21:

`=D3 < MEDIAN($D$3:$D$21)`

To apply such a formula to a range of cells for the purposes of conditional formatting, you need to bear in mind two more things:

- You must enter the reference to the comparison value that changes (such as D3 in the previous formula) as a relative reference.
- You must enter the reference to the comparison value that doesn't change (such as the range $D$3:$D$21 above) as an absolute reference.

This way, when Excel applies the conditional formatting formula to each cell in the range, it adjusts the relative reference accordingly so that the formatting is correctly applied to each cell.

Here are the general steps to follow to set up formula-based conditional formatting:

1. Select the cells to which you want the conditional formatting applied.
2. Choose Home, Conditional Formatting, <u>N</u>ew Rule. Excel displays the New Formatting Rule dialog box.
3. Click Use a Formula to Determine Which Cells to Format.
4. In the F<u>o</u>rmat Values Where This Formula is True range box, type your logical formula.
5. Click <u>F</u>ormat to open the Format Cells dialog box.
6. Use the Number, Font, Border, and Fill tabs to specify the formatting you want to apply and then click OK.
7. Click OK.

Figure 7.23 shows the conditional formatting formula applied to the range D3:D21 that formats those cells with values less than the median.

7

Figure 7.23
You can use a formula as the condition that Excel uses to determine whether to apply formatting.

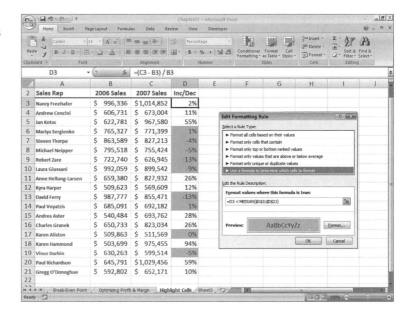

Analyzing Cell Values with Data Bars

Data analysis is often more about the relationships between values in a range than it is about the values themselves. For example, in a table of sales where one product sells 600 units and another sells 300, you might be interested only in the fact that the former sold twice as much as the latter, regardless of the actual sales. Excel 2007 comes with a new tool that enables you to quickly and easily perform these kinds of relative analyses: *data bars*. Data bars are colored, horizontal bars that display "behind" the values in a range. Their key feature is that the length of the data bar that displays in each cell depends on the value in that cell: the larger the value, the longer the data bar. The cell with the highest value has the longest data bar, and the data bars that display in the other cells have lengths that reflect their values. (For example, a cell with a value that is half of the largest value has a data bar that's half as long as the longest data bar.)

To apply data bars to the selected range, choose Home, Conditional Formatting, Data Bars, and then choose the color you prefer. Figure 7.24 shows a worksheet of product sales, with data bars applied to the values in the Units column.

Excel configures its default data bars with the longest data bar based on the highest value in the range and the shortest data bar based on the lowest value in the range. However, what if you want to visualize your values based on different criteria? With test scores, for example, you might prefer to see the data bars based on values between 0 and 100 (so for a value of 50, the data bar always fills only half the cell, no matter what the top mark is).

Figure 7.24
A worksheet with Excel 2007's new data bars applied to the Units column.

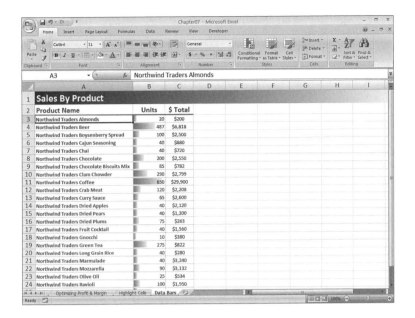

To apply custom data bars, select the range and then choose Home, Conditional Formatting, Data Bars, More Rules to display the New Formatting Rule dialog box. In the Edit the Rule Description group, make sure Data Bar displays in the Format Style list. Notice that there is a Type list for both the Shortest Bar and Longest Bar. The type determines how Excel applies the data bars. You have five choices:

Lowest/ Highest Value	This is the default data bar type: The lowest value in the range gets the shortest data bar, and the highest value in the range gets the longest data bar.
Number	Use this type to base the data bar lengths on values that you specify in the two Value text boxes. For the Shortest Bar, any cell in the range that has a value less than or equal to the value you specify will get the shortest data bar; similarly, for the Longest Bar, any cell in the range that has a value greater than or equal to the value you specify will get the longest data bar.
Percent	Use this type to base the data bar lengths on a percentage of the largest value in the range. For the Shortest Bar, any cell in the range that has a relative value less than or equal to the percentage you specify will get the shortest data bar; for example, if you specify 10 percent and the largest value in the range is 1,000, then any cell with a value of 100 or less will get the shortest data bar. For the Longest Bar, any cell in the range that has a relative value greater than or equal to the percentage you specify will get the longest data bar; for example, if you specify 90 percent and the largest value in the range is 1,000, then any cell with a value of 900 or more will get the longest data bar.

7

Formula	Use this type to base the data bar lengths on a formula.
Percentile	Use this type to base the data bar lengths on the percentile within which each cell value falls given the overall range of the values. In this case, Excel ranks all the values in the range and assigns each cell a position within the ranking. For the Shortest Bar, any cell in the range that has a rank less than or equal to the percentile you specify will get the shortest data bar; for example, if you have 100 values and specify the 10th percentile, the cells ranked 10th or less will get the shortest data bar. For the Longest Bar, any cell in the range that has a rank greater than or equal to the percentile you specify will get the longest data bar; for example, if you have 100 values and specify the 75th percentile, then any cell ranked 75th or higher will get the longest data bar.

One thing you can't do directly with data bars is apply multiple colors. This is a handy way to, say, display particularly low values in red or particularly high values in green. You can apply different colored data bars multiple times to a given range, but Excel always displays only the most recent data bars.

You can work around this problem by manipulating some range properties via VBA. Each Range object has an associated FormatConditions collection, which holds all the conditional formatting rules that have been applied to the range. If you've applied two rules to the range, for example, then the first one you applied is FormatConditions(1) and the second is FormatConditions(2). Each of these returns a FormatCondition object, which in turn has a Formula property.

Applying Percentile-Based Icon Sets

When analyzing a data set, it's often handy to rank where a certain value falls within the data. Excel has functions that enable you to calculate both the ordinal and percentage rank of each value in a set.

For the ordinal (first, second, third, and so on) rank, you use the RANK() function:

RANK(*number*, *ref*[, *order*])

number	The number for which you want to find the rank.
ref	A reference, range name, or array that corresponds to the set of values in which *number* will be ranked. (Note that *ref* must include *number*.)
order	An integer that specifies how *number* is ranked within the set. If *order* is 0 (this is the default), Excel treats the set as though it was ranked in descending order; if *order* is any nonzero value, Excel treats the set as though it was ranked in ascending order.

For example, if a test result is in cell C3 and the full results are in the range C5:C35, then the following formula returns the ordinal rank of the test result:

```
=RANK(C3, C5:C35)
```

The ordinal rank is only occasionally useful. In data analysis, you're more likely to work with the percentage rank. This is useful when you want to know what value in the set corresponds to what percentile. For example, if you want to know what test scores fall in the top 10 percent, you'd calculate the 90th percentile, and every score above that is in the top 10 percent. To calculate the percentage rank, you use the PERCENTILE() function:

```
PERCENTILE(array, k)
```

> *array*   A reference, range name, or array of values for the set of data.
>
> *k*   The percentile, expressed as a decimal value between 0 and 1.

For example, if the test scores are in the range C5:C35, then the following formula calculates the value at which the 90th percentile occurs:

```
=PERCENTILE(C5:C35, 0.9)
```

If you want to see which values are above or below a particular percentile, then you need to turn once again to Excel's conditional formatting tools. For example, if you want to see only those values that are above the 90th percentile, then you can apply a custom highlight cells rule. Choose Home, Conditional Formatting, <u>H</u>ighlight Cells Rules, <u>M</u>ore Rules to open the New Formatting Rule dialog box. In the Format Only Cells With section, choose Cell Value and Greater Than and then enter your PERCENTILE() function in the range box, as shown in Figure 7.25.

Figure 7.25
You can use the
PERCENTILE()
function to apply a
conditional format.

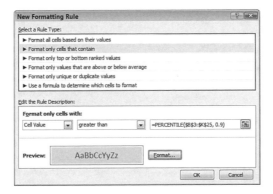

 What if you want to also see those values that lie within the 10th percentile? When you want to visualize multiple relationships in a data set, the ideal tool is Excel 2007's new *icon sets* feature. Like data bars, you use icon sets to visualize the relative values of cells in a range. In this case, however, Excel adds a particular icon to each cell in the range, and that icon tells you something about the cell's value relative to the rest of the range. For example,

7

the highest values might get an upward pointing arrow, the lowest values a downward pointing arrow, and the values in between a horizontal arrow.

To apply an icon set to the selected range, choose Home, Conditional Formatting, Icon Sets, and then choose the set you want. For more complex operations, you can create a custom icon set rule:

1. Select the cells to which you want the conditional formatting applied.
2. Choose Home, Conditional Formatting, Icon Sets, More Rules. Excel displays the New Formatting Rule dialog box.
3. Use the Icon Style list to click the icon set you want to use.
4. For all but the last icon in the set, choose an operator, a Value, and a value Type (Number, Percent, Formula, or Percentile). For example, Figure 7.27 shows the New Formatting Rule dialog box set up to show an upward pointing arrow in cells with values above the 90th percentile, and a downward pointing arrow in cells with values below the 10th percentile.
5. Click OK.

Figure 7.27 shows the icon set rule from Figure 7.26 applied to a data set of gross domestic product growth rates.

Figure 7.26
An icon set rule that uses percentiles.

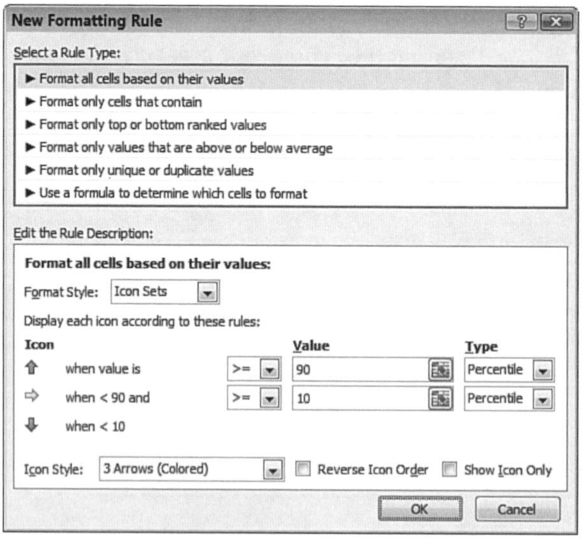

7

Figure 7.27
The conditional formatting applied by the icon set rule shown in Figure 7.27.

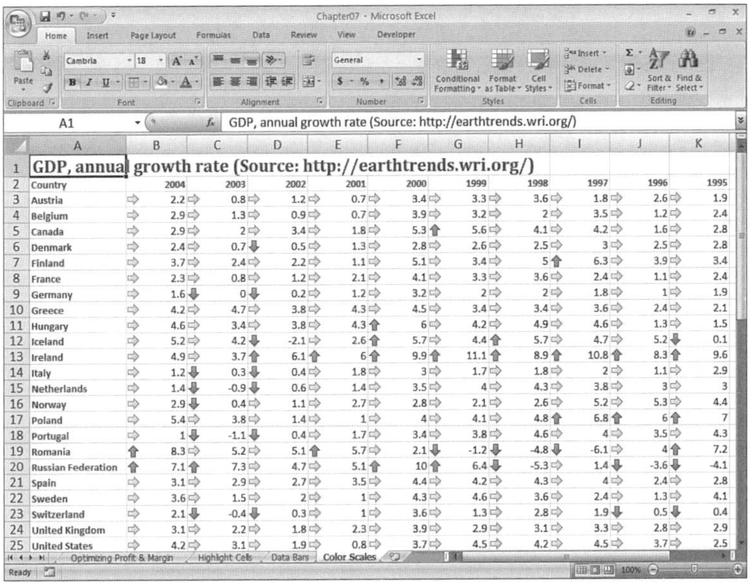

GDP, annual growth rate (Source: http://earthtrends.wri.org/)

Country	2004	2003	2002	2001	2000	1999	1998	1997	1996	1995
Austria	2.2	0.8	1.2	0.7	3.4	3.3	3.6	1.8	2.6	1.9
Belgium	2.9	1.3	0.9	0.7	3.9	3.2	2	3.5	1.2	2.4
Canada	2.9	2	3.4	1.8	5.3	5.6	4.1	4.2	1.6	2.8
Denmark	2.4	0.7	0.5	1.3	2.8	2.6	2.5	3	2.5	2.8
Finland	3.7	2.4	2.2	1.1	5.1	3.4	5	6.3	3.9	3.4
France	2.3	0.8	1.2	2.1	4.1	3.3	3.6	2.4	1.1	2.4
Germany	1.6	0	0.2	1.2	3.2	2	2	1.8	1	1.9
Greece	4.2	4.7	3.8	4.3	4.5	3.4	3.4	3.6	2.4	2.1
Hungary	4.6	3.4	3.8	4.3	6	4.2	4.9	4.6	1.3	1.5
Iceland	5.2	4.2	-2.1	2.6	5.7	4.4	5.7	4.7	5.2	0.1
Ireland	4.9	3.7	6.1	6	9.9	11.1	8.9	10.8	8.3	9.6
Italy	1.2	0.3	0.4	1.8	3	1.7	1.8	2	1.1	2.9
Netherlands	1.4	-0.9	0.6	1.4	3.5	4	4.3	3.8	3	3
Norway	2.9	0.4	1.1	2.7	2.8	2.1	2.6	5.2	5.3	4.4
Poland	5.4	3.8	1.4	1	4	4.1	4.8	6.8	6	7
Portugal	1	-1.1	0.4	1.7	3.4	3.8	4.6	4	3.5	4.3
Romania	8.3	5.2	5.1	5.7	2.1	-1.2	-4.8	-6.1	4	7.2
Russian Federation	7.1	7.3	4.7	5.1	10	6.4	-5.3	1.4	-3.6	-4.1
Spain	3.1	2.9	2.7	3.5	4.4	4.2	4.3	4	2.4	2.8
Sweden	3.6	1.5	2	1	4.3	4.6	3.6	2.4	1.3	4.1
Switzerland	2.1	-0.4	0.3	1	3.6	1.3	2.8	1.9	0.5	0.4
United Kingdom	3.1	2.2	1.8	2.3	3.9	2.9	3.1	3.3	2.8	2.9
United States	4.2	3.1	1.9	0.8	3.7	4.5	4.2	4.5	3.7	2.5

The icon set formatting shown in Figure 7.27 is useful, but it does suffer from a drawback in this case: We're not all that interested in the values that lie between the 10th and 90th percentiles (the ones formatted with horizontal arrows). Unfortunately, Excel doesn't offer options for excluding particular icons from a set. However, you can work around this limitation. The trick is to create a second highlight cells rule that applies to the values you want to exclude and that does *not* apply any formatting. Here's how to set it up:

1. Select the cells to which you want the conditional formatting applied.
2. Choose Home, Conditional Formatting, Highlight Cells Rules, More Rules. Excel displays the New Formatting Rule dialog box.
3. Choose Cell Value in the first list.
4. In the list of operators, choose Between. Excel displays two range boxes.
5. In the first range box, type the lower value that you want excluded from the formatting. For example, to start the exclusion at the 10th percentile, you'd enter the following formula (where *range* is the range you're formatting):
   `=PERCENTILE(`*`range`*`, 0.1)`
6. In the second range box, type the upper value that you want excluded from the formatting. For example, to end the exclusion at the 90th percentile, you'd enter the following formula (where, again, *range* is the range you're formatting; see Figure 7.28):
   `=PERCENTILE(`*`range`*`, 0.9)`
7. Click OK. (Notice that we didn't specify any formatting.)
8. Choose Home, Conditional Formatting, Manage Rules. Excel displays the Conditional Formatting Rules Manager.

7

Figure 7.28

This example uses PER-CENTILE() functions to specify the range of values to exclude from the conditional formatting.

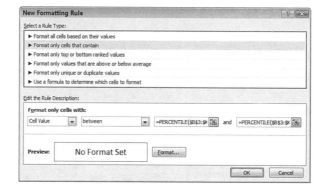

9. The rule you just created should display above your Icon Set rule. If not, click the new rule and then click the up arrow to move it above the Icon Set rule.

10. Besides your new rule, click to activate the Stop If True dialog box, as shown in Figure 7.29.

> **NOTE** If you have multiple conditional format rules applied to a range, Excel applies the rules in order (from top to bottom as shown in the Conditional Formatting Rules Manager) one cell at a time. When you activate the Stop If True check box for a rule, Excel first applies the rule to the cell. If the rule returns FALSE, then Excel continues on to the next rule; if the rule return TRUE, instead, then Excel doesn't apply any more rules to the cell.

11. Click OK. Excel reapplies the rules.

Figure 7.30 shows the result: The data displays with just the upward and downward pointing arrows.

Figure 7.29

Move your no formatting rule to the top and activate the Stop If True check box.

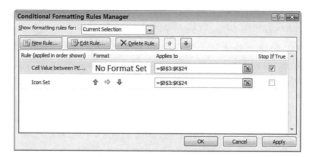

Figure 7.30
The conditional formatting rules from Figure 7.29 applied to the GDP data.

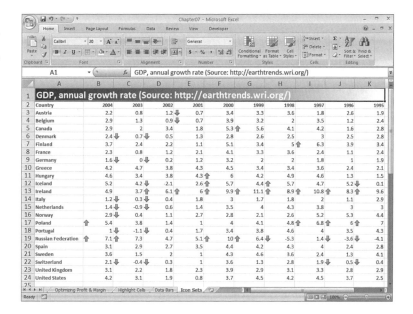

From Here

- For more about calculating loan payments, **see** "Calculating the Principal and Interest for a Loan," **p. 130**.

- You can also analyze data by graphing the trend; **see** "Plotting a Best-Fit Trendline," **p. 213**.

- Access has a query option that enables you to view the top 10 results; **see** "Selecting the Top Values with a Query," **p. 388**.

Chart Tricks

8

One of the best ways to analyze your worksheet data—or get your point across to other people—is to display your data visually in a chart. Excel gives you tremendous flexibility when you create charts; it enables you to place charts in separate documents or directly on the worksheet itself. Not only that, but you have dozens of different chart formats to choose from, and if none of Excel's built-in formats is just right, you can further customize these charts to suit your needs.

Building basic charts in Excel 2007 is easy: You select the data you want to chart, click the Insert tab, and then click the chart type you want using the controls in the Charts group. Of course, as with many Excel features, getting a basic chart is easy, but getting the chart you *want* almost always requires more work on your part. The Chart Tools that display when you click an existing chart give you Ribbon access to three tabs—Design, Layout, and, Format—that offer many useful controls for enhancing and modifying your charts. However, if you want to take your charting to an even higher level, then you need to know a few charting tricks. This chapter takes you through some of my personal favorites.

Using Worksheet Text in a Chart

It's often handy to include worksheet text in a chart. For example, if the underlying worksheet has a title, you might also want to use that text as your chart title. Similarly, you might have a worksheet value that's related to the chart, such as an average of the values in a series, and you might want to include that value as part of the chart title or the value axis title. You can simply edit the appropriate chart object's text by hand to include the value. However, if that value is subject to change (particularly if it's a calculated value such as an average), then you need to always update the chart object by hand. Ideally, it is great to use a method whereby the chart text gets updated automatically whenever the worksheet text changes.

In previous versions of Excel, you can do this quite easily by linking a chart text object to a worksheet cell. You do this by selecting the chart text object, typing an equals sign (=) to let Excel know that you want to enter a formula, clicking the worksheet cell containing the text you wanted, and then pressing Enter to confirm the formula. Alas, that easy and straightforward method was dropped in Excel 2007, which now treats chart text objects as pure text boxes that cannot include formulas.

Fortunately, there's a way to work around this limitation using a bit of VBA code that takes advantage of the fact that chart text objects have a `Text` property. The idea is that you use VBA to set an object's `Text` property equal to the value of a worksheet cell. For example, the chart title corresponds to the `ChartTitle` object, so you modify the `ChartTitle.Text` property.

For example, suppose the worksheet title is in cell A1. If you want to use the same text in the chart title, you click the chart to activate it and then enter the following code in the Visual Basic Editor's Immediate window:

> **NOTE** With the Visual Basic Editor open (press Alt+F11), you display the Immediate window by choosing View, Immediate Window, or by pressing Ctrl+G.

```
ActiveChart.ChartTitle.Text = ActiveSheet.Range("A1")
```

This gives you a static chart title. That is, if you change the title in cell A1, the chart title doesn't automatically update. That's not a problem for a title that doesn't change, but what if you use a volatile value such as an average as part of the chart title? For example, given a worksheet that displays the average of a data series in cell C3, here's a procedure that includes the average in the chart title text:

```
Public Sub WriteChartTitle()
    With ActiveSheet.ChartObjects(1).Chart
        .ChartTitle.Text = "Close (Average = " & _
        Format(ActiveSheet.Range("C3"), "00.0") & ")"
    End With
End Sub
```

Figure 8.1 shows the chart with the text added. (Note that in this procedure I used a more elaborate reference to the chart—`ActiveSheet.ChartObjects(1).Chart`. This means the chart doesn't have to be activated to set the title.)

> **NOTE** You can find the workbook that contains this chapter's examples here:
> www.mcfedries.com/Office2007Gurus/

Figure 8.1
This chart's title includes the average value calculated in cell C3.

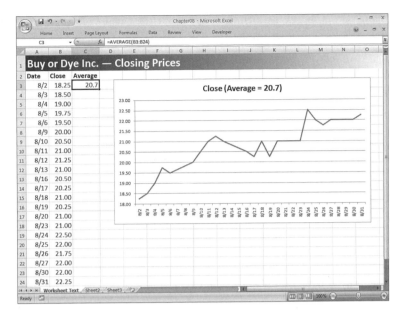

That's fine, but the title text is still static. How can we get Excel to update the chart title automatically if the average changes? It would be nice if Excel 2007 offered a direct way to do this, but it doesn't, so we have to take a more roundabout route. Specifically, we have to take advantage of the fact that in Excel, you can trap the `SheetChange` event, which fires whenever cell data changes in any worksheet. Follow these steps to create a handler for this event:

1. In the Visual Basic Editor, use the Project window to open the VBA project that corresponds to the workbook that contains your chart.

2. Double-click the ThisWorkbook item in the project. The Visual Basic Editor opens a module window for the `ThisWorkbook` object.

3. In the module window, pull down the Object drop-down list (at the top of the module, it's the list on the left) and select Workbook.

4. Pull down the Procedure drop-down list (at the top of the module, it's the list on the right) and select SheetChange. The Visual Basic Editor adds the following procedure stub:

```
Private Sub Workbook_SheetChange(ByVal Sh As Object, ByVal Target As Range)

End Sub
```

5. Type your event handler code between the `Sub` and `End Sub` statements.

In the procedure stub, the `Sh` variable represents the worksheet on which the value changed, and the `Target` variable represents the `Range` object (that is, the cell) that was changed. In the example, you should check to see if the name of the sheet is the same as name of the sheet on which the chart resides (`Worksheet Text`, in this case). If it is, you call the procedure that writes the chart title. Here's the code:

```
Private Sub Workbook_SheetChange(ByVal Sh As Object, ByVal Target As Range)
    If Sh.Name = "Worksheet Text" Then
        WriteChartTitle
    End If
End Sub
```

Plotting the Average on the Value Axis

When you plot numeric data, it is useful if you can get an indication on the chart where the average value lies. (I use the average in this section, but you can easily apply the techniques I show you here to other values such as the median or mode.)

Probably the easiest way to do this is to create an entirely new data series where each value is the average of the series you want to analyze. For example, in Figure 8.2, you see a worksheet that has stock closing prices in column B. I've added a new column for the average in column C. Here are the steps you need to follow to insert the average values:

1. Select the entire range into which you want to add the average values (in Figure 8.2, this is C3:C24).

2. Type (but don't confirm) the `AVERAGE()` function formula, making sure that you use absolute cell references for the data you want to average (in Figure 8.2, we average the range $B$3:$B$24).

3. When you are ready to confirm the formula, press Ctrl+Enter. Excel adds the same formula to all the selected cells.

TIP You can use a similar technique to plot standard deviation lines, which are lines that represent values that are one standard deviation above and below the average. For the values one standard deviation above the mean, press Ctrl+Enter after the formula, as shown in the following:

```
=AVERAGE($B$3:$B$24) + STDEV($B$3:$B$24)
```

The formula for the values one standard deviation below the mean is similar:

```
=AVERAGE($B$3:$B$24) - STDEV($B$3:$B$24)
```

When you are ready to add the new series to the chart, here's a quick method you can use:

1. Select the range, including the header, and then press Ctrl+C to copy it.

2. Select the chart and then press Ctrl+V to paste it. Excel adds the new series, as shown in Figure 8.3.

Figure 8.2
To insert the same formula into each cell in a range, select the range, type the formula using absolute cell references, and then press Ctrl+Enter.

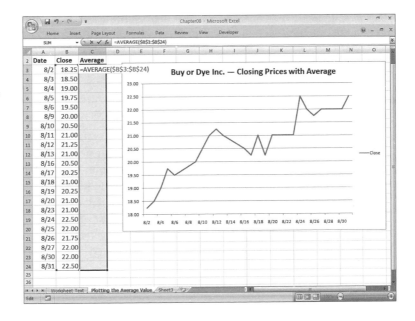

8

NOTE

For more control over the pasting of the new series, copy the data, select the chart, choose the Home tab, click the bottom half of the Paste split button, and then click Paste Special. In the Paste Special dialog box that displays, you can see the options that you can use to tell Excel more about your data.

Figure 8.3
Copy and paste the Average range into the chart to add the new data series.

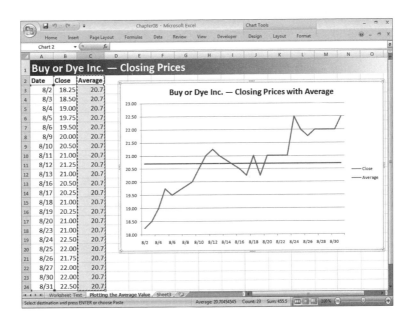

This technique is handy and useful, but it does clutter your chart with an extra data series. If you prefer to show just the original series, you can use a trick to plot just the average on the vertical (y) axis. For this to work, you must do three things:

- Using the same worksheet, add a formula that calculates the average of the series values.
- Convert your chart to an XY (Scatter) type: Click the chart, choose Design, Change Chart Type, click a layout in the XY (Scatter) category, and then click OK.
- Make sure the minimum value of the horizontal (x) axis is the same as the first category value in your data series. For example, in the stock price worksheet shown in Figure 8.3, the first category value is August 2, 2007 (the number 39296), so the minimum value for the horizontal axis should be the same date (that is, the value 39296). If you need to change the minimum value for the horizontal axis, click the axis and then choose Layout, Format Selection to display the Format Axis dialog box. In the Axis Options tab, click the Minimum: Fixed option, type the initial category value in the text box, and then click Close.

You can now follow these steps to add a vertical axis marker for the average value:

1. Click the chart and then choose Design, Select Data. Excel displays the Select Data Source dialog box.
2. Click Add to display the Edit Series dialog box.
3. (Optional) Type a Series Name.
4. Click inside the Series X Values range box and then click the first category value in the original data series.
5. Click inside the Series Y Values range box, delete the default value, and then click the cell that contains the average. Figure 8.4 shows the completed Edit Series dialog box.

Figure 8.4
Use the Edit Series dialog box to select the first category value in the original series and the cell containing the average value.

6. Click OK to return to the Select Data Source dialog box.
7. Click OK. Excel adds the new data series.
8. Choose the Layout tab, click the new series in the Chart Elements list, and then click Format Selection to display the Format Data Series dialog box.
9. Click the Marker Options tab, click the Built-in option, use the Type list to select a marker style, and then click Close.

10. Choose Layout, Data Labels, and then click where you want the label to display.

11. Click the label once to select it and then click it again to get a cursor inside for editing.

12. Delete the value, type **Average**, and then click outside the label.

13. Format the label as desired.

Figure 8.5 shows the stock price chart with the Average value added to the vertical (y) axis.

Figure 8.5
The Average value in C3
is plotted on the chart's
vertical (y) axis.

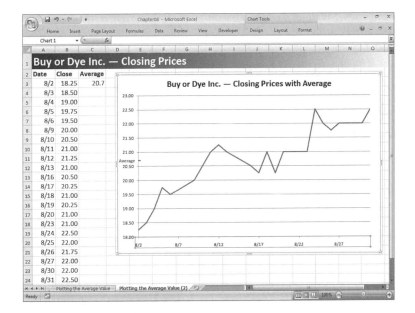

Stacking a Picture as a Bar Chart Data Marker

By default, bar chart data markers use a solid fill. That's usually the effect you want because a solid fill makes it easier to compare markers and analyze the data presented in the chart. On the downside, solid-fill data markers don't compare well when printed on a black-and-white laser printer, and they are, well, dull. For a different twist to your bar charts, you can replace the data markers' solid fills with graphic images, such as clip art pictures or graphics files on your computer. By default, Excel stretches the image according to the number that the marker represents. This tends to distort most images, so it's better to *stack* the image, which means that Excel uses multiple copies of the original image to fill in each data marker. (The bigger the marker, the more copies Excel uses to create the stack.)

8

Here are the steps to follow to stack a picture as a bar chart data marker:

1. Click the data series to select it.
2. Choose Layout, Format Selection to display the Format Data Series dialog box.
3. Click the Fill tab.
4. Click the <u>P</u>icture of Texture Fill option.
5. Click the stacking option you prefer:
   - **Stac<u>k</u>**—Click this option to stack the original image in the data markers.
   - **Stack and Scale <u>w</u>ith *X* Units/Picture**—Click this option to adjust the scale that Excel uses when creating the stacks. Use the text box to specify the number of data units you want Excel to use for each picture. For example, if your data values run from 0 to one million, you can specify 100,000 as the units per picture value.
6. Click Close.

Figure 8.6 shows an example of a bar chart with the solid-fill data markers replaced by stacked pictures.

Figure 8.6
A bar chart with stacked pictures as the data markers.

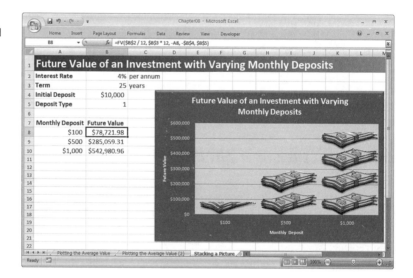

Charting a Dynamic Range

Most chart data consists of an entire range of cells, but it's sometimes necessary to chart only a portion of a range. If you have stock data, for example, you may want to visualize only a particular 7-, 14-, or 30-day portion of the data. If the chart doesn't exist yet, just select the portion of the range you want to work with and then insert the chart. If the chart already exists, there are two methods you can use to adjust the data series:

- Click the chart and then choose Design, Select Data to open the Select Data Source dialog box. For the value range, click the Edit button in the Legend Entries (Series) section to display the Edit Series dialog box, adjust the Series Values reference, and then click OK. For the categories, click the Edit button in the Horizontal (Category) Axis Labels section to display the Axis Labels dialog box, adjust the Axis Label Range reference, and then click OK.

- Click the chart, click any point in the data series, and then adjust the range references used in the SERIES() function that displays in the formula bar. I explain the function as follows.

Here's the syntax for the SERIES() function:

```
SERIES([name,][ category_labels,] values, order)
```

name	A string or cell reference that specifies the series name.
category_labels	The range that holds the labels that display on the category (X) axis. If you omit this argument, Excel uses consecutive integers as labels.
values	The range that holds the values that Excel plots.
order	The plot order for the series.

For example, here's the SERIES() function for the line chart that displayed earlier in Figure 8.1:

```
=SERIES('Worksheet Text'!$B$2,'Worksheet Text'!$A$3:$A$24,
➡'Worksheet Text'!$B$3:$B$24,1)
```

However, what do you do if the sub-range you want to plot changes over time? For example, in a stock price worksheet where you enter prices daily, it is useful to use chart that always shows, say, the most recent 7 days of price data. Is it possible to set this up without having to redefine the series ranges by hand? Absolutely! Using a couple of tricks, you can create a chart that automatically plots a dynamic range.

As an example, I show you how to set up a chart that automatically plots the most recent 7 days of stock data. This task is made easier by Excel 2007's new structured table references. I won't go into this in detail except to say that when you convert a range to a table, Excel 2007 defines a name for that table. Most importantly for our purposes, as you add data to or remove data from the table, Excel 2007 dynamically adjusts the references associated with the table name.

NOTE For a more detailed look at Excel 2007's structured table referencing, see my book *Formulas and Functions with Microsoft Excel 2007* (Que 2007; ISBN 0-7897-3668-3).

8

Therefore, the first thing you need to do is convert your worksheet data to a table. Select your data (including any column headers) and choose Insert, Table to display the Create Table dialog box. Make sure the range is correct, activate the <u>M</u>y Table Has Headers check box, and then click OK. Make a note of the table name (select the table data—don't include the headers—and see the name that displays in Excel's Name box). The default name is Table*n*, where *n* means this is the nth table you've added to the current workbook.

The next stage is to create two dynamic range names—one for the category axis labels and one for the data series values. A dynamic range name is one that automatically adjusts based on the results of the function or functions used to define the name. In this case, you want to create names that dynamically adjust to always return the last seven items in the table you just created.

To make the range name formulas easier to understand, add the range length you want (7, in this case) to a cell and then name that cell Length.

> **TIP** The easiest way to apply a range name to a cell is to click the cell, type the name in the Name box (the text box that displays to the left of the formula bar), and then press Enter.

There are several methods you can use to create a dynamic range name. I like to use the OFFSET() function, which returns a range offset from some original range by a specified number of rows and columns:

OFFSET(*reference*, *rows*, *cols*[, *height*][, *width*])

reference	The original range. In this task, this reference must be absolute.
rows	The number of rows to offset.
cols	The number of columns to offset.
height	The number of rows in the new range. If you omit this argument, the new range uses the same number of rows as the *reference* range.
width	The number of columns in the new range. If you omit this argument, the new range uses the same number of columns as the *reference* range.

Our goal is to create an OFFSET() formula that returns the last *length* number of items in the table, where *length* is the value you stored in the cell named Length, earlier. You do this by offsetting to the *length*-last item in the table and then setting the *height* argument equal to *length*.

For the category (X) axis labels, assuming the category labels start at cell A3 in the table, then the following OFFSET() formula does the job:

=OFFSET($A$3, ROWS(Table1) - Length, 0, Length, 1)

To use this formula as the basis of a dynamic range name, follow these steps:

1. Choose Formulas, Name Manager to open the Name Manager dialog box.

2. Click <u>N</u>ew to open the New Name dialog box.

3. Type the range name (for example, **Categories**) in the <u>N</u>ame text box.

4. Type the OFFSET() formula in the <u>R</u>efers To box.

5. Click OK and then click Close.

For the data series values, assuming the series values start at cell B3 in the table, the following OFFSET() formula does the job:

```
=OFFSET($B$3, ROWS(Table1) - Length, 0, Length, 1)
```

To use this formula as the basis of a dynamic range name, follow the same steps that I outlined previously (entering a different range name, such as **Values**).

Now, all that remains is to adjust the chart references to point at these two new dynamic range names. Use the techniques I mentioned earlier in this section (using the Select Data Source dialog box or editing the SERIES() function directly). For best results, include the workbook name in the references, as shown here:

```
=SERIES($B$2,Chapter08.xlsm!Categories,Chapter08.xlsm!Values,1)
```

Figure 8.7 shows a chart based on these dynamic named ranges.

→ For an example of another chart trick that uses dynamic named ranges, **see** "Creating a Scrolling Chart," **p. 209**

Figure 8.7
A chart based on
dynamically named
ranges.

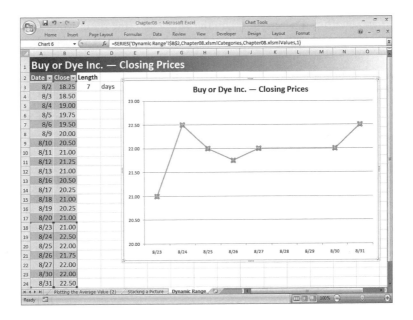

8

Automatically Expanding a Chart to Include New Data

Most charts use static data as their data source. However, it's not uncommon for a chart to use a data source that constantly expands. On a stock price worksheet, for example, you might enter daily prices for a given month. Rather than wait until the end of the month to create the chart, it is useful to chart the existing data and update the chart as you add new prices each day.

The hard way to accomplish this is to edit the range references for the category axis labels and data series values each time you add new data. Fortunately, Excel 2007 gives you a much easier method. As with the dynamic ranges you learned about in the previous section, the trick is to convert your data to a table. When the category axis label range and data series range are part of a table, Excel automatically expands the chart to include any new data that you add to the table. Note that you get this advantage without any other fuss and bother. As soon as you convert the data range to a table, your chart becomes dynamic based on the table data. You don't need to edit the SERIES() function or perform any other arcane tasks.

> **NOTE**
> Another advantage you get with this trick is that it doesn't matter when you convert the data to a table. You can perform the conversion either before or after you've created your chart; Excel will still expand the chart automatically to accommodate new table data.

Displaying a Second Vertical Axis

If you plot two different series on the same chart, the result won't look good if the two series use wildly different data ranges. A good example is a stock chart that includes one series for closing prices and another series for volume. The prices might be measured in tens of dollars, whereas the volumes might be measured in tens of thousands of units. How can you combine these two disparate data sources so that you can see both series properly?

The trick here is to add another vertical axis—called the *secondary axis*—and tell Excel to plot one of the series using that axis. Here are the steps to follow:

1. Click the chart to select it.
2. Click the data series that you want to plot on the secondary axis.
3. Choose Layout, Format Selection to display the Format Data Series dialog box.
4. In the Series Options tab, click the Secondary Axis option.
5. Click Close.

Figure 8.8 shows an example chart with two vertical axes—the primary axis (on the left) plots the Close series, and the secondary axis (on the right) plots the Volume series.

Figure 8.8
If you have series with wildly different data values, plot one of them on the secondary axis.

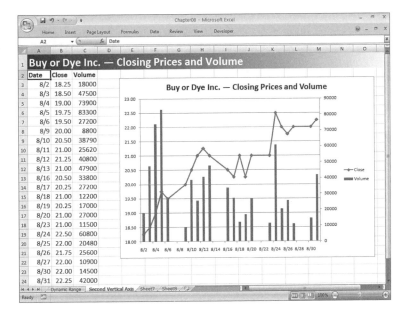

Exploding a Slice from a Pie Chart

A *pie chart* shows the proportion of the whole that is contributed by each value in a single data series. The whole is represented as a circle (the "pie"), and each value is displayed as a proportional "slice" of the circle. You can use pie charts to represent sales figures proportionally by region or by product, or to show population data such as age ranges or voting patterns.

To create a pie chart, select your data, choose Insert, Pie, and click the pie chart type you want. In the pie chart gallery, notice that Excel includes an Exploded Pie type. In pie chart lingo, *exploding* a slice means separating that slice by some amount so that it appears on its own. This is a useful way to highlight a special slice. However, the Exploded Pie type explodes *every* slice, which isn't that useful. If you want to explode just a single slice, you need insert a regular pie chart and then follow these steps:

1. Click the pie chart to select it.

2. Click any slice to select the series and then click the slice you want to explode. This should now be the only data point selected.

3. Choose Layout, Format Selection to display the Format Data Point dialog box.

4. In the Series Options tab, click and drag the Point Explosion slider towards the Separate end (to the right). You can also enter a percentage value in the associated text box.

8

> **NOTE** An explosion value of 100% means that the tip of the slice lies on the circumference of the pie. A value greater than 100% means the slice will be displayed completely outside of the pie.

5. If you want the exploded slice to display in a particular position within the chart, you probably need to rotate the pie. You do this by clicking and dragging the Angle of First Slice slider.

6. Click Close.

Figure 8.9 shows a pie chart that plots the proportions of Earth's elements, with the Others slice exploded so that a shape can point out extra information about the slice's value.

Figure 8.9
A pie chart showing the proportions of terrestrial elements, with the Others slice exploded.

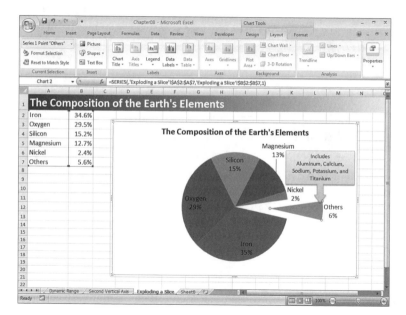

Charting Small Values with a Bar of Pie Chart

In Figure 8.9, I exploded one of the pie chart slices and then added a shape with some explanatory data about the composition of the Others slice. In most pie charts, you use an "Others" slice because the components data that makes up this item are too small to show properly on the pie chart. That is, the slices would be so thin that they'd be hard to pick out from the surrounding slices.

If you want others to see the data represented by an "Others" slice, Excel offers another pie chart type that's ideal: The Bar of Pie type. With this chart type, the smallest data items are gathered into a single slice, as before, but then the separate items that comprise that slice are displayed in a separated stacked bar marker.

To create a Bar of Pie chart, select your data, choose Insert, Pie, Bar of Pie. Figure 8.10 shows an example.

Figure 8.10
A Bar of Pie chart shows the data series' small values in a separate stacked bar marker.

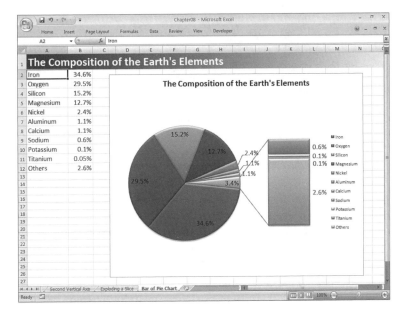

Creating a Scrolling Chart

Earlier in this chapter, you learned how to create a chart that expands automatically as you add new data points (see "Automatically Expanding a Chart to Include New Data"). It's a useful trick that I use all the time, but it does lead to one problem: You can end up with a lot of data points in the chart, and after awhile you have to resize the chart horizontally to maintain the visual integrity of the plot. Of course, that leads to an entirely different problem: Eventually your chart becomes wider than the Excel window, so you need to use the horizontal scroll bar to see different parts of the chart.

A better solution is to keep your chart the same size but add a scrolling element to it that enables you to move back and forth through the data. You set this up by adding a scroll bar to the worksheet and using the values generated by the scroll bar to create dynamically named ranges that change as the scroll bar value changes. Then, as you saw earlier in this chapter (see "Charting a Dynamic Range"), you configure your chart to use these dynamically named ranges. The result is that as you scroll forward and backward in the scroll bar, the data plotted on the charts moves forward and backward by the same amount.

You begin by converting your worksheet data to a table. Figure 8.11 shows the example data that I use in this section. It's a table (named Table2) of monthly sales that runs from January, 1998 to December, 2007. I plot the Month and Actual columns in the chart.

8

Figure 8.11
As an example in this section, I create a scrolling chart for 10-year's worth of monthly sales data.

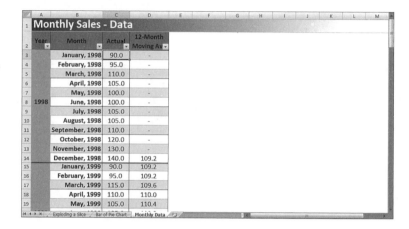

Next, you add the scroll bar. First, insert two values in the worksheet:

- **The initial value of the cell that you'll link to the scroll bar**—Start off this cell with the value **1**. This cell's value changes as you scroll, and you set things up so that this cell represents the starting value Excel plots on the chart. For example, the initial value is 1, so the chart initially begins with the first value in the table. Later, if this cell displays, say, 50, then the chart shows the 50th value in the table as its starting point. You should also name this cell to make your dynamically named range formulas easier to read. In the monthly sales example, I named this cell Starting_Month.

- **The number of values to display in the chart**—This tells Excel how many data points to display at a time. For the monthly sales, I want to see a year's worth of data at a time, so I enter 12 in this cell. In the monthly sales example, I named this cell Months_to_Display.

You are now ready to add the scroll bar to the worksheet. Here are the steps to follow:

1. Choose Developer, Insert, and in the Form Controls gallery, click the Scroll Bar control.

> **NOTE**
> If you don't see the Developer tab, choose Office, Excel Options to open the Excel Options dialog box. In the Popular tab, click to activate the Show Developer tab in the Ribbon check box and then click OK.

2. At the point on the worksheet where you want the scroll bar to display, click and drag a thin rectangle that is the size and shape you want for your scroll bar and then release the mouse button. Drag to the right to create a horizontal scroll bar; drag down to create a vertical scroll bar.

> **TIP** If you want to resize the scroll bar or make other changes to it, you first need to select it. To do this, hold down Ctrl and then click the scroll bar.

3. Choose Developer, Properties to display the scroll bar's Format Control dialog box.

4. Modify the following values:

   - **Current Value**—Set this to 1.
   - **Minimum Value**—Set this to 1.
   - **Maximum Value**—Set this to the number of records in the table you chart.
   - **Incremental Change**—Set this to the number of data points that you want Excel to scroll when you click the scroll bar arrows. In most cases, you should leave this value at 1.
   - **Page Change**—Set this to the number of data points that you want Excel to scroll when you click between the scroll bar and a scroll bar arrow. For the monthly sales example, I set this value to 12.
   - **Cell Link**—Click inside this range box and then click the cell that you set up earlier to hold the current value of the scroll bar (this is $G$3 in the monthly sales example).

5. Click OK.

Figure 8.12 shows the Monthly Sales worksheet with the scroll bar added and its filled in Format Control dialog box. For future reference, note that I have applied the named Months_to_Display to cell G2 and the name Starting_Month to cell G3.

Next, you need to define your dynamically named ranges. As before, you need to use the OFFSET() function, which you should set up as follows:

- The reference point (the OFFSET() function's *reference* argument) is the table header.

- The number of rows to offset (the OFFSET() function's *rows* argument) is the current value of the scroll bar. That is, this should be a reference to the scroll bar's linked cell. In the monthly sales example, this is the Starting_Month named range (cell G3).

- The number of rows in the offset range (the OFFSET() function's *height* argument) is the cell value that defines the number of data points you want to display in the chart. In the monthly sales example, this is the Months_to_Display named range (cell G2).

Figure 8.12
A scroll bar added to the worksheet and configured for the monthly sales data.

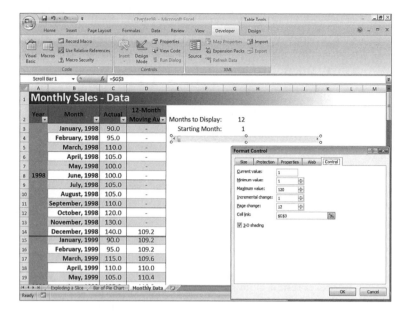

In the monthly sales example, I created the name Monthly_Sales_Categories and assigned it the following formula:

```
=OFFSET(Table2[[#Headers],[Month]],Starting_Month, 0, Months_to_Display, 1)
```

I also created the name Monthly_Sales_Values and assigned it the following formula:

```
=OFFSET(Table2[[#Headers],[Actual]],Starting_Month, 0, Months_to_Display, 1)
```

→ To learn the steps to follow to define a dynamically named range, **see** "Charting a Dynamic Range," **p. 202**

Finally, create a chart and set up the type and formatting you want to use. It's important, however, to *not* plot the entire table. Instead, just plot the same number of points that you want to display in the chart. In the monthly sales example, I want to display 12 months at a time, so I plotted only the first 12 months of data in the table. When that's done, modify the references to the category labels and series values, as described in this chapter's "Charting a Dynamic Range" section.

Figure 8.13 shows the scrolling chart for the monthly sales data. Notice that the current scroll bar value is 13 (see cell G3) and that the chart plot begins with January, 1999, which is the 13th value in the table.

Figure 8.13
The scrolling chart for the monthly sales table.

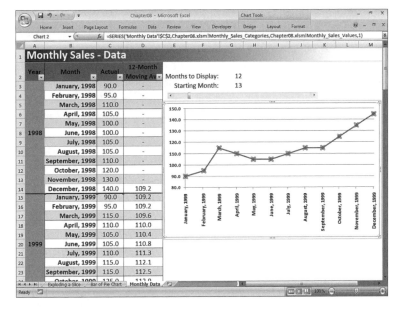

Plotting a Best-Fit Trendline

In these complex and uncertain times, forecasting business performance is increasingly important. Today, more than ever, managers at all levels need to make intelligent predictions of future sales and profit trends as part of their overall business strategy. By forecasting sales six months, a year, or even three years down the road, managers can anticipate related needs such as employee acquisitions, warehouse space, and raw material requirements. Similarly, a profit forecast enables the planning of the future expansion of a company.

> **NOTE**
> The next two sections are excerpts from my book, *Formulas and Functions with Microsoft Excel 2007* (Que 2007; ISBN 0-7897-3668-3). Please see that book for a much more detailed description of Excel's trendline and forecasting tools.

Business forecasting has been around for many years, and various methods have been developed—some more successful than others. The most common forecasting method is the qualitative "seat-of-the-pants" approach, in which a manager (or a group of managers) estimates future trends based on experience and knowledge of the market. This method, however, suffers from an inherent subjectivity and a short-term focus because many managers tend to extrapolate from recent experience and ignore the long-term trend. Other methods (such as averaging past results) are more objective but generally useful for forecasting only a few months in advance.

8

In business, it's becoming increasingly popular to use a statistical tool called *regression analysis* to determine the relationship between one phenomenon that depends on another. For example, car sales might be dependent on interest rates, and units sold might be dependent on the amount spent on advertising. The dependent phenomenon is called the *dependent variable* or the *y-value*, and the phenomenon upon which it's dependent is called the *independent variable* or the *x-value*. (Think of a chart or graph on which the independent variable is plotted along the horizontal [x] axis and the dependent variable is plotted along the vertical [y] axis.)

Given these variables, you can do two things with regression analysis:

- Determine the relationship between the known x- and y-values and use the results to calculate and visualize the overall trend of the data.
- Use the existing trend to forecast new y-values.

With linear data, the dependent variable is related to the independent variable by some constant factor. For example, you might find that car sales (the dependent variable) increase by one million units whenever interest rates (the independent variable) decrease by 1 percent. Similarly, you might find that division revenue (the dependent variable) increases by $100,000 for every $10,000 you spend on advertising (the independent variable).

You make these sorts of determinations by examining the trend underlying the current data you have for the dependent variable. In linear regression, you analyze the current trend by calculating the *line of best-fit*, or the *trendline*. This is a line through the data points for which the differences between the points above and below the line cancel each other out (more or less).

The easiest way to see the best-fit line is to use a chart. Note, however, that this works only if your data is plotted using an XY (scatter) chart. For example, Figure 8.14 shows a worksheet with quarterly sales figures plotted on an XY chart. Here, the quarterly sales are the dependent variable, and the period is the independent variable. (In this example, the independent variable is just time, represented, in this case, by fiscal quarters.)

The following steps show you how to add a trendline to a chart:

1. Click the chart to select it.
2. If more than one data series is plotted, click the series with which you want to work.
3. Choose Layout, Trendline, Linear Trendline. Excel inserts the trendline.

Figure 8.15 shows the best-fit trendline added to the chart.

> ┌─ **CAUTION** ─────────────────────────────
> It's important not to view the trendline values as somehow trying to predict or estimate the actual y-values (sales). The trendline simply gives you an overall picture of how the y-values change when the x-values change.

Figure 8.14
To see a trendline through your data, first make sure the data is plotted using an XY chart.

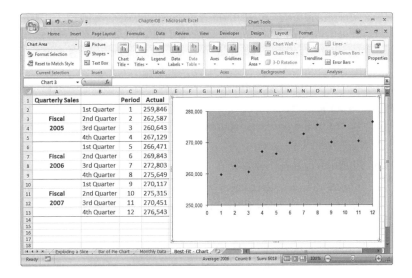

Figure 8.15
The quarterly sales chart with a best-fit trendline added.

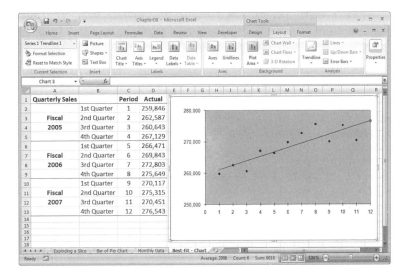

Plotting Forecasted Values

Knowing the overall trend a data set exhibits is useful because it tells you the broad direction that sales or costs or employee acquisitions is going, and it gives you a good idea of how related the dependent variable is on the independent variable. But a trend is also useful for making forecasts in which you extend the trendline into the future (what will sales be in the first quarter of next year?) or calculate the trend value given some new independent value (if we spend $25,000 on advertising, what will the corresponding sales be?).

How accurate is such a prediction? A projection based on historical data assumes that the factors influencing the data over the historical period will remain constant. If this is a reasonable assumption in your case, the projection is a reasonable one. Of course, the longer you extend the line, the more likely it is that some of the factors will change or that new ones will arise. As a result, best-fit extensions should be used only for short-term projections.

If you want just a visual idea of the forecasted trend, you can extend the chart trendline that you created in the previous section. The following steps show you how to add a forecasting trendline to a chart:

1. Click the chart to select it.

2. If more than one data series is plotted, click the series with which you want to work.

3. Choose Layout, Trendline, More Trendline Options to display the Format Trendline dialog box.

4. On the Trendline Options tab, click Linear.

5. Use the Forward text box to select the number of units you want to project the trendline into the future. (For example, to extend the quarterly sales number into the next year, you set Forward to 4 to extend the trendline by four quarters.)

6. Click OK. Excel inserts the trendline and extends it into the future.

Figure 8.16 shows the quarterly sales trendline extended by four quarters.

Figure 8.16
The trendline has been extended four quarters into the future.

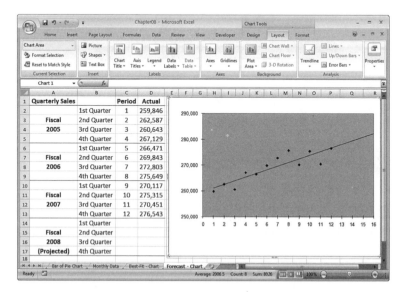

From Here

- If you want to track loan or mortgage payments on a chart, **see** "Calculating the Principal and Interest for a Loan," **p. 130**.

- If you want to track investments on a chart, **see** "Calculating the Future Value of an Investment," **p. 134**.

- You can add stock price quotes to your sheets for plotting; **see** "Adding a Live Stock Price Quote to a Worksheet," **p. 149**.

- It's often more convenient to use Excel 2007's new in-cell data bars rather than creating a separate bar chart; **see** "Analyzing Cell Values with Data Bars," **p. 186**.

Microsoft PowerPoint Tricks

III

Slide and Presentation Tricks

9

Among all the documents that you can create with the Microsoft Office Suite, PowerPoint presentations are unique in that they are the only ones that other people regularly critique. If someone sends you a Word document or an Access database, you rarely begin by casting a critical eye on the layout and formatting. Among spreadsheet jockeys, there is a worksheet aesthetic that looks for a certain amount of elegance in model building, but the main concern is getting the right answer. A PowerPoint presentation, on the other hand, must first meet a certain standard of visual appeal before we even consider the information it's trying to impart. Why? Perhaps it's because presentations seem to be just one small step removed from entertainment: We sit in a darkened room looking at text and pictures on a screen while a person tells us a story about what we're seeing. Or perhaps it's because we've all seen more than our fair share of PowerPoint presentations, and the idea of sitting through another lackluster series of slides is just too much to bear.

Whatever the reason, if you create PowerPoint presentations for your job, you need to know what Office gurus know: Your presentations—every one of them—must be knockouts. That doesn't mean you need to create something that has your audience cheering and on its feet at the end of the show. Rather, it means having your audience look forward to seeing your presentation and actually learning something from it.

This chapter presents a number of tricks that can help you create such presentations, including custom footers and bullets, recoloring pictures, creating custom slide layouts and custom blank presentations, maintaining a slide library, and much more. The focus is on avoiding so-called *PowerPointlessness*—those fancy formats, transitions,

9

sounds, and other effects that have no discernible purpose, use, or benefit. Instead, you get practical tricks and techniques that serve the goal of creating a knockout presentation.

Converting a Word Outline into a PowerPoint Presentation

PowerPoint slides have a built-in hierarchical structure; the slide title is the topmost item, the main bullet points are the second level items, sub-bullets are the third level items, and so on. This hierarchy is easy to see if you click the Outline tab in the PowerPoint Navigation pane. (If you don't see the Navigation pane, choose View, Normal or click the Normal button in the status bar.) In fact, you can use the Outline tab to create a basic presentation:

1. In the Outline tab, type the slide's title and press Enter to create the next slide. Repeat this until you've created the slides you need.

2. For the main bullet points, move the cursor to the end of the title of the slide you want to work with, press Ctrl+Enter, and then type the bullet text. To insert another bullet on the same level, move the cursor to the end of the current bullet and press Enter. Repeat until you've created all the main bullet points you need.

3. For the sub-bullets, move the cursor to the end of the corresponding main bullet, press Enter, press Tab, and then type the bullet text. To insert another bullet on the same level, move the cursor to the end of the current bullet and press Enter. Repeat until you've created all the sub-bullet points you need.

This procedure is handy if you know the text you want to add to the presentation. However, it's also possible that the text resides in a Word document as an outline. If that's the case, you can save yourself a lot of work by importing the Word outline directly into the presentation. PowerPoint can work with Word outlines and convert the outline styles to the corresponding presentation outline levels:

- **Heading 1**—PowerPoint converts this Word style into a slide title. That is, when PowerPoint finds a Heading 1 style, it inserts a new slide into the presentation and adds the Heading 1 text to the title of the slide.

- **Heading 2**—PowerPoint converts this Word style to a second-level item in the presentation outline. This means that each paragraph of Heading 2 text becomes a main bullet in the presentation. These bullets display in the slide most recently created from the previous Heading 1 style.

- **Heading 3**—PowerPoint converts this Word style to a third-level item in the presentation outline. Each paragraph of Heading 3 text becomes a sub-bullet in the presentation. These bullets display under the bullet most recently created from a Heading 2 style.

> **NOTE**
>
> You might be wondering whether PowerPoint supports creating an outline from a Word document that uses custom outline levels (see "Creating Custom Outline Levels" in Chapter 4). That would be a great feature, but unfortunately it doesn't work. PowerPoint only supports Word's Heading style.

To convert a Word outline into a PowerPoint presentation, follow these steps:

1. You have two ways to get started:
   - Select Office, <u>O</u>pen to display the Open dialog box and then, in the list of file types, click All Outlines.
   - In the Outline tab, move the cursor to where you want the Word outline to display, choose Home, click the lower half of the New Slide split button, and then click Slides from Out<u>l</u>ine.

2. Select the Word file containing the outline you want to convert.

> **CAUTION**
>
> Before importing, you need to close the Word document containing the outline. If you don't, PowerPoint won't be able to open the file, and the conversion fails.

3. Click Open. PowerPoint converts the Word outline into a presentation.

Figure 9.1 shows a Word outline, and Figure 9.2 shows the document converted into a PowerPoint presentation outline.

Figure 9.1
A Word outline ready to be converted into a PowerPoint presentation.

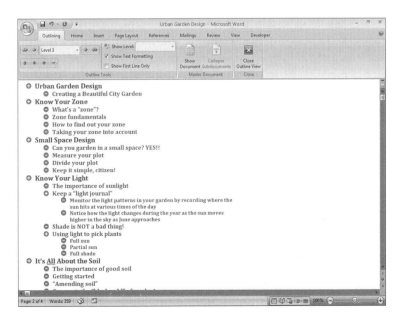

Figure 9.2
The PowerPoint presentation created by converting the Word outline shown in Figure 9.1.

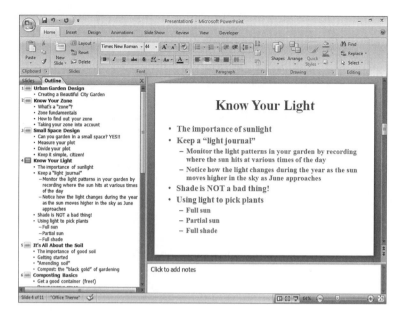

Inserting Custom Text into the Slide Footer

During or after a slide show, it's not unusual for an audience member to have a question about a previously viewed slide. However, unless that slide has some memorable text or graphic, it's often hard for the person to describe which slide he is talking about. It is much easier to display numbers on each slide, which means audience members can then refer to "slide number 5," "slide 12," and so on.

PowerPoint displays slide numbers in the slide footer; a section is located at the bottom of each slide. You can display not only the slide number, but also the date and time (the current values or fixed values), as well as custom text. The latter is useful for displaying things such as copyright messages, your name, your company's name, a project reference, and so on. Here are the steps to follow to display the slide footer and insert a custom text message:

1. Choose Insert, Header & Footer to display the Header and Footer dialog box.

2. In the Slide tab, click to activate the Footer check box.

3. Type your custom text into the Footer text box.

4. To leave the footer text off the presentation's title slide, click to activate the Don't Show on Title Slide check box.

5. Configure the other slide footer options you want to use.

6. Click Apply to All to display the footer on every slide in the presentation. (If you want only the footer on the current slide, click Apply instead.)

Figure 9.3 shows some custom footer text in both the Header and Footer dialog box and the slide.

Figure 9.3
In the Header and Footer dialog box, use the Footer text box to specify your custom footer text.

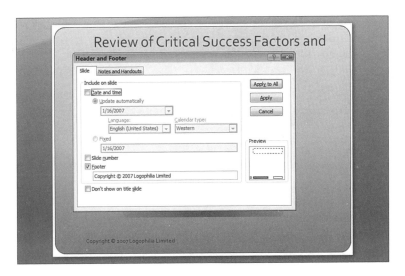

9

The Footer text box in the Slide tab of the Header and Footer dialog box enables you to add static text that displays in a placeholder. However, you may prefer something more dynamic, such as the full pathname of the presentation file. You can do this with a relatively simple VBA script that modifies the Footer object's Text property.

Listing 9.1 shows one such script.

NOTE The PowerPoint file used for the examples in this chapter are located on my Web site at www.mcfedries.com/OfficeGurus.

Listing 9.1   A Script That Inserts a Presentation's Pathname into the Footer Placeholder

```
Sub AddPathToFooter()
    Dim txtPath As String
    Dim s As Slide
    With ActivePresentation
        '
        ' Build the presentation's pathname
        txtPath = .Path & "\" & .Name
        '
        ' Add the pathname to the Slide Master's footer
        .SlideMaster.HeadersFooters.Footer.Text = txtPath
        '
        ' Loop through all the slides
        For Each s In .Slides
            '
            ' Add the pathname to the slide
            s.HeadersFooters.Footer.Visible = msoTrue
            s.HeadersFooters.Footer.Text = txtPath
    End With
End Sub
```

This procedure stores the active presentation's folder path (the `Path` property) and filename (the `Name` property) in the txtPath variable. This string is then stored in the Footer object's `Text` property for both the slide master and the existing slides.

Listing 9.2 shows another example.

Listing 9.2   A Script That Inserts the String `"Slide X of Y"` **into the Footer Placeholder**

```
Sub AddSlideXOfYToFooter()
    Dim s As Slide
    With ActivePresentation
        '
        ' Loop through all the slides
        For Each s In .Slides
            '
            ' Add the "Slide X of Y" text
            s.HeadersFooters.Footer.Visible = msoTrue
            s.HeadersFooters.Footer.Text = "Slide " & s.SlideNumber & _
                                " of " & .Slides.Count
        Next 's
    End With
End Sub
```

This procedure loops through all the slides in the active presentation. For each slide s, the Footer object's `Text` property changes to Slide X of Y, where X is given by the Slide object's SlideNumber property, and Y is given by the Presentation object's Slides.Count property.

> **TIP**
>
> If you also want to add custom text to the date and time placeholder, modify the DateAndTime object's Text property:
>
> ```
>     s.HeadersFooters.DateAndTime.Text = "Text"
> ```

Creating Custom Bullets

Many PowerPoint slides consist of a title and an object such as a picture, SmartArt diagram, or other object. However, text is the meat of most PowerPoint slides, and that text almost always displays in the form of bullet points in a content placeholder. They are called bullet points because each paragraph of text is preceded by a symbol—a *bullet*—that's offset from the text and serves to separate the paragraphs and focus the audience's attention.

For a first-level bullet point, the standard bullet is a small, black, filled circle, but each PowerPoint theme comes with its own bullet style, which may be an arrow, a square, an X, or some other symbol. So the easiest way to customize your slide bullets is to apply a different theme to your presentation. (Choose Design and then click a theme in the Themes gallery.)

If you don't want to apply such a drastic change to your presentation, you can also change just the bullets. You can choose another of PowerPoint's built-in bullets, or you can choose a custom picture or symbol. Here are the steps to follow to change the default bullet styles in your presentation:

1. Choose View, Slide Master to display the presentation's Slide Master view.

2. Click the slide master at the top of the Navigation pane. PowerPoint displays the default styles for each bullet level, including the default bullets.

3. Click anywhere within the bullet level you want to change.

> **NOTE** If you want to change the bullet for only one or more paragraphs, don't bother with steps 1–3. Instead, select the paragraph or paragraphs that you want to customize and then proceed with step 4.

4. Choose Home and click the Bullets arrow to display the Bullets list, as shown in Figure 9.4.

Slide master   Bullets list

Figure 9.4
Click the Slide Master to see the default bullet styles and then use the Bullets list to customize them.

Default bullet styles

9

5. You have two choices:

- Click one of the predefined bullet styles. Repeat steps 3–4 to customize the other bullet levels. Continue with step 11.
- Click Bullets and <u>N</u>umbering to display the Bulleted tab of the Bullets and Numbering dialog box. Continue with step 6.

6. Use the <u>S</u>ize spin button to change the bullet size as a percentage of the bullet text.

7. For bullets that are symbols (not pictures), use the <u>C</u>olor palette to click the bullet color you want to use.

8. Click one of the following buttons:

- **<u>P</u>icture**—Click this button to assign a custom picture as the bullet. In the Picture Bullet dialog box, either click a displayed picture (make sure the Include Content from <u>O</u>ffice Online check box is activated) or click Import to use the Add Clips to Organizer dialog box to choose a custom image. Click OK.
- **C<u>u</u>stomize**—Click this button to assign a custom symbol as the bullet. In the Symbol dialog box, click the symbol you want to use and then click OK.

9. Click OK. PowerPoint applies the custom bullet to the selected level.

10. Repeat steps 3–9 to customize any other bullet levels you want to work with.

11. Choose Slide Master, Close Master View to return to the Normal view. PowerPoint applies the new bullets to your entire presentation.

→ To learn how to animate individual bullets, **see** "Making Bullets Display Individually," **p. 257**

Replacing Fonts Throughout a Presentation

It's important to maintain design consistency throughout your presentation. This means using the same typeface and type size for all your titles, using consistent bullet styles throughout the presentation, using the same or similar background images on all slides, and placing the company logo in the same position on each slide. The more consistent you are, the less work your audience has interpreting the formatting for each slide, so the more it can concentrate on your content.

In a large presentation, you may find that your fonts aren't as consistent as you'd like:

- If you applied a different theme to one or two slides, chances are those themes use fonts that are different than the ones in your main theme.
- If you imported slides from another presentation, those slides may use different fonts.
- If you're collaborating with one or more people, those users may apply different typefaces.

When this happens, the last thing you want to do is run through the entire presentation fixing font inconsistencies. You have, I'm sure, better things to do with your precious time.

Fortunately, PowerPoint comes with a tool called Replace Font that enables you to restore font consistency with just a few mouse clicks. Here are the steps to follow:

1. Choose Home, Replace, Replace Fonts to display the Replace Font dialog box, shown in Figure 9.5.

Figure 9.5
PowerPoint's Replace Font tool enables you to quickly replace all instances of one font with another.

2. In the Replace list, click the font you want to replace.

3. In the With list, click the font you want to use as the replacement.

4. Click Replace.

5. If you have other fonts to replace, follow steps 2–4 for each font.

6. Click Close.

Recoloring a Picture to Match Your Presentation

It's a common source of presentation frustration: You find the perfect piece of clip art for a slide, but the picture's colors don't go with your color scheme. Rather than rejecting the picture outright, you can use PowerPoint's Recolor feature, which enables you to change one or more of the picture's colors for something more complementary to your presentation design. For example, if your presentation is mostly shades of gray, you might want to change a colorful image to grayscale to blend in.

Here are the steps to follow:

1. Click the picture.

2. Choose Format, Recolor to open the Recolor gallery, as shown in Figure 9.6.

3. You have two choices:
   - Click a recolor option in the gallery.
   - Click More Variations and then click a color swatch from the palette that displays.

 TIP A picture can ruin a slide if its background does not blend in with the slide background. You can fix this problem if the image uses a solid color background. Click the picture and then choose Format, Recolor, Set Transparent Color. Move the mouse pointer over the picture and then click any part of the picture's background. PowerPoint formats the image background as transparent, enabling the slide background to show through.

Figure 9.6
Use the Recolor gallery to change a picture's colors to ones more suitable to your presentation's color scheme.

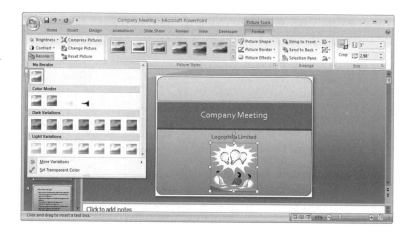

Drawing Shapes at Evenly Spaced Intervals

You can create effective designs by duplicating a particular shape multiple times. Although it's not hard to copy a shape (hold down Ctrl and drag the shape), it's quite difficult to get the same distance between the duplicates. Happily, PowerPoint can do this for you. Click the shape and press Ctrl+D to create the first duplicate. Use your mouse to drag the duplicate to the correct position. This tells PowerPoint how far away you want each duplicate and in which direction. Press Ctrl+D again, and PowerPoint creates a third shape that uses the same spacing as the second. Keep pressing Ctrl+D to create more duplicates, as shown in Figure 9.7.

Figure 9.7
After you establish the spacing between the first and second shapes, press Ctrl+D to create duplicates with the same spacing.

Using Drawing Guides to Precisely Align Objects

When a presentation deadline is looming, one of the first slide design tweaks that many people skip is the alignment of slide objects. They might perform a quick click-and-drag to get objects more or less in line with each other, but getting the alignment exact is (they think) a fiddly, time-consuming, unproductive chore. That's a big mistake, in my mind, because what's the first thing *you* notice in such a presentation? Right: the misaligned objects.

You can make your presentation look more professional by taking minimal extra time to get objects properly aligned. Yes, clicking-and-dragging to align things is hard and not always successful, but the good news is that PowerPoint offers quite an array of tools that take the drudgery and difficulty out of aligning objects.

Your main alignment tools are on the Align menu, which displays in the Format tab when you select the objects with which you want to work. The Align menu has eight commands you can use:

- **Align Left**—Click this command to align the objects on the left edges of their frames. The objects are aligned with the leftmost object.

- **Align Center**—Click this command to align the objects on the horizontal center of their frames. The objects are aligned on a point halfway between the leftmost and rightmost object.

- **Align Right**—Click this command to align the objects on the right edges of their frames. The objects are aligned with the rightmost object.

- **Align Top**—Click this command to align the objects on the top edges of their frames. The objects are aligned with the topmost object. The objects are aligned on a point halfway between the topmost and bottommost object.

- **Align Middle**—Click this command to align the objects on the vertical middle of their frames.

- **Align Bottom**—Click this command to align the objects on the bottom edges of their frames. The objects are aligned with the bottommost object.

- **Distribute Horizontally**—Click this command to align the objects so that they are evenly spaced horizontally.

- **Distribute Vertically**—Click this command to align the objects so that they are evenly spaced vertically.

Another useful alignment tool are the *drawing guides*, which are dashed lines—one horizontal line and one vertical line—that are located in the slide area. When you use your mouse to drag an object near one of the drawing guides, PowerPoint snaps the object to the line.

The easiest way to add the drawing guides to the slide area is to press Alt+F9. (If you prefer the hard way, right-click an empty part of a slide, click Grid and Guides, activate the Display Drawing Guides On Screen check box, and then click OK.) You can then click and drag the guides to position them where you want. You can also use the following techniques to work with the guides:

- To add another guide, hold down Ctrl and then click and drag an existing guide.
- To delete an extra guide, click and drag it to any edge of the current slide.

TIP

At times, you might need to make subtle adjustments to the position of one object relative to another, such as when you're overlaying images to achieve an effect. In such cases, the Align commands and the drawing guides don't help. To position an object precisely, use your mouse to drag the object into its approximate position and then do one of the following:

- Press the left, right, up, or down arrow key. This tells PowerPoint to nudge the object in the arrow's direction by 0.083 inches (one twelfth of an inch), which is the default grid spacing. To change this value, right-click an empty part of a slide, click Grid and Guides, and then use the Spacing combo box to type or select the grid spacing you want to use.
- Hold down Ctrl and press the left, right, up, or down arrow key. This tells PowerPoint to nudge the object in the arrow's direction by one pixel.

Figure 9.8 shows the drawing guides on a slide.

Figure 9.8
Drag an object to a
drawing guide to align
the object with that
guide.

Creating a Custom Slide Layout

Each new PowerPoint presentation comes with a slide master that determines the overall look and layout of the presentation. If you change the slide master's fonts, bullets, or theme, PowerPoint applies those changes to every existing slide as well as every new slide you add. You can also add images and text to the slide master, and those elements display on every slide. Working with the slide master is a great way to ensure a consistent design for your presentation, and all PowerPoint gurus should be comfortable using the Slide Master view (choose View, Slide Master).

However, a PowerPoint presentation is also populated with a number of *layout masters*, which are master slides that control the look and configuration of the various layouts that you can apply to your slides. There's a Title Slide Layout master for title slides, and Title and Content Layout for title and content slides, and so on. To see these layout masters, choose View, Slide Master. As you can see in Figure 9.9, the layout masters are located below the Slide Master in the Navigation pane. In Figure 9.9, the Title Slide Layout is selected.

> **TIP**
> PowerPoint can tell you which slides use a particular layout. Move the mouse pointer over a slide layout, and PowerPoint responds with a ScreenTip that shows the layout master name followed by the numbers of the slides that use the layout master:
>
> ```
> Title and Content Layout: used by slide(s) 2-8, 10, 12
> ```

Figure 9.9
Each presentation comes with a number of layout masters that you can customize.

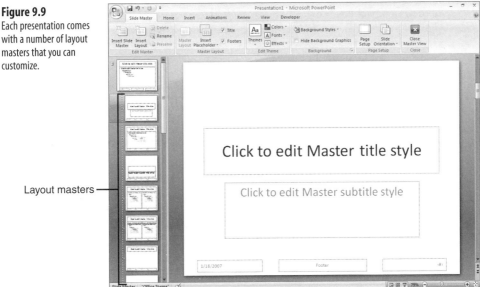

Layout masters

You can create a custom slide layout by either customizing an existing layout master or by creating a new layout master from scratch. Here are the steps to follow:

1. Choose View, Slide Master if you're not already in Slide Master view.

2. Choose the master you want to customize:

   - If you're creating a slide master from scratch, click the layout master before which you want the new layout to display, and then choose Slide Master, Insert Layout.

   > **TIP** If you want your new custom layout to be similar to an existing layout, right-click the existing layout master and then click <u>D</u>uplicate Layout. PowerPoint creates a copy of the layout master, and you can then customize that copy.

   - If you're customizing an existing layout, click the layout master with which you want to work.

3. Add a placeholder by choosing Slide Master, clicking the bottom half of the Insert Placeholder split button, clicking the type of placeholder you want, and then drawing the placeholder on the layout. Repeat for any other placeholders you want to include in the layout.

4. To remove a placeholder, click its border to select it, and then press Delete. (To remove the entire footer from the layout, choose Slide Master and then click to deactivate the Footers check box.)

   > **NOTE** It's okay to delete a placeholder from a layout master that you use for one or more slides. Any text that you added to that placeholder on those slides is preserved in a text box.

   > **TIP** You'd think that deleting a footer placeholder from the Slide Master would also delete the same placeholder from all the layout masters, but that's not the case. After you delete the footer placeholder from the Slide Master, you need to display each layout master, choose Slide Master, click Footer to deactivate it, and then click Footer again to activate it. Only then does PowerPoint remove the placeholder. If you later want to restore any deleted Slide Master placeholder, choose Slide Master, Master Layout, click to activate the placeholder's check box, and then click OK. To then restore the placeholder on any layout master, click the master and then choose Slide Master, Footer.

5. Set up any other options you want for the layout, including the theme, colors, fonts, background, images, static text, and so on.

6. If you created a new layout master in step 2, choose Slide Master, Rename to open the Rename Layout dialog box, type a name in the <u>L</u>ayout Name text box, and then click <u>R</u>ename.

7. Choose Slide Master, Close Master View.

It's important to note that PowerPoint normally maintains certain links between slides and their layout masters. For example, there's a link between a layout master's Title placeholder and the Title placeholders on all the slides that use that layout. This means that any changes you make on the layout master are propagated via those links to the slides that use the layout. However, if you customize a slide, then the link to the layout master is broken. For example, if you change the font of a slide's title and later change the font in the Title placeholder for the slide's layout master, PowerPoint won't apply the change to the slide's title because the link is broken. If you want to restore the link, right-click the slide and then click Reset Slide.

> **TIP** PowerPoint also maintains links between the Slide Master and the layout masters. For example, if you change the formatting of the Title placeholder in the Slide Master, PowerPoint propagates that change to all the Title placeholders in the layout masters. Again, however, if you format a placeholder on a layout master, the link to the Slide Master is broken for that placeholder. Unfortunately, PowerPoint doesn't have an equivalent of the Reset Slide command for restoring the link. Instead, display the Slide Master, copy the placeholder, display the layout master, delete the placeholder, and then paste the placeholder from the Slide Master.

Hiding a Slide Master Object on One Slide

If you add a shape, image, or other object to the Slide Master, it displays on all the presentation's slides. This is a great way to add an image that's common to all the slides, such as a logo, a project or department emblem, or a piece of clip art that relates to the presentation subject. However, you might find that the object isn't appropriate on some slides. For example, you might want to use a certain background color or image on a particular slide, and the Slide Master object might clash with that background.

PowerPoint gives you three ways to remove a Slide Master object from an individual slide:

- To remove *all* the Slide Master images from the slide, display the slide, choose the Design tab, and then click to activate the Hide Background Graphics check box.

- To remove a single Slide Master object from a slide that uses a solid-color background, display the slide, and then choose Insert, Shapes, Rectangle. Draw the rectangle on the slide so that it completely covers the object you want to hide. You now need to use the following steps to format the rectangle:

    1. Choose Format, Shape Fill, and then click the color that matches the slide's background color. If the background uses a texture, click Texture and then click the appropriate texture in the gallery that displays.

    2. Choose Format, Shape Outline, No Outline.

    3. Choose Format, Send to Back. This prevents the rectangle from also hiding any text on your slide.

- To remove a single Slide Master object from a slide that uses a complex background, first create a duplicate of the Slide Master, as described in the next section. In the duplicate Slide Master, remove the object that you want to hide. Return to the slide, choose Home, Insert, and then select a layout that doesn't include the object.

Using Multiple Slide Masters

Consistency among your slides is a laudable presentation goal, but it's not an absolute one. There is not a law that says you *must* make every slide look exactly the same. In fact, some of the most interesting and effective presentations I have seen apply different designs to groups of slides that are related in some way. Here are some ideas to help you get started thinking about this:

- For a budget or financial presentation, use a green color scheme on income-related slides and a red color scheme on expense-related slides.

- For a presentation that includes confidential or sensitive material, add "Confidential" or "For Internal Use Only" text to those slides.

- For a presentation that covers multiple products, place a small picture of the product on each slide related to that product.

- For a presentation that has two or more authors, display the author's name, signature, or picture on each of the slides he worked on.

With these and similar ideas, it probably seems as though we are moving away from the efficiency and usefulness of the Slide Master. That is true if you are restricted to using just a single Slide Master for a presentation. However, PowerPoint lets you add other Slide Masters to your presentation. This means that you can format one Slide Master for one set of related slides, a second Slide Master for another set of related slides, and so on.

To create a new Slide Master, first choose View, Slide Master to open the Slide Master view. PowerPoint now gives you two ways to proceed:

- If you want the new Slide Master to be similar to an existing Slide Master, right-click the existing Slide Master and then click Duplicate Slide Master.

- To create a new Slide Master, choose Slide Master, Insert Slide Master (or press Ctrl+M).

CAUTION

PowerPoint keeps a new Slide Master in the presentation only as long as at least one slide is used. If you change all your slides to use a layout from, say, the original Slide Master, PowerPoint automatically deletes the custom Slide Master. To avoid this, choose View, Slide Master, click your custom Slide Master, and then click to activate the Preserve toggle button. This tells PowerPoint to keep the Slide Master in the presentation, even if it's not used by any slides.

To use a layout from your custom Slide Master, choose Slide Master, Close Master View to turn to the Normal view. Click the slide you want to work with and then choose Home, Layout to display the gallery of layouts. As you can see in Figure 9.10, the gallery shows the layouts from both Slide Masters. (In this case, the Slide Masters are named Office Theme and Paper.) The layouts associated with the slide's current master are displayed at the top. Note that you see a similar gallery if you click the lower half of the New Slide split button.

Current Slide Master layouts

Figure 9.10
Choose Home, Layout to see a gallery of your layouts for your original and custom Slide Masters.

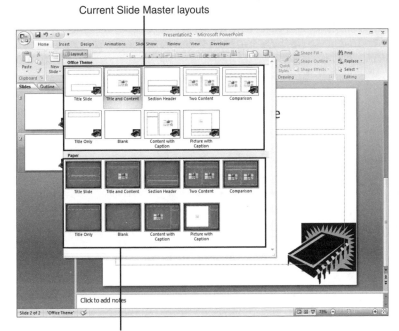

Custom Slide Master layouts

Creating a Custom Blank Presentation

When you choose Office, New, PowerPoint displays the New Presentation dialog box. In the Blank and Recent category, there is a Blank Presentation icon. When you click this icon and then click Create, a new presentation that uses PowerPoint's default blank presentation starts. This presentation has the following characteristics:

■ It uses the Office Theme.
■ It includes a single slide based on the Title Slide Layout.

> **TIP**
> You can quickly create a default blank presentation by pressing Ctrl+N.

This gives you a nice blank slate from which to get started. However, what if you always perform certain customizations when you start a new presentation? For example, you might always change to a particular theme, add a specific number of slides that use certain layouts, add an icon or logo to the Slide Master, set the footer text, and so on. Repeating these and other tweaks every time you start a new presentation is pure drudgery and a waste of valuable time.

One way to work around this is to configure your presentation the way you want and then save the results as a template:

1. Choose Office, Save As to open the Save As dialog box.
2. In the Save as Type list, click PowerPoint Template.

CAUTION

When you choose PowerPoint Template in the Save as Type list, PowerPoint automatically switches to your user profile's `Templates` folder. In Windows Vista, this folder is located at:

`%UserProfile%\AppData\Roaming\Microsoft\Templates`

You may be tempted to save the template in a different folder, but I don't recommend it. By storing your template in the `Templates` folder, PowerPoint automatically locates the template when you select the My Templates category in the New Presentation dialog box, as described later in this section.

---

3. Click Save.

To use the template, choose Office, New and click the My Templates category in the New Presentation dialog box. PowerPoint opens another New Presentation dialog box, which now shows a list of your templates (that is, all the PowerPoint templates in your user profile's `Templates` folder). Click the template and then click OK.

Templates are easy to work with, but there's no doubt it's even easier to work with the default blank presentation, particularly because you can create a new one just by pressing Ctrl+N. Fortunately, PowerPoint enables you to have the best of both worlds: a default blank presentation that you've customized to suit your needs. Here are the steps to follow to set this up:

1. Configure a presentation with the formatting, slides, layouts, and objects that you want included in your future blank (so to speak) presentations.
2. Choose Office, Save As to open the Save As dialog box.
3. In the Save as Type list, click PowerPoint Template.
4. In the File Name text box, type **blank**.
5. Click Save.

Maintaining a Slide Library

As you probably know from hard-won experience, crafting a PowerPoint slide that's both attractive and effective is a great deal of work. Getting the fonts, colors, and alignment just so, tweaking the layout, adding transitions and animations, and, of course, writing the text can all add up to a serious chunk of time. So what happens when you're working on another presentation and realize you need to use the same slide that took you so long to craft? Office gurus know that the cardinal rule of Office productivity is to avoid reinventing any wheels. In this case, this means you shouldn't recreate the same slide from scratch. Instead, PowerPoint gives you several ways to reuse slides.

The most straightforward method is the good old copy-and-paste technique:

1. Open the presentation containing the slides you want to reuse.

2. Select the slides you want to reuse, and then press Ctrl+C to copy them to the Office Clipboard.

3. Open the presentation to which you want to copy the slides.

4. In the Navigation pane, click the slide below which you want to insert the copied slides.

5. Press Ctrl+V to paste the slides. PowerPoint inserts the copied slides.

> **TIP** When PowerPoint inserts the copied slides, it applies the current presentation's theme to each slide. If you prefer to keep the slide's original formatting, click the Paste Options smart tag and then click the Keep Source Formatting option.

PowerPoint also comes with a Reuse Slides pane that enables you to reuse slides without having to open the other presentation. Here's how it works:

1. Choose the Home tab, click the lower half of the New Slide split button, and then click Reuse Slides. PowerPoint displays the Reuse Slides task pane.

2. Click Open a PowerPoint File. The Browse dialog box displays.

3. Click the presentation containing the slides you want to reuse and then click Open. PowerPoint displays thumbnail versions of the presentation's slides in the Reuse Slides pane, as shown in Figure 9.11.

4. In the Navigation pane, click the slide below which you want to insert the slide.

5. If you want PowerPoint to keep the reused slide's original formatting instead of applying the current presentation's theme, click to activate the Keep Source Formatting check box.

> **TIP** To get a closer look at a slide, hover the mouse pointer over the slide's thumbnail.

Figure 9.11
You can use the Reuse
Slides task pane to add
slides from another pre-
sentation.

6. Click the slide you want to reuse. PowerPoint inserts the slide into your presentation.

7. Repeat steps 4–6 for any other slides you want to reuse.

8. Click the Close button (X) in the Reuse Slides task pane.

These techniques are fine if you want to reuse slides from your own presentations. However, what if you want to reuse slides from other people's presentations or make your slides available to other people? For example, your company might require a standard opening or closing slide or a slide with a legal disclaimer. In these cases, you'll want to have the most up-to-date versions of the slides available to a wide group of people. Similarly, you may work with a department or with a project team, and the members of that department or team may require access to common slides.

One solution is to store those slides in one or more presentations and then place those files on shared network folders. However, this works only for network users who have permission to access that folder. Also it seems wasteful to have to open or access an entire presentation when you need only a single slide.

If your company's intranet runs SharePoint Server 2007 or SharePoint Services 2007, you can use a *slide library*. This is a special folder on the SharePoint site that's designed to store individual slides. Users who can access the SharePoint site can then reuse those slides in their presentations.

Here are the steps to follow to publish one or more slides to a slide library:

1. Open the presentation that contains the slide or slides you want to publish.

2. Choose Office, P̲ublish, Publish S̲lides. PowerPoint displays the Publish Slides dialog box shown in Figure 9.12.

Figure 9.12
Use the Publish Slides dialog box to choose the slides you want to publish and the location of the SharePoint slide library.

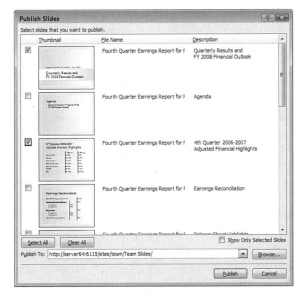

3. Click to activate the check box for each slide you want to publish.

4. In the P̲ublish To text box, type the address of the slide library on the SharePoint site.

5. Click Publish. If your SharePoint site requires a login, the Connect dialog box displays.

6. Type your user name and password and then click OK. PowerPoint publishes the selected slides to the slide library.

After you have saved at least one slide to the slide library, you can then reuse slides from that library in your presentations. Earlier, when you opened the Reuse Slides task pane, you may have noticed that it included an Open a Slide Library link. As you might have guessed by now, the Reuse Slides task pane is your ticket to reusing slides from the SharePoint library. Here are the steps to follow:

1. Choose the Home tab, click the lower half of the New Slide split button, and then click Reuse Slides. PowerPoint displays the Reuse Slides task pane.

2. Use the Insert Slide From text box to type the address of the SharePoint site's slide library and then click the Go (->) button. PowerPoint connects to the SharePoint site and then displays a list of published slides.

3. In the Navigation pane, click the slide below which you want to insert the slide.

4. If you want PowerPoint to keep the reused slide's original formatting instead of applying the current presentation's theme, click to activate the Keep Source Formatting check box.

5. If you want PowerPoint to let you know when someone else has modified the slide, click to activate the Tell Me When This Slide Changes check box.

6. Click the slide you want to reuse. PowerPoint inserts the slide into your presentation.

7. Repeat steps 4–6 for any other slides you want to reuse.

8. Click the Close button (X) in the Reuse Slides task pane.

> **NOTE** If you activate the Tell Me When This Slide Changes check box when you insert a slide, you can later check for an updated version of the slide. In the Navigation pane, right-click the slide in the Slides tab, click Check for Updates, and then click Check This Slide for Changes.

> **NOTE** You can also reuse a slide directly from the SharePoint site's slide library. This is useful for large slide libraries because the browser window is larger than the Reuse Slides pane, to let you see more slides, get a better view of the slide properties (including the slide's name and description), and even edit those properties.
>
> Log on to the SharePoint site, click the link to the slide library, and then click to activate the check box beside each slide you want to send to PowerPoint. Click the Copy Slide to Presentation button, choose whether you want the slides to display in a new presentation or in an open presentation, and then click OK.

Converting a Slide into an Image

If you have a slide that contains a lot of interesting information or that has content that fits well with other material you have, you might want to display that slide in a document you create in another application, or perhaps add it to a Web page. There's isn't a direct way to embed a PowerPoint slide in another document. However, there's a trick you can use to make a copy of the slide as a graphics file, which you can then paste into any document that accepts images, or you can display it on a Web page. Here are the steps to follow:

1. Display the slide you want to convert to an image.

2. Choose View, Notes Page. PowerPoint switches to the Notes Page view.

3. Right-click the slide image and then click <u>S</u>ave as Picture, as shown in Figure 9.13. PowerPoint displays the Save As Picture dialog box.

Figure 9.13
In the Notes Page view, right-click the slide and then click Save as Picture.

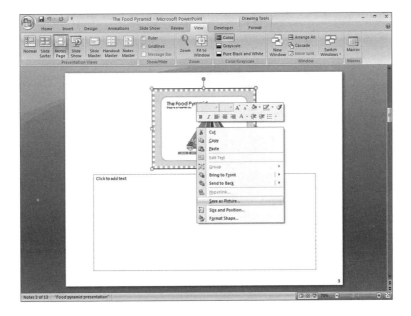

4. Select a folder for the image file and type a File <u>N</u>ame.

5. In the Save as <u>T</u>ype list, click the graphic file format you want to use.

> **TIP**
>
> The file type you choose depends on whether the slide uses complex colors, special effects, or even a photo. In that case, you can maintain high-image quality by selecting Tag Image File Format (TIFF) in the Save as Type list. If you want to use the slide image on a Web page or send it as an e-mail attachment, select JPEG File Interchange Format in the Save as Type list instead. This compresses the image for easier downloading.

6. Click <u>S</u>ave. PowerPoint saves the slide as a graphic file.

Creating a Summary Slide with a Macro

Previous versions of PowerPoint come with a Summary Slide feature that creates a slide titled "Summary Slide" at the end of the presentation, and, for each selected slide, it includes a bullet with the slide title. It is a handy and easy method for creating a bare-bones summary of your presentation.

Alas, that feature is not included in PowerPoint 2007. Not to worry, though, because the VBA procedure shown in Listing 9.3 performs the same function. Before running this procedure, use the Navigation pane or Slide Sorter view to select the slides that you want to include in the summary.

Listing 9.3   A VBA Procedure that Creates a Summary Slide from the Titles of the Selected Slides

```vba
Public Sub CreateSummarySlide()
    Dim objSlide As Slide
    Dim objShape As Shape
    Dim strSlideTitle As String
    Dim strSummary As String
    Dim nVerticalTabPos As Integer
    '
    ' Gather all titles by running through the selected slides
    '
    For Each objSlide In ActiveWindows.Selection.SlideRange
        strSlideTitle = ""
        '
        ' Run through all the shapes on the slide
        '
        For Each objShape In objSlide.Shapes
            '
            ' Does it have a text frame?
            '
            If objShape.HasTextFrame Then
                '
                ' If so, save the text for the summary
                '
                strSlideTitle = objShape.TextFrame.TextRange.Text
                '
                ' Does the text include a vertical tab (ASCII 11)?
                '
                nVerticalTabPos = InStr(strSlideTitle, Chr(11))
                '
                ' If so, strip out the vertical tab and
                ' everything that comes after it
                '
                If nVerticalTabPos <> 0 Then
                    strSlideTitle = Left(strSlideTitle,nVerticalTabPos-1)
                End If
                '
                ' We have the title for this slide, so exit
                '
                Exit For
```

```
            End If
        Next 'objShape
        '
        ' Did we get a title for this slide?
        '
        If strSlideTitle = "" Then
            '
            ' If not, just use the slide name
            '
            strSlideTitle = objSlide.Name
        End If
        '
        ' Append the slide title to the summary text
        '
        strSummary = strSummary & strSlideTitle & vbCrLf
    Next 'objSlide
    '
    ' Create and populate the summary slide
    '
    With ActivePresentation.Slides
        '
        ' Create a new slide at the end of the presentation
        '
        .Add Index:=.Count + 1, Layout:=ppLayoutText
        '
        ' Add the text
        '
        With ActivePresentation.Slides(.Count)
            '
            ' Add the title
            '
            .Shapes(1).TextFrame.TextRange.Text = "Summary"
            '
            ' Add the summary text
            '
            .Shapes(2).TextFrame.TextRange.Text = strSummary
        End With
    End With
End Sub
```

The procedure begins with a For Each...Next loop that runs through the selected slides in the active window. A second For Each...Next loop runs through the shapes in the current slide. For each shape, the procedure tests the HasTextFrame property: If it returns True, then the shape's text is stored in the strSlideTitle variable. Some slide titles include multiline text, and some slides don't have titles at all, but just bullets, which are also multiline text. In both cases, we want the summary to show just the first line of the text. To strip out everything else, the code looks for the vertical tab character (ASCII 11), which is what PowerPoint uses to create separate lines of text. After that's done, we have the text we want for the summary, so the code exits the second For Each...Next loop. Just in case you come across a slide that has no text (you should exclude such slides from your selection), the code checks to see if strSlideTitle is still empty. If so, the code just sets it to the name of the slide.

Now that we have the summary text, the code adds a new Title and Content slide to the end of the presentation, sets the Title placeholder text to Summary, and sets the Content placeholder text to the summary string. Figure 9.14 shows an example of a summary slide this procedure creates.

Figure 9.14
A summary page created by the VBA procedure shown in this section.

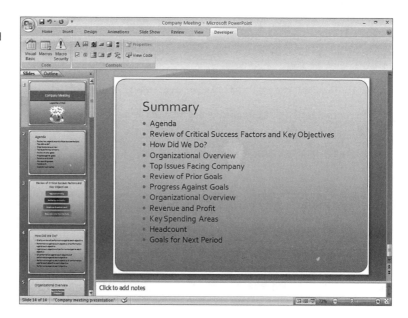

Using Word to Custom Format Handouts

You can create simple handouts in PowerPoint to go along with your presentations. However, if you want to spruce up the handouts, you need the more powerful text and paragraph formatting available in Word. Here are the steps to follow to export your handouts to Word so that you can format the text:

1. In PowerPoint, choose Office, Publish, Create Handouts in Microsoft Office Word. The Send To Microsoft Office Word dialog box displays, as shown in Figure 9.15.

2. Click the page layout you want to use.

3. Activate the Paste Link option.

4. Click OK. The presentation displays in Word.

5. Add, edit, and format your handout text.

Figure 9.15
Use this dialog box to configure the page layout of the presentation handouts that you create in Word.

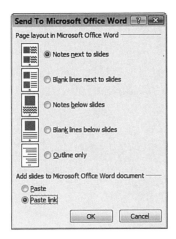

From Here

- For some Word formatting tricks that you can use with your PowerPoint handouts, **see** "Formatting Tricks," **p. 35**.
- To learn how to animate individual bullets, **see** "Making Bullets Appear Individually," **p. 257**.
- To learn some tricks related to animation in PowerPoint, **see** "Animation Tricks," **p. 249**.
- To learn some tricks related to running a slide show, **see** "Slide Show Tricks," **p. 275**.

9

Animation Tricks

For many people, a presentation just isn't complete until they have added slide transitions and other animated effects. These can certainly pump up the wow factor in your work, and any presentation that seeks the knockout adjective had better incorporate some animation into its design. But animation is a complex business, and without a few tricks up your sleeve, even an Office guru can ruin his presentation by blowing the animation stage. This section helps you prevent that fate by showing you a number of advanced but useful tricks and techniques not only for doing animation well, but for getting the most out of this powerful PowerPoint feature.

Before you get to the tricks and techniques, it's worth taking a second to put this animation business into some perspective. After all, advanced knowledge of animation is one thing, but putting that knowledge to good use is another. Here are some dos and don'ts to bear in mind when adding the animation touches to your presentations:

- Do use transitions. They add visual interest, give the audience short breaks between slides, and help you control the pace of your presentation.

- Don't overuse transitions. Nobody objects to fade-ins, dissolves, and other simple transitions, but don't have multiple objects flying in from all corners of the screen.

- Do keep your audience in mind when planning your animations. In a flashy presentation for sales and marketing types, you can probably get away with more elaborate animations; in a no-nonsense presentation to board members or bankers, animations and transitions should be short and sweet.

- Don't use a number of different transitions and animations in a single presentation. Just as your slide text looks awful if you use too many fonts, your presentations can look amateurish if you throw every effect in the book at your audience.

- Do keep your animations snappy, particularly transition effects. It might not seem like a long time, but if your slide transitions are taking 10 or 15 seconds or longer, your audience's mood can degenerate from frustration to anger to outright hostility. Unless your presentation is for kids (who, naturally, prefer elaborate animations), the transition from one slide to another should never take more than a few seconds.

- Don't overshadow your content. The goal of any animation is to highlight a slide element or keep up your audience's interest. If you start adding effects just for fun, I guarantee your audience will *stop* having fun and will look for the nearest exit.

Now on to the tricks....

Applying a Custom Sound to a Transition

A *transition* is a visual (and sometimes auditory) effect that plays during the switch from one slide to another. The most common transition is a fade, where the next slide begins as a black screen and then gradually displays. Similarly, in a push transition it appears as though the slide is being pushed onto the screen. PowerPoint 2007 comes with more than 50 preset transitions, and you can see them when you choose the Animations tab and click the More button in the Transition to This Slide group. Hover the mouse pointer over a transition, and PowerPoint demonstrates the effect on the current slide.

Most transitions occur silently, and that's as it should be for the vast majority of presentations. However, there are times when you want a sound effect to accompany a particular transition, such as:

- A slide that announces a major new product or service might transition with a drum roll.

- A transition to a slide containing a photo might be accompanied by a camera shutter that clicks.

- The transition to the last slide in the presentation might merit an applause effect (if only to encourage your audience to follow suit).

- A presentation to young children might add a variety of sound effects—chimes, explosions, lasers, wind, and so on—to keep the youngsters engaged.

PowerPoint 2007 comes with nearly 20 built-in transition sounds, including Applause, Camera, Drum Roll, Explosion, Laser, and Wind. On the Animations tab, pull down the Transition Sound list to select the sound effect you want to use.

If none of the ready-to-run sound effects suit your needs, PowerPoint also enables you to specify a custom sound effect, which needs to be a sound file in the WAV format.

10

Here are the steps to follow to apply a custom sound effect to a slide transition:

1. Navigate to the slide with which you want to work. (If you want to apply the transition to multiple slides, select those slides using either the Navigation pane or the Slide Sorter view.)

2. Choose Animations, click the More button in the Transition to This Slide group, and then click the transition effect you want to use. (Note that this step is optional; you can add a transition sound effect without also using a transition visual effect.)

3. Choose Transition Sound, Other Sound. PowerPoint displays the Add Sound dialog box.

4. Click the sound file you want to use.

5. Click OK.

6. If you want PowerPoint to keep playing the sound effect until the next sound effect begins, choose Transition Sound, Loop Until Next Sound.

CAUTION

Be careful with the Loop Until Next Sound command. This feature is best used with an enjoyable piece of music that loops smoothly or with an effect that requires a bit of time to unfold, such as a ticking clock. In most other cases, the constant noise will, at best, drive your audience to distraction (or, at worst, to thoughts of harming the presenter).

TIP

While you present, if you have a long (or looped) sound effect playing and you want it to stop, quickly press **W** twice in succession. This toggles the slide show's white screen on and off, but it also serves to stop the sound effect. (Toggling the white screen on and off works best with presentations that use a white or light background. If your presentation uses a black or dark background, press **B** twice to toggle the black screen on and off.)

Creating a Custom Animation

A transition is a visual (or auditory) effect applied to the entire slide and ends after the entire slide is displayed. By contrast, an *animation* is a visual effect applied to a specific slide object, such as the slide title, the bullet text, or an object such as an image or chart. For example, one highly useful (and so highly requested) visual effect is to display bullet points one at a time. To set that up, you create a custom animation that applies a visual effect to each bullet point.

➔ To learn the specific steps required to animate bullets one-by-one, **see** "Making Bullets Display Individually," **p. 257**

You build a custom animation by adding *effects* to one or more slide elements. An effect is a visual flourish applied to the element. PowerPoint supports four types of effects:

- **Entrance**—These effects determine how the slide element enters the slide. Normally, each slide element displays immediately along with the rest of the slide. If you add an entrance effect to an element, however, the element displays after the slide, and usually it does not display until after you click the mouse. PowerPoint has nearly 50 different entrance effects.

- **Emphasis**—These effects enable you to emphasize an element by changing certain properties of the text. PowerPoint has 30 different emphasis effects, and they include applying bold or underline formats, changing the font size, adding color, and flashing the text.

- **Exit**—These effects determine how the slide element leaves the slide. These effects run when you navigate to the next slide. PowerPoint offers more than 50 exit effects.

- **Motion Paths**—These effects determine the path that the slide element follows when it enters the slide. The more than 60 motion paths offered by PowerPoint include geometric figures such as diamonds and trapezoids, various curves, and special paths such as a figure 8. You can also define a custom motion path by drawing it yourself.

The next few sections take you through specific examples of custom animation. For now, here are the general steps to follow to create a custom animation:

1. Select the slide with which you want to work. (Although you can apply a transition to multiple slides, a custom animation requires that you work with only one slide at a time.)

> **TIP** If you want to apply a custom animation to a specific object in all your slides—for example, the title—select View, Slide Master, and then apply the animation to an object on the Slide Master.

2. Choose Animations, Custom Animation. PowerPoint displays the Custom Animation pane.

3. Select the slide element or elements that you want to animate. Note that you can apply animations to any object, including the title and text placeholders, individual bullets (select the bullet text), and objects such as text boxes, shapes, clip art, pictures, and SmartArt diagrams.

4. Click Add Effect and then select one of the four effects categories described earlier: Entrance, Emphasis, Exit, or Motion Paths. PowerPoint displays a few examples of the effects in the category you choose.

5. If you see the effect you want, click it and skip to Step 8. Otherwise, click More Effects to see the complete list of effects in that category. For example, Figure 10.1 shows the Add Entrance Effect dialog box, which lists the available effects for the Entrance category.

Figure 10.1
Click More Effects to see
the full list of effects in
the selected category.

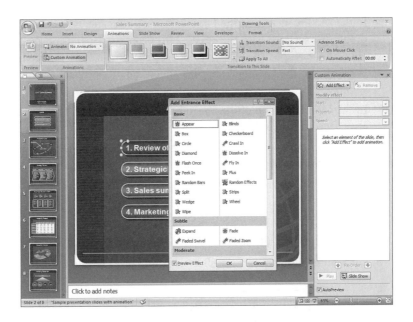

6. Click an effect. If you have the Preview Effect check box activated (this is the default),
   PowerPoint temporarily applies the effect to the selected element.

7. When you have selected the effect you want, click OK. PowerPoint adds the effect to
   the Custom Animation pane and previews the effect.

8. In the Modify section of the Custom Animation pane, use the Start list to determine
   how the effect begins. You have three choices:

   - **On Click**—This option means that PowerPoint runs the animation when you
     click the mouse. (The effects run in order; that is, the first effect runs when you
     first click the mouse, the second effect runs when you click a second time, and
     so on).

   - **With Previous**—This option means that the current effect runs simultaneously
     with the previous effect.

   - **After Previous**—This option means that the current effect runs immediately
     after the previous effect is done.

> **TIP**
>
> If you choose After Previous, you can control the amount of time between the end of the previous
> effect and the start of the current effect. Click the current effect's drop-down list, click Timing, and
> then use the Delay spin button to specify the time interval, in seconds.

9. In the Modify section of the Custom Animation pane, use the middle list to change the property associated with the effect. This property depends on the effect. For the Fly In effect, for example, the property is Direction (From Bottom, From Left, and so on). Similarly, for the Change Font Size effect, the property is Font Size (Tiny, Huge, and so on).

10. In the Modify section of the Custom Animation pane, use the Speed list to select a relative speed for the effect (Very Slow, Slow, Medium, Fast, or Very Fast).

11. To change the order in which the effects occur, select the effect and then use the Re-Order arrows to move the object up or down in the animation order.

12. Repeat steps 3–11 to apply animation effects to other elements on the slide.

To view the animation, you have two choices:

- Click Play to play all the animations without interaction.
- Click Slide Show to start the slide show and play the animations with interaction.

10

> **TIP**
>
> Custom animations apply to only one slide. If you are creating a complex animation for an object such as a slide title, PowerPoint does not offer a direct way to apply the animation to a title on a different slide. You can work around this limitation by copying the animated slide element, navigating to the other slide, and then pasting the slide element. The pasted object includes the animation, so you can now copy the text from the unanimated object and then paste it into the animated object.

Figure 10.2 shows a slide with various custom animation effects applied. Notice the numbers attached to some of the slide objects. These numbers represent the slide's animation order. That is, when you click once, the animation effect runs for the objects with a 1 next to them; when you click a second time, the animation runs for the objects labeled with 2, and so on. Note also that each effect has a drop-down list. You can use that list to change various options related to the effect.

The sections that follow take you through some specific examples of custom animations.

→ PowerPoint doesn't include animations when it converts a presentation to a Web page file. If you want the animations included in your Web page, **see** "Enabling Animations on the Web," **p. 296**

These numbers represent the
slide's animation order

Click the drop-down arrow
to see the effect's options

Figure 10.2
A slide with a custom
animation added.

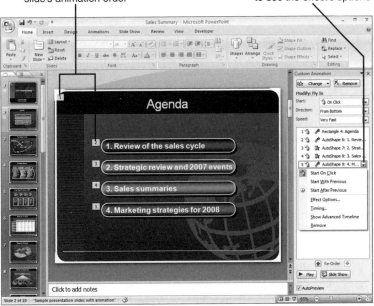

Using Triggers to Display and Hide a Slide Object

In a typical animation, you click anywhere on the slide and PowerPoint applies the effect
to the object associated with the animation. However, it's also possible to set up the animation so that you have to click a particular object on the screen to initiate the effect for the
animated element. The object you click to launch another object's animation is called a
trigger. For example, you can put a shape in the corner of the slide and set it up as a trigger
so that the slide's bullet points run their entrance effect only when you click that shape.

There are many uses for triggers. For example, in an interactive kiosk presentation that
presents educational material, you can set things up so that a slide displays only certain
material or moves on to the next slide only if the user clicks the "correct" part of the slide,
which you've set up as a trigger. However, my favorite use for triggers is to help overcome
an annoying limitation inherent in PowerPoint animations. That is, there's no easy way to
repeat an animation; when you click the slide, the animation runs, and that's it. Yes, you
can apply multiple effects to the same element, but that just gets messy, particularly when
your other animated elements are on the same slide.

A good example that illustrates the usefulness of repeating animation is a slide in which
you want to show both text and a large image. A typical slide isn't likely big enough to
show both at once, so you add two effects to the image: an entrance effect and an exit
effect. This lets you click once to display the image when you're ready for it and then click
again to remove the image when you are done with it. Of course, as soon as the image is

gone, an audience member asks to see it again. Unfortunately, with regular animation effects, the only way to do that is to move back to the previous slide, navigate ahead to the current slide, and run the animations from the beginning. This is not very professional, to say the least.

Fortunately you can easily overcome this kind of problem by setting up a trigger to run the effect. You can click the trigger anytime you like, and PowerPoint will repeat the effect. For something like the image animation, you can set up one trigger to show the image and a second trigger to make it disappear.

Here are the steps to follow to configure a slide object with two triggers—one to display it and one to hide it:

1. On the slide containing the element you want to animate, insert the objects you want to use as triggers. Good trigger candidates are shapes because you can add text to them.

2. Click the element you want to animate and then add the first effect (for example, an Entrance effect).

3. Drop down the first effect's list and then click <u>T</u>iming. The effect's dialog box displays (for example, if you're working with the Fly In effect, you see the Fly In dialog box).

4. In the Timing tab, click <u>T</u>riggers, then click Start effect on <u>c</u>lick of, and then use the associated list to click the object that you want to use as a trigger for the effect. If the object includes text, PowerPoint shows that text along with the object's name, as shown in Figure 10.3. Click OK. PowerPoint adds the trigger to the list of effects.

Figure 10.3
Use the Timing tab to set up another object as a trigger for the effect.

5. Click the element you want to animate and then add the second effect (for example, an Exit effect).

6. Drop down the second effect's list and then click <u>T</u>iming. The effect's dialog box displays.

7. Repeat Step 4 to assign a different trigger to the second effect.

Figure 10.4 shows a slide with some text obscured behind a large image. The slide also includes two Rounded Rectangle shapes used as triggers. Clicking View Map displays the image; clicking Hide Map hides the image.

Figure 10.4
The View Map and Hide Map shapes are triggers that display and hide the large image.

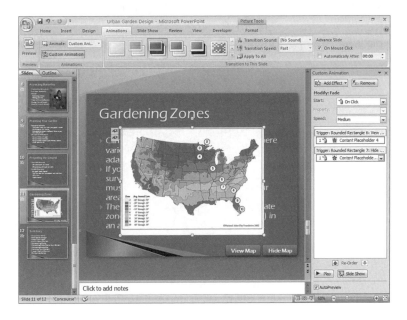

Making Bullets Display Individually

When you apply an entrance effect to a placeholder that contains bullets, PowerPoint does not create a single effect for the entire placeholder. Instead, it sets up several sub-effects according to the following rules:

- Each first-level bullet gets its own effect.
- Each second-level bullet gets the same effect as its corresponding first-level bullet.

To make this clearer, take a look at the slide shown in Figure 10.5. The first main bullet (The importance of sunlight) has a 1 beside it, meaning that it displays with the first mouse click. The second main bullet (Keep a "light journal") has a 2 next to i it, meaning that it displays with the second mouse click. Notice, however, that the second bullet's sub-bullets also have 2s next to them. This means that when you click the second time, you see not only the second bullet, but also its sub-bullets. The fourth main bullet (Using light to pick plants) is set up the same way.

Click to expand the effect's contents

Figure 10.5
When you apply an effect to a bullet place-holder, bullets and sub-bullets get the same number in the animation order.

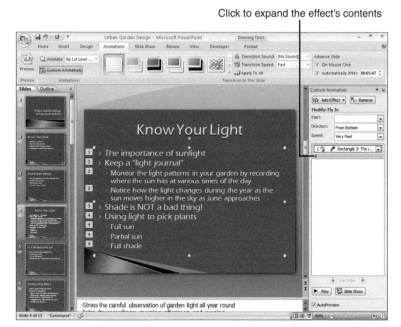

It's nice that PowerPoint applies separate animation effects to the main bullets, but you might prefer that the sub-bullets display one at a time. This gives you extra control not only over the timing of each bullet's entrance, but also over the various effects. Here are just a few ideas you can implement by animating bullets individually:

- You can prevent audience members from looking ahead to bullets that come after the one you are discussing. Delivering a presentation is about telling a story; you don't want people to get ahead of your tale.

- You can maintain suspense if you present the bullets in a special order. For example, if you announce contest prizewinners, you can start with the runners-up and work your way up to the winner.

- You can maximize the "wow" factor. If your slide contains a major result, a break-through, or a surprise announcement, you can hold off on that part of the slide until you are ready to unleash it on your audience.

- You can increase visual interest by applying a different effect to each bullet. Again, however, you want to judge your audience and your material here. There just aren't that many situations where five or six different entrance effects are required or appreci-ated. The key, always, is to avoid animation overload.

> **TIP**
> In some cases, you might want the bullets in a placeholder to display at the same time. To do this, click inside the placeholder and then select every bullet. When you then apply your animation effect, PowerPoint applies a single effect to the entire text. When you click during the presentation, all of the bullets enter the presentation at the same time.

Follow these steps to create separate effects for bullets that PowerPoint has grouped into a single effect:

1. Click the placeholder containing the animated bullets.
2. In the Custom Animation pane, click the Expand Contents button (two downward pointing arrows; see Figure 10.5). PowerPoint displays all of the bullets, as shown in Figure 10.6.

Objects with a mouse icon are animated one by one when you click the mouse

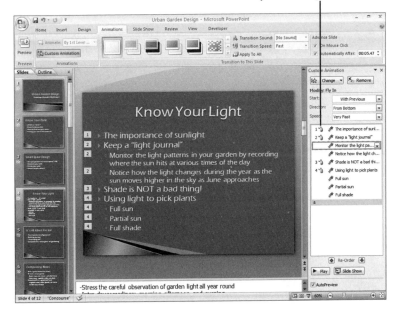

Figure 10.6
After you apply an effect to the entire placeholder, expand the contents to see each bullet.

3. Click a bullet with which you want to work.
4. To change the animation effect for the bullet, click Change, select an effect category, and then select the effect you want.
5. In the Start list, select On Click. PowerPoint renumbers the animation order.
6. Customize the other effect settings as needed.
7. Repeat steps 3–6 to configure the animation for each bullet.

> **NOTE** It's usually easiest to apply an effect to an entire placeholder and then modify each bullet, as described in this section. However, if you want to use different animations for each bullet, it's usually easier to work with the bullets one by one from the start. To apply a custom animation to a bullet, select the bullet text, click Add Effect, and then select the effect you want.

Animating Chart Elements

If you use charts in your presentations, you can animate the components of the chart. Depending on the chart, you have up to five animation possibilities:

- **As one object**—Animates the entire chart.
- **By series**—Animates each data series individually. For example, if you have a bar chart that shows quarterly sales figures by region, you can display the bars one quarter at a time.
- **By category**—Animates each data category individually. For example, if you have a bar chart that shows quarterly sales figures by region, you can display the bars one region at a time.
- **By element in series element**—Animates each data marker in each series one marker at a time. For example, if you have a bar chart that shows quarterly sales figures by region, you can display the bars for each region one quarter at a time.
- **By element in category**—Animates each data marker in each category one marker at a time. For example, if you have a bar chart that shows quarterly sales figures by region, you can display the bars for each quarter one region at a time.

Follow these steps to animate a PowerPoint chart object:

1. Select the chart object.
2. Choose Animations, Custom Animation.
3. Click Add Effect, click an effect category, and then select the animation effect you want.
4. In the animation list, drop down the chart animation's menu and then click Effect Options. PowerPoint displays a dialog box of options for the effect.
5. Click the Chart Animation tab.
6. In the Group chart list (see Figure 10.7), click the animation option you want.
7. If you choose an animation option other than As One Object, PowerPoint enables the Start Animation By Drawing the Chart Background check box. If you want the chart background to be the item that displays when you first click the mouse, leave this check box activated. If you prefer that the chart background display on the slide before you start the chart animation, deactivate this check box.
8. Click OK.

Figure 10.7
Use the list in the Chart Animation tab to select the chart components to animate.

Animating an Organization Chart

If you use SmartArt organization charts in your presentations, you can animate the charts to display the hierarchy in various ways:

- **As one object**—Animates the entire chart.
- **All at once**—Animates all the positions at once, with slightly different timing for each position.
- **By branch one by one**—Animates each position in each branch one position at a time.
- **By level at once**—Animates all the positions in each level, one level at a time.
- **By level one by one**—Animates each position in each level one position at a time.

Here are the steps to follow to animate a SmartArt organization chart:

1. Insert the SmartArt organization chart into a PowerPoint slide. (Choose Insert, SmartArt, click Hierarchy, click Organization Chart icon, and then click OK.)
2. Select the organization chart object.
3. Choose Animations, Custom Animation.
4. Click Add Effect, choose an effect category, and then choose the animation effect you want.
5. In the animation list, drop down the organization chart effect's menu and then click Effect Options. PowerPoint displays a dialog box of options for the effect.
6. Display the SmartArt Animation tab.
7. In the Group Graphic list (see Figure 10.8), click the animation option you want.
8. If you choose an animation option other than As One Object, PowerPoint enables the Reverse Order check box. Activate this check box to animate the organization chart elements in reverse (that is, from the lowest elements to the highest).
9. Click OK.

Figure 10.8
Use the list in the SmartArt Animation tab to select the organization chart components to animate.

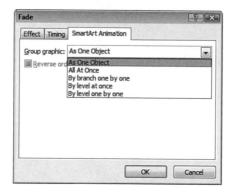

Uncovering Parts of an Image, One at a Time

In Chapter 9, "Slide and Presentation Tricks," I present a technique that enables you to hide a Slide Master object on a single slide by covering it with a rectangle shape that has a fill that matches the slide background. You can use a similar technique to hide different parts of an image, and you can then use animation to uncover each part one at a time.

→ To learn the technique for hiding Slide Master objects, **see** "Hiding a Slide Master Object On One Slide," **p. 235**

For example, your graphics department might have come up with an image split into, say, four quadrants with a sales result, product image, or contest winner in each quadrant. PowerPoint doesn't have a feature that can break up an image into parts that you can animate separately. (The exception is clip art, which you can ungroup into its component parts; see "Animating Separate Elements of a Clip Art Image," next.) However, by covering the image with rectangles or other shapes formatted to look like the slide background, you can apply animation to those shapes to get the effect you want. This technique works best with a slide that has a solid-color background or a texture.

Here are the steps to follow:

1. Choose Insert, Shapes and then click the shape you want to use to hide part of the image (this is the Rectangle in most cases).

2. Draw the shape on the slide so that it covers the part of the image you want to hide.

3. Choose Format, Shape Fill, and then click the color that matches the slide's background color. If the background uses a texture, click Texture and then click the appropriate texture in the gallery that displays.

4. Choose Format, Shape Outline, No Outline.

5. Choose Animations, Custom Animation.

6. Choose Add Effect, Exit, and then select the exit effect you want the shape to use.

7. Repeat steps 1–6 to add more shapes that cover the other parts of the image.

8. In the Custom Animation pane, use the Re-Order arrows to move the shape animations into the order that you want the image uncovered.

Animating Separate Elements of a Clip Art Image

In the previous section, you learned how to hide different parts of an image and then uncover them one at a time using separate exit effects. This was necessary because PowerPoint doesn't have a feature that lets you animate portions of an image. If you use clip art, however, it *is* possible to apply animation effects to different parts of the drawing. This is made possible by the fact that most clip art images are actually composed of many separate shapes. In a drawing of a building, for example, the background, exterior shell, windows, and doors might be separate images. These are grouped together to form a single image, but in most cases, you can ungroup the clip art to work with its component shapes directly. For example, you can give each shape a different entrance effect so that the clip art image appears to assemble itself on-the-fly when you click to activate the animation.

Here are the steps to follow to ungroup a clip art image and to apply animation effects to the component shapes:

1. Choose Insert, Clip Art, use the Clip Art pane to search for and insert the image you want, and then click Close (X) to remove the Clip Art pane.

2. With the clip art image selected, choose Format, pull down the Group menu (it's in the Arrange group), and then click <u>U</u>ngroup.

3. In most cases, PowerPoint will ask you if you want to convert the image to a Microsoft Office drawing object. If so, click <u>Y</u>es.

4. If PowerPoint has to convert the image to a Microsoft Office drawing object, repeat Step 2 to ungroup the drawing object. PowerPoint separates out the various shapes and selects them.

5. Choose Animations, Custom Animation to display the Custom Animation task pane.

6. Choose Add Effect, select an effect category, and then select an effect. PowerPoint applies the effect to every shape.

7. Use the Custom Animation pane to apply a different effect property to each shape. For example, if you applied the Fly In effect, use the Direction list to apply a variety of directions to the shapes: From Bottom, From Left, From Top-Right, and so on.

8. If you want the shapes to run at the same time (this is the default), click any shape effect in the Custom Animation pane, press Ctrl+A to select all of the shapes, and then use the Start list to choose With Previous.

If there's a downside to this technique, it's that some clip art images contain *dozens* of component shapes. Tweaking each shape by hand to vary the effects becomes a chore. A better idea in this case it to use a VBA macro to assign effects randomly.

PowerPoint VBA comes with a number of `PpEntryEffect` constants that represent the different types of entry effects. Table 10.1 lists these constants, their numeric values, and the effects they produce.

> **NOTE**
> VBA's `PpEntryEffect` constants are a quirky group. Some of them—such as Cover and Uncover—don't correspond with entrance effects in the PowerPoint interface. There also seems to be quite a few missing. For example, the Circle effect has an Out direction but not an In direction, and there are no constants for effects such as Expand, Float, and Sling.

Table 10.1   VBA's `PpEntryEffect` Constants

Name	Value	General Effect	Property
ppEffectAppear	3844	Appear	
ppEffectBlindsHorizontal	769	Blinds	Horizontal
ppEffectBlindsVertical	770	Blinds	Vertical
ppEffectBoxOut	3073	Box	Out
ppEffectBoxIn	3074	Box	In
ppEffectCheckerboardAcross	1025	Checkerboard	Across
ppEffectCheckerboardDown	1026	Checkerboard	Down
ppEffectCircleOut	3845	Circle	Out
ppEffectCombHorizontal	3847	Comb	Horizontal
ppEffectCombVertical	3848	Comb	Vertical
ppEffectCoverLeft	1281	Cover	Left
ppEffectCoverUp	1282	Cover	Up
ppEffectCoverRight	1283	Cover	Right
ppEffectCoverDown	1284	Cover	Down
ppEffectCoverLeftUp	1285	Cover	Left Up
ppEffectCoverRightUp	1286	Cover	Right Up
ppEffectCoverLeftDown	1287	Cover	Left Down
ppEffectCoverRightDown	1288	Cover	Right Down
ppEffectCrawlFromLeft	3341	Crawl	From Left
ppEffectCrawlFromUp	3342	Crawl	From Up
ppEffectCrawlFromRight	3343	Crawl	From Right
ppEffectCrawlFromDown	3344	Crawl	From Down
ppEffectCut	257	Cut	
ppEffectCutThroughBlack	258	Cut	Through Black
ppEffectDiamondOut	3846	Diamond	Out
ppEffectDissolve	1537	Dissolve	

Name	Value	General Effect	Property
ppEffectFade	1793	Fade	
ppEffectFadeSmoothly	3849	Fade	Smoothly
ppEffectFlashOnceFast	3841	Flash	Once Fast
ppEffectFlashOnceMedium	3842	Flash	Once Medium
ppEffectFlashOnceSlow	3843	Flash	Once Slow
ppEffectFlyFromLeft	3329	Fly In	From Left
ppEffectFlyFromTop	3330	Fly In	From Top
ppEffectFlyFromRight	3331	Fly In	From Right
ppEffectFlyFromBottom	3332	Fly In	From Bottom
ppEffectFlyFromTopLeft	3333	Fly In	From Top Left
ppEffectFlyFromTopRight	3334	Fly In	From Top Right
ppEffectFlyFromBottomLeft	3335	Fly In	From Bottom Left
ppEffectFlyFromBottomRight	3336	Fly In	From Bottom Right
ppEffectMixed	–2	Mixed	
ppEffectNewsflash	3850	Newsflash	
ppEffectNone	0	None	
ppEffectPeekFromLeft	3337	Peek	From Left
ppEffectPeekFromDown	3338	Peek	From Down
ppEffectPeekFromRight	3339	Peek	From Right
ppEffectPeekFromUp	3340	Peek	From Up
ppEffectPlusOut	3851	Plus	Out
ppEffectPushDown	3852	Push	Down
ppEffectPushLeft	3853	Push	Left
ppEffectPushRight	3854	Push	Right
ppEffectPushUp	3855	Push	Up
ppEffectRandom	513	Random	
ppEffectRandomBarsHorizontal	2305	Random Bars	Horizontal
ppEffectRandomBarsVertical	2306	Random Bars	Vertical
ppEffectSpiral	3357	Spiral	
ppEffectSplitHorizontalOut	3585	Split	Horizontal Out
ppEffectSplitHorizontalIn	3586	Split	Horizontal In
ppEffectSplitVerticalOut	3587	Split	Vertical Out

continues

10

Table 10.1 Continued

Name	Value	General Effect	Property
ppEffectSplitVerticalIn	3588	Split	Vertical In
ppEffectStretchAcross	3351	Stretch	Across
ppEffectStretchLeft	3352	Stretch	Left
ppEffectStretchUp	3353	Stretch	Up
ppEffectStretchRight	3354	Stretch	Right
ppEffectStretchDown	3355	Stretch	Down
ppEffectStripsUpLeft	2561	Strips	Up Left
ppEffectStripsUpRight	2562	Strips	Up Right
ppEffectStripsDownLeft	2563	Strips	Down Left
ppEffectStripsDownRight	2564	Strips	Down Right
ppEffectStripsLeftUp	2565	Strips	Left Up
ppEffectStripsRightUp	2566	Strips	Right Up
ppEffectStripsLeftDown	2567	Strips	Left Down
ppEffectStripsRightDown	2568	Strips	Right Down
ppEffectSwivel	3356	Swivel	
ppEffectUncoverLeft	2049	Uncover	Left
ppEffectUncoverUp	2050	Uncover	Up
ppEffectUncoverRight	2051	Uncover	Right
ppEffectUncoverDown	2052	Uncover	Down
ppEffectUncoverLeftUp	2053	Uncover	Left Up
ppEffectUncoverRightUp	2054	Uncover	Right Up
ppEffectUncoverLeftDown	2055	Uncover	Left Down
ppEffectUncoverRightDown	2056	Uncover	Right Down
ppEffectWedge	3856	Wedge	
ppEffectWheel1Spoke	3857	Wheel	1 Spoke
ppEffectWheel2Spokes	3858	Wheel	2 Spokes
ppEffectWheel3Spokes	3859	Wheel	3 Spokes
ppEffectWheel4Spokes	3860	Wheel	4 Spokes
ppEffectWheel8Spokes	3861	Wheel	8 Spokes
ppEffectWipeLeft	2817	Wipe	Left
ppEffectWipeUp	2818	Wipe	Up

Name	Value	General Effect	Property
ppEffectWipeRight	2819	Wipe	Right
ppEffectWipeDown	2820	Wipe	Down
ppEffectZoomIn	3345	Zoom	In
ppEffectZoomInSlightly	3346	Zoom	In Slightly
ppEffectZoomOut	3347	Zoom	Out
ppEffectZoomOutSlightly	3348	Zoom	Out Slightly
ppEffectZoomCenter	3349	Zoom	Center
ppEffectZoomBottom	3350	Zoom	Bottom

You use these constants with the Shape object's AnimationSettings collection, which has an EntryEffect property. In our case, we want to assign the effects randomly among the ungrouped clip art shapes. To do that, you use Table 10.1 to find the General Effect you want and then examine the range of values associated with that effect. For example, the general Fly In effect has eight associated effects: From Left to From Bottom Right, the values of which range from 3329 to 3336. In VBA, you use the Rnd function to generate random numbers, and you generate a random number between (or equal to) two numbers by using the following general expression:

```
Int((highest - lowest + 1) * Rnd + lowest)
```

Here, *lowest* is the lowest number in the range, and *highest* is the highest number in the range. So for example, the following expression generates random numbers between 3329 and 3336:

```
Int((3336 - 3329 + ) * Rnd + 3329
```

You can use a formula similar to this to run though the shapes in an ungrouped clip art image and assign the random values to the EntryEffect property. Listing 10.1 shows some VBA code that does this:

Listing 10.1 A VBA procedure That Applies Random Effects to a Clip Art's Ungrouped Shapes

```
Sub RandomizeAnimation()
    Dim objShape As Shape
    Dim nEffectFirst As Integer
    Dim nEffectLast As Integer
    Dim nEffect As Integer
    '
    ' Specify the lowest and highest values in the range
    '
    nEffectFirst = 1281
    nEffectLast = 1288
    '
```

continues

Listing 10.1 Continued

```
' Run through all the shapes in the ungrouped clip art
'
For Each objShape In ActiveWindow.Selection.ShapeRange
    '
    ' Seed the randomizer to get a truly random number
    '
    Randomize
    '
    ' Generate a random number in the specified range
    '
    nEffect = Int((nEffectLast - nEffectFirst + 1) * Rnd + nEffectFirst)
    '
    ' Apply it to the EntryEffect property
    '
    objShape.AnimationSettings.EntryEffect = nEffect
Next 'objShape
End Sub
```

You supply the nEffectFirst and nEffectLast variables with, respectively, the lower and upper values in the range of effects you want to use. The code then runs through the selected shapes in the ungrouped clip art, using the formula from earlier in this section to choose a random effect and apply it to the EntryEffect property.

Playing a Video to Introduce a Slide

When you display a slide, it's often desirable to play a short video clip to introduce the slide content. This might be a short movie related to the slide's topic, a message from the company president or other person, an animated clip that demonstrates the task described in the slide, and so on. To add a movie to a slide, choose the Insert tab, click the top half of the Movie split button, and then use the Insert Movie dialog box to select the video file you want to play on the slide.

> **TIP**
>
> PowerPoint (indeed, all of the Office 2007 applications) comes with a large number of animated GIF images. (An animated GIF is essentially a sequence of GIF still images combined into a single file.) These are part of Office 2007's Clip Art collection. To add an animated GIF to your slide, choose the Insert tab, click the lower half of the Movie split button, and then click Movie from Clip Organizer. In the Clip Art window that displays, you see a clip for all the available animated GIFs.

In this kind of situation, it's ideal to display the slide, run the video, remove the video from the slide, and then display the slide's regular content. This requires several animation effects, as described in the following steps:

1. Add and format your regular slide.

2. Insert the video clip into your slide. When PowerPoint asks how you want the movie to start, click <u>A</u>utomatically. This means that PowerPoint will begin running the video right away when you navigate to the slide.

3. Move and size the video as needed. If the video now covers the placeholder for any of the slide's content, select the video, choose the Options tab, and then click the top half of the Send to Back split button.

4. Choose Animations, Custom Animation to display the Custom Animation task pane. Note that PowerPoint has added two items to the animation list: one for the video itself (numbered 0) and one for a trigger created by PowerPoint (which you can ignore).

5. In the animation list, pull down the menu associated with the video and then click Effect Options. PowerPoint displays the Play Movie dialog box.

6. Click the Movie Settings tab and then click to activate the <u>H</u>ide While Not Playing check box. This ensures that the video window disappears when it stops playing.

7. Click OK.

8. Select all the content placeholders on the slide, including the title and bullets.

9. In the Custom Animation task pane, click Add Effect, click Entrance, and then click the effect you want to use to bring the content onto the slide.

10. In the Start menu, click After Previous. This tells PowerPoint to bring in the slide content after the video has stopped playing.

> **TIP**
> You may find that PowerPoint brings in the slide content one object at a time. That happens because you applied the After Previous value to the content objects. If you want all of the slide content to display at the same time, select the content effects, except the first one, and then use the Start menu to click With Previous.

> **TIP**
> In some cases, the slide content displays a little before the video finishes. To stop this from happening, add a slight delay to the content effect. In the animation list, select all of the content effects, pull down the menu associated with those effects, and then click Effect Options. In the Timing tab, change the <u>D</u>elay setting to 0.5 seconds and then click OK.

Emphasizing the Current Bullet Point

When you put together and present a PowerPoint slide show, you should avoid a malaise that is sometimes called *triple delivery*—having the same text on the screen, on a handout, and spoken aloud. Most presenters avoid the triple delivery problem by making their bullet points relatively terse and then expanding on the point orally. Unfortunately, when your speech departs significantly from the bullet text, your audience may forget which bullet is the current one. You can solve that problem by reiterating the bullet text from time to time or by pointing at the text as you speak.

Neither of these solutions is that great because you need to remember to perform them while you're extemporizing. A much better solution is to have the current bullet point emphasized by, say, bold or underlined text or by applying a different font size or color. These effects are available in the Emphasis category. However, you need to be careful: In most cases, PowerPoint doesn't reverse the effect automatically. Ideally, you want the emphasis applied to only one bullet at a time. That is, when you apply the emphasis effect to the next bullet, PowerPoint should remove the effect from the previous bullet.

The easiest way to set this up is to use the Change Font Style effect, which enables you to emphasize bullet text by applying bold, -italic, or underline. Best of all, the Change Font Style effect comes with a property that enables you to automatically remove the font style from the current bullet when you move to the next bullet.

Follow these steps to set this up:

1. Select the placeholder containing the bullets you want to animate.
2. Choose Animations, Custom Animation to display the Custom Animation task pane.
3. Choose Add Effect, E̲mphasis, Change Font Style.
4. In the Custom Animation task pane, use the Font Style list to click the style you want to apply: B̲old, I̲talic, or U̲nderline.
5. Use the Duration list to click Until Next Click.

Most of the other effects in the Emphasis category don't have the handy Duration property. In these cases, you need to "de-emphasize" the effect by hand by adding a second emphasis effect that reverses the original one.

For example, I occasionally like to emphasize text using the Grow/Shrink effect. (For text, this gives the same result as the Change Font Size effect.) For example, I might grow the text to 125 percent of its original size to make it stand out from the other bullets. Reversing this is a bit tricky, however, because you can't just return the text to 100 percent. Instead, you need to apply the effect to the text's *current* size. So if you grow the text using 125 percent, you reverse that by shrinking it using 80 percent.

 TIP One relatively easy way to calculate the correct shrinking percentage is to use fractions. Convert the growth percentage to a fraction and then reverse the top and bottom. The resulting fraction gives you the shrink percentage. For example, 125 percent is 125/100 which reduces to 5/4 (dividing the top and bottom by 25), so reversing that gives 4/5, which expands to 80/100 (multiplying the top and bottom by 20) or 80 percent. Similarly, a growth of 150 percent is 3/2, so the reverse is 2/3, or about 67 percent for the shrink factor.

In this case, you must work with the bullets individually; you cannot work with the place-holder. There are a number of ways to go about this, but I find the following method the easiest one to manage:

1. For each bullet, select the text of the bullet and then choose Add Effect, Emphasis, Grow/Shrink.

2. Select all the effects you created in step 1, pull down the Size list, use the Custom text to enter a growth value (that is, a percentage greater than 100), and then press Enter.

3. For each bullet except the last one, select the text of the bullet and then choose Add Effect, Emphasis, Grow/Shrink.

> **NOTE** Why skip the last bullet in Step 3? Because clicking after you are done with this bullet should take you to the next slide.

4. Select all the effects you created in Step 3, pull down the Size list, use the Custom text box to enter a shrink value (that is, a percentage less than 100) that reverses the growth value from Step 2, and then press Enter.

5. With the effects from Step 3 still selected, use the Start list to click With Previous. This tells PowerPoint to apply the shrink effect on the current bullet at the same time as it applies the grow effect to the next bullet.

6. For each effect you created in Step 3, click the effect and then use the Re-Order arrows to position the effect below the growth effect of whatever bullet follows it. For example, if you have four slides A, B, C, and D, the order should look like this (see Figure 10.8 for an example):

   A - Grow

   B - Grow

   A - Shrink

   C - Grow

   B - Shrink

   D - Grow

   C - Shrink

7. In the Custom Animation pane, press Ctrl+A to select all of the effects. (If you have other effects in the list, hold down Ctrl and click all of the effects from Steps 1 and 3, instead.) Use the Speed list to click Very Fast. (Grow/Shrink effects look best at top speed.)

Figure 10.9 shows a slide with five bullets that have grow (125 percent) and shrink (80 percent) effects applied.

Grow effects

Shrink effects

Figure 10.9
A slide with both grow and shrink effects added to the bullets.

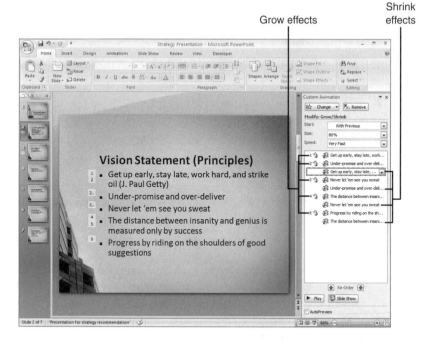

Adding Scrolling Credits

If you create a Top 10 Most Requested Effects list, at or near the top of that list is the display scrolling credits on the last slide. It's always a good idea to acknowledge those who had a hand in creating a presentation, and scrolling credits look professional. The good news is that PowerPoint makes this easy to set up with a built-in Credits effect that sets things up for you automatically. Here are the steps to follow:

1. Insert a blank slide at the end of the presentation. (The easiest way to do this is to right-click below the last slide and then click <u>N</u>ew Slide.)

2. Choose Insert, Text Box, and then draw the text box placeholder. Be sure to position the text box in the horizontal center of the slide. (An easy way to do this is to choose Format, Align, Align <u>C</u>enter.) PowerPoint preserves the text box's horizontal position when running the animation, so centered text looks best.

3. Type your credits into the text box and format the text as desired.

4. Choose Animations, Custom Animation to display the Custom Animation pane.

5. With the text box selected, choose Add Effect, <u>E</u>ntrance, <u>M</u>ore Effects to display the Add Entrance Effect dialog box.

6. In the Exiting section, click Credits, and then click OK.

7. If you want the credits to start as soon as you display the last slide, use the Start list to click After Previous.

8. The default speed is 15 seconds, which should work for most credits. If you have a long list of credits, however, you might prefer a longer time. Pull down the effect's list and click Timing. In the Speed text box, type the time (in seconds) and then click OK.

Note that it does not matter where your text box displays on the slide. PowerPoint starts the text box below the slide, and then it slowly moves it up toward the top of the slide, and then scrolls it off the top.

From Here

- To learn how to hide Slide Master objects, **see** "Hiding a Slide Master Object On One Slide," **p. 235**.
- If you want animations included in your Web page, **see** "Enabling Animations on the Web," **p. 296**.
- You can initiate custom actions when viewing a slide show; **see** "Linking to the Last Slide Viewed," **p. 292**, and "Linking to a Hidden Slide," **p. 290**.

10

Slide Show Tricks

Over the past two chapters, you have seen quite a few tricks and techniques for sprucing up your slides, perking up your presentations, and augmenting your animations. I have stressed the idea that you should always tailor your PowerPoint tweaks to suit your material and your audience and, most importantly, to not get in the way of your message. The same ideas apply to the end result of all your hard work: the slide show itself. Your goal should always be to avoid having people think about *how* you present and, instead, concentrate solely on *what* you present. This means that no matter what material you show or who you show it to, your slide show presentation must be seamless, smooth, and as professional as possible.

The tricks you learn in this chapter help you do just that. From adding narration to and rehearsing the slide show to creating automatic and custom slide shows to creating on-slide links that anticipate audience needs and questions, this chapter shows you how to take your presentation to a higher plane.

Rehearsing a Slide Show

Good public speakers can tell you that one of the secrets to their success is that they always rehearse a speech, usually several times. This helps them learn their material, discover problem areas (too-long sentences, tongue-tripping phrases, and so on), and internalize the speech to the extent that when they finally get up in front of their audience, their delivery sounds unforced, natural, and conversational.

Good presenters also rehearse their slide shows, and they get the same benefits as their speech-giving colleagues. However, PowerPoint also comes with some technology that gives you even more benefits for rehearsal. This technology is

PowerPoint's Rehearse Timings feature, which enables you to run through your presentation and keep track of how long you spend on each slide and the total presentation time. There are several ways you can take advantage of this information to improve your slide show:

■ You can look for slides that take substantially more time than the other slides in your presentation. For example, you might find that most of your slides take 3 or 4 minutes, but you have one slide that takes 10 minutes. That's almost always an indication that the longer slide contains too much information or is too complex. You should consider dividing the slide into two or three shorter or simpler slides.

→ When looking for anomalous slide times, it might help to know the average slide time. **See** "Calculating the Average Slide Time," **p. 279**

■ You can look for slides that take substantially less time than the other slides. For example, you might have several slides that take only 20 or 30 seconds. This indicates either that you're rushing through your material or, more likely, that those short slides contain too little information or are too simple. Consider either expanding the material in those slides or combining some of those slides into a single slide.

■ You can ensure that your presentation falls within whatever time constraints you have been given. Most presenters are given a time limit, and professional presenters never wear out their welcome by exceeding that limit. The Rehearse Timings feature also tracks the overall elapsed time on your presentation, so you know whether your delivery goes over your allotted time. If it does, you can cut some material to reduce the delivery time.

■ You can ensure that you have enough material to fill your time slot. Few things are as embarrassing as a presentation that falls significantly short of its allotted time. This means that you raced through your material, didn't explain your slides thoroughly, or that you didn't have enough material in the first place. With Rehearse Timings, you can identify when a presentation is woefully short and take steps to fix the problem.

→ You can also use Rehearse Timings to set up a slide show that runs automatically. For the details, **see** "Setting Up an Automatic Slide Show," **p. 282**

Begin by opening your slide show presentation. For accurate timing, use the same computer that you'll use to run the slide show, particularly if you use large graphics or lots of complex transitions since it can take PowerPoint much longer to process these effects on a less powerful computer. Now follow these steps to rehearse the timing for a slide show:

1. Choose Slide Show, Rehearse Timings. PowerPoint launches the slide show and displays the Rehearsal toolbar, as shown in Figure 11.1. The Slide Time box tells you the amount of time you have spent on the current slide, and then the Presentation Time box tells you the amount of time you spent on the presentation as a whole.

Figure 11.1
When you choose Rehearse Timings, PowerPoint starts the slide show and displays the Rehearsal toolbar.

2. For each slide, present the material just as you would during an actual presentation. Speak at your normal pace, and be sure to run though all your animations. When it's time to move to the next slide, you can click the screen as usual, or you can click Next in the Rehearsal toolbar.

> **TIP**
> When you present a slide, you might make a mistake that throws off the slide's timing. In that case, click the Repeat button in the Rehearsal toolbar. PowerPoint subtracts the current slide time from the overall presentation time and resets the Slide Time box to 0:00:00.

> **NOTE**
> If the phone rings or you're otherwise interrupted during the rehearsal, click the Pause button in the Rehearsal toolbar to temporarily suspend the timers.

3. When you're done, PowerPoint displays a dialog box that shows you the total presentation time and asks if you want to keep the slide timings. Click Yes.

With the rehearsal complete, PowerPoint drops you off in the Slide Sorter view and displays the slide times under each slide, as shown in Figure 11.2.

Time for current slide

Figure 11.2
After you complete the rehearsal, PowerPoint displays the Slide Sorter view, which shows the time beneath each slide.

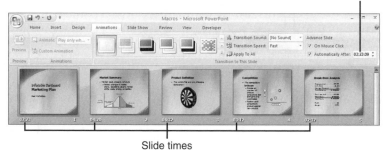

Slide times

Assigning Slide Times with a Macro

When you use the Rehearse Timings feature as described in the previous section, you might get interrupted during a slide and forget to click the Pause button in the Rehearsal toolbar. Rather than starting from scratch, you can complete the slide show and then adjust the time for the interrupted slide by hand. To do this, navigate to the slide (either in Normal view or Slide Sorter view), choose the Animations tab, and then adjust the time displayed in the Automatically After spin button (pointed out earlier in Figure 11.2).

> TIP
> When you specify a time using the Automatically After control, it's often faster to use the text box to type the time. That is, you select the entire displayed time and then type the new time using the *mm:ss* format, where *mm* is the number of minutes and *ss* is the number of seconds.

What if you need to adjust the time of multiple slides? If want to assign the same time to each slide, select all the slides and then edit the time displayed in the Automatically After control. PowerPoint assigns that time to all the selected slides.

A more likely scenario is that the slides you want to change require different times. In this case, you don't have any choice except to modify the slide times one by one using the Automatically After control.

However, what if you need to adjust all the times by the same amount? For example, you might decide that you rushed through the rehearsal and that the time for each slide should be increased by 30 seconds. Similarly, if you set up an automatic slide show that has 20 slides and the total time is 5 minutes (300 seconds) less than what is required, you can fix the problem by adding 15 seconds to each slide.

You can adjust the timing of each slide by hand, of course, but this is the sort of repetitive task for which VBA was made. Listing 11.1 presents a macro that adjusts the time of every slide in the active presentation by a specified number of seconds.

NOTE   You can download the presentation that contains this chapter's macro code from my Web site:
`www.mcfedries.com/OfficeGurus2007/`

Listing 11.1   A VBA Macro that Adjusts the Advance Time of Each Slide by a Specified Number of Seconds

```
Sub AdjustSlideTimes()
    Dim objSlide As Slide
    Dim varAdjustTime As Variant
    '
    ' Get the adjustment time, in seconds
    '
    varAdjustTime = InputBox("Enter the number of seconds by which to " & _
                             "adjust the slide times:")
    '
    ' Was Cancel clicked?
    '
    If varAdjustTime = "" Then Exit Sub
    '
    ' Run through each slide in the active presentation
    '
    For Each objSlide In ActivePresentation.Slides
        '
        ' Add the adjustment to the slide's advance time
        '
        With objSlide.SlideShowTransition
            .AdvanceTime = .AdvanceTime + Int(varAdjustTime)
        End With
    Next 'objSlide
    '
    ' Switch to Slide Sorter view to see the new times
    '
    ActiveWindow.ViewType = ppViewSlideSorter
End Sub
```

The procedure begins by using the `InputBox` function to prompt for the number of seconds by which the slide times are to be adjusted (this can be a positive or negative number). This value is stored in the `varAdjustTime` variable. After making sure that Cancel isn't clicked (if it were, the procedure exits), the macro then uses a `For Each...Next` loop to run through all the slides in the active presentation. For each slide's `SlideShowTransition` object, the `varAdjustTime` value is added to the `AdvanceTime` property. When the loop is done, the macro switches to Slide Sorter view to see the new timings.

Calculating the Average Slide Time

When I discussed the rationale behind using the Rehearse Timings feature at the beginning of this chapter, I mentioned that it helps you look for slide times that are out of whack with the rest of the presentation. You can usually do this by eyeballing the slide times in Slide

Sorter view. However, in more complicated presentations, it might help to know the average slide time, which you can then use as a comparison for individual slides.

If you write down the total time after you complete a rehearsal, you can divide that time by the number of slides in the presentation. However, dividing minutes and seconds by an integer value is not a straightforward calculation, and it is unlikely anyway if you adjust your slide timing by hand or by using the macro shown in the previous section.

To get quick and easy slide time averages, use the VBA macro shown in Listing 11.2.

Listing 11.2   A VBA Macro that Calculates the Average Slide Time

```vba
Sub GetAverageSlideTime()
    Dim objSlide As Slide
    Dim nTotalTime As Integer
    Dim nAverageTime As Integer
    nTotalTime = 0
    '
    ' Run through each slide in the active presentation
    '
    For Each objSlide In ActivePresentation.Slides
        '
        ' Add the slide's advance time to the total
        '
        nTotalTime = nTotalTime + objSlide.SlideShowTransition.AdvanceTime
    Next 'objSlide
    '
    ' Calculate the average time
    '
    nAverageTime = nTotalTime / ActivePresentation.Slides.Count
    '
    ' Display the total time and average time
    '
    MsgBox "Total time: " & Format(TimeSerial(0,0,nTotalTime), "h:mm:ss") & _
            vbCrLf & _
            "Avg. time: " & Format(TimeSerial(0,0,nAverageTime), "h:mm:ss")
End Sub
```

This procedure begins by running through all the slides in the active presentation. For each slide, the value of the AdvanceTime property is added to the nTotalTime variable. When the loop exists, the average time is calculated by dividing the value of nTotalTime by the number of slides in the presentation. Finally, a message is displayed showing the total time and the average time, as seen in Figure 11.3.

Figure 11.3
The macro in Listing 11.3 displays the total presentation time and the average slide time.

Microsoft PowerPoint

Total time: 0:57:34
Avg. time: 0:03:12

OK

Adding Narration to a Slide Show

Not all slide shows are presented in person. As you learn in the next section, you can set up a slide show to run automatically in a kiosk or booth. More commonly, you might share a presentation with remote users. For example, you can send a presentation to another person as an email attachment or on a CD, you can put the presentation on a shared network folder, or you can publish the presentation to a Web site. In all these scenarios, you obviously cannot present the slide show in person. However, you can do the next best thing and record narration to go along with each slide. When remote users open your presentation and run the slide show, they hear your voice along with each slide. PowerPoint can also store slide timings with your narration.

> ⌐ C A U T I O N ─────────────────────────────
>
> Note that unlike Rehearse Timings, PowerPoint's Narration feature doesn't give you any way to start over on a particular slide. Therefore, make sure you're comfortable with your presentation before you begin. You might want to have your notes or handouts on hand, just in case you need them.

Here are the steps to follow to add narration to a slide show:

1. Plug in your computer's microphone, if you haven't done so already.

2. Choose Slide Show, Record Narration. PowerPoint displays the Record Narration dialog box, shown in Figure 11.4.

Figure 11.4
Use the Record Narration dialog box to set up the microphone level and sound quality for your narration.

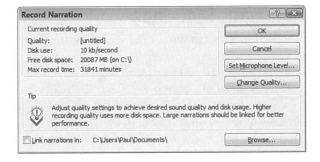

3. Click Set <u>M</u>icrophone Level to open the Microphone Check dialog box. Talk normally into the microphone, and PowerPoint adjusts the sound level to match your voice. When the level stabilizes (that is, when the green bars that signal the audio level stop moving), click OK.

4. Click <u>C</u>hange Quality to open the Sound Selection dialog box. Either use the <u>N</u>ame list to select a predefined sound quality (CD Quality, Radio Quality, or Telephone Quality) or use the <u>A</u>ttributes list to select a specific quality level. (The higher the

11

kb/sec value, the better the quality and the more disk space the recording uses.) Click OK when you're done.

5. If you want PowerPoint to create separate .wav files for the narration (one for each slide), click to activate the Link Narrations In check box. (The default location is your user profile's Documents folder; it's My Documents in pre-Vista computers. You can change that by clicking the Browse button.)

6. Click OK.

7. For each slide, present the material just as you would during an actual presentation. Speak at your normal speed and voice level. If you need to stop temporarily, right-click the slide and then click Pause Narration.

8. When the slide show ends, PowerPoint asks if you also want to save the slide timings. Click Save to preserve the timings or Don't Save to discard them.

When the recording is done, PowerPoint switches to Slide Sorter view.

> **TIP**
>
> What do you do if you already have existing audio that you want to apply to a slide? For example, you might have a message from the company CEO or audio from a training video. In this case, navigate to the slide, choose Insert, and click the top half of the Sound split button to display the Insert Sound dialog box. Click the audio file you want to apply to the slide and then click OK. In the dialog box that displays, click Automatically, which tells PowerPoint to play the audio clip as soon as you navigate to this slide in the presentation.

Setting Up an Automatic Slide Show

At times, you might need to set up an unattended slide show that runs automatically and continuously. In a trade show booth, for example, you might want to run a slide show next to a product display. You might also want a slide show to run continuously in a store window or in a kiosk. None of these situations is conducive to having a person around to stop and restart the show, much less to actually present the material. In such cases, it's better to configure the slide show to run automatically until it's interrupted. The following steps show you how this is done:

1. Rehearse the slide show to set up the timings, as described earlier (see "Rehearsing a Slide Show").

2. Add narration to the slide show, if needed, as described earlier (see "Adding Narration to a Slide Show"). At the end of the show, be sure to click Don't Save so that PowerPoint doesn't overwrite your slide show timings.

3. Choose Slide Show, Set Up Slide Show. PowerPoint displays the Set Up Show dialog box, shown in Figure 11.5.

Figure 11.5
Use the Set Up Show dialog box to configure a slide show to run automatically.

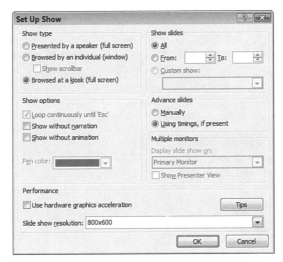

4. In the Show Type group, click Browsed at a Kiosk (Full Screen). (Note that PowerPoint automatically activates and disables the Loop Continuously until 'Esc' check box, as shown in Figure 11.5.)

5. In the Advance Slides group, click Using Timings, If Present.

6. If the slide show displays on a monitor that supports a specific screen resolution, use the Slide Show Resolution list to click that resolution.

7. Click OK.

When you're ready to start the automatic slide show, choose Slide Show, From Beginning. PowerPoint loads the show and uses the slide timings to advance each slide automatically. When the last slide is complete, PowerPoint returns to the first slide and starts the slide show over again.

Playing CD Tracks During a Slide Show

PowerPoint enables you to add a sound file that plays automatically when you navigate to a slide. These are normally short audio clips that play sound effects, messages, or snippets of music. However, there might be times when you prefer to play a longer sound clip. For example, you might want a particular song to accompany a slide, or you might want to play several cuts of music during a break in the slide show. The best way to set up these longer sound effects is to have PowerPoint play them directly from a CD. Here is how it works:

> **CAUTION**
>
> The license that comes with a commercial audio CD probably doesn't allow you to play large chunks of the disc in a public setting. Short samples are fair use, but you need to be careful when using longer bits.

1. Insert the CD containing the audio track or tracks you want to use. (If you see the AutoPlay window, click the Close button or press Esc.)

2. In PowerPoint, navigate to the slide into which you want to insert the CD audio.

3. Choose the Insert, click the bottom half of the Sound split button, and then click Play CD Audio Track. PowerPoint displays the Insert CD Audio dialog box, shown in Figure 11.6.

Figure 11.6

Use the Insert CD Audio dialog box to specify the CD tracks you want to play with the current slide.

4. Use the Start at Track spin box to set the starting track number.

5. Use the End at Track spin box to set the ending track number.

> **TIP**
>
> If you want to play only part of a single track, specify the track's number in both the Start at Track spin box and then End at Track spin box. Then use the Time spin box next to End at Track to specify the length of the clip.

6. If you want PowerPoint to keep playing the audio, click to activate the Loop Until Stopped check box.

7. To set the playback level, click the Sound Volume button and then use the Volume slider to set the level.

8. PowerPoint normally displays a sound icon on the slide. If you don't want this icon to appear, click to activate the Hide Sound Icon During Slide Show check box.

9. Click OK. PowerPoint displays a dialog box that asks how you want the audio to start in the slide show.

10. Click Automatically to have the audio start right away; if you want to start the audio only when you click the sound icon (and assuming you didn't opt to hide the sound icon in step 8), click When Clicked, instead.

Creating a Custom Slide Show

The content you have in a slide show isn't always suitable or appropriate for every audience. For example, a slide show about your company might contain secret corporate data. That's fine for internal use, but it's not something you would want to show in a public forum. Similarly, a financial slide show for company executives might contain sensitive payroll data that you wouldn't want to appear if you also presented the show to lower-level managers.

For these and similar situations, you don't need to build multiple versions of your presentation with material tailored to each audience. Instead, PowerPoint enables you to work with a single presentation file, but build custom slide shows from that file. A custom slide show is a show that displays only those slides that you specify.

Follow these steps to create a custom slide show:

1. Choose Slide Show, Custom Slide Show, Custom Sho<u>w</u>s. PowerPoint displays the Custom Shows dialog box.

2. Click <u>N</u>ew. PowerPoint displays the Define Custom Show dialog box.

3. Type a name in the Slide Show <u>N</u>ame text box.

4. In the Slides in <u>P</u>resentation list, click a slide that you want to add to the custom show. (If you want to add multiple slides, hold down Ctrl and click each slide.)

5. Click <u>A</u>dd. PowerPoint adds the slide to the S<u>l</u>ides in Custom Show list, as shown in Figure 11.7.

Figure 11.7
Use the Define Custom Show dialog box to create a custom slide show that includes a subset of the current presentation's slides.

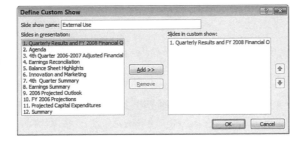

6. Repeat steps 4 and 5 to specify all the slides you want to include in the custom show.

7. Click OK to return to the Custom Shows dialog box.

8. Click Close.

To play a custom show, choose Slide Show, Custom Slide Show, Custom Sho<u>w</u>s to display the Custom Shows dialog box, click the custom show you want to play, and then click <u>S</u>how.

Presenting a Slide Show Using Two Monitors

When you run a slide show, the operative phrase is "What You See Is What They Get." In other words, what you see on your monitor is what your audience sees on the projection screen. That's not a problem if the slide show goes smoothly, but if you have to access the slide show menu during the presentation (for example, to select a different pointer or to navigate to another slide), the appearance of the menu not only distracts your audience, but it also looks unprofessional. This is doubly true if you need to access something in another Windows program (by pressing Ctrl+T during the slide show), resulting in the sudden intrusion of the Windows taskbar and Start menu into the proceedings.

You can work around this problem by using PowerPoint's Presenter view on a system that has two monitors attached. Presenter view displays the full-screen slide show on one monitor, and on the other its displays a special Speaker view, which divides the screen into three sections: the current slide, the current slide's Notes page, and a strip containing thumbnail images of the presentation's slides. You can use the Speaker view to navigate the slide show and change options, and the audience members are none the wiser because they just see the current slide.

To use Presenter view, first attach a second monitor to your computer and then configure that monitor in Windows, as described in the following steps:

1. In Windows Vista, choose Start, Control Panel and then under Appearance and Personalization, click Adjust Screen Resolution. (In Windows XP, choose Start, Control Panel, Display.)
2. Click the 2 icon.
3. Click <u>E</u>xtend the desktop onto this monitor, as shown in Figure 11.8.
4. Adjust the <u>r</u>esolution and <u>c</u>olors for the second monitor as needed.
5. Click OK.
6. If Windows asks if you want to keep the new settings, click Yes.

Now that Windows knows about your second monitor, the next step is to tell PowerPoint that you want to use another monitor during your presentation. Here are the steps to follow:

1. Choose the Slide Show tab.
2. In the Monitors group, use the Show Presentation On list to click the monitor that you want to use to display the slides to the audience (see Figure 11.9).

3. If the presentation monitor requires a special resolution, use the Resolution list to click the setting you want to use.

4. Click to activate the Use Presenter View check box.

Figure 11.8
First you need to tell Windows that a second monitor is attached to your computer.

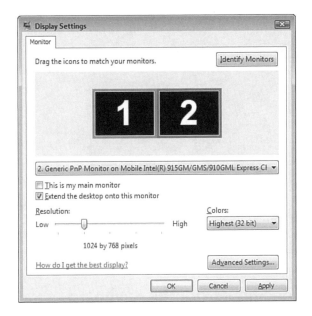

Figure 11.9
Use the Slide Show tab's Monitors group to set up your presentation to run on two monitors.

The next time you start the slide show, PowerPoint uses the Presenter view: The monitor you selected in Step 2 displays the current slide in full-screen mode, whereas the other monitor gives you the Speaker view, which is shown in Figure 11.10.

Most of today's video adapters come with a *graphics coprocessor*, a microprocessor that performs graphics chores such as 2D and 3D rendering which would otherwise be handled by the computer's CPU. This can help speed up the display on your monitor. If you have this type of hardware in your computer, click the Slide Show tab and then click Set Up Slide Show to display the Set Up Show dialog box. Click the Use Hardware Graphics Acceleration check box and then click OK.

Current slide   Notes

Figure 11.10
In the Presenter view,
you see the Speaker
view, which includes the
current slide, its notes,
and slide thumbnails.

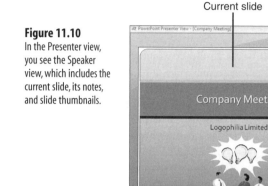

Thumbnails

Controlling a Slide Show from the Keyboard

Most of the time, you use your mouse to operate and navigate a slide show. You can use these two basic techniques:

- Click to move to the next slide in the presentation or to run the next animation in the current slide.

- Turn the mouse wheel backward (toward you) to move to the next slide in the presentation or to run the next animation in the current slide; turn the mouse wheel forward (away from you) to advance to return to the previous slide in the presentation or to reverse the most resent animation in the current slide.

For more control over the slide show, either click the Slide Show Menu icon or right-click the slide show. The menu you see contains the following commands:

- **Next**—Moves to the next slide in the presentation.

- **Previous**—Moves to the previous slide in the presentation.

- **Last Viewed**—Jumps to the last slide that you displayed in the presentation. Note that this won't be the same as the presentation's previous slide if you used the Go to Slide command (see the next item in this list), a hyperlink, or an action button to jump to the current slide from elsewhere in the presentation.

- **Go to Slide**—Displays a menu of the slides in the presentation. When you click a slide in the list, PowerPoint jumps to that slide.

TIP

You can jump back to the first slide by holding down the left and right mouse buttons for a couple of seconds.

- **Custom Show**—Displays a menu of the custom slide shows that you've defined for the current presentation. When you click an item in the list, PowerPoint switches to the custom show.

→ For the details on setting up a custom show, **see** "Creating a Custom Slide Show," **p. 285**

- **Screen**—Displays a menu of screen option. Click either Black Screen or White Screen to blank the screen temporarily. (You return to the presentation by clicking the screen.) You can also click Show/Hide Ink Markup to turn ink annotations on and off, or click Switch Programs to display the Windows Start menu and taskbar.

- **Pointer Options**—Displays a list of annotation tools, such as the pen type, ink color, and arrow options.

- **Pause**—Temporarily stops the slide show. To restart the presentation, right-click the screen, and then click Resume.

- **End Show**—Stops the slide show.

Besides these mouse-based techniques, there are also several keyboard techniques you can use to navigate and operate a slide show. Many presentation gurus have these keyboard shortcuts memorized because this enables them to avoid the slide show menu, which can be distracting and looks unprofessional, and using the keyboard is almost always faster than using the mouse. Table 11.1 lists PowerPoint's slide show keyboard shortcuts.

11

Table 11.1	**Navigating a PowerPoint Slide from the Keyboard**
Key	**Description**
N	Advances to the next slide or runs the next animation. PowerPoint also supports the following keys for this task: spacebar, Enter, right arrow, down arrow, or Page Down.
P	Returns to the previous slide or reverses the most recent animation. PowerPoint also supports the following keys for this task: Backspace, left arrow, up arrow, or Page Up.
n, Enter	Jumps to slide number *n*.
S or +	Pauses or resumes an automatic slide show.
B or .	Toggles the black screen on and off.
W or ,	Toggles the white screen on and off.
A	Toggles the mouse pointer and slide show navigation tools on and off.

continues

Table 11.1	**Continued**
Key	**Description**
Ctrl+A	Changes the mouse pointer to an arrow, if the mouse is currently displayed as a pen or eraser.
Ctrl+T	Displays the Windows taskbar.
Esc	Ends the slide show. PowerPoint also ends the slide show if you press hyphen [-] or Ctrl+Break.

Linking to a Hidden Slide

When you put together your presentation, part of your preparation should always involve anticipating possible audience questions, comments, or concerns. This enables you to provide quick and accurate responses, which impresses a lot of people and enhances the overall message of your presentation.

Most of the time, you can write down possible questions, answers, and other material in the notes pages of your slides. However, you might think of an audience question that requires a more formal response in the form of a separate slide. The only problem is that you don't want to include that slide in your presentation because the question or comment that leads to it might never come up. The solution is to include the slide in the presentation anyway but mark it as hidden. This means that the slide doesn't display in your slide show and doesn't print in your handouts.

> **TIP**
>
> If you want to print your hidden slides, choose Office, Print to display the Print dialog box. Click to activate the Print Hidden Slides check box and then click OK.

To hide a slide, select it in the Normal or Slide Sorter view and then choose Slide Show, Hide Slide. PowerPoint lets you know a slide is hidden by displaying a rectangle with a diagonal slash behind the slide number. (In Normal view, a hidden slide looks as if it is washed out in the Slides tab.)

How do you view a hidden slide when you need it? PowerPoint gives you two methods:

- Display the Slide Show menu, choose Go to Slide, and then click the hidden slide. Note that in the list of slides the hidden slide displays with parentheses around its slide number. For example, a slide might normally display in the list as 12 Review, but if you hide the slide it displays as (12) Review.
- Set up a hyperlink or action button that, when clicked, takes you to the hidden slide.

If you want to configure some text in one of your slides as a hyperlink that takes you to the hidden slide, follow these steps:

1. Select the text you want to use as a link.

2. Choose Insert, Hyperlink (or press Ctrl+K) to display the Insert Hyperlink dialog box.

3. Click Place in This Document. PowerPoint displays the Select a place in this document list, which consists of the slides in the presentation, including your hidden slide (which displays with parentheses around its slide number).

4. Click the hidden slide to which you want to link, as shown in Figure 11.11.

5. Click OK.

Figure 11.11
Use the Insert Hyperlink dialog box to set up a text link to your hidden slide.

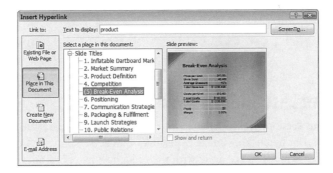

If you don't want a link to appear in your presentation text, you can create a separate action button instead. An action button is a small graphic image that you configure to run a particular action when clicked. In this case, you want the action button to display your hidden slide. Here are the steps to follow:

1. Display the slide on which you want to display the action button.

2. Choose Insert, Shapes to display the Shapes gallery and then click an icon in the Action Buttons section. (It doesn't matter which one you choose, but one of the button icons might be more appropriate for your needs. For example, if your hidden slide anticipates a possible question, then you should use the Help button, which comes with a question mark (?) icon.)

3. Click and drag your mouse on the slide to create the action button. When you release the mouse button, PowerPoint displays the Action Settings dialog box.

4. Click the Hyperlink To option.

5. In the list under the Hyperlink To option, click Slide. PowerPoint displays the Hyperlink to Slide dialog box.

6. Click your hidden slide and then click OK. The name of the slide displays in the Action Settings dialog box, as shown in Figure 11.12.

7. Click OK.

Figure 11.12
Use the Action Settings dialog box to set up an action button to link to your hidden slide.

Linking to the Last Slide Viewed

In the previous section, you learned how to navigate to a hidden slide by using the Go To Slide command or by clicking a text hyperlink or an action button. That works well, but in almost all cases, when you are done with the hidden slide, you should return to the slide you previously viewed. Again, PowerPoint offers two methods:

- Display the slide show menu and choose Last Viewed.
- Set up an action button that, when clicked, takes you to the previously viewed slide.

Here are the steps to follow to create such an action button:

1. Display the slide on which you want to display the action button.
2. Choose Insert, Shapes to display the Shapes gallery and then click an icon in the Action Buttons section. (In this case, a suitable shape is the Back or Previous button.)
3. Click and drag your mouse on the slide to create the action button. When you release the mouse button, PowerPoint displays the Action Settings dialog box.
4. Click the Hyperlink To option.
5. In the list under the Hyperlink To option, click Last Slide Viewed.
6. Click OK.

Protecting a Presentation by Distributing It as a Slide Show File

If you want other people to view your presentation without you, the easiest way is to either send the presentation file via email as an attachment or to place the presentation file in a shared network folder. The users can then open the presentation in PowerPoint and use the standard Ribbon commands or keyboard methods to run the slide show.

The drawback with this method is that the other users have the presentation open in PowerPoint, so they can make changes to it. If you don't want that to happen, one solution is to set up the presentation with a modification password. This means that the user cannot change the presentation in any way without providing the correct password. Here are the steps to follow to set this up:

1. Choose Office, Save As (avoid the arrow) to open the Save As dialog box.
2. Choose Tools, General Options to open the General Options dialog box.
3. Type a password in the Password to Modify text box.
4. Click OK. PowerPoint displays the Confirm Password dialog box.
5. Type the password again and click OK.
6. Click Save. PowerPoint asks if you want to replace the existing file.
7. Click Yes.

Now when another user opens the presentation, he sees the Password dialog box. The user must either enter the correct password or must click the Read Only button.

Applying a modification password keeps the presentation safe from unwanted changes, but it still means that another user can open the file in PowerPoint and see your notes, animation settings, and other design features. If you'd like to avoid that, or if the other user is a PowerPoint novice who does not know how to start a slide show, you can save your presentation as a separate file that uses the PowerPoint Show (PPS) format (which has the .ppsx file extension; normal PowerPoint files have the .pptx extension). When the user launches the PPS file (by double-clicking it in Windows Explorer, for example), PowerPoint runs the slide show right away without displaying the PowerPoint interface. When the user finishes the slide show, PowerPoint exits.

Follow these steps to save a copy of your presentation as a PowerPoint Show file:

1. Choose Office, click the Save As arrow, and then choose PowerPoint Show. PowerPoint displays the Save As dialog box with PowerPoint Show selected in the Save as Type list.

> **CAUTION**
>
> The PowerPoint Show file type works only with PowerPoint 2007. Users who have an earlier version of PowerPoint (specifically, 2003, XP, 2000, or 97) must use the Save as Type list to click PowerPoint 97-2003 Show.

2. Select a location for the PowerPoint Show file.
3. Use the File Name text box to name the file.
4. Click Save.

Publishing a Slide Show to the Web

Ever since Microsoft's belated 1995 realization that the Internet was something big that ought to factor into the company's plans, it has crammed the Office suite with Net-friendly features and added Office-friendly features to Internet Explorer. The goal has always been to blur the previously hard-edged distinction between here—your computer and your LAN—and there—the Web, FTP sites, and other online locations.

What do you do if you have existing documents, worksheets, and presentations that you want to mount on the Web? Internet Explorer can work in conjunction with Office to display these files, but all your readers might not have that capability. To make sure *anyone* who surfs to your site can access your data, you need to convert your files into the Web's *lingua franca:* HTML. Fortunately, Office applications make this easy by including features that convert documents from their native format into HTML.

> **TIP** Before you save your presentation as a Web page, you might want to tell PowerPoint which browser or browsers your users surf with because this determines the features PowerPoint uses to render the Web page XML or HTML. For example, if you tell PowerPoint that your users browse with Netscape Navigator 4.0 or later, PowerPoint disables the MHTML format (described in the steps that follow). Choose Office, PowerPoint Options, click Advanced, click Web Options, and then display the Browsers tab. Use the People Who View This Web Page Will Be Using list to click your target browser. Note, too, that you can use the check boxes in the Options list to customize the Web page features.

Publishing a PowerPoint presentation to the Web is becoming increasingly common. After a conference, for example, many people make their presentations available online for those who did not attend. Also with business travel budgets tightening, "presenting" online saves the expense of either traveling to the audience or bringing the audience to you.

PowerPoint gives you extensive page-publishing options, as the following steps show:

1. Open the presentation you want to publish.
2. Choose Office, Save As (avoid the arrow) to open the Save As dialog box.
3. Select a location for the new file.
4. In the Save As Type list, you choose from two possibilities:
   - **Single File Web Page**—This is the MIME Encapsulation of Aggregate HTML Documents (MHTML) format. It combines the HTML and references to external files such as images into a single file that uses the .mht extension. Note that only Internet Explorer supports this file type.
   - **Web Page**—This is a regular HTML Web page that uses the .htm file extension. PowerPoint also creates a folder named *Filename*_files (where *Filename* is the text in the File Name text box) that includes any external files such as images required by the Web page.

TIP To save the supporting files in the same folder as the Web page, choose Office, PowerPoint Options, click Advanced, click Web Options, display the Files tab, and deactivate the Organize Supporting Files in a Folder check box.

5. Use the File Name text box to change the name of the file, if necessary. If you don't, PowerPoint changes the document's extension to .mht or .htm (depending on the file type you chose in step 4).

6. Click Publish to display the Publish as Web Page dialog box, as shown in Figure 11.13.

Figure 11.13
Use the Publish as Web Page dialog box to configure your presentation's Web page options.

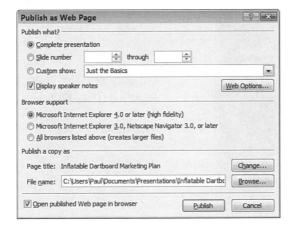

7. To determine how much of the presentation you publish, PowerPoint gives you three options:

- **Complete Presentation**—Activate this option to publish every slide in the presentation.

- **Slide Number *X* Through *Y***—Activate this option to publish only the range of slides you specify using the two spin boxes.

- **Custom Show**—Activate this option to publish the custom slide show you select in the associated list. (PowerPoint disables this option if the presentation has no custom slide shows.)

→ For the details on creating custom shows, **see** "Creating a Custom Slide Show," **p. 285**

8. If you also want to include your speaker notes, leave the Display Speaker Notes check box activated.

9. Use the options in the Browser Support group to set the target browser for your users.

10. To change the page title (the text that displays in the browser's title bar), click Change, enter the new title, and click OK.

11. Click Publish. PowerPoint publishes the presentation to a Web page.

11

PowerPoint sets up the presentation Web page with an ActiveX control that displays the slide show content. By default, Internet Explorer doesn't display ActiveX controls for security reasons (and browsers such as Firefox don't display them at all). Therefore, when you launch the presentation Web page, Internet Explorer displays the Information Bar, which tells you that the program prevents an ActiveX control from running. Click the Information Bar, click Allow Blocked Content, and then click <u>Y</u>es when Outlook Express asks if you are sure. Figure 11.14 shows a published presentation.

Figure 11.14
A PowerPoint presentation published as a Web page.

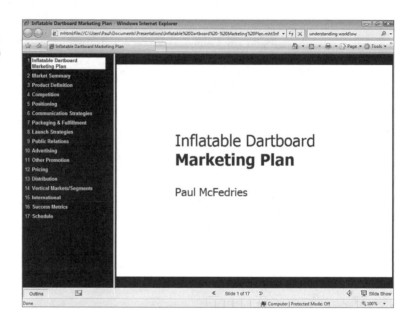

Enabling Animations on the Web

If you want put your presentation on the Web, you should know that PowerPoint doesn't include animations when it converts a presentation to a Web page file. This helps improve the performance of the slide show, particularly for users running a dial-up connection. If you want the animations included in your Web page (for example, if you know that most of your users have a broadband connection), you need to follow these steps to set this up:

1. Choose Office, PowerPoint Opt<u>i</u>ons to open the PowerPoint Options dialog box.
2. Click Advanced.
3. Click Web O<u>p</u>tions to open the Web Options dialog box.

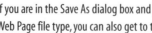
TIP   If you are in the Save As dialog box and you have selected either the Single File Web Page or the Web Page file type, you can also get to the Web Options dialog box by clicking <u>P</u>ublish and then clicking <u>W</u>eb Options.

4. Click the General tab.

5. Click to activate the Show Slide Animation While Browsing check box.

6. Click OK to return to the PowerPoint Options dialog box.

7. Click OK.

Copying the Presentation to a CD

Saving a presentation to the Web (as described earlier, see "Publishing a Slide Show to the Web") is a great way to enable nonPowerPoint users to see your material. However, this isn't a perfect solution. For one thing, your user might not have access to the Web when he wants to view your presentation (a person might be on a plane, for example). For another, the Web version of a presentation never looks as good as the original, so much of your formatting work is lost, which can detract from your message.

To create a version of your presentation that nonPowerPoint users can view without an Internet connection and that appears exactly as you designed it, you need to use PowerPoint's Package for CD command. This feature takes your presentation and its associated files and works with your computer's CD burner to burn the files to a disc. (Note that you can only burn to a CD, not to a DVD.) PowerPoint also includes the PowerPoint Viewer 2007 utility, which enables anyone to view any PowerPoint file (including files created with earlier versions of PowerPoint: 2003, XP, 200, and 97). The CD also comes with an AutoRun feature, so all the other user has to do is insert the CD, and the slide show runs automatically.

Here are the steps to follow to burn a copy of your presentation on a CD:

1. Choose Office, Publish, Package for CD.

2. Depending on your presentation, PowerPoint might display a dialog box letting you know that it will convert your files to the PowerPoint 97-2003 format. If so, click OK.

3. In the Package for CD dialog box (see Figure 11.15), use the Name the CD text box to type a name for the CD.

> **NOTE** Bear in mind that the name you give to the CD is the name that is next to the CD drive letter in Windows Explorer when the user inserts the disc. You have a maximum of only 16 characters to work with when naming the disc, but try to make the name as descriptive as you can.

4. If you have any other files that you want to include on the CD, click Add Files, use the Add Files dialog box to select them, and then click Add.

5. Insert a recordable CD into your CD burner.

11

Figure 11.15
A PowerPoint presentation published as a Web page.

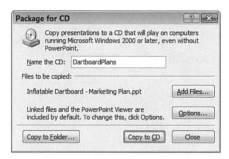

6. Click Copy to <u>C</u>D. PowerPoint asks if you want to include linked files on the CD. (Linked files are external files that you insert into your presentation, including sound clips and video files.)

7. Click <u>Y</u>es. PowerPoint begins copying the files to the CD. When it is done, the Microsoft Office PowerPoint dialog box displays; it asks if you want to copy the same files to another CD.

8. If you want to burn another CD, insert the disc and click <u>Y</u>es; otherwise, click <u>N</u>o to return to the Package for CD dialog box.

9. Click Close.

From Here

- Another way to present PowerPoint information to people who don't have the program is to convert one or more slides into images; **see** "Convert a Slide into an Image," **p. 242**.

- To ensure your slide show handouts look their best, you can format them in Word; **see** "Using Word to Custom Format Handouts," **p. 246**.

- To learn how to add animations to a presentation, see "Creating a Custom Animation," **p. 251**.

Microsoft Outlook Tricks

Email Tricks

If you are a writer, a financial analyst, or a database administrator, you probably spend the bulk of your work day using Word, Excel, or Access. Everyone else dips into and out of these programs (and PowerPoint) throughout the day. However, there's one member of the Office family that most of us leave open and use all day long: Outlook. Whether it's handling our ever-growing email load, organizing our calendar, or managing our contacts, Outlook gets a real workout in a typical business day.

With that in mind, this chapter presents a number of techniques designed to help you get the most out of Outlook's email capabilities, and Chapter 13, "Calendar and Contacts Tricks," helps you take Outlook's scheduling and contact management features to the Office guru level.

As far as email is concerned, you are probably too busy reading, composing, and managing your email to give much thought to what your life was like back in the early 1990s when most of us had barely heard of email or rarely used it beyond sending out the odd internal message to a colleague or two. Now email is, hands-down, the most often used and, arguably, the most important business tool in the modern-day business arsenal. It is so important that I think it is a crime if you don't become an expert email user, particularly an expert on Outlook's prodigious email capabilities. If you take a few minutes now to learn the ins and outs of the Outlook Inbox, you can save *hours* of time every week because your email work will go faster and more efficiently. This chapter shows you a few techniques to get you well on your way to becoming an Outlook email expert.

Customizing the Inbox Message Fields

In Outlook's default layout, the message list is located in the middle of the window and the Reading pane is on the right. This brain-dead layout makes the message list practically useless because it crams the message data—including the sender name (or address), the subject line, and icons such, as the flag and categories—into a tiny, two-line rectangle—this is called *compact mode*. A much better arrangement is to have the Reading pane below the message list. You can set this up by choosing <u>V</u>iew, <u>R</u>eading Pane, <u>B</u>ottom.

> **TIP**
>
> If you like the Reading Pane on the right, you can make compact mode easier to work with by increasing the number of lines that Outlook displays for each item. Choose <u>V</u>iew, <u>A</u>rrange By, Cust<u>o</u>m, click <u>F</u>ields and then choose a higher number in the <u>M</u>aximum Number of Lines in Compact Mode list (the default is 2).

With that bit of business out of the way, the Inbox message list expands to reveal ten fields of message data:

- **Importance**—Shows the priority settings the sender applies to a message: High (a red exclamation mark), Low (a downward-pointing blue arrow), or Normal (no icon).
- **Reminder**—Displays a bell icon for messages for which you have set a due date with a reminder.
- **Icon**—Displays an icon that gives you information about a message's status. For example, unread messages show a closed envelope icon, read messages show an open envelope icon, messages you reply to add a left-pointing purple arrow, and messages you forward add a right-pointing blue arrow.
- **Attachment**—Displays a paperclip icon for messages that have one or more files attached.
- **From**—Shows the name (or sometimes just the email address) of the person or organization that sent the message.
- **Subject**—Displays a message's topic.
- **Received**—Shows the date and time you receive a message.
- **Size**—Shows a message's size in KB or MB.
- **Categories**—Shows the categories you assign to a message.
- **Flag Status**—Displays the flag you apply to a message.

This is good information, to be sure, but it's not the only information that Outlook maintains for each message. In fact, there are dozens of data fields for each message, including useful fields such as Cc (the recipients who received copies of the message), E-mail Account (the name of the account to which the message was sent), and Sent (the date and time the message was sent). You can add any of these fields to the Inbox message list.

12

Here are the steps to follow to customize the message fields:

1. Right-click any field header and then click Field Chooser to display the Field Chooser dialog box, as shown in Figure 12.1.

> **TIP**
> Outlook also offers a Field Chooser button on the Advanced toolbar. To display this toolbar, choose View, Toolbars, Advanced.

Figure 12.1
Use the Field Chooser dialog box to customize the fields displayed in the message list.

2. In the drop-down list at the top of the dialog box, choose All Mail Fields.

3. Drag a field from the Field Chooser dialog box and drop it inside the field headers at the point where you want the field to display.

4. Repeat Step 3 for any other fields you want to add.

5. Click the Close (X) button to shut down the Field Chooser dialog box.

6. To move a field, drag its header left or right within the column header area and then drop it into the position you want.

7. To size a field, drag the right edge of the field's header to the left or right or right-click the field header and then select Best Fit (which sizes the field to be as wide as its widest entry).

8. To remove a field, drag it up or down until you see a large X display over the field and then release the mouse.

Instead of working with the message list fields directly, you can also use a dialog box to add and remove fields. Here's how it works:

1. Choose View, Arrange By, Custom to display the Customize View: Messages dialog box.

2. Click Fields to display the Show Fields dialog box (see Figure 12.2).

12

Figure 12.2
You can also use the Show Fields dialog box to customize the fields displayed in the message list.

3. Use the Select Available Fields From list to choose the message field category you want to use.

4. To add a field, click the field name in the Available Fields list and then click Add. The field displays in the Show Fields In This Order list.

5. To reorder the fields, click the field you want to work with in the Show Fields In This Order list and then click the Move Up and Move Down buttons.

6. To remove a field, click it in the Show Fields In This Order list and then click Remove.

7. Click OK to return to the Customize View: Messages dialog box.

8. Click OK.

TIP

Outlook also enables you to create custom fields where the displayed value is based on a formula that you build. Display the Field Chooser dialog box and click New. (Alternatively, display the Show Fields dialog box and click New Field.) In the New Field dialog box, type a Name for the field and then use the Type list to select Formula. Type the formula into the Formula text box or click Edit to use the Formula Field dialog box, which offers lists of the available fields and functions. For example, suppose you create a field named "Conference" and you want it to display "Yes" if the message subject contains the word "Conference." Here's the formula to use:

```
IIf(Instr([Subject],"Conference") <> 0, "Yes", "")
```

This formula uses the Instr function to see if the [Subject] field contains the word Conference. If so, the word Yes is returned; otherwise, a blank string is returned. After you create the field, it displays in the User-Defined Fields in Inbox category, and you can add it to the Inbox fields from there.

Setting the Junk E-mail Protection Level

It's probably safe to say that there are no longer any spam-free zones. If you have an Internet-based email account, then you get spam, end of story. And if you're like most people, you don't get just one or two spams a day, but more like one or two dozen (or, shudder, one or two *hundred*, which is, sadly, no longer an unusually high amount). That's not surprising because spam now accounts for the majority of the billions of messages sent every day, and on some days, it even accounts for 90 percent of all sent messages!

It is no longer possible to avoid spam, but there are some things you can do to minimize how much of it you have to wade through each day:

- Never use your actual email address in a newsgroup account. The most common method that spammers use to gather addresses is to harvest them from newsgroup posts. One common tactic you can use is to alter your email address by adding text that invalidates the address, but is still obvious for other people to figure out:

  `user@myisp.remove_this_to_email_me.com`

- When you sign up for something online, use a fake address if possible. If you need or want to receive email from the company and must use your real address, make sure you deactivate any options that ask if you want to receive promotional offers. Alternatively, use an address from a free Web-based account (such as a Hotmail account), so that any spam you receive goes there instead of to your main address.

- Never open suspected spam messages or display them in the Reading pane because doing so can sometimes notify the spammer that you've opened the message, which confirms your address is legitimate.

A *Web bug* is an image that resides on a remote server and is added to an HTML-formatted email message by referencing a URL on the remote server. (Images and other objects that reside on a remote server and are not embedded in the message are called *external content*.) When you open the message, Outlook uses the URL to download the image for display within the message. That sounds harmless enough, but if the message is junk email, it's likely that the URL will also contain either your email address or a code that points to your email address. When the remote server gets a request for this URL, it knows not only that you've opened their message, but also that your email address is legitimate.

Fortunately, Outlook 2007 is hip to the Web bug menace, and it's set up to automatically block *any* external content (including sound files). When you receive an HTML message with links to remote images, Outlook blocks the images and, for each one, displays instead a placeholder containing a red X and a message telling you that the image has been blocked. The Information pane also tells you that the message's pictures have been blocked. If you know the message isn't spam, you can view the images by clicking the Information pane and then clicking Download Pictures.

To make sure that Outlook 2007 is set up to block image downloads, choose Tools, Trust Center, click Automatic Download, and then make sure the Don't Download Pictures Automatically in HTML E-mail Messages or RSS Items check box is activated.

12

If you block image downloads, you can configure Outlook to always display images from someone you trust. You do that by adding that person to your Safe Senders list. If you have a message from that person, click the message and then choose Actions, Junk E-mail, Add Sender to Safe Senders List. If you don't have a message, choose Actions, Junk E-mail, Junk E-mail Option, select the Safe Senders tab, click Add, and then type the person's address in the Add Address or Domain dialog box. (If you want Outlook to trust everyone from a certain domain, type the domain name, instead.)

- Never, I repeat, *never*, respond to spam, even to an address within the spam that claims to be a "removal" address. By responding to the spam, you prove that your address is legitimate, so you'll just end up getting *more* spam.

If you do get spam despite these precautions, Outlook's Junk E-mail feature is your next line of defense. This feature is a *spam filter* that examines each message you receive to look for telltale signs of *spamminess* (as anti-spam types call it). If Outlook determines that a message is spam, it automatically shuffles the message to the Junk E-mail folder so that you don't have to deal with it directly. Fortunately, the default level used by the Junk E-mail filter is, for most people, a good tradeoff between protection and convenience. That is, it catches the vast majority of spam, but it also only rarely flags legitimate messages as spam (this is called a *false positive*). However, you can change the filter's protection level if you find that you're still getting lots of spam in your Inbox, or if Outlook is generating too many false positives. Choose Actions, Junk E-mail, Junk E-mail Options to open the Junk E-mail Options dialog box, display the Options tab (see Figure 12.3), and then choose one of the following protection levels:

- **No Automatic Filtering**—Shuts off the Junk E-mail filter but still moves messages from blocked senders to the Junk E-mail folder (which I discuss later in this section). You should go with this level only if you use a third-party spam filter or if you handle spam using your own message rules.

- **Low**—Moves messages with obvious spam content to the Junk E-mail folder. This is the default protection level.

- **High**—Moves messages with at least slight spam content to the Junk E-mail folder. This level should catch all incoming spam, but it also can generate a few false positives. You should need to move up to this level only if your spam situation is out of control. If you do choose this level, be sure to check the Junk E-mail folder several times a day to look for false positives.

T I P Checking the Junk E-mail folder is never fun because it means dealing directly with messages that are usually either offensive or annoying (or both). To make this distasteful chore less onerous, turn off the Reading pane (by choosing <u>V</u>iew, <u>R</u>eading Pane, <u>O</u>ff) the next time you display the Junk E-mail folder. (Outlook remembers this setting and turns off the Reading pane automatically the next time you display the folder.)

N O T E If you see a false positive in the Junk E-mail folder, let Outlook know. Right-click the message and then choose <u>J</u>unk E-mail, <u>M</u>ark as Not Junk. In the Mark as Not Junk dialog box that displays, leave the Always Trust E-mail <u>F</u>rom "*address*" check box activated (where *address* is the address of message sender). This tells Outlook not to mark messages from that sender as spam in the future. Outlook does this by placing the address on your Safe Senders list.

If the message is sent to a mailing list, the list's address displays in the Always Trust E-mail <u>S</u>ent to the Following Addresses list. In this case, activate the check box beside the address to tell Outlook to include that address in your Safe Recipients list.

- **Safe Lists Only**—Handles all messages as spam, unless a message comes from an address or domain that you've added to your Safe Senders or Safe Recipients lists. Outlook uses these lists as so-called *whitelists* (the opposite of blacklists), that defines who can legitimately send you email. This is a useful level if you receive only nonspam email from people you know or from mailing lists you subscribe to.

Figure 12.3
In the Junk E-mail Options dialog box, use the Options tab to set the junk email protection level.

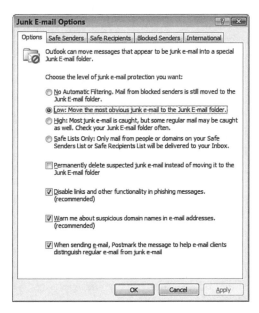

Blocking Messages from a Particular Person or Domain

If you notice that a particular address or domain name is the source of spam that Outlook doesn't catch, you can force Outlook to filter the spam to the Junk E-mail folder by telling it to block all incoming messages from that address or domain. Outlook maintains a Blocked Senders list to watch out for these shunned addresses and domains.

You can add an address or domain to the Blocked Senders list by following these steps:

1. Choose Actions, Junk E-mail, Junk E-mail Options to open the Junk E-mail Options dialog box.
2. Click the Blocked Senders tab.
3. Click Add to open the Add Address or Domain dialog box.
4. Type the individual address or domain name (use the form *domain.com* or *@domain.com*) and then click OK.
5. Repeat Steps 3–4 to add more addresses to your Blocked Senders list.
6. Click OK.

> **TIP**   If you have a message from someone you want to block, click the message and then choose Actions, Junk E-mail, Add Sender to Blocked Senders List.

Blocking Foreign or Non-English Messages

As I write this, the United States remains the number one spam-producing country in the world, generating about a 22 percent of all spam. Still, it means that the other 78 percent of spam comes from foreign countries (assuming you live in the U.S.), and much of that spam is written in a language other than English. The biggest non-U.S. spam generators are China, South Korea, France, Spain, and Poland.

> **TIP**   To get the latest on which countries generate the most spam, look for the annual Sophos Security Threat Report published near the start of each year by the security firm Sophos Plc: www.sophos.com.

This information can help you fine-tune Outlook's Junk E-mail filter because you can block incoming messages that originate from a particular country. Outlook does this by using the *top-level domain* (TLD), which is the final suffix that displays in a domain name. There are two types: a *generic top-level domain* (gTLD), such as com, edu, and net, and a *country code top-level domain* (ccTLD), such as ch (China) and kr (South Korea). Outlook uses the latter to filter spam that comes from certain countries.

12

Outlook can also filter messages that are written in a foreign language. The character set of a foreign language always displays using a special *encoding* unique to that language. (An encoding is a set of rules that establishes a relationship between the characters and their representations.) Outlook uses this encoding to filter spam that displays in a specified language.

Here are the steps to follow to block messages from specific countries and languages:

1. Choose <u>A</u>ctions, <u>J</u>unk E-mail, <u>J</u>unk E-mail Options to open the Junk E-mail Options dialog box.

2. Choose the International tab.

3. To block one or more countries, click <u>B</u>locked Top-Level Domain List, activate the check box beside each of the countries you want to filter (see Figure 12.4), and then click OK.

Figure 12.4
Use the Blocked Top-Level Domain List to select the countries you want to block.

4. To block one or more languages, click B<u>l</u>ocked Encodings List, activate the check box next to each of the languages you want to filter and then click OK.

5. Click OK.

Avoiding Viruses by Reading Mail in Plain Text

Dealing with the ever-growing onslaught of spam is bad enough, but our Inboxes are also under siege from another threat: viruses and Trojan horse programs disguised as legitimate message attachments, often from someone you know. When you open the attachment, the virus infects your computer, and then, behind the scenes, it uses Outlook to send virus-laden messages to people in your Contacts folder.

You can avoid getting infected by one of these viruses by implementing a few common-sense procedures:

- Never open an attachment that comes from someone you don't know.
- Even if you know the sender, if the attachment isn't something you expect to receive, assume the sender's system is infected. Write back and confirm that the sender sent the message.

12

- Some viruses come packaged as scripts that are hidden within messages that use the HTML format. This means that the virus can run as soon as you view the message! If a message looks suspicious, don't open it, just delete it. (Note that you need to turn off the Outlook Reading pane before deleting the message. Otherwise, when you highlight the message, it displays in the Reading pane and sets off the virus. Select <u>V</u>iew, <u>R</u>eading Pane, <u>O</u>ff.)

- Install a top-of-the-line antivirus program, particularly one that checks incoming email. Also be sure to keep your antivirus program's virus list up-to-date. As you read this, there are probably dozens, maybe even hundreds, of morally challenged scumnerds designing even nastier viruses. Regular updates help you keep up.

In addition to these general procedures, Outlook also comes with its own set of virus-protection features. For example, Outlook automatically disables certain types of attachments, such as executable files. However, if you want to ratchet up the security level in Outlook, you need to switch to a diet of plain text. That is, you need to tell Outlook to ignore HTML and Rich Text formatting and, instead, display all your messages using text with no special fonts, colors, HTML tags, images, backgrounds, or sounds: just simple, unadorned text where no virus or other malicious content can hide. Here are the steps to follow:

1. Choose <u>T</u>ools, Tru<u>s</u>t Center to open the Trust Center dialog box.

2. Click E-mail Security.

3. Click to activate the Re<u>a</u>d All Standard Mail in Plain Text check box.

4. Click OK.

When you receive an HTML or rich text message, Outlook converts the message to plain text when you view it either in the Reading pane or in its own window, as shown in Figure 12.5. The Information pane also includes the following message:

`This message was converted to plain text.`

Figure 12.5
When you view an HTML or rich text message, Outlook converts it to plain text.

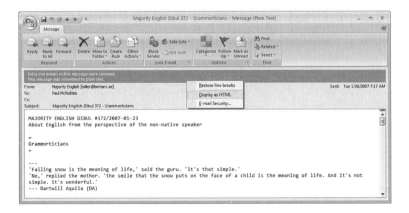

> **TIP** The only downside to reading email in plain text is that the 10-point Courier New font is down-right ugly. To pick a nicer plain text font, choose <u>T</u>ools, <u>O</u>ptions to open the Options dialog box. Click the Mail Format tab, and then click Stationery and Fonts to open the Signatures and Stationery dialog box. In the <u>P</u>ersonal Stationery tab, click the Fo<u>n</u>t button in the Composing and Reading Plain Text Messages section and then use the Font dialog box to specify your preferred font (such as Calibri or, my favorite, Verdana).

Allowing a Blocked File Type as an Attachment

As I mentioned in the previous section, most viruses are now transmitted via email. It's sobering to contemplate the billions of dollars and hundreds of thousands of man hours lost because of major virus outbreaks over the past few years. It's saddening to realize that almost all those outbreaks were started and escalated by a simple action repeated thousands of times: opening an email attachment. For Microsoft, it was no doubt frightening to realize that most of the damage was caused by Outlook users because, in most cases, these viruses took advantage of security holes to not only infect each user's PC, but also to pass along copies of the virus to other users.

Chastened by all of this, Microsoft designed Outlook 2003 with a grim determination to avoid similar problems. Most drastically, Microsoft identified around 70 file types that might potentially cause problems as attachments and then simply did not allow users to open those files. Note that Microsoft didn't merely make it inconvenient to open these file types; no, they made it *impossible* without high-level tweaks (I show you this later). If someone sends you, for instance, a file with the .exe extension (an executable file), Outlook displays the following message in the Information pane:

```
Outlook blocked access to the following potentially unsafe attachments: filename
```

Here, *filename* is the name of the blocked file. If you select the File, Save Attachments command, the blocked file does *not* display in the submenu. There is, in short, no way to view, open, or save the attachment.

Microsoft has continued this hard-line approach in Outlook 2007. Table 12.1 runs through the file types and their associated extensions that Outlook 2007 blocks.

Table 12.1   File Extensions Blocked by Outlook on Incoming Attachments

Extension	File Type
.ade	Access Project Extension
.adp	Access Project
.app	Executable Application
.asp	Active Server Page

continues

Table 12.1   Continued

Extension	File Type
.bas	BASIC Source Code
.bat	Batch File
.cer	Internet Security Certificate
.chm	Compiled HTML Help
.cmd	Command File for Windows NT
.com	Command File
.cpl	Windows Control Panel Extension
.crt	Security Certificate
.csh	UNIX C Shell Script
.exe	Executable File
.fxp	FoxPro Compiled Source
.hlp	Windows Help File
.hta	Hypertext Application
.inf	Information or Setup File
.ins	IIS Internet Communications Settings
.isp	IIS Internet Service Provider Settings
.its	Internet Document Set
.js	JavaScript Source Code
.jse	JScript Encoded Script File
.ksh	UNIX korn Shell Script
.lnk	Windows Shortcut File
.mad	Access Module Shortcut
.maf	Access Form Shortcut
.mag	Access Diagram Shortcut
.mam	Access Macro Shortcut
.maq	Access Query Shortcut
.mar	Access Report Shortcut
.mas	Access Stored Procedures
.mat	Access Table Shortcut
.mau	Media Attachment Unit
.mav	Access View Shortcut

12

Extension	File Type
.maw	Access Data Access Page
.mda	Access Add-in
.mdb	Access Application, Access Database
.mde	Access MDE Database File
.mdt	Access Add-in Data
.mdw	Access Workgroup Information
.mdz	Access Wizard Template
.msc	Microsoft Management Console Snap-in Control File
.msi	Windows Installer File
.msp	Windows Installer Patch
.mst	Windows SDK Setup Transform Script
.ops	Office Profile Settings File
.pcd	Visual Test Script
.pif	Windows Program Information File
.prf	Windows System File
.prg	Program File
.pst	Outlook Personal Folder File
.reg	Registry Data File
.scf	Windows Explorer Command
.scr	Windows Screen Saver
.sct	Windows Script Component, Foxpro Screen
.shb	Windows Shortcut into a Document
.shs	Shell Scrap Object File
.tmp	Temporary File/Folder
.url	Internet Uniform Resource Locator
.vb	VBScript File, Visual Basic Source
.vbe	VBScript Encoded Script File
.vbs	VBScript Script, VBA Script
.vsmacros	Visual Studio .NET Binary-based Macro Project
.vss	Visio Stencil
.vst	Visio Template

12

continues

Table 12.1   Continued

Extension	File Type
.vsw	Visio Workspace File
.ws	Windows Script File
.wsc	Windows Script Component
.wsf	Windows Script File
.wsh	Windows Script Host Settings File

There is, to be sure, much that is potentially dangerous in Table 12.1, but also much that is potentially useful: Registry files, screen savers, Access databases, and batch files, to name just a few. How do you sneak such files past Outlook in cases where you know the files are safe? Here are some ideas:

- Compress the file into a ZIP archive. Outlook doesn't block the .zip extension, so your recipient can easily open or save the archive, and then it extract the original file.

- Rename the file's extension to one that isn't listed in Table 12.1. For example, rename script.wsh to script.wsh.delete. When recipients save the attachment, they can remove the extra extension to restore the original filename.

- If you have a Web site, put a copy of the file on the site and then send the file's URL in the message instead of the file itself. The recipients can then download the file directly to their system, bypassing Outlook altogether.

- If you are working on a network, put a copy of the file in a shared network folder and then put the folder's network address in your message instead of attaching the file.

> **CAUTION**
>
> No matter how you fool or bypass Outlook's attachment security, you still need to be smart about the attachments themselves. That is, always scan the files for viruses before opening them.

If you regularly get attachments of a certain file type, the preceding solutions can be more of a hassle than they're worth. Fortunately, there is a Registry tweak you can perform that enables you to specify one or more extensions that Outlook should open with less paranoia. Notice that I didn't say with *no* paranoia; even with the tweak, you still have a hurdle or two to jump through. To see why, first understand that the file types in Table 12.1 are what Microsoft calls *Level 1* file types. With Level 1, you don't get access to the files, period. However, Microsoft also defines *Level 2* file types. With these file types, you can access them as attachments, but *only* by first saving the files to your hard disk. That is, you can't open the files directly from the message. The assumption here is that saving the files to your hard disk gives you the opportunity to virus-check the files before opening them.

To specify a file type as Level 2 (there are no default Level 2 file types in Outlook 2007), follow these steps:

1. Open the Registry Editor. (Press Windows Logo+R to open the Run dialog box, type **regedit**, and click OK. Note that Windows Vista asks you for your User Account Control credentials before allowing you to open the Registry Editor.)

2. Navigate to the following key:
   `HKEY_CURRENT_USER\Software\Microsoft\Office\12.0\Outlook`

3. If you don't see a Security subkey, choose <u>E</u>dit, New, Key, type **Security**, and press Enter.

4. With the Security subkey selected, choose <u>E</u>dit, New, String Value, type **Level1Remove** and press Enter.

5. Press Enter to open the Level1Remove setting.

6. Type the extension of each file type you want to move to Level 2, separated by semicolons. For example, the following string moves the Registry Data File, Screen Saver, and Access Database file types to Level 2:
   `.reg;.scr;.mdb`

7. Shut down and restart Outlook to put the new setting into effect.

When you attempt to open a Level 2 file type attachment from a message, Outlook displays the Attachment Security Warning dialog box shown in Figure 12.6. You need to click the <u>S</u>ave to Disk button to save the attachment to your hard disk before you can open it.

Figure 12.6
You can work with Level 2 file types, but you must save them to your hard disk before you can open them.

Setting a Message Follow-Up Reminder

Outlook enables you to quickly flag a selected message for follow-up by clicking the message's Flag Status field. This sets the default Today flag. For other flags (Tomorrow, Next Week, and so on), you have three choices:

- Right-click the message's Flag Status field
- Click the Follow Up toolbar button
- Choose <u>A</u>ctions, Follow <u>U</u>p

Despite the fact that Outlook offers several flag types, these flags have limited value because everyone tends to ignore them after a while, so the follow-up percentage tends to drop over time. If you have a message that requires you follow up, you can take things to the next level by setting a reminder. Here's how it works:

1. Select the message with which you want to work.

2. Right-click the message's Flag Status field (or choose <u>A</u>ctions, Follow <u>U</u>p) and then click Add Reminder. Outlook displays the Custom dialog box, shown in Figure 12.7.

Figure 12.7
Use the Custom dialog box to set a message follow-up reminder.

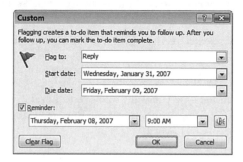

3. In the <u>F</u>lag to list, click the reason for the flag (Call, Forward, Reply, and so on).

4. Use the <u>D</u>ue date calendar to click the date by which the follow-up must occur.

5. Make sure the <u>R</u>eminder check box is activated and then use its associated calendar and time list to select the date and time you want Outlook to display the reminder.

6. Click OK.

Supplementing a Reminder with an Email Message

Setting up a reminder to follow up on an email message, as described in the previous section, is a useful way to prod yourself to move on handling that email. Unfortunately, reminders don't do you much good if you're not there to see them. For example, you might be out of the office when the reminder displays. If you are away from your desk only for a short time, it is no big deal because you will see the reminder when you get back. However, if you are gone for an extended period, the reminder isn't useful.

You can work around this problem by configuring Outlook to send an email message to any account that you have access to while away from the office. You do this using a VBA procedure, such as the one shown in Listing 12.1.

> **NOTE** The VBA code used in this chapter is available on my Web site:
>
> www.mcfedries.com/Office2007Gurus/chapter12.txt

> ┌─ **C A U T I O N** ───
>
> By default, Outlook 2007 is set up to disable all macro projects that aren't signed with a security certificate. To get your own code to run, choose Tools, Trust Center to open the Trust Center dialog box. Click Macro Security and then click the Warnings For All Macros option. Click OK to put the new setting into effect and then close and restart Outlook.

Listing 12.1   A VBA Procedure that Sends an Email Message When Outlook Processes a Reminder

```vba
Private Sub Application_Reminder(ByVal Item As Object)
    Dim msg As MailItem
    '
    ' Create a new message
    '
    Set msg = Application.CreateItem(olMailItem)
    '
    ' Set up the message with your address and the reminder subject
    '
    msg.To = "youraddress@wherever.com"
    msg.Subject = Item.Subject
    msg.Body = "Reminder!" & vbCrLf & vbCrLf
    '
    ' Set up the message body using properties
    ' appropriate to the different reminder types
    '
    Select Case Item.Class
        Case olAppointment
            msg.Body = "Appointment Reminder!" & vbCrLf & vbCrLf & _
            "Start: " & Item.Start & vbCrLf & _
            "End: " & Item.End & vbCrLf & _
            "Location: " & Item.Location & vbCrLf & _
            "Appointment Details: " & vbCrLf & Item.Body
      Case olContact
            msg.Body = "Contact Reminder!" & vbCrLf & vbCrLf & _
            "Contact: " & Item.FullName & vbCrLf & _
            "Company: " & Item.CompanyName & vbCrLf & _
            "Phone: " & Item.BusinessTelephoneNumber & vbCrLf & _
            "E-mail: " & Item.Email1Address & vbCrLf & _
            "Contact Details: " & vbCrLf & Item.Body
      Case olMail
            msg.Body = "Message Reminder!" & vbCrLf & vbCrLf & _
            "Sender: " & Item.SenderName & vbCrLf & _
            "E-mail: " & Item.SenderEmailAddress & vbCrLf & _
            "Due: " & Item.FlagDueBy & vbCrLf & _
            "Flag: " & Item.FlagRequest & vbCrLf & _
            "Message Body: " & vbCrLf & Item.Body
      Case olTask
            msg.Body = "Task Reminder!" & vbCrLf & vbCrLf & _
            "Due: " & Item.DueDate & vbCrLf & _
            "Status: " & Item.Status & vbCrLf & _
            "Task Details: " & vbCrLf & Item.Body
    End Select
    '
```

12

continues

Listing 12.1 Continued

```
    ' Send the message
    '
    msg.Send
    '
    ' Release the msg object
    '
    Set msg = Nothing
End Sub
```

The `Application_Reminder` procedure is an event handler that runs whenever Outlook processes a reminder, and the `Item` variable that's passed to the procedure represents the underlying Outlook item: an appointment, contact, message, or task. You can paste this procedure into the `ThisOutlookSession` module in Visual Basic Editor.

> **NOTE** To open the `ThisOutlookSession` module in Visual Basic Editor, first choose <u>T</u>ools, <u>M</u>acro, <u>V</u>isual Basic Editor (or press Alt+F11). In the Visual Basic Editor's Project pane, open the Project1 branch, open the Microsoft Office Outlook Objects branch, and then double-click ThisOutlookSession.

The procedure declares a `MailItem` (message) variable named `msg`, uses it to store a new message, and then sets up the message's To, `Subject`, and initial `Body` properties. Then a `Select Case` statement processes the four possible `Item` classes: `olAppointment`, `olContact`, `olMail`, and `olTask`. In each case, the message body is extended to include data from the item. Finally, the message is sent using the `Send` method, and the `msg` variable is released.

> **NOTE** If you want to send the email to multiple recipients, one option is to use the `MailItem` object's Cc or Bcc properties. If you prefer to place multiple addresses in the message's To field, use the `Recipients.Add` method as often as needed, like so:
>   `msg.Recipients.Add "another@domain.com"`

Creating Custom Color Categories

When you glance at your Inbox message list, all the messages look more or less the same. You might see icons in the Flag Status, Reminder, or Attachment columns, but the message data itself is a sea of sameness. By contrast, you probably don't *think* of those messages in the same way. Instead, you might have an informal classification scheme that you use to slot each message into a particular category: colleagues, your boss, receipts, projects, and so on.

Rather than keeping these categories in your head, you can configure Outlook to use the categories you want, and you can then apply those categories to your messages. These categories and their associated color icons display in the Categories field, so you can easily see which message belongs to which category, and you can even sort on the Category field to see related message together in the message list.

Outlook comes with several generic categories predefined for you: Red Category, Yellow Category, Purple Category, and so on. The default is Red Category, and you can apply it by clicking the message's Categories field. The first time you do this, Outlook displays the Rename Category dialog box, shown in Figure 12.8. This isn't too surprising because Red Category isn't exactly a descriptive name. Type a new name in the Name text box, select a Color, and assign a Shortcut Key, if you want. (Assigning a shortcut key is what you do so that you can apply this category to the current message just by pressing that key combination.) Click Yes when you are done.

Figure 12.8
When you click inside the Categories field for the first time, Outlook asks if you want to rename the Red Category item.

To apply other categories, you have three choices:

- Right-click the message's Categories field
- Click the Categorize toolbar button
- Choose Actions, Categorize

With the list of categories displayed, click the category you want to apply. As with the default Red Category, the first time you select a category, Outlook displays the Rename Category dialog box so that you can customize the category.

Rather than customizing the categories one-by-one, Outlook offers the Color Categories dialog box, which enables you to customize existing categories, create new categories, and delete categories you don't use. Here are the steps to follow:

1. Choose Actions, Categorize, All Categories. (You can also right-click the message's Categories field or click the Categorize toolbar button and then click All Categories.) Outlook displays the Color Categories dialog box, shown in Figure 12.9.
2. Click the category you want to customize.
3. To change the name, click Rename, type the new name, and then press Enter.
4. Use the Color list and click the category color.
5. Use the Shortcut Key list to associate a shortcut key with the category.
6. To create a new category, click New to open the Add New Category dialog box (which is similar to the Rename Category dialog box shown earlier in Figure 12.8). Type a Name, choose a Color and (optionally) a Shortcut Key, and then click OK.

Figure 12.9
Use the Color Categories dialog box to customize your category names, colors, and shortcut keys.

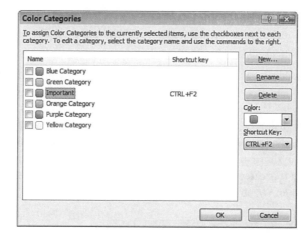

7. To apply one or more categories to the current message, click to activate the check box for each category you want to apply.

8. To remove a category, select it and then click <u>D</u>elete.

9. When you're done, click OK.

Applying Colors to Messages from Specific Senders

As I mentioned in the previous section, as the Inbox message list fills up, it quickly turns into an undifferentiated mass of text. Applying different categories helps, but if you really want messages to stand out, Outlook gives you another tool: applying a color to messages that come from a particular person. This is handy if you are on the lookout for messages from that person, especially if you operate a busy Inbox. By showing that person's message in, say, a red font, you can tell at a glance if you have received messages from that person.

Follow these steps to color messages from a particular person:

1. In the Inbox message list, click a message from the person whose message you want to color. (You can skip this step if you don't currently have a message from that person.)

2. Choose <u>T</u>ools, Organi<u>z</u>e. Outlook displays the Ways to Organize Inbox pane.

3. Click Using Colors to display the controls shown in Figure 12.10.

Figure 12.10
Click Using Colors and then use the controls to apply a color to a sender's messages.

4. If you didn't select a message in Step 1, use the Color Message From text box to type the name of the person. (Note that Outlook looks at the From field to decide whether to apply the color to a message.)

> **TIP** You don't have to type the person's full name. If you just type a partial name, Outlook applies the color to any message where the From field contains the partial name. Note, too, that it doesn't matter if you type the name using the First Last format (for example, Paul McFedries) or the Last, First format (for example, McFedries, Paul); Outlook still matches the name no matter which format displays in the From field.

5. Use the Color Messages From…In list to click the color you want to apply to the person's messages.

6. Click Apply Color. Outlook applies the color to all the person's messages.

7. Click Close (X) to close the pane.

> **NOTE** To stop Outlook from coloring a person's messages, choose Tools, Organize, click Using Colors, and then click Automatic Formatting. In the Automatic Formatting dialog box, click the rule that applies the color and then click Delete.

Downloading Mail for a Single Account Using Multiple Computers

It's a modern-day dilemma: How do you keep tabs on your work email when you're not at your desk or in the office? If you have a notebook computer or PDA with you, or if you have a computer at home, you can set up any of these machines to also check for messages on your work account. Unfortunately, after you download a message to the other machine, Outlook deletes it from the server. This means that the message is gone when you go to check your email on your work computer, which is almost certainly not what you want.

You can solve this dilemma by configuring Outlook to leave a copy of your incoming messages on the server after you download them. That way, no matter which machine you use to check your email, a copy of the message is still available when you check messages using another machine. Note that this does *not* mean that Outlook will keep downloading the same messages over and over each time you check your mail. After you download a message once to any computer, Outlook won't download the same message again to that computer.

12

Here are the steps to follow to configure your account to leave a copy of incoming messages on the server:

1. Choose <u>T</u>ools, <u>A</u>ccount Settings. Outlook display the Account Settings dialog box.

2. In the E-mail tab, click the account you want to configure.

3. Click Ch<u>a</u>nge. Outlook displays the Change E-mail Account dialog box.

4. Click <u>M</u>ore Settings. Outlook displays the Internet E-mail Settings dialog box.

5. Click the Advanced tab.

6. Click to activate the <u>L</u>eave a Copy of Messages on the Server check box.

7. If you want Outlook to delete the message from the server after a while, click to activate the <u>R</u>emove from Server After *X* Days check box and then specify the number of days after which you want Outlook to automatically delete the messages from the server.

8. If you click to activate the Re<u>m</u>ove from Server When Deleted from 'Deleted Items' check box, Outlook deletes the messages from the server when you permanently delete the messages.

9. Click OK to return to the E-mail Accounts dialog box.

10. Click <u>N</u>ext.

11. Click Finish to return to the Account Settings dialog box.

12. Click <u>C</u>lose.

Note that you probably want to configure your main computer and your secondary computers or devices a little differently:

- **Main computer**—Activate the <u>L</u>eave a Copy of Messages on the Server check box *and* the <u>R</u>emove from Server After *X* Days check box. For the number of days, choose a value that gives you enough time to download the messages using your other devices. Even if you don't download the messages on your other machines, at least they won't pile up on the server.

- **Your other devices**—Activate only the <u>L</u>eave a Copy of Messages on the Server check box.

Creating an Email Shortcut for a Recipient

I mentioned at the beginning of the chapter that many Outlook users run the program all day, which makes sense if you constantly send and receive messages. However, many people rebell against the incessant interruptions created by email. They believe that constantly checking for new messages reduces productivity by inducing a state known as *continuous partial attention*, where most of your attention is on a primary task, but where you also monitor several background tasks (such as incoming email) just in case something more important or interesting happens.

The result is that many people now leave Outlook off most of the time, and they check for new mail only once or twice a day. When they need to send a message, they launch Outlook, compose the new message, send it, and then close Outlook again. To me, this seems like a great deal of work just to send a message. If there are some people with whom you correspond regularly, you can save yourself a few steps by creating email shortcuts for those recipients. When you launch the shortcut, a new Outlook message window displays. The message is already addressed to the recipient, so you just fill in the rest of the message and send it, which adds the message to Outlook's Outbox folder. Note that all of this happens without the main Outlook program starting. The next time you start Outlook, it sends any messages waiting in the Outbox folder.

Follow these steps to create an email shortcut:

1. Open the folder in which you want to create the shortcut. For easier access, I recommend using the desktop, the Quick Launch toolbar, or the Start menu.

> **TIP**
> If you want the shortcut to display in the Quick Launch toolbar or the Start menu, start by creating the shortcut on the desktop. To move the shortcut to the Quick Launch toolbar, hold Shift, click-and-drag the shortcut, and drop it inside the Quick Launch toolbar. To put the shortcut on the Start menu, click-and-drag the shortcut over the Start button then, when the Start menu displays, drag the icon up into the menu and drop it inside the pinned items area (the part of the Start menu that includes the Internet and E-mail icons).

2. Right-click the folder and then choose New, Shortcut to open the Create Shortcut dialog box.

3. In the Type the Location of the Item text box, type the following (where *address* is the email address of the recipient; see Figure 12.11):

   `mailto:address`

Figure 12.11
In the Create Shortcut dialog box, type `mailto:address` to create an email shortcut for a recipient.

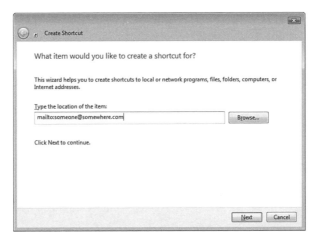

4. Click <u>N</u>ext.

5. In the <u>T</u>ype a Name for this Shortcut text box, type a name for the shortcut. For example, type the recipient's name or email address.

6. Click <u>F</u>inish.

Having Replies Sent to a Different Address

If you have multiple accounts, when you compose a new message or reply to or forward an incoming message, you can click the Account button to choose from which account the message is sent. Normally, any replies to your message are sent to that account. However, that might not be convenient for you. For example, you might send the message from an account that is scheduled to be deleted soon, and you want replies to go to your new account. Or you might prefer that replies go to your assistant or someone else in your department. Similarly, you might send a business message from home and prefer that replies go to your business address.

For these situations, you can specify an alternative address to which replies are sent:

1. In the message window, choose Options, Direct Replies To. Outlook displays the Message Options dialog box, shown in Figure 12.12.

Figure 12.12
Use the Message Options dialog box to specify an alternative address for replies to the message.

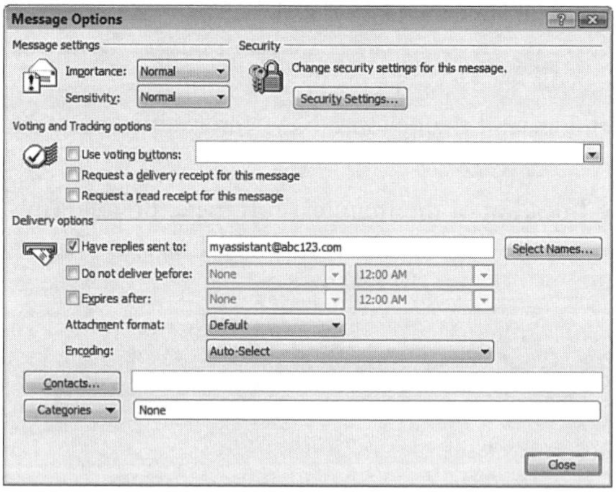

2. Make sure the H<u>a</u>ve replies sent to check box is activated (it should be activated by default).

3. In the text box, type the address you want to use. To choose an address from your Contacts list, click Se<u>l</u>ect Names, choose the recipient, and click OK.

4. Click Close.

Using a Different Outgoing (SMTP) Mail Port

On the Internet, Simple Mail Transport Protocol (SMTP) is the protocol that describes the format of Internet email messages and how messages get delivered. To facilitate this, your Internet service provider (ISP) runs an SMTP server (perhaps more than one) that handles your outgoing mail. When you set up an account in Outlook, it always asks you for the name of this server, which it calls the Outgoing Mail Server (SMTP). This name usually takes the form mail.*isp*.com, where *isp*.com is your ISP's domain name. When you send a message in Outlook, the program contacts the SMTP server and passes along your message. The server then routes the message toward its recipient or recipients.

This admirably straightforward sequence of events is complicated somewhat by the fact that many (now, perhaps most) ISPs insist that all their customers' outgoing mail go through the ISP's SMTP server. This makes sense for your email accounts from that ISP, but it also means that third-party accounts—for example, accounts provided by your Web site or blog-hosting company—have to go through the ISP's SMTP server, as well. This can create problems:

- Your ISP might refuse to send messages that use the third-party account. The usual cause of this is that the ISP believes you're a spammer surreptitiously trying to relay the message through the ISP's SMTP server.

- Your ISP might at some point refuse to send messages from *any* of your accounts because you've bumped up against the ISP's monthly limits on SMTP bandwidth or total messages sent.

- Many ISP SMTP servers are busy, so it might take a while for your message to go through the server, particularly if the ISP gives higher priority to its own accounts.

For all these problems, you are better off if you can send messages from your third-party account directly to the third party's own SMTP server. The third-party server should not think you are a spammer, you are less likely to hit bandwidth or message limits if you split your messages between servers (and many third-parties have no such limits), and your message is likely to be routed faster.

Unfortunately, you usually can't just plug in the third party's SMTP server address in the Outgoing Mail Server (SMTP) field of your account in Outlook. The problem here is that by default, outgoing mail is sent through port 25, and when you use this port, you must also use the ISP's SMTP server.

Fortunately, many third-party hosts help you work around this problem by enabling you to access their SMTP server via a nonstandard port. Here are the steps to follow to configure an email account to use a nonstandard SMTP port:

1. Choose Tools, Account Settings to open the Account Settings dialog box.

2. In the E-mail tab, select the account you want to modify.

3. Click Change to open the Change E-mail Account dialog box.

12

4. Use the <u>O</u>utgoing Mail Server (SMTP) text box to type the domain name of the third-party host's SMTP server.

5. Click <u>M</u>ore Settings to open the Internet E-mail Settings dialog box.

6. Click the Advanced tab.

7. In the <u>O</u>utgoing Server (SMTP) text box, type the port number specified by the third-party host, as shown in Figure 12.13.

Figure 12.13
Change the Outgoing Server (SMTP) value to the port number used by your third-party host.

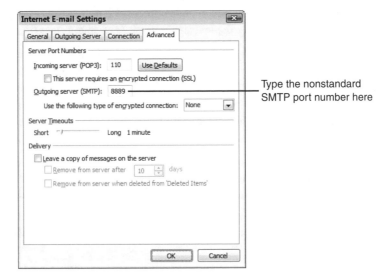

Type the nonstandard SMTP port number here

8. Click OK to return to the Change E-mail Account dialog box.

9. Click <u>N</u>ext.

10. Click Finish.

11. Click <u>C</u>lose.

> **TIP** Your ISP (or, indeed, any of your email hosts) probably implements yet another email security feature called SMTP Authentication, which authenticates the sender of each message. If you find that your messages aren't delivered or generate an error, you may need to tell Outlook that your account requires SMTP Authentication. Follow Steps 1–5 in this section to display the Internet E-mail Settings dialog box. Click the Outgoing Server tab and activate the My <u>O</u>utgoing Server (SMTP) Requires Authentication check box. Most SMTP authentication uses your account username and password, so leave the <u>U</u>se Same Settings as My Incoming Mail Server option activated. If your host uses a separate outgoing logon, activate <u>L</u>og On Using, instead, and fill in your User <u>N</u>ame and <u>P</u>assword.

Prompting to Save Messages in the Sent Items Folder

As you may know, Outlook is set up by default to always save a copy of each outgoing message in the Sent Items folder. If you don't want copies of your message saved for some reason, you can turn this feature off:

1. Choose <u>T</u>ools, <u>O</u>ptions to open the Options dialog box.
2. Click E-<u>m</u>ail Options to open the E-mail Options dialog box.
3. Click to deactivate the Sa<u>v</u>e Copies of Messages in Sent Items Folder.
4. Click OK to return to the Options dialog box.
5. Click OK.

Not saving *any* messages is a bit drastic, of course. You might want to save most of your sent messages, but not all of them. For example, you might not want to save trivial "Thank you!" replies, test messages, forwarded messages, or messages that contain large attachments. It's possible to configure Outlook so that each time you send a message, the program asks you if you want to save a copy of that message in the Sent Items folder.

You set this up using a bit of VBA code. To process outgoing mail in VBA, you need to add code to handle an `Application` object event called `ItemSend`. As with the code shown earlier in Listing 12.1, you set up the event handler by using the `ThisOutlookSession` object, which is part of the default Outlook VBA project. In the Visual Basic Editor, double-click `ThisOutlookSession`, click Application in the Object list and then click ItemSend in the Procedure list. Outlook adds the following stub to the module (see Figure 12.14):

```
Private Sub Application_ItemSend(ByVal Item As Object, Cancel As Boolean)
End Sub
```

Double-click ThisOutlookSession

Select Application in the Object list   Select ItemSend in the Procedure list

12

Figure 12.14
In the Visual Basic Editor, add the stub for the `ItemSend` event handler by selecting Application in the Object list and ItemSend in the Procedure list.

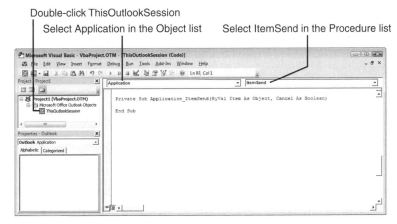

In the procedure's arguments, `Item` represents the message you send, and `Cancel` is a `Boolean` variable that you set to `True` if you don't want Outlook to send the message.

Listing 12.2 shows an event handler for `ItemSend` that prompts you to choose if Outlook should save the outgoing message in Sent Items.

Listing 12.2   An Event Handler for `ItemSend` That Prompts You to Save a Copy of an Outgoing Message in the Sent Items Folder

```
Private Sub Application_ItemSend(ByVal Item As Object, Cancel As Boolean)
    Dim nResult As Integer
    '
    ' Display the prompt
    '
    nResult = MsgBox("Save this message in Sent Items?", vbSystemModal +
vbYesNoCancel)
    '
    ' Check the result
    '
    If nResult = vbCancel Then
        Cancel = True
    End If

    If nResult = vbNo Then
        '
        ' If the user clicked No, don't save the message in Sent Items
        '
        Item.DeleteAfterSubmit = True
    End If
End Sub
```

As A Yes/No/Cancel `MsgBox` function asks if you want the message saved in Sent Items, and the response is stored in the `nResult` variable. If you click the Cancel button, the procedure sets `Cancel` to `True`, which means Outlook does not send the message. (The message stays onscreen.) If you click the No button, instead, the procedure sets the message's `DeleteAfterSubmit` property to `True`, which means Outlook does not store a copy in Sent Items.

Setting Up a Password-Protected Folder

If you use Outlook to exchange messages containing confidential data, such as trade secrets, budget plans, payroll details, or proprietary information, the data might be vulnerable to snooping if you leave your desk. You can prevent this by storing the confidential messages in a folder protected by a password, but, unfortunately, Outlook doesn't give you any way to do this. Fortunately, it's fairly easy to set up a password-protected folder using some VBA code.

In the Visual Basic Editor, double-click `ThisOutlookSession` to open the module and then add the following global variable to the top of the module:

```
Private WithEvents myExplorer As Explorer
```

This enables you to trap events for the `Explorer` object, which represents the Outlook interface. In particular, you want to trap the `BeforeFolderSwitch` event. This event fires when the user tries to display a different folder. The idea is that because this event fires before the other folder is displayed, you can use the event handler to ask the user for a password. If the correct password isn't given, you cancel the folder switch.

To use the `myExplorer` object, display the `ThisOutlookSession` module, click Application in the Object list and then click Startup in the Procedure list. In the `Application_Startup` event handler that VBA adds to the module, add the following statement to set `myExplorer` to Outlook's active `Explorer` object (see Figure 12.15):

```
Set myExplorer = Application.ActiveExplorer
```

Select Application in the Object list   Select Startup in the Procedure list

Figure 12.15
In the Visual Basic Editor, add the stub for the `Startup` event handler by selecting Application in the Object list and Startup in the Procedure list.

With that done, you can now set up the handler for the `BeforeFolderSwitch` event. In the `ThisOutlookSession` module, click myExplorer in the Object list and then click BeforeFolderSwitch in the Procedure list. You can now add the code shown in Listing 12.3.

12

Listing 12.3   An Event Handler That Asks the User for a Password Before Switching to the "Confidential" Folder

```
Private Sub myExplorer_BeforeFolderSwitch(ByVal NewFolder As Object,
➥Cancel As Boolean)
    Dim pwd as String
    '
    ' Are we switching to the "Confidential" folder?
    '
    If NewFolder.Name = "Confidential" Then

        ' If so, ask the user for the password
        '
        pwd = InputBox("Please enter the password for this folder:")
        '
        ' Check the password
        '
        If pwd <> "password" Then
            '
```

continues

Listing 12.3 Continued

```
         ' If the password doesn't match, cancel the switch
         '
            Cancel = True
        End If
    End If
End Sub
```

This procedure accepts an argument named `NewFolder`, which represents the folder to which the user is trying to switch. If this folder's name is Confidential, the procedure asks the user to enter the password. If the password doesn't match, the `Cancel` argument is set to `True`, which means the folder isn't displayed.

> **CAUTION**
>
> The code in Listing 12.3 uses the word password as the folder password. If you use this code on your system, be sure to change the password to a less obvious word or phrase.

You might wonder just how secure this method is if the password displays right in the code. As things stand, it's not secure because a savvy user knows how to examine the VBA code. Therefore, you need to prevent others from viewing the project. Here are the steps to follow:

1. In the Visual Basic Editor, select Tools, *Project* Properties, where *Project* is the name of your VbaProject.OTM project (the default name is Project1).

2. Display the Protection tab, shown in Figure 12.16.

Figure 12.16
Use the Protection tab to prevent unauthorized users from viewing your Outlook VBA code.

3. Click to activate the Lock project for <u>v</u>iewing check box.

4. Type a password into the <u>P</u>assword text box and then type it again in the <u>C</u>onfirm password text box.

5. Click OK.

Shut down Outlook, and then restart it to put the password into effect.

Cutting Your Mailbox Down to Size

The busier your email life is, the larger your Outlook mailbox gets. Having a massive mailbox not only makes it hard to find the messages you want, it also slows down Outlook's performance. To avoid these problems, use the Mailbox Cleanup tool to delete old or large items, archive items, and clean out the Deleted Items folder. To display this tool, choose <u>T</u>ools, Mailbo<u>x</u> Cleanup. Outlook displays the Mailbox Cleanup dialog box, shown in Figure 12.17.

Figure 12.17
Use Mailbox Cleanup to reduce the size of your Outlook mailbox and improve performance.

Here's how you use this tool:

■ Click View <u>M</u>ailbox Size to keep track of the size of the Outlook mailbox. The Folder Size dialog box that displays tells you the overall size of the mailbox as well as the size of each folder. Click Close when you're done.

> **TIP**
> The Folder Size dialog box shows the size of the mailbox and its folders in kilobytes (KB). If you want to convert any value to megabytes, use the Calculator tool (select Start, All Programs, Accessories, Calculator) to divide the KB value by 1,024.

- To find old messages, activate Find Items Older Than X Days and then click Find. The messages are displayed in the Advanced Find window, and from there you can delete or move the messages.

- To find large messages, activate Find Items Larger Than X Kilobytes and then click Find. Again, the messages are displayed in the Advanced Find window, and from there you can delete or move them.

- To archive messages, click AutoArchive.

> **NOTE** To configure the default settings for AutoArchive, select Tools, Options, select the Other tab, and then click AutoArchive. The dialog box that displays enables you to turn archived items on and off, set the AutoArchive frequency, and more. If you want special AutoArchive settings for a particular folder, right-click the folder, click Properties, and then select the AutoArchive tab.

- To clean out the Deleted Items folder, click Empty.

From Here

- To learn how to get Outlook data into Access, **see** "Importing Data from an Outlook Folder," **p. 380**.

- You can use Outlook to collect data for Access; **see**, "Collecting Access Data via E-mail," **p. 384**.

- For the details on working with VBA macros and the Visual Basic Editor, **see** "Appendix A, Working with VBA Macros," **p. 429**.

Calendar and Contacts Tricks

It seems almost redundant to describe modern life as "busy." Everyone works harder, cramming more appointments and meetings into already-packed schedules and somehow finding the time to get their regular work done between crises. As many a management consultant has advised over the years (charging exorbitant fees to do so), the key to surviving this helter-skelter, pell-mell pace is *time management*. Although there are as many theories about time management as there are consultants, one of the keys is that you should always try to make the best use of the time available. Although that often comes down to self-discipline and prioritizing your tasks, an efficient scheduling system can sure help.

That's where Outlook's Calendar feature comes in. At first glance, Calendar just looks like an electronic version of your day planner. You move around from day to day and month to month, entering tasks and appointments at their scheduled times. But Calendar goes far beyond this simple time-keeping function. For example, you can use it to schedule meetings via email and, depending on the responses, automatically update your schedule. You can put your Calendar on a public network folder so that others can see when you are available and set up appointments with you based on this information.

In other words, Calendar helps you spend less time on the process of scheduling, which gives you more time to do real work. The first half of this chapter takes you through several tricks and techniques that will help you get full value from Outlook Calendar feature.

The second half of this chapter looks at Outlook's contact management module—called, appropriately

13

enough, *Contacts*—which gives you amazing flexibility for dealing with your ever-growing network of colleagues, clients, friends, and family. So, yes, you can use Contacts to store mundane information such as phone numbers and addresses, and with more than 140 pre-defined fields available, you can preserve the minutiae of other people's lives: their birth-days and anniversaries, the names of their spouses and children, even their nicknames. I show you a few useful tricks and techniques that can help you take your work in the Contacts folder to the next level.

Starting Outlook in the Calendar Folder

By default, Outlook opens with the Inbox folder displayed, which makes sense because most people use Outlook primarily for email. If most of your Outlook time is spent in the Calendar, instead, you might prefer to display the Calendar folder automatically at startup. Here's how to do it:

1. Choose Tools, Options. Outlook opens the Options dialog box.
2. Select the Other tab.
3. Click Advanced Options. Outlook opens the Advanced Options dialog box.
4. Click Browse. Outlook opens the Select Folder dialog box.
5. Select the Calendar folder.
6. Click OK to return to the Advanced Options dialog box.
7. Click OK to return to the Options dialog box.
8. Click OK to put the new setting into effect.

> **TIP**
> These days, it's not uncommon for Outlook users to spend equal amounts of time in both the Inbox and Calendar folders. Rather than continually switch from one to the other in the main Outlook window, you can display a second Outlook window. This enables you to leave, say, the Inbox folder open in the first window and have the Calendar folder open in the second window. To set this up, right-click Calendar in Outlook's Navigation pane and then click Open in New Window. Note, too, that if you leave the second window open when you exit Outlook, the program "remembers" that you had a second window open and will automatically open it again the next time you start Outlook.

Changing the Number of Days That Calendar Displays

When you click Calendar in the Navigation pane, Outlook displays a calendar grid for today's date. If you want to view or work with some other date, you click that date in the Date Navigator (the calendar or calendars that display at the top of the Navigation pane). Whichever date you click, Calendar just shows a grid for that date. This is the Day calendar, and it's Calendar's default view. However, Calendar has other views that show multiple days, and you can easily create custom views that show as many days as you want.

Outlook comes with several predefined views, and these give you the simplest ways to change the number of days displayed in the Calendar grid:

- Choose <u>V</u>iew, Wo<u>r</u>k Week (or press Ctrl+Alt+2) to switch to the Work Week view, which shows Monday to Friday for whatever date was selected in the Date Navigator. (An alternative method is to display the Week view, discussed next, and then click the Show Work Week option.) For example, if you had today's date selected in the Date Navigator, switching to the Work Week view displays Monday through Friday for the current week.

> **TIP**
>
> It's not at all unusual these days for people to have non-standard work weeks that don't consist of Monday through Friday. For example, someone in retail might work Wednesday through Sunday, while a part-timer or person in a job-sharing arrangement might work Monday, Wednesday, and Friday.
>
> If your work week consists of a collection of days other than Monday through Friday, you can customize Outlook's Work Week view to show those days. Choose <u>T</u>ools, <u>O</u>ptions, and then click <u>C</u>alendar Options to open the Calendar Options dialog box. The Calendar Work Week group has check boxes named Sun, Mon, Tue, Wed, Thu, Fri, and Sat. Activate those check boxes that represent the days in your work week and then click OK in all open dialog boxes.

- Choose <u>V</u>iew, <u>W</u>eek (or click the Week button or press Ctrl+Alt+3) to switch to the Week view, which shows Sunday through Saturday for whatever date was selected in the Date Navigator.

> **TIP**
>
> If you prefer your week to begin on a day other than Sunday, you can customize Outlook to start the week accordingly in its Week view. Choose <u>T</u>ools, <u>O</u>ptions and then click <u>C</u>alendar Options to open the Calendar Options dialog box. Use the First Day of W<u>ee</u>k list to choose the day you prefer to start the week and then click OK in all open dialog boxes.

- Choose <u>V</u>iew, <u>M</u>onth (or click the Month button or press Ctrl+Alt+4 or Alt+=) to switch to the Month view. This view actually shows the five weeks that surround whatever date was selected in the Date Navigator. The days in the same month as the selected date are shown with a white background, and the days in the previous and next months are shown with a light blue background.
- Choose <u>V</u>iew, <u>D</u>ay (or click the Day button or press Ctrl+Alt+1) to return to the Day view.

You will probably use these built-in views most of the time, but there may be times when you need a custom view. For example, you might want to compare appointments for two

13

different dates, or you might want to see only the three days this week where you have appointments scheduled.

Outlook offers a number of techniques that enable you to use the Date Navigator to choose any number of days to display:

- Click and drag the pointer over the days you'd like to see. When you release the button, Outlook displays the selected days.

- To view multiple consecutive dates, click the first date, hold down Shift, and click the last date.

- To view multiple, nonconsecutive dates, click the first date, then hold down Ctrl key, and click the other dates (see Figure 13.1).

- To view an entire week (Sunday through Saturday), move the mouse pointer to the left of the week and click.

- To view multiple consecutive weeks, move the mouse pointer to the left of the first week and then click and drag down or up to select the weeks.

- To view multiple nonconsecutive weeks, move the mouse pointer just to the left of the first week and then click; hold down Ctrl and then for each of the other weeks, move the mouse pointer to the left of the week and click.

Hold down Ctrl and click the days you want to view

Figure 13.1
Outlook can display any number of days in the Calendar.

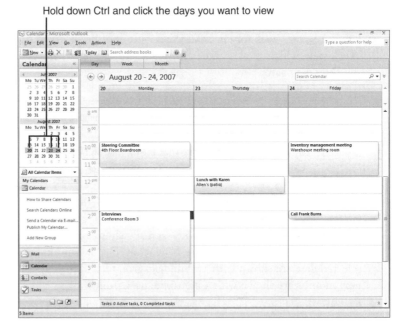

To display *x* number of days, press Alt+*x*, where *x* is a number from 0 to 9. For example, pressing Alt+4 displays the four days beginning with the currently selected day. Pressing Alt+0 displays the ten days beginning with the currently selected day.

Customizing the Day View's Time Scale

In Calendar's Day and Week views, the left side of the grid displays the hours of the day, divided into half-hour segments. This enables you to easily create appointments or meetings that begin on the hour or on the half hour. However, if you regularly set up appointments at other times—for example, at 15 minutes past or 15 minutes to the hour—then the half-hour time scale is a problem because you then have to adjust the appointment start time.

To avoid this extra work, you can tell Outlook to display a finer time scale that breaks down each hour into smaller segments, such as 15 minutes, 10 minutes, or even 5 minutes. On the other hand, if you mostly set appointments for the top of the hour, you can see more hours at a time in the Calendar grid by using a 60-minute time scale.

Here are the steps to follow to customize the time scale:

1. Right-click the Calendar grid and then click Other <u>S</u>ettings. Outlook opens the Format Day/Week/Month View dialog box.
2. Use the Ti<u>m</u>e Scale list to click the scale you prefer: 60, 30, 15, 10, 6, or 5.
3. Click OK.

When you're in Day or Week view, a quicker way to change the time scale is to right-click the time display on the left side of the Calendar grid and then click the time scale you want (such as 6<u>0</u> Minutes or <u>1</u>5 Minutes).

Adding Another Time Zone to the Day and Week Views

The times you see in the Day and Week views are geared to your current time zone, naturally enough. Outlook gets the current time zone from Windows, so if you change your Windows time zone setting, Outlook will also change its time zone.

It's often advantageous to view a second time zone alongside your own. For example, if you're in the Eastern time zone and you regularly communicate with people in the Pacific time zone, it's useful to be able to see the Pacific time alongside Eastern time when you're making appointments. Similarly, if you have colleagues in Europe or you're never quite sure what time it is in Arizona, displaying the appropriate time zone in Calendar can help.

13

Here are the steps to follow to add a second time zone to Calendar's Day and Week views:

1. Switch to the Day or Week view (or the Work Week view) if you haven't done so already.

2. Right-click the time display and then click Change Time Zone. Outlook opens the Time Zone dialog box.

3. In the Current Windows Time Zone group, use the Label text box to type a label for your time zone. This label displays at the top of the current time zone. (Specifying labels for the time zones is good because it enables you to tell at a glance which time zone is which.)

4. Click to activate the Show an Additional Time Zone check box.

5. In the Additional Time Zone group, use the Label text box to type a label for the second time zone.

6. Use the Time Zone list to select the time zone you want to add, as shown in Figure 13.2.

Figure 13.2
Use the Time Zone dialog box to add another time zone to Calendar's Day and Week views.

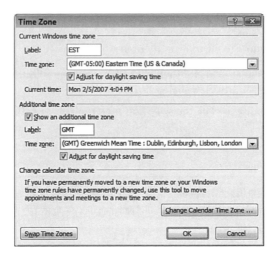

7. Click OK.

Figure 13.3 shows the Day Calendar with two time zones displayed.

> **TIP**
> You can double the number of months that the Date Navigator displays. Move your mouse pointer over the border that separates the Navigation pane and the Calendar so that the horizontal resize pointer displays. Drag the border to the right to roughly double the size of the default Navigation pane. When you release the mouse, Outlook displays four months instead of two in the Date Navigator.

Time zones

Figure 13.3
Outlook's Day view with
the Eastern Time (EST)
and Greenwich Meant
Time (GMT) zones dis-
played.

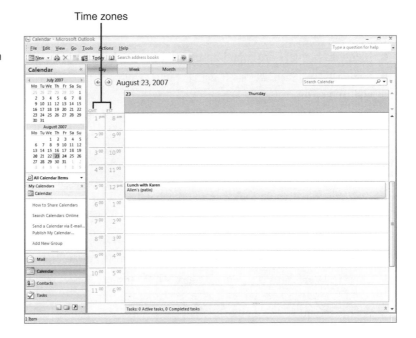

Customizing Calendar's Holidays

By default, Outlook doesn't display holidays in any Calendar view. This is problematic because you often need to know when holidays occur so that you can avoid scheduling appointments on those days and so you can plan other events such as family vacations. Holidays are country-specific, of course, so Outlook arranges holidays by country, with nearly 90 nations represented in all. You'll certainly want to add the holidays for your own country, but you're also free to add holidays from other countries, too. This is a good idea if you regularly deal with colleagues or clients in another country or if you're planning a trip to another country.

Follow these steps to add holidays to the Outlook Calendar:

1. Choose Tools, Options. Outlook opens the Options dialog box.
2. In the Preferences tab, click Calendar Options. Outlook opens the Calendar Options dialog box.
3. Click Add Holidays. Outlook opens the Add Holidays to Calendar dialog box.
4. For each country's holidays that you want to add to the Calendar, click to activate its check box. (In most Outlook installations, the check box for your country is activated by default.)
5. Click OK. Outlook adds the holidays and returns you to the Calendar Options dialog box.
6. Click OK to return to the Options dialog box.
7. Click OK.

13

Besides these standard, country-specific holidays, Outlook also enables you to customize the Calendar with nonstandard holidays, events, or dates, such as

- Religious holidays not found in the Outlook database.

- Company-specific dates such as the company picnic, the office Christmas party, year-end, and so on.

- Personal milestones such as family birthdays, your anniversary, vacation dates, and so on.

Most of the time, you can simply add these nonstandard holidays by hand as events in the Calendar. However, if you have lots of holidays to add, Outlook offers a faster solution: Customize the file that Outlook uses to track holidays. This is a simple text file that records the holiday (or whatever) name and the date on which it occurs. Here are the steps to follow:

1. How you begin depends on which version of Windows you use:

   - In Windows XP, choose Start, Run to open Windows' Run dialog box.

   - In Windows Vista, choose Start, All Programs, Accessories, right-click Command Prompt, click Run as Administrator, and then provide your User Account Control credentials. Vista opens a command prompt session.

2. Type the following:

   ```
   notepad "%Program Files%\Microsoft Office\Office12\1033\outlook.hol"
   ```

3. Press Enter. Notepad opens the Outlook.hol file. Figure 13.4 shows the first few entries in the United States portion of the file.

Figure 13.4

The Outlook.hol text file holds Outlook's holiday data.

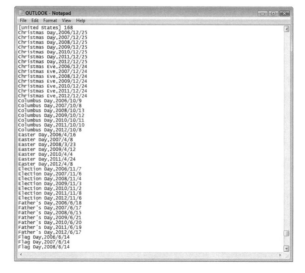

13

4. Scroll to the bottom of the list, start a new line, and type the following, where *Section* is the name of the section you want to add (this is also the name of the check box that

displays in the Add Holidays to Calendar dialog box; make this your company name, family name, or whatever), and *Number* is the number of holidays you're going to list:

[Section] Number

5. For each holiday, start a new line and type the holiday using the following format, where *Name* is the name of the holiday, and *yyyy/m/d* is the date of the holiday (see Figure 13.5):

Name,yyyy/m/d

Figure 13.5
An example of a custom holiday list.

6. Save your work and then close Notepad.

7. Follow the steps from earlier in this section to display the Add Holidays to Calendar dialog box. Click to activate the check box next to your custom holiday list, as shown in Figure 13.6 and then click OK.

Figure 13.6
The section name you added to the Outlook.hol file displays in the Add Holidays to Calendar dialog box.

Printing a Blank Calendar

It's often handy to print out a blank calendar for a particular month. For example, you might want to pin the calendar to a company bulletin board so that people can write in appointments or events. Unfortunately, it's likely you won't be able to print a blank monthly calendar directly from your Outlook Calendar because it's probably filled with appointments and events. However, it's possible to create a second Calendar folder and then print directly from that.

First, here's how you create the blank Calendar folder:

1. Switch to Month view and display the month you want to print. (For a blank day or week calendar, switch to the appropriate view and display the day or week you want to print.)

2. Choose File, New, Folder (or press Ctrl+Shift+E). The Create New Folder dialog box displays.

3. Type a name for the new folder (such as the month and year).

4. Make sure that Calendar Items is selected in the Folder Contains list.

5. Click OK.

Outlook adds the new Calendar folder to the My Calendars list in the Navigation pane.

Now follow these steps to print the blank calendar:

1. Activate the blank calendar's check box in the My Calendars list.

2. Close the main Calendar by deactivating the Calendar check box in the My Calendars list.

3. Choose File, Page Setup, Monthly Style.

4. Click Print to open the Print dialog box.

5. Adjust the Start and End dates to print only those dates you want in the blank calendar.

6. If you want to check the blank calendar before printing, click Preview to open the Print Preview window, shown in Figure 13.7. When you're done, click Print to return to the Print dialog box.

7. Click OK.

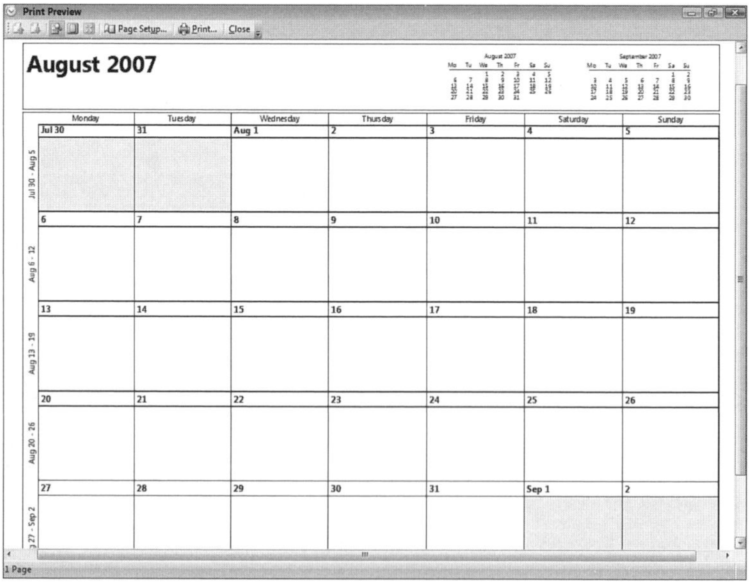

Figure 13.7
A preview of a blank calendar, ready to be printed.

Using Natural-Language Dates and Times

When you create an appointment and need to enter a date in the Start Time field, what do you do if you want the appointment to occur on, say, the first Monday in August? Typically, most people pull down the Start Time calendar control, scroll ahead to August, and then click the first Monday. That works fine, but you may not know that Outlook also enables you to type the following in the Start Time text box:

`first mon in aug`

Outlook understands such natural-language dates and converts them to actual dates (and times). If today is Thursday, August 23, for example, and you type **next fri** in a date box, Outlook will enter Friday, August 31 as the date. Similarly, if you type **noon** in a time box, Outlook automatically converts it to 12:00 PM.

Outlook's capability to understand natural-language dates and times is called AutoDate. Here are some AutoDate examples that should give you some idea about what this feature can do:

- AutoDate converts `yesterday`, `today`, and `tomorrow` into their date equivalents.

- You can shorten day names to their first three letters: `sun`, `mon`, `tue`, `wed`, `thu`, `fri`, and `sat`. (Notice, too, that case isn't important.) You can also shorten month names: `jan`, `feb`, `mar`, `apr`, `may`, `jun`, `jul`, `aug`, `sep`, `oct`, `nov`, and `dec`.

- To specify a date in the current week (Calendar's weeks run from Sunday through Saturday), use the keyword `this` (for example, `this fri`).

- To specify a date from last week or last month, use the keyword `last` (for example, `last aug`).

- To specify a date in the next week or month, use the keyword `next` (for example, `next sat`).

- If you want to use the first day of a week or month, use the keyword `first`. For example, `first mon in dec` gives you the first Monday in December. Similarly, use `last` to specify the last day of a week or month.

- To get a date that is a particular number of days, weeks, months, or years from some other date, use the keyword `from` (for example, `6 months from today`).

- To get a date that is a particular number of days, weeks, months, or years before some other date, use the keyword `before` (for example, `2 days before Christmas`).

> **NOTE** AutoDate also recognizes a number of holidays that fall on the same date each year, including the following: Boxing Day, Cinco de Mayo, Christmas, Christmas Day, Christmas Eve, Halloween, Independence Day, Lincoln's Birthday, New Year's Day, New Year's Eve, St. Patrick's Day, Valentine's Day, Veterans Day, and Washington's Birthday.

13

- To get a date that is a particular number of days, weeks, months, or years in the past, use the keyword ago (for example, `4 weeks ago`).

- AutoDate also accepts spelled-out dates, such as `August 23rd` and `first of January`. These aren't as useful because they probably take longer to spell out than they do to enter the date in the usual format.

For time fields, keep the following points in mind:

- AutoDate converts `0` to 12:00 AM and `12` to 12:00 PM.

- AutoDate converts integers between 0 and 12 to the corresponding morning hours. For example, it converts `4` to 4:00 AM. If you want to specify an afternoon or evening hour, type the integer followed by `PM`. For example, AutoDate converts `8 PM` to 8:00 PM.

- AutoDate converts `noon` and `midnight` into the correct times.

- AutoDate understands military time. So, if you enter `9`, AutoDate converts this to 9:00 AM. However, if you enter `21`, AutoDate changes it to 9:00 PM.

- Use `now` to specify the current time.

- You can specify time zones using the following abbreviations: `CST`, `EST`, `GMT`, `MST`, and `PST`.

Customizing the To-Do Bar

Outlook 2007 comes with a new feature called the To-Do Bar that gives you at-a-glance access to the Date Navigator, your next three appointments, and a list of your pending tasks. The To-Do Bar is a welcome replacement for the TaskPad in previous versions of Outlook, not only because it shows more information, but also because it's far more customizable:

- You can change the number of appointments and toggle the display of appointments on and off.

- You can change the number of months shown in the Date Navigator and toggle the Date Navigator on and off.

- You can toggle the Task List on and off.

First, make sure you're displaying the To-Do Bar by choosing <u>V</u>iew, To-Do <u>B</u>ar, <u>N</u>ormal. The To-Do Bar displays on the right side of the Outlook window, as shown in Figure 13.8.

Task List   Date Navigator

Appointments   To-Do Bar

Figure 13.8
Outlook 2007's new To-Do Bar shows upcoming appointments and pending tasks.

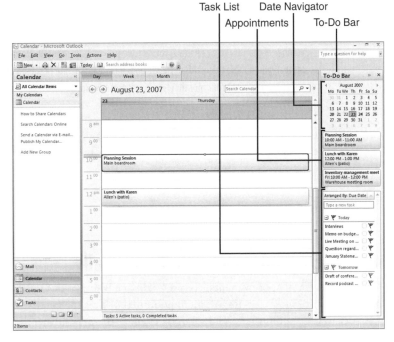

To toggle the three To-Do Bar elements on and off, choose View, To-Do Bar and then choose the element you want to toggle: Date Navigator, Appointments, or Task List. For more customization settings, follow these steps:

1. Choose View, To-Do Bar, Options to open the To-Do Bar Options dialog box, shown in Figure 13.9. (You can also right-click the top of the To-Do Bar and then click Options.)

Figure 13.9
The To-Do Bar Options dialog box enables you to customize the number of month rows and the number of appointments shown in the To-Do Bar.

2. Click the Show Date Navigator check box to toggle the Date Navigator on and off. If you leave the check box activated, use the Number of month rows text box to specify the number of rows that the To-Do Bar uses to display the Date Navigator.

13

> **NOTE** The number of months you see in the To-Do Bar is a function not only of the value in the Number of month rows text box, but also the width of the To-Do Bar. For example, if you change the Number of month rows value to 2, you can see two months in the To-Do Bar using the default width. If you double the width of the To-Do Bar (by clicking and dragging the left edge of the To-Do Bar), you can see four months (two across and two down).

3. Click the Show Appointments check box to toggle the appointments on and off. If you leave the check box activated, use the Number of appointments text box to specify how many appointments you want to display.

4. Click the Show Task List check box to toggle the Task List on and off.

5. Click OK.

Color-Coding Appointments Automatically

If you have a lot of appointments, consider taking advantage of Outlook's capability to color code—or *categorize*—important appointments. This means that you apply a particular category to the appointment, and Outlook changes the appointment's background color to the color associated with the category. I showed you how to customize Outlook's categories in Chapter 12, "Email Tricks."

➔ For the details on customizing Outlook's categories, **see** "Creating Custom Color Categories," **p. 318**

To set the category for an existing appointment, right-click the appointment, click Categorize (you can also click the Categorize toolbar button or choose Edit, Categorize), and then click the category.

Rather than color-coding appointments by hand, you can configure Outlook to automatically apply a color to an appointment based on one or more keywords in the appointment subject or notes field (or both). For example, you can set up Outlook to automatically apply a green background to appointments that include the word *Budget* in the subject or notes. This is called a *rule*, and you can create rules based on keywords, appointment times, meeting attendees, and other conditions.

Follow these steps to set up a rule that applies automatic color-coding:

1. Choose Edit, Automatic Formatting. Outlook opens the Automatic Formatting dialog box.

2. Click Add. Outlook creates a new, empty rule.

3. Type a Name for the new rule.

4. Use the Color list to click the color you want to apply to appointments that satisfy the new rule's conditions.

5. Click Condition. Outlook opens the Filter dialog box (see Figure 3.10).

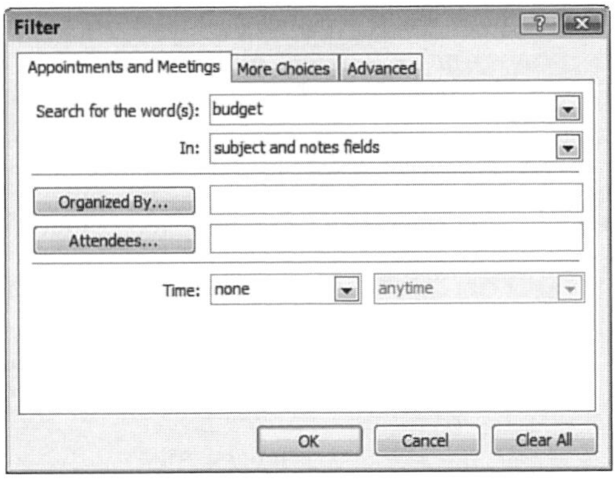

Figure 13.10
Use the Filter dialog box to set up the condition or conditions under which Outlook applies your automatic formatting rule.

6. In the Search for the word(s) text box, type one or more keywords that you want Outlook to match. Note that if you enter two or more words, the appointment must match *all* the words to satisfy the condition.

7. Use the In list to click where you want Outlook to search for the keywords: Subject Field Only, Subject and Notes Fields, or Frequently-Used Text Fields.

> **NOTE** The Frequently-Used Text Fields option includes the following fields: Subject, Location, Categories, Required Attendees, Optional Attendees, and Resources.

8. If you want to color-code appointments and meetings created by another person, click Organized By and then select a contact.

9. If you want to color-code appointments and meetings that have a particular attendee, click Attendees and then select a contact.

10. If you want to color-code appointments by time, use the Time lists to select an operator (Starts, Ends, Created, or Modified) and a time (such as Tomorrow or Next Week).

11. Click OK to return to the Automatic Formatting dialog box.

12. Click OK to put the new rule into effect.

Editing Multiple Contacts at Once

It's not unusual to have several contacts that have one or more fields in common. For example, if you deal with a number of people from a particular company, those contacts have the same value in the Company field, and they may also all have the same values in the Web Page Address, Business Phone Number, Business Fax, and Business Address fields.

13

What happens, however, when the value in a common field changes? For example, the company might change its name or move to a different address. If you only have a couple of contacts that are affected by the change, it's no big deal to update the contact data by hand. However, what if you have half a dozen or more contacts with the same data? Updating all those contacts by hand is a tedious chore, at best. Fortunately, you can take advantage of a trick that enables you to edit all of the affected contacts at once.

You begin by organizing your Contacts folder into groups according to the field you want to change. The easiest way to do this is to select an existing view that corresponds to the changing field. For example, if you're changing the Company field, then you'd click By Company in The Current View section of the Navigation Pane. If Outlook doesn't have a view for the field you want to change, you can create it yourself:

1. Choose View, Current View, Define Views. The Custom View Organizer dialog box displays.

2. Click New. The Create a New View dialog box displays.

3. Use the Name of New View text box to name the view (for example, By *Field*, where *Field* is the name of the field you want to modify), make sure Table is selected in the Type of View list, and then click OK. The Customize View dialog box displays.

4. Click Group By to display the Group By dialog box.

5. In the Group Items By list, click the field you want to modify.

6. Click OK to return to the Customize View dialog box.

7. Click OK to return to the Custom View Organizer dialog box.

8. In the Views for folder 'Contacts' list, click your new view.

9. Click Apply View.

With your contacts grouped on the field you want to work with, you are now ready to make the change. Here are the steps to follow:

1. Choose View, Expand/Collapse Groups, Collapse All Groups. The Contacts folder now shows only the group headers.

2. Locate the group that contains the contacts you want to edit, and then expand that group by clicking its plus sign (+).

3. Edit the field in the group's first contact. Outlook immediately adds a new group for the edited data and moves the first contact into that group.

4. Drag the group header for the rest of the Contacts with the old data and drop it on the group header for the new data (see Figure 13.11). Outlook updates all the Contacts with the new field data.

13

Drag the header of the old field value to the new field value

Figure 13.11
When you drag one group into another, Outlook updates the group field to the value in the new group.

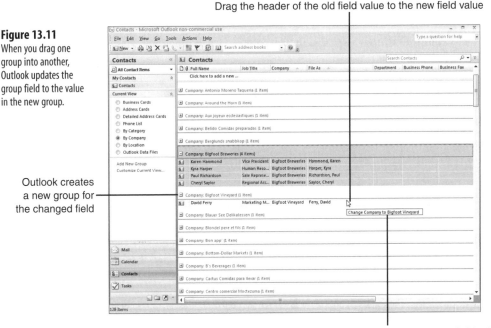

Outlook creates a new group for the changed field

Outlook lets you know it will change the field value

Calling a Contact

Although email seems to have replaced the telephone as the contact medium of choice, it's still often useful and necessary to call the people you work with. If your computer has a modem, then you can get Outlook to initiate the call for you and even make a note of the call in Outlook's Journal folder. For this to work, you need to have a traditional (that is, not wireless) phone on your desk and your phone cables configured as follows:

- Run one phone cable from your modem's "Line" jack to the phone jack on your wall.
- Run another phone cable from your modem's "Phone" jack to your telephone.

Outlook gives you all kinds of ways to initiate a call, but the following two are the easiest:

- In the Contacts folder, right-click the contact and then click Call Contact.
- If the contact you want to call is already open, choose the Contact tab and click the top half of the Call split button (it's in the Communicate group).

Outlook displays the New Call dialog box, shown in Figure 13.12. Before starting your call, you can use the following options in this dialog box:

- **Open Contact**—Click this button to open the Contact window for the current contact.
- **Dialing Properties**—Click this button to select or change the dialing properties for Windows.

13

- **Create New Journal Entry When Starting New Call**—Activate this check box to create an entry in Outlook's Journal for this call.

- **Dialing Options**—Use this button to set up speed-dial numbers, discussed later in this section.

Figure 13.12
Use the New Call dialog box to configure and initiate the contact phone call.

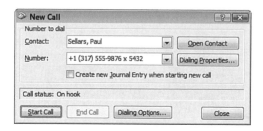

When you're ready to dial, click <u>S</u>tart Call. When the Call Status reads `Connected`, pick up the phone and proceed with your call. When you're done, click <u>E</u>nd Call.

> **TIP**
>
> Outlook keeps track of the last seven calls you dialed. To redial one of these numbers, choose <u>A</u>ctions, <u>Ca</u>ll Contact, <u>R</u>edial or drop down the toolbar's Dial list and then click <u>R</u>edial. Click the number to redial from the menu that displays.

> **NOTE**
>
> If you want to phone someone not in your Contacts list, choose <u>A</u>ctions, <u>Ca</u>ll Contact, <u>N</u>ew Call (or press Ctrl+Shift+D) to display the New Call dialog box. Type the phone number into the <u>N</u>umber text box and then click <u>S</u>tart Call.

You may find that you have several contacts that you call the most. Rather than always right-clicking or opening these contacts to call them, you can place them on Outlook's Speed Dial list, which enables you to initiate calls to those contacts with just a few mouse clicks. Here are the steps to follow to set up a Speed Dial number:

1. Press Ctrl+Shift+D to open the New Call dialog box. (Actually, you can use any method you want to display this dialog box. Unfortunately, Outlook gives you no direct method of defining a specific number as a Speed Dial number. It would be nice if we had an Add to Speed Dial command, but there isn't one.)

2. Click the Dialing Options button. Outlook opens the Dialing Options dialog box, as shown in Figure 13.13.

3. Type the person's name in the <u>N</u>ame text box.

4. Type the person's phone number in the Phone n<u>u</u>mber text box.

5. Click A<u>d</u>d.

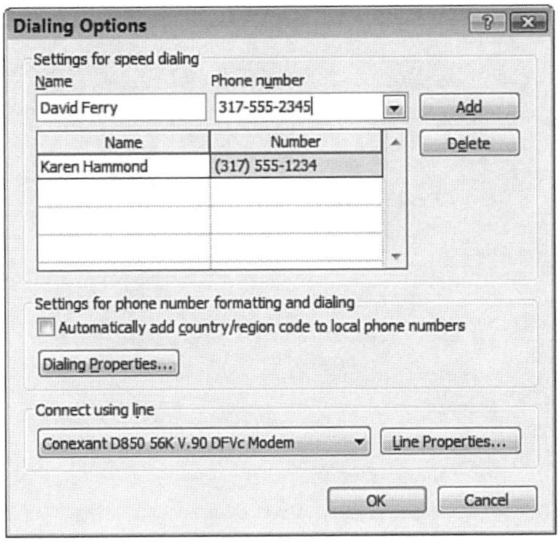

Figure 13.13
Use the Dialing Options dialog box to add a number to Outlook's Speed Dial list.

6. Repeat Steps 3–5 to add other numbers to the Speed Dial list. You can add up to 20 entries.

7. Click OK to return to the New Call dialog box.

8. Click Close.

To start a Speed Dial call, you have two choices:

- Choose Actions, Call Contact, Speed Dial (or drop down the toolbar's Dial list and choose Speed Dial). In the menu that appears, click the person you want to call.

- Display the New Call dialog box, pull down the Contact list, and then click the person you want to call.

Adding a Contact Picture

With digital cameras all the rage, sharing photos is as easy as emailing or, in the case of camera phones, making a phone call. This means it's possible you may have a picture of a contact. If so, you can add that picture to the person's contact data. Here's how:

1. Open the contact.

2. Choose Contact, Picture, Add Picture, or click the Add Contact Picture button. The Add Contact Picture dialog box displays.

3. Select the picture you want to use.

4. Click OK. Outlook replaces the Add Contact Picture button with the picture you selected, as shown in Figure 13.14.

Figure 13.14
The contact with a picture added.

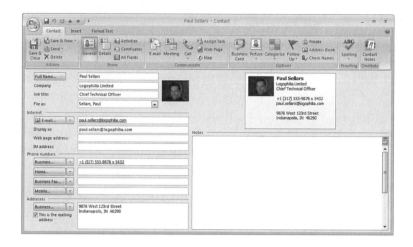

Displaying a Map for a Contact's Address

In the old days (a few years ago!), if you had a contact located in an unfamiliar part of town or even in another city altogether, visiting that person required a phone call or email asking for directions. You'd then write down the instructions, get written directions via email, or perhaps even get a crudely drawn map faxed to you. Those days, fortunately, are long gone thanks to a myriad of online resources that can show you where a particular address is located and even give you driving directions to get there from here (wherever "here" may be).

Even better, Outlook 2007 integrates with Microsoft's Virtual Earth and Live Search services to generate a map of a contact's location based on the person's contact address. Follow these steps to use the Map feature:

1. Open the contact you want to work with.

2. In the Addresses section, on the drop-down list, click the address type you want to use (Business, Home, or Other).

3. Check the address to make sure it's accurate.

4. Choose Contact, Map. Outlook opens Internet Explorer and sends the contact's address to the Live Search service, as shown in Figure 13.15.

13

Figure 13.15
Clicking the Map button in a contact window loads the contact's address into the Live Search service, which displays a map of the contact's location.

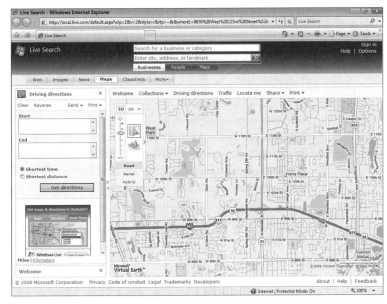

Printing a Phone Directory of Your Contacts

Hard copies of corporate phone directories are increasingly rare these days. That's not surprising because it's so much easier to maintain and distribute phone data electronically. However, there are still occasions when a physical directory is useful. For example, you might require a phone directory in a location (such as a warehouse) that doesn't have a nearby computer. Similarly, you might want to print a directory of your contacts to leave by a phone in a room that doesn't have a computer.

To print your Contacts folder as a phone directory, follow these steps:

1. Select the contacts you want to include in the phone directory. (If you want to print all your contacts, don't select any.)
2. Choose File, Print (you can also press Ctrl+P or click the Print toolbar button). Outlook opens the Print dialog box.
3. Use the Print Style list to click Phone Directory Style.
4. To print just the selected contacts, click the Only Selected Items option.
5. Use the Number of Copies spin box to specify how many copies to print.
6. Click OK. Outlook prints the phone directory.

13

Sharing a Folder with Other Users

In a business environment, it's often useful to share your Outlook data with other users. For example, if you have an assistant, you might want him to view your Outlook Calendar or Contacts. Similarly, the members of a team might need to see each other's Calendar or Tasks.

> **TIP** If you want to share one of your contacts with another person, it's often easier to email the contact information to that person. To do this, open the contact and choose Contact, Send (in the Actions group). If the recipient has Outlook, select In Outlook Format; if the recipient doesn't have Outlook, select In Internet Format (vCard).

Sharing a Folder via Email

For the Calendar folder, an easy way to share is to email some or all of the Calendar details to another user. The other user receives an HTML message that includes the Calendar data. He can also open the attached calendar file to open the calendar in Outlook. Here are the steps to follow to email your Calendar:

1. In the Calendar folder's Navigation Pane, click the Send a Calendar Via E-mail link. Outlook displays the Send a Calendar Via E-mail dialog box, shown in Figure 13.16.

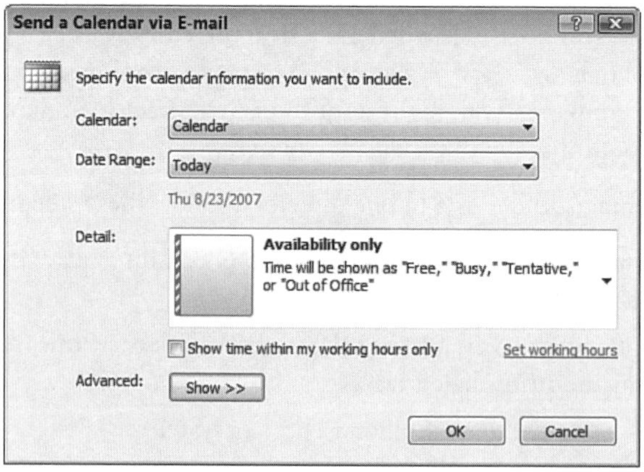

Figure 13.16
Use the Send a Calendar Via E-mail dialog box to specify how much of your Calendar you want to send.

2. If you have more than one Calendar, use the Calendar list to select the one you want to send.

3. Use the Date Range list to select the dates you want to send (Today, Tomorrow, Next 7 Days, Next 30 Days, Whole Calendar, or Specify Dates).

4. Use the <u>D</u>etail list to select how much appointment detail you want the other user to see:

- **Availability Only**—Outlook shows only your time as Free, Busy, Out of Office, and so on. No appointment details display in the Calendar.
- **Limited Details**—Outlook includes your availability as well as the Subject line of each appointment.
- **Full Details**—Outlook includes your availability, the Subject line of each appointment, and appointment details such as the Location.

5. If you choose Availability only in Step 4, you can also click to activate the Show time within my <u>w</u>orking hours only to limit the Calendar to the hours between 8 AM and 5 PM.

> **TIP**
>
> To change your default working hours, choose <u>T</u>ools, <u>O</u>ptions, and then click <u>C</u>alendar Options to open the Calendar Options dialog box. Use the Star<u>t</u> Time list to select the start of your working day, use the E<u>n</u>d Time list to select the end of your working day, and then click OK in the open dialog boxes.

6. Click Show to display the advanced options.

7. If you selected either Limited Details or Full Details in Step 4, you can click to activate the Include Details o<u>f</u> Items Marked Private check box to include private appointments in the Calendar.

> **TIP**
>
> To mark an appointment as private, open it and then choose Appointment, Private (in the Options group).

8. If you selected Full Details in Step 4, you can click to activate the Include A<u>t</u>tachments Within Calendar Items check box to include appointment attachments in the Calendar.

9. Use the <u>E</u>-mail Layout list to select how you want the Calendar items to display in the message:

- **Daily Schedule**—Shows your complete daily schedule, include unscheduled time.
- **List of Events**—Shows only your appointments.

9. Click <u>O</u>K. Outlook gathers the Calendar data, and then it creates a new HTML email message with the Calendar data attached as an iCalendar file and displayed within the body of the message.

10. Address the message, add any body text you think is necessary, and then send the message.

Figure 13.17 shows Calendar data received in a message.

13

Figure 13.17
Calendar data sent via email.

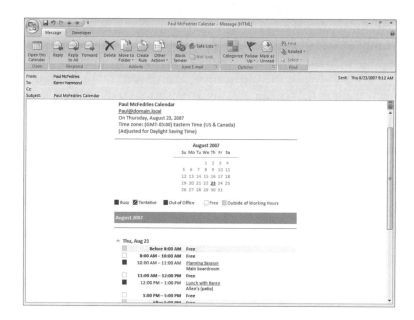

Sharing a Folder via Microsoft Exchange

If your company uses Microsoft Exchange Server, or if you have an account on an Exchange Server host, you can share any of your folders with other Exchange Server users. You can set up the sharing for specific users, and you can apply permissions that determine what actions each user can perform within the folder. Outlook gives you two ways to share your folders: with permissions and with delegate access.

To share any Outlook folder, follow these steps:

1. Select the folder you want to share.

2. Choose File, Folder, Change Sharing Permissions. Outlook opens the folder's Properties dialog box and displays the Permissions tab, shown in Figure 13.18.

3. Click Add to display the Add Users dialog box.

4. For each user you want to allow to open the folder, select the name and then click Add. When you're done, click OK to return to the Properties dialog box.

5. Select the name of the user to whom you want to assign permissions.

6. Use the Permission Level list to select the permission level for the user:

   Owner—User can create, read, edit, and delete all folder items, create subfolders, and can change the permission levels for other users.

   Publishing Editor—User can create, read, edit, and delete all items and create subfolders.

   Editor—User can create, read, edit, and delete all items.

Publishing Author—User can create and read all items and create subfolders but can edit and delete only the user's own items.

Author—User can create and read all items but can edit and delete only the user's own items.

Nonediting Author—User can create and read all items but can delete only the user's own items.

Reviewer—User can only read items.

Contributor—User can only create items. The contents of the folder do not display. (Does not apply to delegates.)

None—User can't open the folder.

Figure 13.18
In the folder's Properties dialog box, use the Permissions tab to configure a folder for sharing with other users on your Exchange Server system.

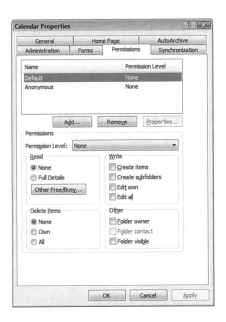

7. Customize the permission level by activating or deactivating the check boxes and option buttons in the Read, Write, Delete Items, and Other groups.

8. Repeat Steps 5–7 to set the permission level for each user.

9. Click OK.

After you configure an Exchange user with folder permissions, the next step is usually to send a sharing invitation to that person. This is an email message that lets the person know that he can access your folder, and you can also use it to ask the person if you can view the same Outlook folder on his system. Here are the steps to follow:

13

1. Open the folder you want to share.

2. In the Navigation Pane, click Share My *Folder*, where *Folder* is the name of the folder you share. (You can also choose File, Folder, Share *Folder*.) Outlook starts a new message with the following Subject line (where *Name* is your name and *Folder* is the shared folder):
   ```
   Sharing invitation: Name - Folder
   ```

3. Address the message to the person with whom you shared the folder.

4. To ask the user for permission to view the same folder in his mailbox, click to activate the Request Permission to View the Recipient's *Folder* check box (again, where *Folder* is the name of the folder you share).

5. Add a brief message to the other person, if desired.

6. Click Send. Outlook asks you to confirm that you want to share the folder.

7. Click Yes. Outlook sends the sharing invitation, and then it lets you know the folder has been shared.

8. Click OK.

Sharing a Folder with Delegate Access via Microsoft Exchange

It's often handy to have another person send new messages, replies, and forwards on your behalf. For example, you may be stuck in a meeting when an important message comes through that must be responded to immediately. Similarly, you might have a deputy or team assistant that you want to give access to your Inbox folder while you're not in the office.

You can do this by sharing your Inbox folder with the other person. However, that's not ideal because other people access your shared folder as themselves. So, if an assistant accesses your shared Inbox and replies to one of your messages, the recipient will see that the reply came from your assistant, not you. If you want the other person to send messages that appear to come from you, and if you're on an Exchange Server network or host, then you can give that person *send-on-behalf-of* permission on your Inbox folder. You do this by setting up the user as a *delegate* who has *delegate access* to your Inbox. Follow these steps:

1. Choose Tools, Options. Outlook opens the Options dialog box.

2. Choose the Delegates tab.

3. Click Add. Outlook opens the Add Users dialog box.

4. Click the user you want to assign delegate access, click Add, and then click OK. Outlook opens the Delegate Permissions dialog box for the user, as shown in Figure 13.19.

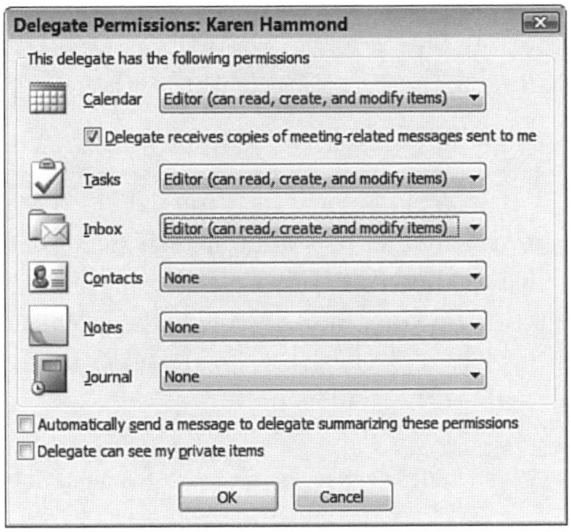

Figure 13.19
In the Delegate Permissions dialog box, specify the permissions for each folder you want the selected delegate to access on your behalf.

Delegate Permissions: Karen Hammond

This delegate has the following permissions

Calendar Editor (can read, create, and modify items)

☑ Delegate receives copies of meeting-related messages sent to me

Tasks Editor (can read, create, and modify items)

Inbox Editor (can read, create, and modify items)

Contacts None

Notes None

Journal None

☐ Automatically send a message to delegate summarizing these permissions
☐ Delegate can see my private items

OK   Cancel

5. For each folder you want the delegate to access, use the associated list to set the user's permissions on that folder:

   Reviewer—The delegate can only read items.

   Author—The delegate can create and read all items but can edit and delete only the delegate's own items.

   Editor—The delegate can create, read, edit, and delete all items.

6. If you want Outlook to send a message to the delegate outlining the permissions you set, click to activate the Automatically send a message to delegate summarizing these permissions check box.

7. If you want the delegate to also see those items that you marked as private, click to activate the Delegate can see my private items check box.

8. Click OK to return to the Options dialog box.

9. Click OK.

Viewing Another User's Shared Folder

Earlier in this chapter you learned how to share a folder with permissions and with delegate access. If another Microsoft Exchange user has given you share permissions or delegate access, you can view the shared folder anytime you like. Here are the steps to follow:

1. Choose File, Open, Other User's Folder to display the Open Other User's Folder dialog box.

2. Type the name of the person who shared the folder. If you're not sure, click Name, use the Select Name dialog box to click the user, and then click OK.

3. In the Folder Type list, click the type of folder you want to access.

4. Click OK. Outlook displays the shared folder.

> **TIP**
>
> For the Calendar, Contacts, Tasks, Notes, and Journal folder, you can also click the Open Shared *Folder* link in the Navigation pane, where *Folder* is the type of folder (for example, Open Shared Calendar).

Figure 13.20 shows Outlook with another person's Calendar folder open alongside the current user's Calendar. Note that the other person's Calendar appears in the Navigation Pane in the People's Calendars section, so you can easily toggle the calendar on and off by activating and deactivating its check box. (A check box for the user's shared folder displays in the Navigation Pane for all nonmessage folders.)

Click to toggle the shared Calendar   Shared Calendar

Figure 13.20
A shared Calendar folder.

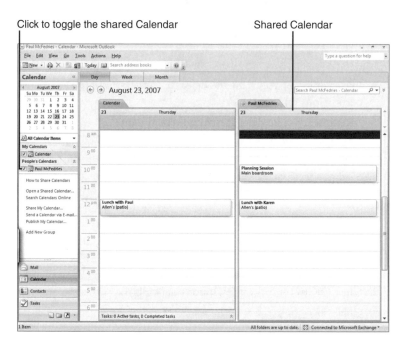

Working with Another Email Account as a Delegate

If you're a delegate with Editor or Author privileges, you have send-on-behalf-of permission, meaning you can send new messages, replies, and forwards using the folder owner's email account. Although you can do this by displaying a shared message folder, it's much easier if you add the owner's email account to your Exchange Server profile. Here's how it's done:

1. Choose Tools, Account Settings to open the Account Settings dialog box.

2. Click your Exchange Server account and then click Change. The Change E-mail Account dialog box displays.

3. Click More Settings to open the Microsoft Exchange dialog box.

4. Display the Advanced tab.

5. Click A<u>d</u>d to open the Add Mailbox dialog box.

6. Type the owner's name and click OK.

7. Click OK to return to the Change E-mail Account dialog box.

8. Click <u>N</u>ext.

9. Click Finish to return to the Account Settings dialog box.

10. Click <u>C</u>lose.

Outlook displays both sets of mail folders, as shown in Figure 13.21.

Figure 13.21
When you add another user's mailbox to your account, Outlook shows both sets of mail folders.

Other user's mail folders

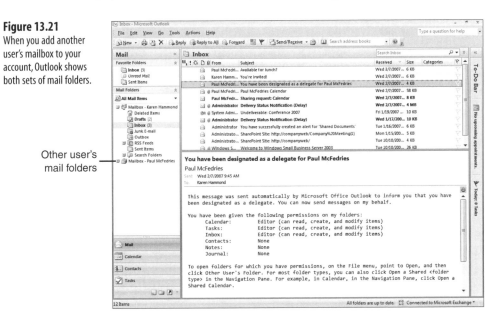

To send a message as a delegate on behalf of the owner, start a new message or reply to or forward an existing message in one of the owner's message folders. Make sure the From field is displayed by choosing Options, Show From. Type the owner's name into the From field, and then fill out and send the message normally. When the recipient receives the message, the From field data has the following format:

```
Delegate Name on behalf of Owner Name
```

From Here

- For the details on customizing Outlook's categories, **see** "Creating Custom Color Categories," **p. 318.**

- To learn how to get Outlook data into Access, **see** "Importing Data from an Outlook Folder," **p. 380.**

13

Microsoft Access Tricks

V

Table and Query Tricks

Microsoft Access is the data powerhouse of the Office suite. It's a full-fledged relational database management system, but it offers easy-to-use features for storing, viewing, and manipulating data. However, Office gurus want to go far beyond these simple data tasks, and they know that Access has the tools that are powerful and flexible enough to handle just about any need. Running through all of these tools would require several books of this size, but I have a few favorite tools, tricks, and techniques that I find are the most useful for bringing Access data down to size. I tell you about these features in this chapter and in Chapter 15, "Form and Report Tricks." In this chapter, you learn a number of techniques for entering data accurately and consistently, including using data validation, input masks, and default field values. You also learn how to relate multiple tables, how to collect Access data via email, and how to create powerful queries that tame even the wildest data.

Validating Data Entry

Access may be a powerful program, but it's not a stretch to say that it's only as useful as its data is accurate. You can create the world's most powerful queries, the most efficient forms, and the best-looking reports, but none of it means a thing if the data in the underlying table is either downright wrong (for example, if digits get transposed) or invalid (for example, a field value falls outside an allowable range of values). Slips of the fingertips always happen during data entry, but Access does offer a few tools that you can use to lessen the chance that you or someone else enters invalid data.

One simple way to help users enter valid data is to include a description for each field in a table. As you can see in Figure 14.1, in the table Design view (right-click the table in the Navigation pane and then click <u>D</u>esign View), you can use the Description column to enter brief descriptions of each field. These descriptions can also include data-entry instructions, such as the following for the Order Date field:

```
The order date in MM/DD/YYYY format.
```

In Datasheet view (choose Design, click the bottom half of the View split button, and then click Datas<u>h</u>eet View), the Description text displays in the Access status bar when the user enters the field, as shown in Figure 14.2.

NOTE   In this chapter and the next, the sample data I use is a modified version of the Northwind sample database that shipped with Access 2003. (There is a new Northwind sample database in Access 2007, but its data is extremely limited and not useful for illustrating database concepts.) You can download the database I use in this chapter from my Web site:

    http://www.mcfedries.com/Office2007Gurus/

Description for the Order Date field

Figure 14.1
You can add Description text for each field in your table.

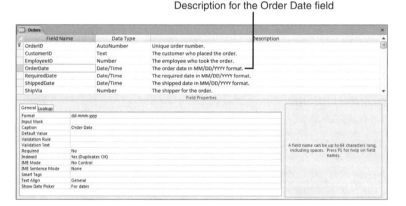

Status bar field descriptions can help users enter data more accurately but, of course, they are useful only if the user actually reads them. Unfortunately, people all too often miss such prompts while in the throes of data entry.

Access helps ensure valid data by alerting the user when he enters data that doesn't conform to the field's data type. Access automatically displays a smart tag with the following message (where *Type* is the field's data type; see Figure 14.3 for an example):

```
The value you entered does not match the Type data type in this column.
```

14

When you enter a field...

Figure 14.2
The current field's
Description text displays
in the status bar.

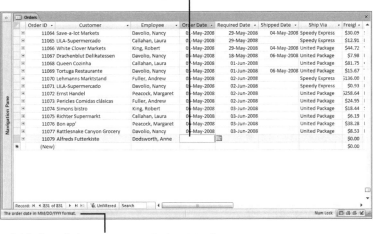

...the field's Description text appears in the status bar

Figure 14.3
If you try to enter a value
that doesn't match the
field's data type, Access
displays a smart tag sim-
ilar to the one shown
here.

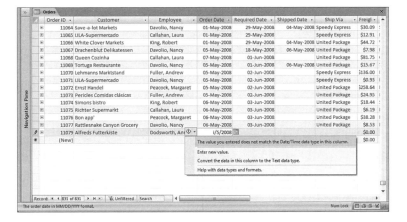

Ensuring data type consistency is just one of the battles that database designers must wage. The other major battle is ensuring that the entered data is accurate and valid. If you want to enhance the accuracy and validity of entered data, you need to automate data checking to a certain extent by implementing *validation rules*. These are conditions that specify the legal values that the user can enter.

For example, in a table of orders placed, suppose you want to avoid order dates that are in the future. In your business, orders are placed today or perhaps in the recent past, but never in the future. To ensure this, you can set up a validation rule that allows the data only if the order date is less than or equal to today's date. For invalid entries, you can define *validation text* that pops up to alert the user that he has entered an invalid value.

14

Here are the steps to follow to set up validation rule:

1. Open the table you want to work with in Design view (right-click the table in the Navigation pane and then click <u>D</u>esign View).

2. Click the field to which you want to apply the validation rule.

3. Click inside the Validation Rule property.

4. Type a formula that specifies the validation criteria. You can either enter the formula directly into the property box, or you can click the ellipsis (…) button and create the formula using the Expression Builder.

5. Click inside the Validation Text property and then specify a message that you want Access to display if the user enters an invalid value.

> **NOTE** If your table already includes data in the field to which you applied the validation rule, it's a good idea to run a test on the existing data to ensure that it satisfies the new rule. In the table Design view, choose Design, Text Validation Rules. Note, too, that Access also prompts you to test your validation rules when you save the table after modifying the Validation Rule property.

Figure 14.4 shows an example validation rule and text for the Orders table's Order Date field. We want this value to be equal to or before today's date, which is given by the Date function:

```
<=Date()
```

Validation rule   Validation text

Figure 14.4
Use the Validation Rule property to enter a data validation expression for a field.

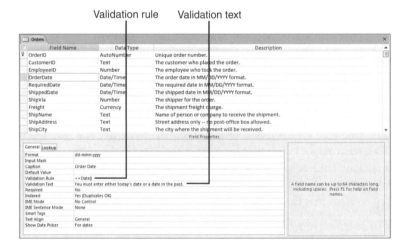

In Figure 14.4, you see that there is also a string in the Validation Text property. If the users enter invalid data (that is, any value for which the Validation Rule expression returns False), the validation text displays in a dialog box, as shown in Figure 14.5.

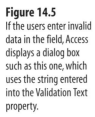

Figure 14.5
If the users enter invalid data in the field, Access displays a dialog box such as this one, which uses the string entered into the Validation Text property.

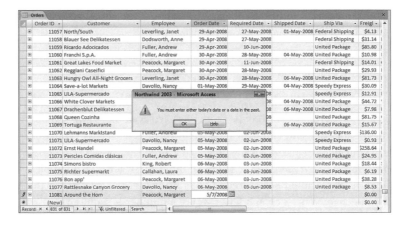

As a slightly more complex example, suppose you have a field for a discount rate and you've set up that field with the Percent number format. (In the table's Design view, select Percent in the Format property.) This speeds data entry because to enter, say, 25 percent, the user needs to enter only the 25, and Access adds the percent sign (%) automatically. Unfortunately, some users might enter 0.25, which means the data goes into the table as 0.0025, which is invalid. In other words, you want users to enter values that are less than or equal to 100, but also either 0 or greater than 1. Here's an expression that you can use in the Validation Rule field to ensure the correct data range for the Discount field:

```
<=1 And (=0 Or >=0.01)
```

This expression says that the data value must be less than or equal to 1 and either 0 or greater than 0.01. (Remember that the validation rule is applied to the data that is actually stored in the field. So even though, in this case, the user enters, say, 25, the data is actually stored in the field as 0.25.)

Using an Input Mask to Ensure Consistent Data Entry

The data in a particular field may be valid, but it can still be problematic if it's not consistent. For example, if your table has a field to store phone numbers, each entry might be valid in the sense that it has ten digits: a three-digit area code and a seven-digit local number. However, there are many ways to enter those ten digits in the table:

```
(317)555-6789
(317) 555-6789
(317)5556789
317-555-6789
317555-6789
31735556789
```

With such inconsistencies, you are going to have all kinds of trouble trying to sort on this field, find data within this field, define query criteria on this field, and so on. Perhaps you might never think of performing these database tasks on a phone number field, but you

14

might on social security numbers, ZIP codes, dates, times, account numbers, and so on, and those items can also get entered inconsistently.

In the previous section, you saw an example where the user was shown status bar text that described exactly how to enter a date (see Figure 14.1 and 14.2):

```
The order date in MM/DD/YYYY format
```

Again, however, it's entirely possible (perhaps even likely) that the user might miss the status bar message and enter the data willy-nilly. As with data validation, you need to configure your field to automatically enter data using the format you prefer. You do that by applying an *input mask* to the field. An input mask acts like a template that lets the user see how the data should be entered. The input mask can also prevent the user from typing invalid characters (such as a letter where a number is required).

Here's an example input mask that you might see when you enter a table's phone number field (Access calls this a *data look*):

```
(___) ___-____
```

Each underscore (_) acts as a placeholder for a character, and you can specify what type of character is valid (numbers, in this case). The other characters in the input mask—the parentheses around the area code, the space that comes after the area code, and dash in the local number—display automatically as the user enters the field. When the user types a digit, the insertion point automatically moves to the next placeholder, skipping over extra characters such as the parentheses, spaces, and dashes. So the user types just the ten digits of the phone number, and the result is a field that looks like this:

```
(317) 555-6789
```

You can type input masks directly, but creating them is easiest when you use the Input Mask Wizard, as shown in the following steps:

1. Open the table you want to work with in Design view (right-click the table in the Navigation pane and then click <u>D</u>esign View) and then click the field with which you want to work.

2. Click inside the Input Mask property.

3. Click the ellipsis (…) button to start the Input Mask Wizard, shown in Figure 14.6.

4. In the Input Mask list, click the input mask with the data look you want (or one that's close to what you want). To check out the resulting input mask, click inside the Try It box and then enter a value.

5. Click <u>N</u>ext.

6. Use the Input Mask text box to make changes to the mask (see Tables 14.1 and 14.2 for the specifics about which symbols to use).

7. Use the Placeholder Character list to choose the character you want to display in the input mask as a placeholder. (Again, you can click inside the Try It box to give the input mask a whirl.)

Figure 14.6
With the Input Mask Wizard, you can either select a predefined input mask or create a custom input mask.

8. Click Next.

9. Access asks how you want the field data stored in the table:

   - **With the Symbols in the Mask**—Click this option if you want the extra symbols (such as the parentheses and dashes in a phone number mask) stored along with the data.

   - **Without the Symbols in the Mask**—Click this option to store only the data.

10. Click Finish.

The Input Mask Wizard lists the most common data looks, but you may have data such as account numbers, part codes, or employee IDs that don't fit any of the wizard's predefined masks. In that case, you need to create a custom input mask, which is a data look that consists of three kinds of characters:

■ **Data placeholders**—These characters (see Table 14.1) are replaced by the actual data typed by the user. The different placeholders specify the type of character the users must enter (such as a digit or letter) and whether the character is optional or required.

■ **Modifiers**—These characters (see Table 14.2) are not displayed in the mask; instead, they are used to modify the mask in some way (such as converting all the entered characters to lowercase).

■ **Literals**—These are extra characters (see Table 14.2) that display in the mask the same as you enter them in the expression. For example, you might use parentheses as literals to surround the area code portion of a phone number.

Table 14.1 lists the data placeholders you can use to build your input mask expressions.

14

Table 14.1 Data Placeholders to Use for Custom Input Masks

Placeholder	Data Type	Description
0	Digit (0–9)	The character is required; the users are not allowed to include a plus sign (+) or a minus sign (–).
9	Digit or space	The character is optional; the users are not allowed to include a plus sign (+) or a minus sign (–).
#	Digit or space	The character is optional; the users are allowed to include a plus sign (+) or minus sign (–).
L	Letter (a–z or A–Z)	The character is required.
?	Letter (a–z or A–Z)	The character is optional.
a	Letter or digit	The character is required.
A	Letter or digit	The character is optional.
&	Any character or space	The character is required.
C	Any character or space	The character is optional.

Table 14.2 lists the modifiers and literals you can use to build your input mask expressions.

Table 14.2 Modifiers and Literals to Use for Custom Input Masks

Modifier	Description
\	Displays the following character as a literal; for example, \(is displayed as (.
"*text*"	Displays the string *text* as a literal; for example, "MB" is displayed as MB.
.	Decimal separator.
,	Thousands separator.
: ; - /	Date and time separators.
<	Displays all the following letters as lowercase letters.
>	Displays all the following letters as uppercase letters.
!	Displays the input mask from right to left when you have optional data placeholders on the left.
Password	Displays the characters as asterisks so that other people cannot read the data.

You can type your input mask data looks directly into the Input Mask property, or you can modify a predefined input mask using the Input Mask Wizard.

For example, suppose your company uses account numbers that consist of four uppercase letters and four digits, with a dash (-) in between. Here's an input mask suitable for entering such numbers:

```
>aaaa\-0000
```

Note, too, that input masks can contain up to three sections separated by semicolons (;):

```
first;second;third
```

> **first**—This section holds the input mask expression.
>
> **second**—This optional section specifies whether Access stores the literals in the table when you enter data. Use 0 to include the literals; use 1 (or nothing) to store only the data.
>
> **third**—This optional section specifies the placeholder character. The default is the underscore (_).

For example, following is an input mask for a ZIP code that stores the dash separator and displays dots (.) as placeholders:

```
00000\-9999;0;.
```

Setting a Default Value for a Field

One of the easiest ways to ensure accurate and valid data entry is to avoid users having to enter any data at all! You can't populate entire records without at least *some* data entry, of course, but most tables include at least one field where the value is either always the same (for example, today's date) or is the same for a majority of records (for example, most of your customers get a 40 percent discount). Yes, you can train users to enter these standard values in the appropriate fields, but why not train Access instead? You do this by specifying a *default value* for a field, which is a value that Access enters into a field automatically each time you create a new record. The default value can either be a literal value (such as 0.4 in the Discount field) or a formula (such as =Date() in the Order Date field).

Here are the steps to follow to specify a default value for a field:

1. Open the table you want to work with in Design view (right-click the table in the Navigation pane and then click <u>D</u>esign View) and then click the field with which you want to work.
2. Click inside the Default Value property.
3. Type the literal value or formula that specifies the default value.
4. Save the table.

14

Requiring a Value for a Field

In some cases, table data is invalid not because it's the wrong data type or some numbers were transposed or the value is out of the allowed range, but because it's missing altogether. When entering orders, for example, it's important to make sure that the Customer and Order Date fields are entered (to name just two), while it's fine to leave the Shipped Date field blank because that is filled in later when the order ships. Mistakes happen, however, and it's easy for the data entry user to skip a field (for example, by accidentally pressing Tab twice).

For a field where the user must enter data, you can set the Required property to Yes. When you do this and the user tries to start a new record without entering a value in that field, Access displays a dialog box telling the user to enter a value in the field, as shown in Figure 14.7.

Figure 14.7
When you set a field's Required property to Yes, Access displays a message similar to this if you leave the field blank.

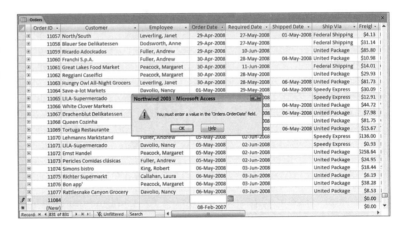

Here are the steps to follow to require a value for a field:

1. Open the table you want to work with in Design view (right-click the table in the Navigation pane and then click <u>D</u>esign View) and then click the field with which you want to work.

2. Click inside the Required property.

3. Use the list to select Yes. (You can also toggle the property between Yes and No by double-clicking inside the property.)

4. Save the table.

Ensuring That No Duplicate Values Display in a Field

It's often useful to have only unique values in a field. For example, fields that you use to uniquely identify records—customer account numbers, employee IDs, product codes, purchase order numbers, and so on—must, by definition, contain no duplicate values. Similarly, fields of customer names, product names, category names, and so on should contain no duplicates.

If you want a field that simply numbers each record or provides some kind of unique value for each record, then the easiest way to avoid duplicates is to apply the AutoNumber data type to the field. Access populates that field with 1 for the first record, 2 for the second record, and so on. With each new record you add to the table, Access increments the most recently used AutoNumber value by one to get a new value for the field. The user can't edit the AutoNumber field, so its values are guaranteed to be unique. Follow these steps to set up a field with the AutoNumber data type:

1. Open the table you want to work with in Design view (right-click the table in the Navigation pane and then click <u>D</u>esign View).

2. For the field you want to work with, pull down the Data Type list and select AutoNumber.

3. Save the table.

The AutoNumber solution has a few drawbacks:

- You can have only one AutoNumber field per table.
- AutoNumber fields generate only numbers, not other data types.
- The numbers generated by AutoNumber aren't meaningful in the same way that, say, an account number or product code is meaningful.

To overcome these limitations, you need to be able to take any existing field and configure it to accept only unique values. You can do this by applying an *index* to the field. An index is a special data structure that (in simplest terms) consists of a sorted list of all the words in a field (assuming you're working with a text field), cross-referenced with the records in which each of those words appear. When you search for a word, Access uses the index to locate the word in the list and then take you to the first record that contains that word. Indexed searches are lightning fast and take only a fraction of the time of a non-indexed search, where Access has to methodically plod through each record to look for your search term.

Access indexes come in two forms: those that accept duplicate values in the field and those that don't. By using the latter index type, you not only ensure that your field contains only unique values, but you also get the benefits of fast searches on that field. Here are the steps required to set up a field with an index that doesn't allow duplicate entries:

1. Open the table you want to work with in Design view (right-click the table in the Navigation pane and then click <u>D</u>esign View).

2. Click the field you want to work with.

3. In the list associated with the Indexed property, select Yes (No Duplicates).

4. Save the table.

14

> **NOTE**
>
> When you save the table after specifying a no-duplicates index for a field, Access may display a dialog box with the following message:
>
> ```
> The changes you requested to the table were not successful
> because they would create duplicate values in the index, primary
> key, or relationship.
> ```
>
> Access is telling you in a roundabout way that your table already contains duplicate data in the field to which you applied the no-duplicates index. Access also suggests changing the data to remove the duplicates, but that's actually impossible while you still have the no-duplicates index applied to the field. (It's impossible because Access won't let you switch to Datasheet view unless you save the table, but saving the table displays the error message.) Click OK to close the dialog box and then click OK again when Access tells you errors were made. Change the field's Indexed property to No or to Yes (Duplicates OK). You can now save the changes, switch to Datasheet view, and then eliminate the duplicate values in the field. After you've done that, you can then return to the Design view and select Yes (No Duplicates) in the field's Indexed property.

Selecting a Field Value from a List

Another great way to keep your data in shape is to avoid freeform text inputs wherever possible. If a data entry user has to type a customer name or product name from memory, that's a sure recipe for inconsistent and error-filled data. Fortunately, in many cases, you can avoid freeform text entry. If there are only a finite number of possible values for a field, you can eliminate this weak link in your data chain by giving users a list of items to choose from. This is called a *lookup column*. A lookup column won't ensure error-free data entry (the user can still choose the wrong item in the list), but it does ensure that the field won't contain typos or inconsistent entries.

Access offers two methods for defining lookup columns: You can take the unique values for a field in an existing table or query, or you can type the list values yourself. The following steps show you how to create a lookup column based on the values in a table or query field:

1. Open the table you want to work with in Design view (right-click the table in the Navigation pane and then click <u>D</u>esign View).

2. Choose Design, Lookup Column. Access starts the Lookup Wizard.

3. Make sure the I Want the Lookup Column to <u>L</u>ook Up the Values in a Table or Query option is activated and then click <u>N</u>ext.

4. Click the table that contains the field you want to use for the lookup column. (For a query, click the Query option and then click the query.) Click <u>N</u>ext.

5. In the Available Fields list, select the field you want to use to populate the lookup column and then click > to add it to the Selected Fields list (see Figure 14.8). Click Next.

14

Figure 14.8
Use this Lookup Wizard
dialog box to choose the
field you want to use to
populate your lookup
column.

6. If you want the lookup column sorted, use the drop-down list to choose the field you selected, click the Ascending (or Descending) toggle button, and then click <u>N</u>ext.

7. Click and drag the right edge of the column header to set the width of the lookup column, and then click <u>N</u>ext.

8. In the final wizard dialog box, use the text box to edit the field name and then click <u>F</u>inish.

9. Save the table.

Figure 14.9 shows a table where the Company Name field is a lookup column of unique values from the Customers table's CompanyName field.

Figure 14.9
The lookup column from
Figure 14.8.

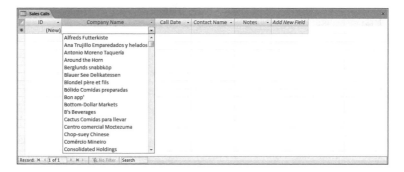

It is often the case that the items you want to see in your lookup column won't exist in any field in a table or query. That's not a problem because the Lookup Wizard also enables you to type the lookup column values by hand. Here's how it works:

1. Open the table you want to work with in Design view (right-click the table in the Navigation pane and then click <u>D</u>esign View).

2. Choose Design, Lookup Column. Access starts the Lookup Wizard.

14

3. Click the I Will Type in the Values That I Want option and then click Next.

4. For each value you want to display in the lookup column, type the item text and press Tab.

5. Click and drag the right edge of the column header to set the width of the lookup column.

6. Click Next.

7. In the final wizard dialog box, use the text box to edit the field name and then click Finish.

8. Save the table.

Entering a Field at the End for Easier Editing

When you view a table in Datasheet view, you can use the keys shown in Table 14.3 to navigate the fields and records.

Table 14.3   Keyboard Techniques for Navigating a Table in Datasheet View

Press	To Move To
Tab or right arrow	The next field to the right or to the first field of the next record if you are in the last field of the current record.
Shift+Tab or left arrow	The previous field to the left or to the last field (the Add New Field column) of the previous record if you are in the first field of the current record.
Home	The first field.
End	The last field (Add New Field).
Ctrl+Home	The first field of the first record.
Ctrl+End	The last field of the last record.

When you use these keystrokes to move into a field that already contains data, Access selects the data. This makes it easy to replace the data because all you have to do is start typing the new value. However, what if most of the time you want to edit the existing field value? In that case, you need to press F2 to get the cursor inside the field. Rather than perform this extra step every time, you can configure Access to immediately place the cursor at the end of the field when you navigate to it using the keyboard. Here are the steps to follow:

1. Choose Office, Access Options to open the Access Options dialog box.

2. Click Advanced.

3. In the Behavior Entering Field group, click Go to End of Field.

4. Click OK.

14

After you activate the Go to End of Field option, you can no longer use the left arrow and right arrow keys to navigate from one field to another. Instead, you can only use Tab and Shift+Tab to navigate fields horizontally.

Inserting Hyperlinks into a Table

As you may know, in Word, Excel, and PowerPoint, you can choose the Insert, Hyperlink command to insert a hyperlink into a document. You can't do this in Access, however. Instead, to work with hyperlinks in Access tables, you have to create a special field. Specifically, you have to create a field that uses the Hyperlink data type. For example, in the sample Northwind database, the Suppliers table, shown in Design view in Figure 14.10, has a HomePage field that uses the Hyperlink data type.

Hyperlink field

Figure 14.10
To add hyperlinks to an Access table, you need to create a field that uses the *Hyperlink* data type.

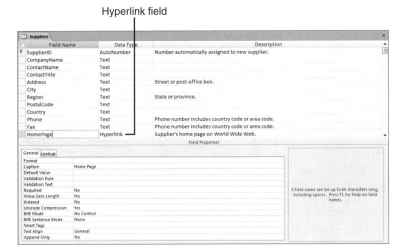

You can also insert a Hyperlink field using the Datasheet view. Choose Datasheet, New Field to display the Field Templates pane and then double-click the Hyperlink field type (it's in the Basic Fields group). Access adds a new field named Hyperlink. To change the name of this field, right-click the field header, click Rename Column, type the new name, and then press Enter.

If your table already includes a text field that contains Web addresses, you can convert that field to use the Hyperlink data type. Click anywhere inside the field, choose the Datasheet tab, pull down the Data Type list, and then choose Hyperlink. Access automatically converts the addresses in the field to links.

14

After you've added the Hyperlink field, switch to Datasheet view. You have two options for inserting a hyperlink into a cell:

- Select the cell and then type the URL, path, or network path for the document to which you want to link.

- Right-click the cell and then choose Hyperlink, Edit Hyperlink to use the Insert Hyperlink dialog box to specify the link.

After the link is in place, click the cell to jump to the specified Web site or document. Figure 14.11 shows the Suppliers table with a few hyperlinks added.

Figure 14.11
The Suppliers table with some sample hyperlinks.

When working with Access hyperlinks, bear in mind that some of the normal Access editing methods don't apply. For example, you might normally edit a cell by first clicking it to get the insertion point cursor and then making changes. With a Hyperlink field, however, you can't get the cursor by clicking (because that just activates the link). Instead, you need to use the keyboard to select the cell and then press F2.

Also you need to be careful when you are editing a hyperlink. In general, Access hyperlinks take the following form:

friendly_name#link_location#

For example, suppose you enter the following into a cell:

```
Click here to load the memo#\\SERVER\public\memo.docx#
```

Access displays only `Click here to load the memo` in the cell.

Access ignores anything you enter *after* the last pound sign. So if you append something to the address, make sure you do it within the pound signs. Note, however, that anything *before* the first pound sign is used as link text. So instead of displaying, for instance, a URL, you can enter a description or name.

Importing Data from an Outlook Folder

If you have used Outlook for any length of time, then your folders are probably chock full of useful data: email messages, contacts, appointments, and so on. There may come a day when you want to analyze this data in some way. For example, you may want to get a sense of how many messages you send or receive each day, find out how many of your contacts are based outside of the country, and so on. This kind of analysis is tough to do in Outlook itself, but it's exactly the kind of thing for which Access was made. Even better, Access comes with an import feature that makes it easy to import data from any Outlook folder. You have three choices:

- Import a snapshot of an Outlook folder's data into a new table. Here, "snapshot" means that the resulting Access data is static, so any changes you make to the folder in Outlook are not reflected in the Access table.
- Append a snapshot of an Outlook folder's data into an existing table.
- Import an Outlook folder's data into a new table and set up a link between Outlook and the new table. This means that any changes you make to the data in Outlook automatically get passed along to the Access table, and vice versa.

Here are the steps to follow to import a snapshot of an Outlook folder's data into a new or existing table:

1. Choose External Data, More (in the Import tab), <u>O</u>utlook Folder. Access displays the Get External Data - Outlook Folder dialog box.

2. Activate one of the following options and then click OK:

    - **Import the Source Data into a New Table in the Current**—Click this option to import the folder into a new table.

    - **<u>A</u>ppend a Copy of the Records to the Table**—Click this option to add the folder items to the table that you select in the list.

3. Access launches the Import Exchange/Outlook Wizard, shown in Figure 14.12. Click the Outlook folder you want to import and then click <u>N</u>ext. If you append the folder items to an existing table, skip to step 8.

4. The wizard displays a table of the folder's columns, which is converted into fields in the Access table. For each column, click the column header and then adjust the following options for the corresponding field in the Access table:

    - **Field <u>N</u>ame**—The name of the field in the Access table.

    - **Data <u>T</u>ype**—The data type of the field in the Access table.

    - **<u>I</u>ndexed**—The index option for the field. Choose No, Yes (Duplicates OK), or Yes (No Duplicates). For an explanation of these index options, see "Ensuring That No Duplicate Values Appear in a Field," earlier in this chapter.

    - **Do No Import Field (<u>S</u>kip)**—Activate this check box if you do not want to include this field in the Access table.

5. Click <u>N</u>ext.

14

Figure 14.12
Use the Import Exchange/Outlook Wizard to choose which Outlook folder you want to import.

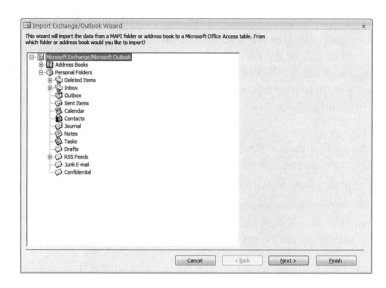

6. The wizard displays the following primary key options:

   • **Let Access Add Primary Key**—Leave this option active to have Access handle the primary key for you. Access adds an ID field to the table and populates it with AutoNumber values.

   • **Choose My Own Primary Key**—Click this option if the folder already has a column of values that uniquely identify each item and then use the list to click the field that contains those values.

   • **No Primary Key**—Click this option to bypass the primary key for this table. This is fine if you do not need to relate the new table to any other tables in the database.

7. Click Next. The final wizard dialog box displays.

8. Use the Import to Table text box to adjust the table name, if necessary, and then click Finish. Access prompts you to save the import steps.

9. If you do not need to repeat this import procedure, click Close and then skip the rest of these steps. Otherwise, if you think you will need to import this folder regularly, click to activate the Save Import Steps check box. Access adds the following controls to the dialog box:

   • **Save As**—Access suggests a default name for the import steps such as Import-Contacts. Edit the name as desired.

   • **Description**—Type an optional description for the import steps. This description displays in the list of saved import operations.

   • **Create Outlook Task**—Click to activate this check box to add a new Task item to Outlook.

10. Click Save Import. Access saves the import steps. If you activated the Create Outlook Task check box, Outlook displays the new Task window, as shown in Figure 14.13.

> **TIP**
>
> If you want Outlook to regularly remind you to run the import task, choose Task, Recurrence, and then use the Task Recurrence dialog box to set up a recurrence pattern (such as Daily or Weekly).

Click Run Import to perform
the import from Outlook

Figure 14.13
You can create an Outlook task that enables you to run the import from within Outlook.

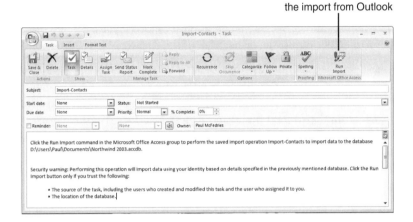

11. Choose Task, Save & Close.

If you saved the import steps, two methods can run the import again:

- In Access, Choose External Data, Saved Imports to open the Manage Data Tasks dialog box. Click the saved import you want to run and then click Run. When Access asks if you want to overwrite the existing table, click Yes.

- In Outlook, click Tasks, double-click the import task, and then choose Task, Run Import (pointed out in Figure 14.13). When Outlook asks you to confirm, click OK.

Here are the steps to follow to import an Outlook folder's data into a new table and set up a link between Outlook and the new table:

1. Choose External Data, More (in the Import tab), Outlook Folder. Access displays the Get External Data - Outlook Folder dialog box.

2. Click to activate the Link to the Data Source by Creating a Linked Table option and then click OK. Access launches the Import Exchange/Outlook Wizard.

3. Click the Outlook folder you want to import and then click Next. The final wizard dialog box displays.

4. Use the Linked Table Name text box to adjust the table name, if necessary, and then click Finish. Access lets you know that it has set up the linked table.

5. Click OK.

Collecting Access Data via E-mail

In the business world, many of our documents are collaborative efforts that are created, edited, or commented upon by multiple people. This kind of teamwork is commonplace in Word, Excel, and PowerPoint, but it's becoming increasingly the norm in Access, as well. The most common Access collaboration scenarios involve placing the database in a shared network folder or moving some or all of the data to a SharePoint site.

These intranet solutions are fine if you only have a few people who collaborate on the data. However, what if you need input from dozens or even hundreds of people? For example, you might need some data from each employee or input from a large number of product managers or department heads. In such cases, it doesn't make sense to give each person permission to access the database. In the past, database administrators usually sent out queries to each person asking for the required data, and then a data entry user would input the responses into the database.

Fortunately, this costly and slow solution will soon be a thing of the past thanks to a new Access 2007 feature called Access Data Collection (ADC). With ADC, you create a form that includes fields for the data you want to collect, place that form in an HTML email message, and then send that message to every person from whom you want to collect the data. Each person fills in the form and returns the message, which is then saved in a special Outlook folder called Access Data Collection Replies. You then synchronize Access (by hand or automatically) with those replies, and the data is added to the underlying table.

CAUTION _____

Many people set up their email clients to read messages in plain text, and that's not good for ADC. First, viewing the ADC message in plain text prevents the user from seeing the form at all. Second, even if the user converts the message to HTML (by clicking the Information bar and then clicking Display as HTML), Access perceives this as a "change" to the form, and it won't process the reply. That is, in the Access Data Collection Replies folder, the Data Collection Status column for the reply says the following:

```
Failure: Cannot process this e-mail message. The form in this
e-mail message is either corrupt or has been modified.
```

The user must turn off the Outlook option to read messages in plain text (choose Tools, Trust Center, click E-mail Security, and then click to deactivate the Read All Standard Mail in Plain Text check box), reply to and fill in the ADC form, and then reset the plain text option.

Creating the Access Data Collection Message

Best of all, creating an ADC form is a snap thanks to an Access wizard that builds the form step by step. Here's how it works:

1. In the Navigation pane, click the table you want to use to store the collected data.

2. Choose External Data, Create E-mail. Access starts the ADC Wizard.

3. Click <u>N</u>ext. The wizard asks whether you want to use an HTML form or an InfoPath form.

4. Click <u>H</u>TML Form and then click <u>N</u>ext.

5. If the table already contains data, the wizard asks whether you want to collect new information or update existing information. Click one of the following options and then click <u>N</u>ext:

   - **Collect Ne<u>w</u> Information Only**—Click this option to send a blank form for new data.

   - **<u>U</u>pdate Existing Information**—Click this option to send existing data for the recipient to edit. The record that contains the recipient's address is the record the recipient edits.

6. For each field you want to include in the form, click the field and then click > (or click >> to add all the fields). Click <u>N</u>ext.

7. If you want Access to automatically synchronize with Outlook when the replies arrive, click to activate the Automatically <u>P</u>rocess Replies and Add Data to *Table* check box (where *Table* is the name of the table you chose in step 1) and then click <u>N</u>ext.

8. Choose how you want to specify the message recipients (click <u>N</u>ext after you make your choice):

   - **Enter the E-mail Addresses in Microsoft Office <u>O</u>utlook**—Click this option to enter the recipients by hand in the Outlook message window that displays later. Skip to Step 10.

   - **Use the E-mail Addresses Stored in a Field in the <u>D</u>atabase**—Click this option if you have the recipients' addresses stored in the current database. Proceed to Step 9.

9. Specify the addresses in the database using one of the following options (click <u>N</u>ext when you are done):

   - **The <u>C</u>urrent Table or Query**—Click this option if the email addresses are stored in the table you use with ADC. Use the associated list to click the field that contains the addresses.

   - **An <u>A</u>ssociated Table**—Click this option if the addresses reside in another table that is related to the current table. First, use the associated list to click the field in the current table upon which the relationship is based. Second, when Access displays a list of fields in the related table, use the list to click the field that contains the email addresses.

14

10. Edit the message Subject and Introduction, as needed. If the addresses came from the Access database, click where you want the addresses added: the To Field, Cc Field, or Bcc Field. Click Next.

11. You now have two ways to proceed:

    • If you choose an Access field for the recipient addresses, click Next. Access displays a list of the recipients with check boxes for each address. Leave the check boxes activated for the recipients you want to receive the message. When you are done, click Send.

    • If you specify recipients via Outlook, click Create to create the message, select the recipients, and then click Send.

Working with Access Data Collection Replies

If you receive an ADC message, you need to fill in the fields and return the message. Here are the steps to follow:

1. Click the Access Data Collection message and then click Reply. Access displays the message window.

2. Scroll down the message body until you see the form, as shown in Figure 14.14.

Figure 14.14
When you reply to an ADC message, fill in each form field in the body of the reply.

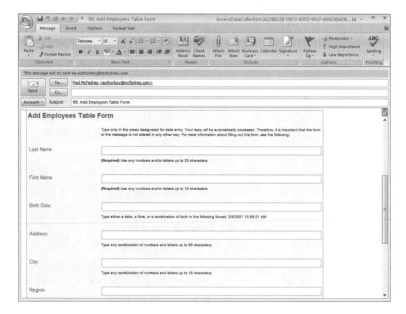

3. Click inside a form field and type the data.

4. Repeat Step 3 for each field.

5. After you fill in each field, click Send.

As mentioned earlier, when you receive replies to your messages, they are automatically routed to the Access Data Collection Replies folder in Outlook. (This is a subfolder of the Inbox folder.) If you didn't set up Access to automatically handle the replies, follow these steps to manually handle a reply:

1. In Outlook, open the reply.
2. Click Export to Access. Outlook asks you to confirm.
3. Click OK. Outlook exports the data.
4. Click OK.

Finding Duplicate Records with a Query

Earlier in this chapter, I showed you how to use a no-duplicates index to make sure that a particular field contains only unique values (see "Ensuring That No Duplicate Values Appear in a Field"). On a larger scale, you might be worried instead about having entire records that are duplicates. This might be an order that was entered twice or an import operation that appends records that already exist in the table. If the table doesn't have an AutoNumber field or a no-duplicates index on a field, then Access does not prevent the duplicate record or records from being entered.

In such cases, a Find Duplicates query can locate these records for you. This query displays a list of a table's duplicate entries (if it has any). You can then either edit or delete one or more records to remove the duplication.

The Find Duplicates Query Wizard sets everything up for you by taking you through the following steps:

1. Choose Create, Query Wizard to open the New Query dialog box.
2. Click Find Duplicates Query Wizard and then click OK. Access launches the Find Duplicates Query Wizard.
2. Click the table you want to use and then click <u>N</u>ext.
3. In the Available Fields list, for each field you want to check for duplicate data, click the field and then click > to add the field to the Duplicate-Value Fields list. When you are done, click <u>N</u>ext.
4. In the Available Fields list, for each other field you want to include in the query, click the field and then click > to add the field to the Additional Query Fields list. When you're done, click <u>N</u>ext.
5. Type a name for the query.
6. Click <u>F</u>inish. Access runs the query and displays the resulting dynaset.

14

Selecting the Top Values with a Query

When you put together an Access query, you add a table, select one or more fields from that table, and then specify your *criteria*: the expression that tells Access which records you want to see. When you then run the query, Access displays a dynaset (that is, a datasheet with the query results) that includes every record in the table that matches your criteria.

However, there are times when you don't need to see every record that satisfies your criteria. For example, in a query of orders for last month, you might be interested in seeing only the biggest orders, whether in terms of the most units or the most dollars. Similarly, in a query of products, you might want to view only the most expensive items or the ones with the least inventory in stock.

For these situations, you can tell Access to restrict the dynaset to a specified number of records or to a percentage of the total:

1. Set up your query table, fields, and criteria.

2. For the field in which you want to see the top values, apply a Descending sort. (If you want to see the bottom values, instead, apply an Ascending sort.)

3. In the Design tab, use the Top Values combo box (see Figure 14.15) to specify how much of the dynaset you want to return in the results:

    - Select a number or percentage value from the list.
    - Type a number or percentage in the text box.
    - Choose All to see every record.

4. Choose Design, Run to see the query results.

Top Values

Figure 14.15
Use the Top Values combo box to tell Access the number or percentage of the top (or bottom) values you want to return.

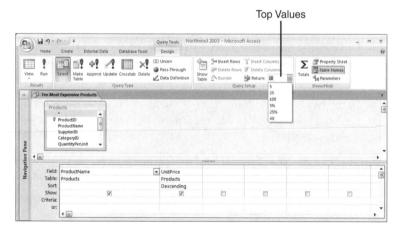

Adding a Custom Calculated Column to a Query

Most queries simply display the raw data for the fields included in the design grid, probably filtered by some criteria. In a business environment, however, you often need to perform some kind of analysis on the dynaset. To do that, you need to introduce calculations into your query by creating what is called a *calculated column*. This is a column in the dynaset where the "field" is an expression and the field values are the results of the expression for each record.

With calculated columns, you can create extremely sophisticated queries that use the full power of Access's expression-building features. Here are just a few examples:

- Suppose you have a table of products with a UnitPrice field and you want to display a new column that shows the unit price for each product plus a five percent increase. You can do that by creating a calculated column based on the following expression:

  `[UnitPrice] * 1.05`

- Suppose you have a table of orders that contains a UnitPrice field and a Quantity field and want a new column that shows the order total. You can do that by creating a calculated column based on this expression:

  `[UnitPrice] * [Quantity]`

- Suppose you have a table of employees that includes FirstName and LastName fields and you want to see the names combined. You can do that by basing a calculated column on the following expression:

  `[FirstName] & " " & [LastName]`

The expression you use for a calculated column can be any combination of operator, identifier, and literal values, and there are many built-in functions you can use.

Building a calculated column is straightforward: Instead of specifying a field name when adding a column to the dynaset, you enter an expression. You type the expression directly into the column header in the design grid using the following general form:

`ColumnName:expression`

Here, `ColumnName` is the name you want to use for the calculated column, and `expression` is the calculation.

> **TIP**
> Calculated column expressions are routinely long, which means you do not see the entire expression in the `Field` cell. One solution is to widen the column to fit the length of the expression. Alternatively, click anywhere inside the expression and press Shift+F2 to display the expression inside the Zoom window.

Figure 14.16 shows two examples of custom calculated columns. The first is the left hand column, which includes the following in the column header:

`Employee: [FirstName] & " " & [LastName]`

As described earlier in this section, this column combines the FirstName and LastName fields with a space in between, the results of which are displayed in a column named Employee.

Figure 14.16
Two examples of custom calculated columns in a query.

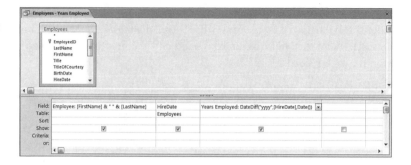

The second example is in the far right column, and it's a bit more complex:

```
Years Employed: DateDiff("yyyy",[HireDate],Date())
```

This expression uses the DateDiff function to calculate how many years each person has been employed with the company. In this case, DateDiff calculates the difference between the employee's hire date (given by the HireDate field) and the current date (given by the Date function). The yyyy string argument tells Access to return the number of years (rounded up to the next highest year).

The DateDiff function uses the following simplified syntax:

```
DateDiff(interval, date1, date2)
```

interval	A string that specifies the time unit to use when calculating the difference between *date1* and *date2*. Table 14.3 lists the string values you can use.
date1, date2	The dates for which you want to calculate the difference.

Table 14.3 Acceptable Values for the DateDiff Function's *interval* Argument

Interval	Date/Time Units
yyyy	Years
y	Days of the year
q	Quarters
m	Months
ww	Calendar weeks
w	Weeks
d	Days
h	Hours
n	Minutes
s	Seconds

Figure 14.17 shows the query results.

Employees - Years Employed

Employee	Hire Date	Years Employed
Nancy Davolio	01-May-1992	15
Andrew Fuller	14-Aug-1992	15
Janet Leverling	01-Apr-1992	15
Margaret Peacock	03-May-1993	14
Steven Buchanan	17-Oct-1993	14
Michael Suyama	17-Oct-1993	14
Robert King	02-Jan-1994	13
Laura Callahan	05-Mar-1994	13
Anne Dodsworth	15-Nov-1994	13

Record: 1 of 9 No Filter Search

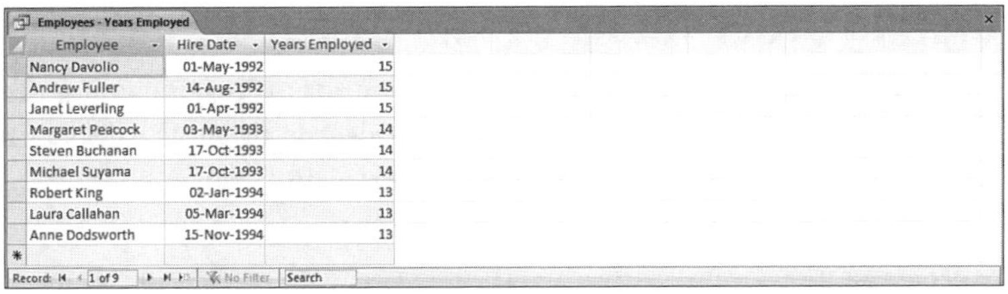

Figure 14.17
The results generated by the query shown in Figure 14.16.

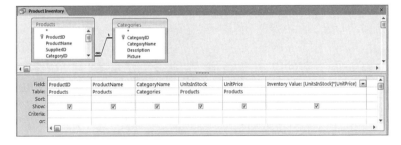

Calculating Inventory Value

The Northwind database's Products table contains both a UnitsInStock field and a UnitPrice field. The *inventory value* is the quantity in stock multiplied by the price of the product. You can set up a calculated column to show the inventory value by entering the following expression as the header of a new column in the design grid, as shown in Figure 14.18 (see Figure 14.19 for the resulting dynaset):

```
Inventory Value:[UnitsInStock]*[UnitPrice]
```

Figure 14.18
This query includes a calculated column that derives its values by multiplying the UnitsInStock field by the UnitPrice field.

Product Inventory

Product ID	Product Name	Category Name	Units In Stock	Unit Price	Inventory Value
1	Chai	Beverages	39	$18.00	$702.00
2	Chang	Beverages	17	$19.00	$323.00
24	Guaraná Fantástica	Beverages	20	$4.50	$90.00
34	Sasquatch Ale	Beverages	111	$14.00	$1,554.00
35	Steeleye Stout	Beverages	20	$18.00	$360.00
38	Côte de Blaye	Beverages	17	$263.50	$4,479.50
39	Chartreuse verte	Beverages	69	$18.00	$1,242.00
43	Ipoh Coffee	Beverages	17	$46.00	$782.00
67	Laughing Lumberjack Lager	Beverages	52	$14.00	$728.00
70	Outback Lager	Beverages	15	$15.00	$225.00
75	Rhönbräu Klosterbier	Beverages	125	$7.75	$968.75
76	Lakkalikööri	Beverages	57	$18.00	$1,026.00
3	Aniseed Syrup	Condiments	13	$10.00	$130.00
4	Chef Anton's Cajun Seasoning	Condiments	53	$22.00	$1,166.00

Record: 1 of 76 No Filter Search

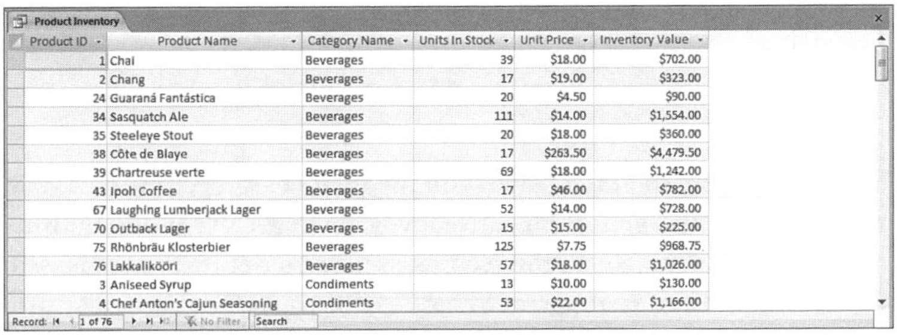

Figure 14.19
The calculated column named Inventory Value contains the results of the expression `[UnitsInStock]*[UnitPrice]`.

> **NOTE**
> Keep in mind that you can always use a calculated column for filtering the dynaset. In other words, you can use the calculated column's `Criteria` cell to enter a criteria expression. For example, if you want to see those products where the inventory value is greater than $3,000, you enter `>3000` in the `Criteria` cell of the calculated column.

14

Calculating Order Totals

Northwind's Order Details table contains data for orders, including the Quantity, UnitPrice, and Discount for each product ordered. To get the discounted total for a product, you multiply the Quantity by the UnitPrice and then subtract the percentage discount. Here's a calculated column expression that returns this discounted product total:

```
Discounted Total:[UnitPrice] * [Quantity] * (1 - [Discount])
```

Figure 14.20 shows the calculated column and Figure 14.21 shows the resulting dynaset (I set up the calculated column to use the Currency format).

Figure 14.20
This orders query includes a calculated column that derives its values by multiplying the quantity by the price and then subtracting the discount.

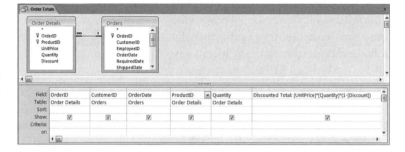

Figure 14.21
The calculated column named Discounted Total contains the results of the expression.

The Discounted Total field gives you the total charge per product, but what if you want to know the total charge for the entire invoice? To get this useful information, you need to tell Access to aggregate all the records in the dynaset that have the same value in the OrderID field. For example, in Figure 14.20, you see that the first three records have the value 10248 in the OrderID field because that order consists of three different products.

You set this up by converting your query to a *totals query*. A totals query groups the results based on a particular field and also includes one or more columns that perform an aggregate operation—such as summing or averaging—on the values of a particular field. A totals query derives either a single value for the entire dynaset or several values for the records that have been grouped within in the dynaset. Table 14.4 outlines the aggregate operations you can use for your totals queries.

Table 14.4   Aggregate Operations Available for Totals Queries

Operation	Purpose
Group By	Groups the records according to the unique values in the field.
Sum	Sums the values in the field.
Avg	Averages the values in the field.
Min	Returns the smallest value in the field.
Max	Returns the largest value in the field.
Count	Counts the number of values in the field.
StDev	Calculates the standard deviation of the values in the field.
Var	Calculates the variance of the values in the field.
First	Returns the first value in the field.
Last	Returns the last value in the field.
Expression	Returns a custom total based on an expression in a calculated column.
Where	Tells Access to use the field's criteria to filter the records before calculating the totals.

In our example, we want to apply the Group By operation to the OrderID field and the Sum operation to the Discounted Total calculated column:

1. Choose Design, Totals (in the Show/Hide group). Access adds a `Total` row to the design grid, and each `Total` cell contains a list of the aggregate operations, and Access applies the Group By operation to each column by default.

2. Make sure that the field upon which the query's groups is based is on the far left of the query design. (To move a column, click the bar above the column header to select the entire column and then click and drag the bar to the new position.)

3. For any field you want to total, use the field's `Total` cell drop-down list to click the function you want to use. In this case, add the Sum operation to the Discounted Total column. For good measure, I also Sum the Quantity column.

4. If you want to restrict the records involved in the aggregate operation, enter the appropriate expression in the field's `Criteria` cell.

5. (Optional) In the dynaset, Access displays *OperationOfFieldName* in the field header, where *Operation* is the aggregate operation you chose in Step 2, and *FieldName* is the name of the field with which you work. If you want to see a more readable name, change the `Field` cell to the following, where *FieldName* is the name you want to use (refer to Figure 14.21 for an example):

   `Field Alias:FieldName`

6. Run the query.

14

Figure 14.22 shows the query shown earlier in Figure 14.20 converted to a totals query. The OrderID column is on the far left, and the Sum operation has been applied to the Discounted Total column and to the Quantity (using the alias Total Units). Figure 14.23 shows the results.

Figure 14.22
To calculate the total charge for each invoice, apply the Sum operation to the calculated Discounted Total field and group the Order Details records by OrderID.

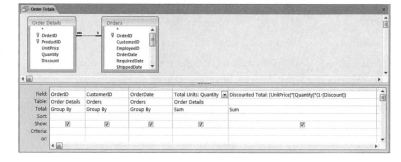

Figure 14.23
The results of the query shown in Figure 14.22.

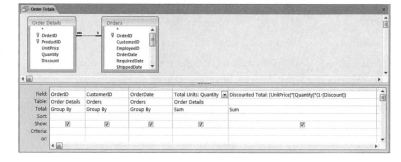

NOTE The other change to note between the query shown in Figure 14.20 and the one shown in Figure 14.22 is the removal of the ProductID field. The values in this field are not groupable (because, for each order, the ProductID field contains a set of unique values), so I needed to remove the field to get Access to group on the OrderID field.

NOTE If you apply an aggregate operation to a calculated field in the manner shown in Figure 14.22 and then close and reopen the query, you can see that Access has changed the calculated field by "moving" the aggregate operation into the field's expression and changing the Total cell to Expression. Access converted the totals query so that it uses an aggregate *function*.

Prompting for Query Criteria

There's a certain satisfaction that comes from working hard to get a query to perform just the way you want it and then getting instant (or close to it) results just by double-clicking the query in the Navigation pane. This assumes that your query does not change over time, which is the case for most queries. You might tweak the query here and there as fields are added, renamed, or removed from the underlying data source, but the rest of the query remains more or less intact.

However, there are times when you need a more dynamic solution. For example, you might have a Products query that filters the data to show only those products in a specified category, such as Beverages. What if you then want to run the same query, only with Seafood as the category? Similarly, your query might filter the Orders table to show only those orders placed on a specific date, and later you might want to run the query using a different date.

The usual solution is to modify the query's design and then run it. That's fine if you make the change only once in a while, but this might be something you do regularly. In that case, it's inefficient to constantly change the query design. A better solution is to have Access prompt you for the criteria you want to use. This kind of query is called a *parameter query*.

Here are the steps to follow to create a basic parameter query:

1. Start a new query and add the table or tables with which you want to work.
2. Add the fields you want to use for the query to the design grid.
3. In the Criteria cell of the field for which you want to prompt for a parameter, enter the prompt text, surrounded by square brackets. For example, if you want to prompt the users to enter a last name, type something like this in the cell:
   ```
   [Enter the product category you want to work with:]
   ```
4. Set up the other criteria and the rest of your query elements.

Figure 14.24 shows a Products and Categories query with the following parameter prompt in the CategoryName field:

```
[Enter the product category you want to work with:]
```

Figure 14.24
This query prompts for a parameter to use as the criteria for the CategoryName field.

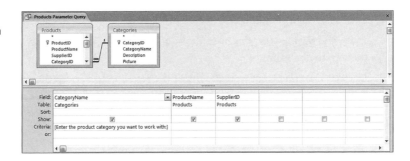

When you run the query, Access displays the Enter Parameter Value dialog box, as shown in Figure 14.25. Notice that the dialog box prompt text is exactly the same as the text entered in the Criteria (minus the square brackets).

Figure 14.25
When you run the query,
Access uses the Enter
Parameter Value
dialog box.

You use the text box to enter the value as the criteria and then click OK. (If you click
Cancel, Access returns you to the query design window without running the query.) Figure
14.26 shows the dynaset that results when Beverages is entered as the criteria.

Figure 14.26
The dynaset that results
when the criteria
entered in Figure 14.25
is applied to the query in
Figure 14.24.

> **NOTE**
>
> You can specify more than one parameter in a single query. Access displays a separate Enter
> Parameter Value dialog box for each parameter.

Access assumes that the parameter values you enter are text. If you want to use other data
types, you need to tell Access which data you prefer to use. Here are the steps to follow:

1. If you already have a parameter prompt text in the query, click inside the Criteria cell
   that contains the prompt text.
2. Choose Design, Parameters. Access displays the Query Parameters dialog box.
3. Enter the prompt text (without the square brackets) in the first available text box in
   the Parameter column.
4. Use the Data Type list to the right of the text box to choose the data type you want for
   the parameter.
5. Repeat Steps 3 and 4 for other parameters you want to enter.
6. Click OK.

14

From Here

- To learn how to create hyperlinks in Word, **see** "Inserting a Hyperlink in a Document," **p. 23**.

- Excel also comes with a data validation feature; **see** "Allowing Only Certain Values in a Cell," **p. 107**.

- To learn how to create calculated controls in an Access form, **see** "Creating Calculated Form Controls," **p. 409**.

14

Form and Report Tricks

15

In Chapter 14, "Table and Query Tricks," I emphasized that your work in Access should strive for one overarching goal: to make your data as accurate and as complete as possible. That worthy theme is also much in evidence in this chapter as you learn even more techniques that help you to reduce as much as possible what computer types call GIGO (garbage in, garbage out). In this case, the "in" part of the equation is related to forms which, if configured properly, can make data entry not only much easier and faster, but also far more accurate; and the "out" part is related to reports which, when done well, put an attractive face on your rather plain data. In this chapter, you learn quite a few tricks and techniques for getting more out of forms and reports.

Opening a Form Automatically When You Load a Database

It's not uncommon in database work to have a table that serves as the focal point of a database. That is, the table contains most of the data and, aside from perhaps a few other related tables, most of your work in that database consists of entering and editing data in the main table and running queries (and, later, reports) on the table data.

In such situations, you probably have a form set up for entering and editing that table's data, and it's likely that the first thing you do each day when you load the database into Access is open that form. In that case, it makes sense to configure Access to display that form automatically when you start the database.

15

Note, too, that there are other ways that displaying a form immediately after launching a database is useful:

- You can display a splash screen that displays the name of the company, department, or project, along with a logo or other image.
- You can display a switchboard form, which consists of a collection of command buttons that perform tasks such as opening other forms or printing reports.
- You can display a list of instructions that covers how to use the database or what the database contains.
- You can display a summary of news or updates related to the database.

Here are the steps to follow to create a startup form:

1. Create and save the form you want to use.
2. Choose Office, Access Options to open the Access Options dialog box.
3. Click Current Database.
4. In the Display Form list, choose the form you want to display at startup.
5. If you don't want the users to also have access to the Navigation pane, deactivate the Display Navigation Pane check box.
6. Click OK.
7. When Access warns you that you must restart the database to put the options into effect, click OK, and then close and reopen the database.

> **TIP**
> Choosing not to display the Navigation pane at startup adds a bit of extra security to your database. However, what if you need to work with the database window yourself? Hold down the Shift key when you start the database to bypass all the startup options.

> **TIP**
> If you only work in a single database in Access, you still have to open that database each time you start the program. To save yourself a few startup steps, you can configure Access to always load the most recently used database at startup. Choose Office, Access Options to open the Access Options dialog box. Click Advanced and then scroll down to the Advanced section. Click to activate the Open Last Used Database When Access Starts check box and then click OK.

Automatically Moving to the Last Record When You Open a Form

Data entry in Access is often a "What have you done for me lately?" affair. That is, when you open a form, you often display the most recently entered record, which can help you get your bearings for entering more records. In most forms, you display the most recently entered record by moving to the last record, which you can do by clicking the Last Record button (or by choosing Home, Go To, Last). If you always do this when you open a particular form, you can save yourself a step by configuring the form to always automatically move to the last record.

To understand how to do this, you need to know that when certain actions occur in Access, the program fires an *event*, which is just a programmatic indication that the action has occurred. For example, when you navigate to a new record in a form, Access fires the Current event because the form now has a new current record. For any event, you can use VBA to create an *event handler*, a procedure that runs each time its associated event fires. For the current event, for example, your event handler can move the focus to a particular field.

For our purposes in this section, we want to take advantage of the Open event, which fires each time you open a form. In this case, we use the Open event handler to automatically move to the last record. Here are the steps to follow:

1. With the form open in Design view (right-click the form in the Navigation pane and then click Design View), choose Design, Property Sheet to open the Property Sheet pane.

2. In the Selection Type list, click Form.

3. Click the Event tab.

4. Click inside the On Open property, and then click the … button. Access displays the Choose Builder dialog box.

5. Click Code Builder and then click OK. The Visual Basic Editor and the basic code for the Open event handler display

   ```
   Private Sub Form_Open(Cancel As Integer)

   End Sub
   ```

6. Between the Sub and End Sub statements, type the following statement code (where *form* is the name of your form; see Figure 15.1):

   ```
   DoCmd.GoToRecord acDataForm, "form", acLast
   ```

7. Choose File, Close and Return to Microsoft Office Access.

The next time you view the form, Access automatically navigates to the last record.

Figure 15.1
Use the Open event handler to configure the form to automatically navigate to the last record when you open it.

> **TIP**
>
> If you have a form where you always start a new record for data entry as soon as you open the form, you can use the Open event handler to automatically start a new record for you. Follow the steps in this section, and in Step 6, add the following statement (again, where *form* is the name of your form):
>
> ```
> DoCmd.GoToRecord acDataForm, "form", acNewRec
> ```

Creating a Switchboard Form

If your database is used by novice or inexperienced users, you might not want them navigating the often confusing and (in the wrong hands) dangerous Access interface. Instead, you can create an easy-to-use front-end that gives these users a limited set of choices, such as opening a form or two or printing a report. This front-end is a special type of Access form called a *switchboard* that has no associated data source. Instead, the switchboard just displays a set of command buttons, each of which performs a specific action, such as opening a form.

Here are the steps to follow to create a switchboard:

1. Choose Database Tools, Switchboard Manager.
2. If Access tells you that it cannot find a valid switchboard and asks if you want to create one, click <u>Y</u>es. Access creates a basic switchboard form and displays the Switchboard Manager dialog box.
3. Click <u>E</u>dit to open the Edit Switchboard Page dialog box.
4. Click <u>N</u>ew to open the Edit Switchboard Item dialog box.
5. Use the <u>T</u>ext box to type a name for the new switchboard command.
6. Use the Command list to select the command you want the item to run:
   - **Go to Switchboard**—Opens another switchboard. Use the Switchboard list to select the switchboard you want to open.
   - **Open Form in Add Mode**—Opens a form but displays only a new record. The user can't edit any existing records. Use the <u>F</u>orm list to select the form you want to use (see Figure 15.2).
   - **Open Form in Edit Mode**—Opens a form and makes all the records available for editing. Use the <u>F</u>orm list to select the form you want to use.
   - **Open Report**—Opens the report you specify using the <u>R</u>eport list.
   - **Design Application**—Displays the Switchboard Manager dialog box.
   - **Exit Application**—Shuts down Microsoft Access.
   - **Run Macro**—Runs the Access macro that you specify using the <u>M</u>acro list.
   - **Run Code**—Runs the VBA function procedure that you specify using the <u>F</u>unction Name list.

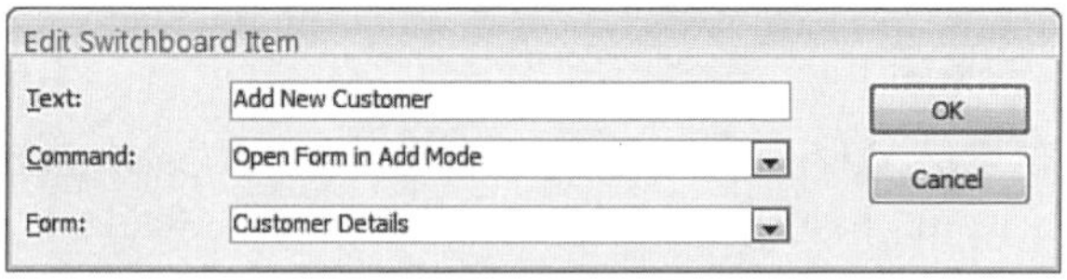

Figure 15.2
Use the Edit Switchboard
Item dialog box to create
a new item for your
switchboard.

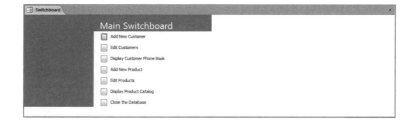

7. Click OK to return to the Edit Switchboard Page dialog box.
8. Repeat Steps 4–7 to add up to eight items to the switchboard.
9. Click Close to return to the Switchboard Manager dialog box.
10. Click Close.

To run your switchboard, double-click the Switchboard item in the Navigation Pane. Figure 15.3 shows an example of a switchboard. You also probably want the switchboard form to load automatically when you start your database. See "Opening a Form Automatically When You Load a Database," earlier in this chapter.

Figure 15.3
An example switch-
board.

Using a Toggle Button for a Yes/No Field

You use Yes/No fields in tables when you have a quantity that you can represent in one of two states: on (Yes, True, or –1) or off (No, False, or 0).

When you create a Yes/No field in the table Design view, the Display Control property (it's in the Lookup tab) defaults to Check Box. This means that when you add a Yes/No field to a form, Access automatically represents the field with a check box control (along with a label that displays the name of the field or the field's Caption property). For something a bit different, you can use a toggle button, instead. A toggle button is a cross between a check box and a command button: Click it once, and the button stays pressed; click it again, and the button returns to its normal state. The button can either display a caption or a picture. Here are the steps to follow to insert a toggle button and bind it to a Yes/No field:

1. In the Design tab's Controls group, click Toggle Button.
2. Draw the toggle button on the form.
3. Choose Design, Property Sheet to open the Property Sheet pane.

4. In the Format tab, you have two choices that determine what appears on the face of the button:
   - `Caption`—Use this property to specify text that displays on the face of the button. (For clarity, it's best to use the name of the `Yes/No` field.)
   - `Picture`—Use this property to specify an image that displays on the button face. Click the ellipsis button (...) to display the Picture Builder dialog box, shown in Figure 15.4. Either use the Available Pictures list to click an image or click Browse to choose an image from the Select Picture dialog box (although note that Access can use only BMP or icon files).

> **CAUTION**
>
> If you want to use a custom picture, bear in mind that if the image is larger than the toggle button, Access won't shrink the image to fit inside the button—it just centers the image in the button and displays as much as can fit. Therefore, always choose a bitmap or icon that is the same size or smaller than the toggle button.

> **TIP**
>
> It's often useful to have the toggle button's caption or picture change as the button's state changes. For example, you could change the caption to `On` when the button is pressed and change it to `Off` when the button isn't pressed. To set this up, display the button's Property Sheet, select the Event tab, click inside the After Update property, click the ellipsis button (...), and then click Code Builder. Use the `AfterUpdate` event handler to change the button's `Caption` or `Picture` property depending on the button's current `Value`. Here's an example:
>
> ```
> Private Sub Toggle0_AfterUpdate()
>     If Toggle0.Value = True Then
>         Toggle0.Caption = "On"
>     Else
>         Toggle0.Caption = "Off"
>     End If
> End Sub
> ```

Figure 15.4
Use the Picture Builder dialog box to choose an image to display on the face of the toggle button.

5. In the Data tab, use the `Control Source` property to choose the name of the `Yes/No` field you want bound to the toggle button.

6. In the `Default Value` property, enter the initial value for new records. For the "pressed" state, use `Yes`, `True`, or `-1`; for the "unpressed" state, use `No`, `False`, or `0`.

Preventing Changes to the Form's Data Source

It's sometimes useful to create a form that only displays the data in its associated record source. For example, in a table of financial data from a previous fiscal year where the books are closed, you wouldn't want anyone to add, edit, or delete table data. In such situations, you can configure the form to prevent additions, deletions, edits, or any combination of these three actions. Here's how:

1. Open the Design view for the form you want to work with (right-click the form in the Navigation pane and then click <u>D</u>esign View).

2. Choose Design, Property Sheet to open the Property Sheet pane.

3. In the Selection Type list, click Form.

4. Click the Data tab.

5. Adjust the following properties, as needed (in each case, double-clicking the property toggles its value between Yes and No):

   - **Allow Additions**—Set this property to No to prevent users from adding new records.

   - **Allow Deletions**—Set this property to No to prevent users from deleting existing records.

   - **Allow Edits**—Set this property to No to prevent users from making changes to existing records.

6. Close the Property Sheet pane and save your changes.

Customizing the Form's Tab Order

When you have a form open in Form view, you can navigate from one field to another using the keyboard: Press the Tab key to move forward through the fields, and press Shift+Tab to move backward through the fields. Because you use the Tab key to navigate the fields, the order in which the controls are selected is called the *tab order*. The default tab order is the order in which you added the controls to the form. Unfortunately, this initial order doesn't always correspond to the "natural" order of the controls. For example, when entering an address, it's natural to enter the street address, then the city, state or region, country, and ZIP or postal code, in that order. However, if you didn't add the fields in that order, pressing Tab causes the user to navigate the fields unnaturally. Similarly, rearranging the form fields after adding them can cause the focus to jump haphazardly around the form.

To fix these and similar Tab navigation problems, you can customize the tab order to suit the form design. Here are the steps to follow:

1. Choose Arrange, Tab Order. Access displays the Tab Order dialog box, shown in Figure 15.5.

15

Selection buttons

Figure 15.5
Use the Tab Order dialog
box to customize the
order in which the user
navigates the form when
pressing the Tab key.

> **TIP**
>
> If you're customizing the tab order because you've rearranged the form fields, you can probably save yourself a bit of work by clicking the Auto Order button. This tells Access to set the tab order by working left-to-right and down through the form fields. This should give you a tab order that's pretty close to what you want, so you may only need to make a few small adjustments to get the order just right.

2. Use the Section list to click the form section with which you want to work.

3. In the Custom Order list, select the control you want to work with by clicking the selection button to the left of the control.

4. Click and drag the control's selection button to move the control up or down in the Custom Order list.

5. Repeat Steps 2–4 for other sections and controls you want to move.

6. Click OK.

Creating Shortcut Keys for Form Controls

Forms are almost always used as data entry tools, which means that most of your interaction with a form is via the keyboard. Yes, you can place mouse-friendly controls such as check boxes, toggle buttons (see "Using a Toggle Button for a Yes/No Field," earlier in this chapter), option buttons, and list boxes on a form. However, most of your form time is spent typing entries into text boxes. This means that, in most cases, data entry in a form is most efficient when your hands stay on the keyboard as much as possible. This is helped by the fact that you can use Tab and Shift+Tab to navigate the form fields, as discussed in the previous section.

However, what if you need to skip over a number of fields? For example, you may edit a record and need to make changes to two fields that aren't close on the form. Pressing Tab repeatedly isn't efficient, and neither is taking one hand off the keyboard to click inside the next field with your mouse. A faster and more efficient solution is to define a *shortcut key* for each form field. A shortcut key is a letter or number that enables you to select the control from the keyboard by holding down Alt and pressing the character. This character is usually underlined on the control's label. For example, if you see a field named Address, and the *A* is underlined, then you can select that field by pressing Alt+A while the form is displayed.

Here are the steps to follow to define a shortcut key for a form control:

1. Assuming the control automatically comes with a label, insert the control. If the control already exists on the form, skip to Step 2.
2. Click the label associated with the control.
3. Choose Design, Property Sheet to open the Property Sheet pane.
4. Click the Format tab.
5. In the Caption property, edit the label text by inserting the ampersand character (&) before the character you want to use as the accelerator key. For example, if the label has the text Address, editing the text to &Address sets up the letter A as the shortcut key (meaning that Alt+A will select the control associated with the label; see Figure 15.6).

Ampersand appears before
A in the Caption property

Figure 15.6
Precede a character with the ampersand character (&) to set up that character as the control's shortcut key.

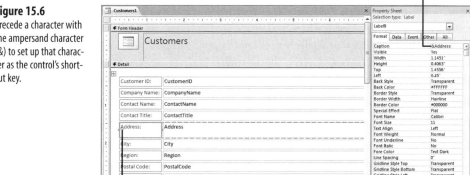

A is underlined in the label

TIP

If you want to associate another label with a control, first select the control's current label and delete it. Add the new label (if you haven't done so already) and then click the smart tag that displays. In the menu, click <u>A</u>ssociate Label with a Control, use the Associate Label dialog box to click the control you want to use with the label and then click OK.

CAUTION

To avoid confusion, make sure each control on the form has a unique shortcut key. If you accidentally use the same shortcut on two controls, Access displays a smart tag on both labels notifying you of the problem. Click the smart tag and then click <u>C</u>hange Caption to see some suggested alternatives for the shortcut key.

If, for some reason, it's unavoidable that two controls use the same shortcut key, note that you can navigate to the second control by pressing the shortcut key combination twice. For example, suppose you have the labels &Name and &Number on the form, in that order. Pressing Alt+N first selects the Name control, and pressing Alt+N again selects the Number control.

Applying Formatting to Special Form Values

In Chapter 14, you learned how to reduce erroneous or invalid data entries by applying a validation rule to a field. You can also apply validation rules to form controls. Click the control, choose Design, Property Sheet, display the Data tab, and then edit the Validation Rule property in the same way as described in Chapter 14.

→ To learn how to set up field validation rules, **see** "Validating Data Entry," **p. 365**

However, what if your goal isn't to prevent the user from entering certain data values in a field, but to monitor that field for values that are in some way special or anomalous? For example, in a Products form where you enter the list price and cost price, you can then set up a calculated control that displays the gross margin for each product (see "Creating Calculated Form Controls," later in this chapter). In this case, you might want to monitor the gross margin calculation for results that are below some target value.

Access enables you to monitor form values by automatically applying a particular format—such as a font or background color—when a control value meets a specified condition. This is called *conditional formatting*, and you apply it by following these steps:

1. Select the field to which you want the conditional format applied.
2. Choose Design, Conditional. Access displays the Conditional Formatting dialog box, shown in Figure 15.7.
3. If you want to specify the format to use when the condition is *not* met, use the formatting buttons in the Default Formatting group.

Figure 15.7
Use the Conditional Formatting dialog box to specify font or background formatting to apply to a control when its value meets a specific condition.

15

4. Select the type of condition you want to use:

- **Field Value Is**—The condition is applied to the current value of the field or unbound control. In this case, you construct the condition by selecting a comparison operator (such as Between or Less Than) in the second list and then by entering one or two values (depending on the operator).

- **Expression Is**—The condition is met when the logical expression you enter returns True. For example, if you enter Date()=#8/23/2007#, the formatting is applied only on August 23, 2007.

- **Field Has Focus**—The condition is met when the field or unbound control has the focus (that is, when the cursor is inside the field).

5. Click the formatting buttons to specify the font formatting to apply to the control when the condition is met.

6. If you want to apply another condition, click <u>A</u>dd and repeat Steps 4 and 5 for the new condition.

7. Click OK.

Creating Calculated Form Controls

Your forms aren't restricted to just the fields in the underlying data source. Access also enables you to create form controls that perform calculations. For example, you can add a control that shows the current date or time. On a more complex level, given a UnitPrice field and a ListPrice field in a Products table, you can create a control that calculates the gross margin for each product.

You set up a calculated form control by adding a text box to the form and then setting its Control Source property to the formula you want to calculate. This formula can use any of the Access operators, operands, and functions, and it can use the values in both bound and unbound controls. When you switch to Form view, the text box displays the results of the formula for each record.

To add a text box to your form, follow these steps:

1. Choose the Design tab.

2. In the Controls group, click Text Box.

15

3. On the form, click and drag a rectangle to draw the text box in the size and shape you need. When you release the mouse button, Access adds the text box and an associated label.

4. Edit the label text, as necessary.

5. Click the text box to select it.

6. Choose Design, Property Sheet to display the control's property sheet. (You can also press Alt+Enter or double-click the control.)

7. Choose the Data tab.

8. Type the formula in the Control Source property. (You can also click ... to create your expression using the Expression Builder.)

9. Apply other text box properties, as required.

10. Choose the Format tab.

11. Use the Format property to define the format used to display the result. You can either select a predefined format (such as General Date or Percent) or type a format string.

12. Use the Decimal Places property to define the number of decimal places to display in the result.

13. Close the property sheet.

For example, Figure 15.8 shows two calculated text box controls. In the Form Header section, you see a text box that contains the expression =Date(). In the Detail section, the Gross Margin text box has the following formula as its Control Source property:

```
=([ListPrice] - [UnitPrice]) / [UnitPrice]
```

In the Form view in Figure 15.9, you can see that the Form Header text box displays the current date. (Note that I entered the format string mmmm d", "yyyy in the text box's Format property to get the date format shown in Figure 15.9.) In the Detail, the Gross Margin text box shows the results of the formula (I configured this control with the Percent numeric format.)

NOTE

Users can't edit the text in a calculated text box. They can move the insertion point cursor within the control and then select and copy the control text, but if they try to edit the text, Access beeps the PC's internal speaker and displays the following in the status bar (where *expression* is the expression in the Control Source property):

```
Control can't be edited; it's bound to the expression 'expres-
sion'.
```

Type the formula here

Figure 15.8
To create a calculated control, enter an expression in a text box's `Control Source` property.

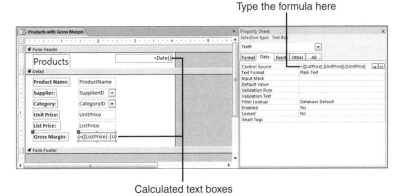

Calculated text boxes

Figure 15.9
In the Form view, the text boxes display the results of the calculations.

Creating Custom Report Groups

One easy method you can use to make your Access reports more readable is to sort the records. For example, a report based on the Customers table can be sorted on the values in the CompanyName field. Here are the steps you follow to sort a report:

1. Choose Design, Group & Sort to open the Group, Sort, and Total pane.

2. Click Add a Sort. Access adds a Sort By list to the Group, Sort, and Total pane.

3. Use the Sort By list to select the name of the field on which you want to sort. Access adds a Sort Order list to the Group, Sort, and Total pane.

4. Use the Sort Order list to choose either an ascending or descending sort. Note that the name of the sort depends on the field type. For example, for text fields, you see `With A on Top` (an ascending sort) and `With Z on Top` (descending); for numeric fields, you see `From Smallest to Largest` (an ascending sort) and `From Largest to Smallest` (descending)

5. Repeat Steps 2–4 to sort the report on other fields, as needed.

For even more control over the report output, you can also create report groups. A *group* is a collection of related records. In a Customers report, for example, you can organize the records in groups by country. Similarly, in an invoice report you can create groups of invoices for each customer.

Why not just sort the report on the appropriate field, instead? That would work, too, but grouping gives you a big advantage over sorting: You get two new report sections—a *group header* and a *group footer*. You can use these sections to display text and calculations. For example, you can use the group header to identify the group, and you can use the group footer to print summary information about the group (such as the sum of a particular field or the total number of records in the group).

To group your report, follow these steps:

1. Choose Design, Group & Sort to open the Group, Sort, and Total pane.

2. Click Add a Group. Access adds a Group On list to the Group, Sort, and Total pane.

3. Use the Group On list to select the field you want to use as the basis of the grouping.

4. Use the Sort Order list to select a sort order for the groups. (Note that this doesn't sort the records *within* the group. If you want sorting within each group, see Step 12.)

5. Click More to display a list of properties for the field.

6. Use the Group By list to specify how Access creates the groups:

   - To create a group for each unique value in the field, choose By Entire Value (this is the default).

   - If the field is numeric, click a predefined option, such as By 5s or By 100s. Alternatively, click Custom and then use the Interval text box to enter the numeric value to use as the group basis interval. For example, if you enter 20, the records are grouped in intervals of 20 (such as 1–20, 21–40, and so on) according to the values in the field.

   - If the field is text, choose either By First Character or By First Two Characters. Alternatively, click Custom and then use the Characters text box to enter the number of characters to use as the group basis. For example, when you enter 4, the records are grouped according to the first four letters in the field.

   - If the field contains dates or times, choose one of the various predefined grouping options: By Day, By Week, By Month, By Quarter, or By Year. You can also click Custom and then use the By text box and list to set the number of Minutes, Hours, Days, Weeks, Months, Quarters, or Years to use as the grouping.

7. Use the Totals list to choose either With No Totals or to select the field on which you want the totals to display for each group. See "Adding Calculations to a Report," later in this chapter, for more details.

8. Use the With Title control to specify a title, which displays in the group header section.

9. For the group header, choose either With a Header Section or Without a Header Section.

10. For the group footer, choose either With a Footer Section or Without a Footer Section.

11. Use the keep together list to specify if you want Access to keep the group header and footer with the group detail on the same page:

- **Do Not Keep Group Together On One Page**—Choose this item if you don't care about this.

- **Keep Whole Group Together On One Page**—Choose this item if you want Access to display the entire group—the group header, detail (records), and group footer—on the same page. (If this isn't possible, Access ignores this setting.)

- **Keep Header and First Record Together On One Page**—Choose this item if you want Access to display the group header on the same page as the first group record. This prevents the group header from being *orphaned*, or displaying by itself at the bottom of a page.

12. If you want the records sorted within each group, click Add a Sort and then choose a sort field and sort order.

13. Click the Close button (X) to close the Group, Sort, and Total pane.

Figure 15.10 shows a completed Group, Sort, and Total pane that groups the Products by Category report on the CategoryName field. Notice that the Design view includes the group header and group footer sections. (These sections are given the names *FieldName* Header and *FieldName* Footer, where *FieldName* is the name of the field specified in the Group, Sort, and Total pane.)

Figure 15.10
Use the Group, Sort, and Total pane to sort the report records and group the records based on the values in one or more fields.

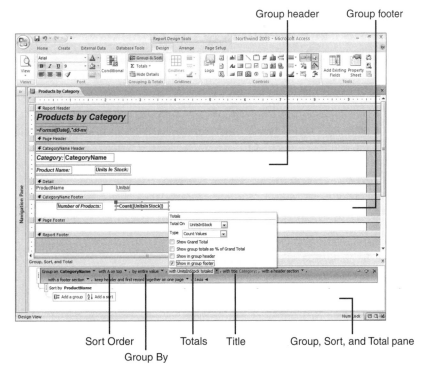

I added a Count Values calculation for the UnitsInStock field, and I activated the Show in group footer check box to place the total in the group footer (see Figure 15.11). Access added the =Count([CategoryName]) calculated control to the footer, and I added the explanatory text box (Number of Products:).

Figure 15.11
A preview of the report shown in Figure 15.10.

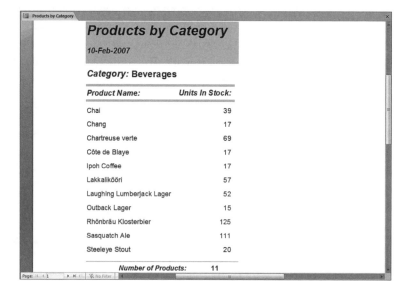

Inserting Page Numbers in the Report

If your report is only a page or two, you don't need to worry too much about adding page numbers for the printout. For longer reports, however, page numbers are a good idea because they make it easier for the reader to keep track of the pages. Follow these steps to add page numbers to the report:

1. Choose Design, Insert Page Number. Access displays the Page Numbers dialog box, shown in Figure 15.12.

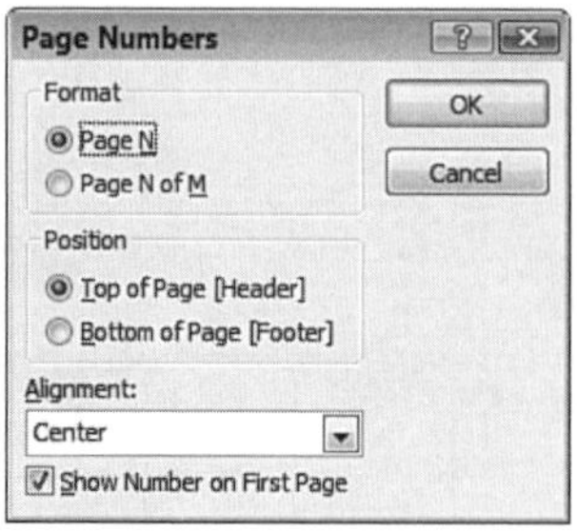

Figure 15.12
Use the Page Numbers dialog box to insert page numbers into your report.

2. In the Format group, activate one of the following options:

   - **Page N**—This option inserts the text Page N on each page, where N is the page number.
   - **Page N of M**—This option inserts the text Page N of M on each page, where N is the page number, and M is the total number of pages in the report.

3. In the Position group, activate one of the following options:

   - **Top Of Page [Header]**—This option inserts the page number control in the Page Header section.
   - **Bottom Of Page [Footer]**—This option inserts the page number control in the Page Footer section.

4. In the Alignment list, select the alignment you want to use for the page number control: Left, Center, or Right. If you select Inside, the page numbers are placed to the left on odd pages and to the right on even pages; if you select Outside, the page numbers are placed to the right on odd pages and to the left on even pages.

5. If you don't want the page numbers to display on the report's first page, deactivate the Show Number on First Page check box.

6. Click OK. Access adds the page number controls to the report

7. Move and format the page number controls, if necessary.

Inserting the Current Date in a Report

When a person reads a report, one thought that's always in the back of (or, often, right in the front of) his mind is, "How current is this data?" Nobody wants to waste time looking at data that's out-of-date or no longer relevant because it's not current. If the report uses date-related data, it helps to include those dates in the report. If that's not possible, the next best thing is to add a label that says something like, "This report printed on," and then, next to it, insert the current date (the Report Header and Report Footer are good locations for the date). This information tells the readers when the report was published so they know at a glance which version of the report they're reading or how old the data is.

Follow these steps to add the date to the report:

1. Choose Design, Date & Time. Access displays the Date and Time dialog box.

2. To add the date, leave the Include Date check box activated and then click an option button to choose the desired date format.

3. To add the time, as well, leave the Include Time check box activated and then click an option button to choose the desired date format.

4. Click OK. Access adds the date and/or time controls to the Report Header.

5. Move and format the date and time controls, if necessary.

15

Access displays the date and time using the Date() and Time() functions to build calculated controls. This means the values of these controls change every time the report is previewed. This doesn't matter for a printed report, but it might not be what you want in a report distributed electronically. In that case, you need to use a label to enter the date and time manually.

Adding Page Breaks after Report Sections

Some reports are nothing but a continuous series of data-filled pages, with no relief in the form of white space anywhere in sight. This can be tiring to read, and it also means your report has no structure. Think of a book that's one continuous chapter or an essay that's one continuous paragraph. To make your reports easier on the eyes and brains of your readers, you should start different sections of the report (such as the report groupings) on a new page. You can configure your report with automatic page breaks by modifying each section's Force New Page property. Here are the steps to follow:

1. Open the report in Design view.
2. Select the section you want to work with.
3. Choose Design, Property Sheet to display the section's property sheet.
4. Display the Format tab.
5. Use the Force New Page list to choose one of the following values:
   - **Before Section**—Choose this option to force a page break before the section. This ensures that the section begins at the top of a new page.
   - **After Section**—Choose this option to force a page break after the section. This ensures that the next section begins at the top of a new page.
   - **Before & After**—Choose this option to force page breaks before and after the section. This ensures that the section appears on a page by itself.
6. Close the property sheet.
7. Print preview the report to confirm that each section is formatted the way you want.

Note, too, that you can also add a page break by hand by inserting a Page Break object in the report. A Page Break object tells the printer to start a new page no matter how much of the current page is filled. In the report Design view, the Controls group includes a Page Break button that enables you to insert a page break anywhere within the report. This capability is useful when you need to break down a particular section into two or more subsections. For example, you can insert a page break into the Report Header section and thus divide the header into two separate pages. You can use the first page for the report title and possibly the company logo, and you can use the second page to provide the reader with an introduction to the report or instructions for interpreting the report data.

Follow these steps to insert a page break into your report:

1. Choose the Design tab.

2. In the Controls group, click the Insert or Remove Page Break button.

3. Click inside the report at the spot where you want the page break to display. Access displays six dots to mark the page break location.

Preventing Widowed Report Records

One of your report goals should be to avoid having single items (such as a record or control) display by itself at the top of a page. An item that displays by itself at the top of a page is called a *widow*, and it's not only a waste of paper (if you're printing the report), but it also makes the report harder to read because chances are that the widowed item belongs with some or all of the items on the previous page. Fortunately, you can force all the elements of a section to display together on one page. You can do this by modifying the section's Keep Together property. Here are the steps to follow:

1. Open the report in Design view.

2. Select the section with which you want to work.

3. Choose Design, Property Sheet to display the section's property sheet.

4. Display the Format tab.

5. In the Keep Together property, choose Yes.

6. Close the property sheet.

7. Print preview the report to verify that each section is formatted the way you want.

Starting Report Sections at the Top of a Row or Column

In the next section, "Creating a Multiple-Column Report," you learn how to configure a report to use multiple columns. You will see that one of the options you can select is called Down, Then Across, which means that the records are printed down each column, and the columns run across the page. You can improve the readability of your report by forcing each new section to start at the top of the next column. (If you use the opposite column configuration—Across, Then Down—where the records are printed across each row, and the rows run down the page, you can then configure sections to always start at the beginning of the next row.) You do this by modifying the section's New Row or Col property. Here are the steps to follow:

1. Open the report in Design view.

2. Select the section with which you want to work.

3. Choose Design, Property Sheet to display the section's property sheet.

4. Display the Format tab.

5. Use the New Row or Col list to choose one of the following values:

- **Before Section**—Choose this option to force the section to begin at the top of a new row or column.

- **After Section**—Choose this option to force the next section to begin at the top of a new row or column.

- **Before & After**—Choose this option to force the section to display in a new row or column by itself.

6. Close the property sheet.

7. Print preview the report to confirm that each section is formatted the way you want.

Creating a Multiple-Column Report

Access reports come in two basic formats: tabular, which uses a datasheet-like layout with fields in columns and records in rows, and columnar, which uses a form-like layout with the fields arranged in a single, vertical column for each record. For this reason, the columnar layout is also called the *single-column* layout.

The single-column format is useful when you have wide fields because each field can use up to the entire width of the page. If your fields aren't that wide, however, the columnar layout is wasteful because you end up with a great deal of whitespace to the right of the fields. The tabular layout can get rid of the whitespace, but it's not as nice looking as the columnar layout.

Instead of compromising, it's possible to get the efficiency of the tabular layout combined with the attractive look of the columnar layout. You do this by creating a *multiple-column* report that takes the basic columnar format and bends the records so that they now snake through two or more columns. (Which is why this is sometimes called a *snaked-column* layout.)

The multiple-column effect displays only when you preview or print the report. In other words, it's not something that you set up within the report Design window (that is, by manipulating the position of the fields and field labels). However, that doesn't mean that you can apply the multiple-column layout to any report. When building your report, bear in mind that the page is going to be divided into columns, and that the width of each column is the width of the page divided by the number of columns, less the left and right page margins and the amount of space you want between each column.

For example, suppose you want two columns a half-inch apart on a page 8.5 inches wide. Assuming the left and right margins are one inch, that leaves six inches for the two columns, or three inches each. Therefore, when building the report, you need to make sure that no part of the report is wider than three inches. (Use the horizontal ruler to monitor the width of the report. If you don't see the ruler, choose the Arrange tab and then click to activate the Ruler toggle button in the Show/Hide group.)

Finally, after your controls are set to the proper width, change the width of the report itself so that it's no wider than the column width you want.

You set up a report to use multiple columns by modifying the Page Setup options. Here are the steps to follow:

1. Choose Page Setup, Page Setup to display the Page Setup dialog box.

2. In the Print Options tab, make note of the left and right margin widths, as given by the values in the Left and Right text boxes. You need these values to calculate the optimal column width.

3. Display the Columns tab.

4. In the Grid Settings group, use the Number of Columns text box to type how many columns you want to use in your report. As shown in Figure 15.13, when you enter a value greater than 1, Access enables the Column Layout group.

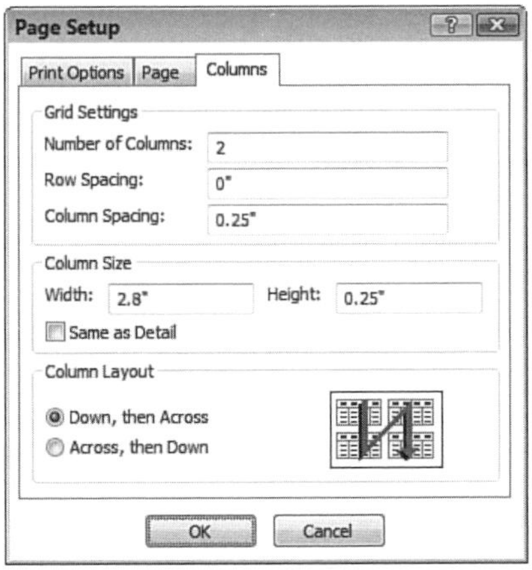

Figure 15.13
Use the Columns tab to set up your report to use multiple columns.

5. If you want to include extra space between each record, type the spacing value (in inches) in the Row Spacing text box.

6. Use the Column Spacing text box to specify the amount of space (in inches) to allow between each column.

7. In the Column Size group, the Width text box should already be set to the width of your report. (Assuming the Same as Detail check box is activated.) If not, use the Width text box to enter the width you want to use for each column. You can also use the Height text box to specify the height of each record.

8. Use the Column Layout group to choose one of the following options:

   • **Down, then Across**—With this option, the records are printed down each column, and the columns run across the page.

   • **Across, then Down**—In this case, the records are printed across each row, and the rows run down the page.

9. Click OK.

10. Preview the report to make sure your columns look the way you want.

Figure 15.14 shows a two-column report with data from the Northwind Customers table. (The Contact Name field combines the First Name and Last Name fields from that table.)

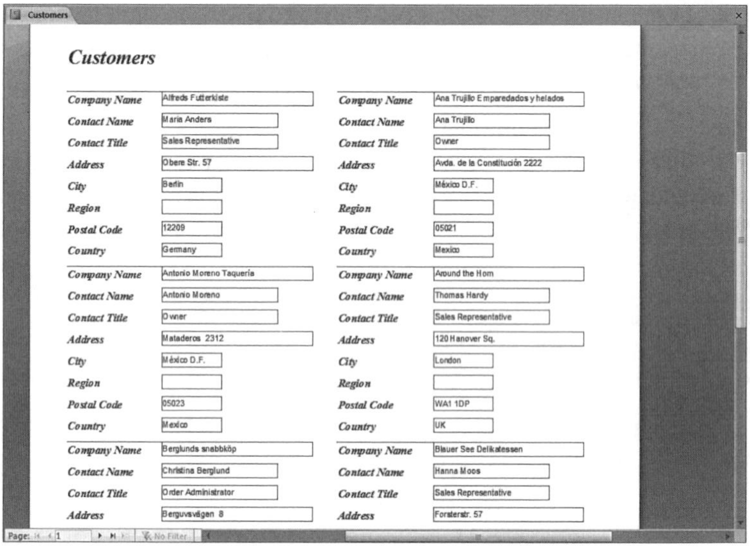

Figure 15.14
An example of a two-column report.

If your columns don't all fit on the page, Access displays the dialog box shown in Figure 15.15.

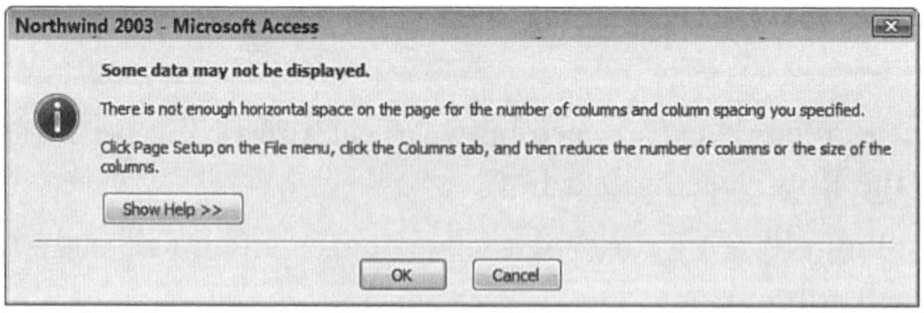

Figure 15.15
Access displays this dialog box if your columns don't all fit the width of the page.

Here are some solutions to try:

- Reduce the number of columns. For example, if three columns won't fit on the page, trying using only two.

- Reduce the width of each column. In the Columns tab of the Page Setup dialog box, reduce the value of the Width text box in the Column Size group.

- Reduce the width of your report by reducing the width of the controls and the report itself. If this prevents a field text box from displaying all its data, try increasing the height of the text box to compensate.

- In the Margins tab of the Page Setup dialog box, reduce the Left and Right values accordingly. The smaller your margins, the more room Access can devote to the columns.

> **CAUTION** ————————————————————————————————
>
> Most printers don't support margins much smaller than about 0.25 inches.

- In the Page tab of the Page Setup dialog box, choose Landscape instead of Portrait.

Creating Mailing Labels

When you examine the output of the report shown in Figure 15.14, you might be struck by the report's uncanny resemblance to a sheet of mailing labels. You are well within your rights to think just that because a multiple-column layout is exactly how you build a mailing label report in Access. After all, what is a sheet of mailing labels but a collection of stick-ons, each with a specific width and height, repeated in a row-and-column format? What is a multiple-column report? Why, it's the same thing: a collection of records, each with a specific width and height, repeated in a row-and-column format.

So if you want to print mailing labels from a table of address data, you need only use that data as the source of a multiple-column report, where each column is configured to precisely match the width and height of your labels. Of course, you also need to take into account the row and column spacing to match the layout on the mailing label sheet, so some tweaking is required.

Rather than go through that, Access provides you with an easier method: the Label Wizard. This wizard takes you step-by-step through the entire label-making process. It supports all the standard mailing label formats, so the tweaking and guesswork are taken out of the process.

Here are the steps to follow to build a set of mailing labels using the Label Wizard:

1. In the Navigation pane, choose the table or query you want to use as the data source for the report.
2. Choose Create, Labels. Access launches the Label Wizard, as shown in Figure 15.16.
3. Use the What label size would you like? list to click the label size you want to use. You can also use the following controls to change the displayed labels:
   - **Unit of Measure**—Click either the English or the Metric option.
   - **Label Type**—Click either the Sheet Feed or the Continuous option.
   - **Filter by manufacturer**—In the drop-down list, click the name of the label manufacturer. (If you don't see the manufacturer listed, choose Avery because many off-brand labels are manufactured to the Avery standard.)

Figure 15.16
Use the initial Label Wizard dialog box to choose the label size you want to use.

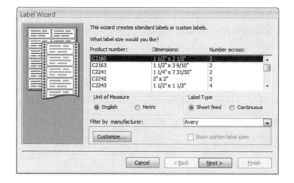

4. Click <u>N</u>ext. The Label Wizard prompts you for font information.

5. Use the Font Name, Font Size, Font Weight, and Text Color controls to choose the font specifics for the label text. You can also choose to italicize and underline the text by activating the Italic and Underline check boxes.

6. Click <u>N</u>ext. The wizard asks you to define the layout of the label.

7. Build the label by using the following techniques (see Figure 15.17 for an example):

   • To add a field, click the field name in the Available Fields list and then click >.

   • To start a new line in the label, move to the end of the current line and then press Enter.

   • To add text to the label, position the cursor where you want the text to display and then type the text.

Figure 15.17
Define the label layout by adding fields, new lines, and text.

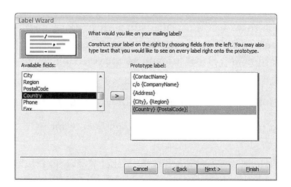

8. Click <u>N</u>ext. The wizard prompts you for the report sort order.

9. Click the field you want to use as the sort basis in the Available Fields list and then click >. If you want to sort on multiple fields, repeat in the sort order you want.

10. Click <u>N</u>ext. The wizard prompts you for a report name.

11. Type the name in the text box provided. You also need to choose your next action:

   - **See The Labels As They Will Look Printed**—Choose this option to display the report in Print Preview.

   - **Modify The Label Design**—Choose this option to display the report in the Design view.

12. Click <u>F</u>inish.

Figure 15.18 shows an example report.

Figure 15.18
A report ready to be printed as mailing labels.

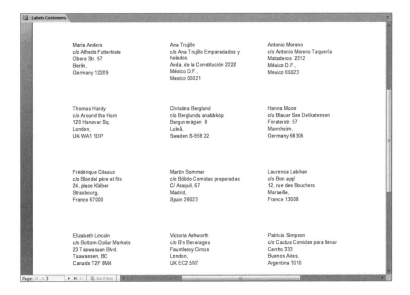

If the Label Wizard does not recognize your mailing labels or if you need a custom job for some other reason, the wizard enables you to design your own custom label size. Here are the steps to follow:

1. In the Navigation pane, choose the table or query you want to use as the data source for the report.

2. Choose Create, Labels to start the Label Wizard.

3. Click Customize. The wizard displays the New Label Size dialog box.

4. Click <u>N</u>ew. The New Label dialog box displays.

3. Use the <u>L</u>abel Name text box to type a name for the custom label.

4. In the Unit of Measure group, click Englis<u>h</u> or <u>M</u>etric.

5. In the Label Type group, click <u>S</u>heet Feed or <u>C</u>ontinuous.

6. In the Orientation group, click <u>P</u>ortrait or Lan<u>d</u>scape.

7. Use the <u>N</u>umber Across text box to type the number of columns of labels you require.

8. Use the text boxes in the Enter Label Measurements In Inches/Centimeters area to specify the label dimensions as well as the margin widths, row and column spacing, and other measurements. Figure 15.19 shows an example.

9. Click OK.

Figure 15.19
Use the New Label dialog box to design a custom label size.

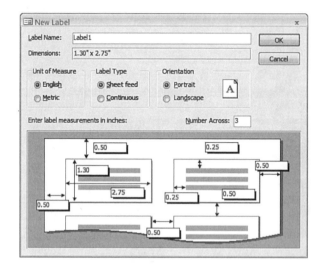

Distributing a Report Snapshot

After you finish your report, you might want to share its contents with other people. You can simply print the report and distribute hard copies, but that seems a bit old fashioned nowadays (not to mention environmentally unfriendly). To distribute an electronic version of the report, Access gives you a number of options (in each case, you need to display the report before proceeding):

- If your readers can use an Access database in a shared network location, choose External Data, More (in the Export group), Access Database, choose the remote database, and then click OK.

- If your readers have access to a SharePoint site, choose External Data, Move to SharePoint.

- To convert your report to the RTF file format that can then be viewed in Word, choose External Data, Word (in the Export group), choose a location, and then click OK.

- To convert your report to a Web page, choose External Data, More (in the Export group), HTML Document, choose a location, and then click OK.

The RTF and HTML file formats are useful if your readers don't have Access and so can't view your report in its native format. Unfortunately, some reports don't convert to these formats perfectly, so your report might not look exactly the way you set it up. If you want to ensure report fidelity, you can convert the report to the Snapshot file format and then ask your readers to view the snapshot file using the Microsoft Snapshot Viewer program, which shows the report exactly as you configured it in Access.

> **NOTE** You can find a link to download the Snapshot Viewer program on the following Microsoft page: support.microsoft.com/kb/175274

Here are the steps to follow to convert your report into a snapshot file:

1. Display the report in Report view.
2. Choose External Data, More (in the Export group), Snapshot Viewer. Access displays the Export - Snapshot Viewer dialog box.
3. Use the File Name text box or the Browse button to choose a location for the snapshot file.
4. If you have the Snapshot Viewer program installed and you want to open the snapshot file in the program after the conversion is complete, click to activate the Open the Destination File after the Export Operation is Complete check box.
5. Click OK. Access converts the report to a snapshot file.
6. Click Close.

With the snapshot file created, you can now distribute it on the network or as an email attachment. For the latter, note that Access gives you a more direct way to email a report snapshot:

1. Display the report in Report view.
2. Choose Office, E-mail. Access displays the Send Object As dialog box.
3. In the Select Output Format list, click Snapshot Format.
4. Click OK. Access converts the report to the snapshot file, and then it opens a new Outlook message window with the file attached.
5. Fill out the message details (recipient address, subject, and so on).
6. Click Send.

From Here

- You can also apply conditional formatting in Excel; **see** "Highlighting Cells Above or Below a Certain Value," **p. 182**.
- To learn how to set up field validation rules, **see** "Validating Data Entry," **p. 365**.

Appendixes

Working with VBA Macros

Office gurus know a secret that's crucial for mastering any or all of the Office applications: There are things you can make a program do that are not available via the program's interface (that is, its Ribbon commands and shortcut keys). To accomplish these extra tricks and techniques, you have to go under the program's hood and use Visual Basic for Applications (VBA), the programming language that comes with the Office suite. You use VBA to build small sets of instructions called scripts, or, more commonly, macros. With these instructions, you can make the program perform multiple tasks in a single operation or, as I mentioned earlier, perform tasks that are not part of the interface.

This book isn't designed to teach you VBA, but it *is* designed to offer you numerous and useful techniques to help you get the most out of Office and get your work done faster and more efficiently. VBA is a big help because you can use it to perform manual tasks that are inordinately time-consuming or downright impossible. As proof, most of the chapters in this book offer a few VBA macros. These procedures show you many techniques for programming the Office applications, but, more importantly, I chose the macros because they are truly useful and time-saving. So, even if you have no desire to learn VBA, you can still implement the macros on your own system to work faster and more efficiently.

In this appendix, you learn how to run existing macros, record program actions as a macro, and the basics of creating your own macros.

> **NOTE** This appendix presents only a minimal introduction to using VBA macros. However, VBA is a relatively easy language to learn and is well worth the effort if you want to create truly custom functions that are designed to suit your needs and solve your Office problems. If you want to take the plunge into VBA programming, may I not-so-humbly suggest my book *VBA for the 2007 Microsoft Office System* (Que Publishing, 2007)?

Activating the Ribbon's Developer Tab

If you run VBA code regularly or create your own VBA code, you can make some coding chores a bit more efficient by displaying the new Developer tab in the Office 2007 Ribbon. This tab gives you one-click access to many VBA-related features, so it's worth displaying. Follow these steps:

1. Choose Office, *Application* Options (where *Application* is the name of the current Office program, such as Word or Excel).

2. In the Popular tab, click to activate the Show Developer Tab in the Ribbon check box.

3. Click OK.

Note that displaying the Developer tab in one Office program displays it in all of them. Figure A.1 shows the Developer tab displayed in Word.

Figure A.1
Display the Developer tab for easier access to some VBA features.

Running a VBA Macro

VBA macros come in two forms:

- **Command macro**—This is code that performs an action that usually has an effect on the program's environment. For example, the macro might insert text into a worksheet cell or change a Word option. In general, you can think of a command macro as being akin to a program menu command.

- **Function macro**—This is code that returns a result. A function often takes one or more values as inputs, manipulates those values in some way, and then sends back the result of those manipulations. In general, you can think of a function macro as being akin to an Excel worksheet function or a Word formula field.

You can run both command and function macros from within other macros and functions, but I ignore that here. Instead, the next few sections show you the techniques you need to use the macro examples provided throughout this book.

Using the Example Code

To use the macros presented in this book, you need to copy the code into a VBA module on your computer. A *module* is an object that you insert into a document. The purpose of a module is to store VBA code, so to work with a module, you need to know how to get to the Visual Basic Editor, which I discuss later (see "Working with the Visual Basic Editor").

Using the Macro Name List

The Macro Name list is a list of your stored command macros. This means that your recorded macros are as little as four mouse clicks away, as you see in the following steps:

A

1. Set up the document so that it's ready to handle the tasks that the macro will run (for example, open a document, move the cursor into position, or select text).

2. Choose Developer, Macros (or choose the View tab and click the top half of the Macros split button; you can also press Alt+F8). Word displays the Macros dialog box (see Figure A.2); in Excel and PowerPoint, it's called the Macro dialog box.

Figure A.2
Use the Macro Name list to select the macro you want to run.

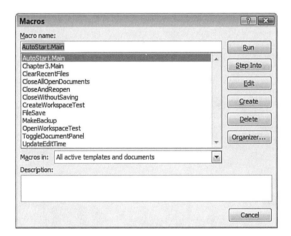

3. (Optional) Use the Macros In list to click the template or document that contains the macro.

4. In the Macro Name list, click the macro you want to run.

5. Click Run. The program runs the macro.

Assigning Shortcut Keys to Word Macros

If you have a macro that you frequently use, even the few mouse clicks required to run the macro from the Macro Name list can seem excessive. A faster alternative is to assign a shortcut key to the macro, which means you can run the macro by pressing the shortcut key.

To assign a shortcut key in Word, follow these steps:

1. You have two ways to get started:
   - If you're recording a macro (see "Recording a VBA Macro," later in this chapter), either choose Developer, Record Macro or choose View, pull down the Macros list, and then choose Record Macro. Fill in the macro details (name, storage location, and description) first, and then click Keyboard. Skip to Step 4.
   - For an existing macro, choose Office, Word Options, click Customize, and then click the Customize button next to the Keyboard Shortcuts text.

2. In the Customize Keyboard dialog box, use the Categories list to click Macros. Word displays your macros in the Macros list.

3. In the Macros list, click the macro you want to work with.

4. Click inside the Press New Shortcut Key box and then press the shortcut key you want to use. One of two things will happen:
   - Word displays Currently Assigned To, followed by [unassigned], as shown in Figure A.3. This means no other command uses the shortcut key, so proceed to Step 5.

Figure A.3
Use Word's Customize Keyboard dialog box to assign a shortcut key to a macro.

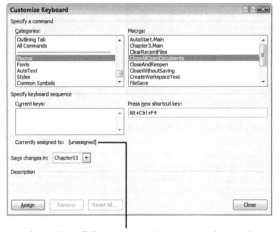

You see [unassigned] if no command uses your shortcut key

- Word displays Currently Assigned To, followed by the name of a command. This means that another Word command (or macro) already uses the shortcut key. Repeat Step 4 until you find an unassigned shortcut key.

> **CAUTION**
>
> It's best to avoid overwriting any of Word's built-in shortcuts because you may use them now or in the future. By using key combinations that include some or all of the Shift, Ctrl, and Alt keys, you can almost always find an unassigned shortcut for your macros. If you have overwritten some Word shortcuts and you'd like to reset them, select Office, Word Options, click the Customize tab, and then click the Customize button to open the Customize Keyboard dialog box. Click Reset All and then click Yes when Word asks you to confirm.

> **TIP**
>
> If you have trouble remembering your keyboard shortcuts, you can get Word to print out a list of them. Choose Office, Print to open the Print dialog box. In the Print What list, click Key Assignments, and then click OK.

5. Click Assign.
6. Click Close.
7. If you opened the Word Options dialog box earlier, click OK.

Assigning Shortcut Keys to Excel Macros

If you want to assign a shortcut key to an Excel macro, you have two ways to get started:

- If you're recording a macro (see "Recording a VBA Macro," later in this chapter), either choose Developer, Record Macro or choose View, pull down the Macros list, and then choose Record Macro. Fill in the macro details (name, storage location, and description) first and then click Keyboard. Skip to Step 4.

- For an existing macro, choose Developer, Macros (you can also choose View, Macros or press Alt+F8) to display the Macro dialog box. Click the macro you want to work with and then click Options to display the Macro Options dialog box shown in Figure A.4.

Figure A.4
Use the Macro Options dialog box to assign a shortcut key to a macro.

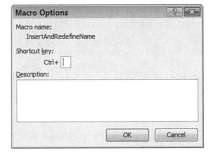

In the Shortcut <u>K</u>ey Ctrl+ text box, type the letter you want to use with Ctrl for the key combination. For example, if you type **e**, you can run the macro by pressing Ctrl+E. Click OK.

Creating a Quick Access Toolbar Button for a Macro

The only problem most people have with assigning shortcut keys to macros is remembering which shortcut runs which macro! The more shortcuts you assign, the harder it gets to remember them and the more likely it is that you'll press an incorrect shortcut key by mistake. What many VBA veterans do is assign just a few shortcut keys to their most frequently used macros, and other macros that they need handy, they assign to the Quick Access toolbar. This is a great way to run oft-used macros because they're only a click away, and you can assign different icons to each macro to help you differentiate them.

Follow these steps in either Word or Excel to create a Quick Access toolbar button for a macro:

1. Click the Customize Quick Access Toolbar button (see Figure A.6) and then choose <u>M</u>ore Commands. The application's Options dialog box displays with the Customize tab displayed.

2. In the <u>C</u>hoose Commands From list, click Macros. A list of your macros displays.

3. Click the macro you want to work with and then click <u>A</u>dd. The program adds the macro to the list of Quick Access toolbar buttons.

4. To change the macro button's icon, click the macro in the list of Quick Access toolbar buttons and then click <u>M</u>odify. The Modify Button dialog box displays, as shown in Figure A.5.

Figure A.5
Use the Modify Button dialog box to assign an icon and display name to your macro button.

5. Use the Symbol list to click the icon you want to use for the macro button.

6. Use the Display name text box to type the name you want to display when you hover the mouse pointer over the button.

7. Click OK.

8. Repeat Steps 3–7 to assign other macros to buttons.

9. Click OK.

Figure A.6 shows a macro button added to Word's Quick Access toolbar.

Macro button   Customize Quick Access Toolbar button

Figure A.6
A macro button added to the Quick Access toolbar.

> **TIP**
>
> In its default position above the Ribbon, the Quick Access toolbar can display only so many buttons. If you want to add a lot of buttons for your macros (or other program commands), move the Quick Access toolbar under the Ribbon. Click the Customize Quick Access Toolbar button and then choose Show Below the Ribbon.

Using a Function Macro

You use functions as part of Excel worksheet formulas or as part of Access expressions that build calculated fields.

In Excel, as with the program's built-in functions, you can either type the function into the formula by hand, or you can use the Insert Function method. Assuming you edit a cell formula, you can enter a VBA function into the formula by hand using the following general format:

```
WorkbookName.xls!FunctionName(arguments)
```

Here, *WorkbookName* is the file name of the workbook that contains the function, *FunctionName* is the name of the function, and *arguments* is the list of values for the arguments accepted by the function.

To use the Insert Function method, follow these steps:

1. Choose Insert, Function to display the Insert Function dialog box.
2. In the Or Select a Category list, click All to make sure that all the VBA functions are included in the Select a Function list.
3. The VBA functions display in the list using the same *WorkbookName.xls!FunctionName* format that I described earlier. Therefore, first look for the workbook name in the list and then select the function you want.
4. Click OK.
5. If the function accepts arguments, enter them and click OK.

In Access, you can enter the function into an expression either by hand or by using the Expression Builder. To insert a function by hand, place the cursor in the query Field cell or form text box and type the function using the following format:

```
FunctionName(arguments)
```

Here, *FunctionName* is the name of the function, and *arguments* is the list of values for the arguments accepted by the function.

To use the Expression Builder, follow these steps:

1. Place the cursor in the query Field cell or form text box.
2. Choose Design, Builder to display the Expression Builder dialog box.
3. In the left list, open the Functions branch.
4. Select the name of your database.
5. In the middle list, select the name of the module that contains your function.
6. In the right list, double-click the function you want to insert. Access inserts the function into the expression.
7. (Optional) Fill in the rest of your expression.
8. Click OK.

Recording a VBA Macro

By far the easiest way to create a command macro is to use the Macro Recorder. With this method, you start the recorder, and then you run through the task you want to automate (including selecting text, running menu commands, and choosing dialog box options). The Recorder translates everything into the appropriate VBA statements and copies those statements to a command macro in a module. You can then use the recorded macro to replay the entire procedure any time you like. This section shows you how to record a command macro in Word and Excel. (The other programs in the Office suite don't have macro recording capabilities.)

Recording a Word Macro

Before getting started, make sure that Word is set up so that it's ready to record. If you want to perform your actions on a specific document, for example, make sure that document is open. Similarly, if you want to record a series of formatting options, select the text you want to work with. Here are the steps to follow to record a macro in Word:

1. Choose Developer, Record Macro (or choose View, pull down the Macros menu and then choose <u>R</u>ecord Macro). The Record Macro dialog box displays, as shown in Figure A.7.

> **TIP** You can also start a recorded macro by clicking the Macro Recording button in the status bar. If you don't see the Macro Recording button, right-click the status bar and then click <u>M</u>acro Recording.

Figure A.7
Use Word's version of the Record Macro dialog box to name and describe your macro.

2. Word proposes a name for the macro (such as Macro1), but you should use the <u>M</u>acro name text box to change the name to something more meaningful. However, you must follow a few naming conventions:

   - No more than 255 characters. (That sounds like a lot, and it is. Because you may occasionally have to type macro names, I recommend keeping the names relatively short to save wear and tear on your typing fingers.)
   - The first character must be a letter or an underscore (_).
   - No spaces or periods are allowed.

> **NOTE**
>
> You saw earlier in this chapter that one way to run a recorded macro is to select it from a list of all your recorded macros. If you create a lot of macros this way, that list will get long in a hurry. Therefore, when naming your recorded macros, make sure you assign names that will make it easy to differentiate one macro from another. Names such as `Macro1` and `Macro2` tell you nothing, but names such as `AdjustWindowSize` and `NewDocumentTasks` are instantly understandable.

3. Use the Store macro in drop-down list to specify where the macro will reside. I recommend keeping the default All Documents (Normal.dotm) option. This saves the macro in the Normal template, which makes it available all the time. (You can also store the macro in any open template, which makes the macro available to any document that uses the template, or in any open document, which makes the macro available only to that document.)

4. Enter an optional description of the macro in the Description text box.

5. Click OK. The application returns you to the document and starts the recorder.

6. Perform the tasks you want to include in the macro. Here are some things to bear in mind during the recording:

   - Word gives you two indications that a recording is in progress: The mouse pointer includes what looks like a cassette tape icon, and the status bar's Record Macro button changes to a blue square.

   - The mouse works only for selecting Ribbon commands and dialog box options. If you need to change the document cursor position or select text, you need to use the keyboard.

   - Because the macro recorder takes note of *everything* you do, be careful not to perform any extraneous keyboard actions or mouse clicks during the recording.

7. When you finish the tasks, choose Developer, Stop Recording (or choose View, pull down the Macros menu, and then choose Stop Recording; you can also click the Macro Recording button in the status bar).

Recording an Excel Macro

Before launching your recording in Excel, make sure the program is set up as required. For example, open the workbook and select the worksheet you want to use during the recording. Here are the steps to follow to record a macro in Excel:

1. Choose Developer, Record Macro (or choose View, pull down the Macros menu, and then choose Record Macro). Figure A.8 shows the Excel version of the Record Macro dialog box that displays.

As in Word, you can also start a recorded macro in Excel by clicking the Macro Recording button in the status bar. If you don't see the Macro Recording button, right-click the status bar and then click Macro Recording.

Figure A.8
Use Excel's Record Macro
dialog box to name and
describe your macro.

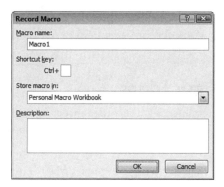

2. Use the Macro name text box to change the name to something memorable or descriptive. (Follow the same naming conventions outlined in the previous section).

3. In Excel, you can use the Shortcut Key: Ctrl+ text box to assign a shortcut key to the macro. Note, however, that this is optional because VBA offers other ways to run your recorded macros (see "Running a VBA Macro," earlier in this chapter).

4. Use the Store macro in drop-down list to specify where the macro will reside. You can store the macro in the current workbook, a new workbook, or in the Personal Macro Workbook. If you use the Personal Macro Workbook, your macros will be available to all your workbooks.

NOTE

Excel's Personal Macro Workbook doesn't exist until you assign at least one recorded macro to it. After you do that, the Personal Macro Workbook (its file name is PERSONAL.XLSB) opens automatically every time you start Excel. This is useful because any macros contained in this file will be available to all your workbooks, which makes them easy to reuse. Note, however, that you don't see the Personal Macro Workbook when you start Excel because the file is hidden. If you want to see this workbook, you have to first unhide it: Choose the View, Unhide command, select Personal in the Unhide dialog box, and then click OK.

5. Enter an optional description of the macro in the Description text box.

6. Click OK. Excel returns you to the workbook and starts recording.

7. Perform the tasks you want to include in the macro. Here are some things to bear in mind during the recording:

- Excel gives you just one indication that a recording is in progress: The status bar's Record Macro button changes to a blue square.
- Unlike Word, Excel makes the mouse available for all actions.
- Because the macro recorder takes note of *everything* you do, be careful not to perform any extraneous keyboard actions or mouse clicks during the recording.

8. When you finish the tasks, choose View, pull down the Macros menu, and then choose Stop Recording (or click the Macro Recording button in status bar).

Working with the Visual Basic Editor

To add existing macro code to a module, edit a recorded macro or build your own macros from scratch, you use the Visual Basic Editor. You have two ways to open the Visual Basic Editor:

- If you want to edit a specific macro, choose Developer, Macros (or choose View and click the top half of the Macro split button; you can also press Alt+F8). In the dialog box, click the macro you want to work with and then click Edit.
- Choose Developer, Visual Basic (or press Alt+F11).

The Visual Basic Editor is a so-called *integrated development environment*, which means it has tools and objects that enable programmers to write and edit VBA code. The Visual Basic Editor is divided into three areas (as shown in Figure A.9):

- **Project Explorer**—This area shows the open VBA projects as well as a hierarchical view of the contents of each project. These contents include the open application objects (worksheets, documents, slides, and so on), any modules that have been created either by recording a macro or by creating one from scratch (explained later), and any user forms that you've built.
- **Properties window**—This area shows the various properties available for whatever object is highlighted in the Project Explorer. The Properties window is divided into two columns. The left column shows you the names of all the properties associated with the object, and the right side shows you the current value of each property. To change the value of a property, click the appropriate box in the right column and then either type in the new value or select it from a drop-down list (the method you use depends on the property).
- **Work area**—This is where the module windows you work with are displayed.

Project Explorer

Insert list   Object list   Procedure list

Figure A.9
The Visual Basic Editor is
a complete program-
ming environment.

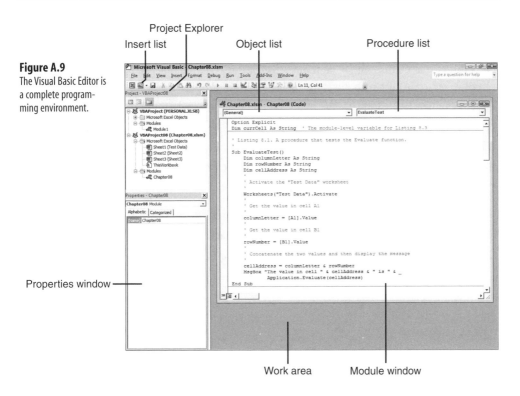

Properties window

Work area   Module window

A

Creating a Module

To create a module, follow these steps:

1. In the Visual Basic Editor, use the Project pane to click the project in which you want to insert the module. For example, if you want to use the Personal Macro Workbook in Excel, click the PERSONAL.XLSB project.

2. Choose Insert, Module or drop down the Insert list (pointed out in Figure A.9) and select Module. The Visual Basic Editor adds a Modules branch (if one doesn't already exist) to the project and opens the module window.

Opening a Module

Later, when you've created modules in various workbooks, you'll need to know how to open the module that contains the code you want. You have two choices:

- Choose Developer, Macros (or choose View and click the top half of the Macro split button; you can also press Alt+F8). In the dialog box, click the macro you want to work with and then click Edit. The program launches the Visual Basic Editor and opens the module containing the macro.

- In the Visual Basic Editor, use the Project window to open the branch of the workbook that contains the module, open that project's Modules branch, and then double-click the name of the module you want to open.

I should also point out that each module window has two drop-down lists under the title bar (refer to Figure A.9):

- **Object list**—This control contains a list of the available objects. Modules don't have objects, so this list contains only (General) for a module window.

- **Procedure list**—This is a list of all the command macros and function macros in the module. Until you add a macro, this list shows only (Declarations).

Running a Command Macro from the Visual Basic Editor

After you create a command macro, you can run it directly from the Visual Basic Editor:

1. Open the module containing the command macro.

2. Place the insertion point anywhere inside the macro.

3. Choose Run, Run Macro. (You can also click the Run Macro toolbar button or press F5.)

Office 2007 Keyboard Shortcuts

B

There are many secrets to computer productivity, and I hope the tricks and techniques you've learned in this book help you achieve new heights of efficiency and speed. However, there's one productivity booster that many people overlook: the efficient use of the keyboard. By efficient, I'm talking about keeping your hands on the keyboard when you're typing. Nothing slows down a typing session like having to constantly move your right (or left) hand over to the mouse to navigate a document, select an object, or run a command. This not only slows you down, but it is also dangerous. Studies have shown that repetitive stress injuries—long thought to be caused by excessive keyboarding—are more often caused by constant use of the mouse. Even that seemingly innocuous movement of pivoting your arm to move from keyboard to mouse and back again is fraught with peril and can cause the painful malady known as mouse elbow.

To help you keep your hands on the keyboard as much as possible, it helps to know how to use the keyboard to perform many everyday chores such as navigating and editing text, selecting data, applying formatting, working with documents and windows, and running program commands. Fortunately, Office 2007 is loaded with hundreds of keyboard tricks and shortcuts that you can take advantage of. This appendix presents a complete list of these keyboard techniques.

General Office 2007 Keyboard Shortcuts

Press	To
Accessing the Ribbon	
Ctrl+F1	Hide or show the Ribbon (the tabs remain in view).
Alt+F	Display the Office menu.
Alt or F10	Move the focus to the active tab. This also displays the KeyTips over the tabs. (Press a KeyTip character to display the associated tab.)
Alt, left arrow	Select the next tab.
Alt, right arrow	Select the previous tab.
Alt, Tab	Select the next command in the active tab.
Alt, Shift+Tab	Select the previous command in the active tab.
Spacebar or Enter	Display the selected gallery or menu.
Editing a Document	
Ctrl+C	Copy the current selection to the Clipboard.
Ctrl+X	Cut the current selection to the Clipboard.
Ctrl+V	Paste the most recently cut or copied selection from the Clipboard.
Ctrl+Alt+V	Open the Paste Special dialog box.
Ctrl+F	Open the Find and Replace dialog box with the Find tab displayed.
Ctrl+H	Open the Find and Replace dialog box with the Replace tab displayed.
Ctrl+K	Open the Insert Hyperlink dialog box.
Ctrl+Y or F4	Redo the most recent action.
Ctrl+Z	Undo the most recent action.
Ctrl+Alt+V	Copy the formatting of the currently selected text or object.
Ctrl+Shift+V	Paste the most recently copied formatting to the selected text or object.
Formatting Text	
Ctrl+B	Apply bold to the selected text.
Ctrl+I	Apply italics to the selected text.
Ctrl+U	Apply underline to the selected text.
Working with Documents	
Ctrl+N	Create a new document.
Ctrl+O or Ctrl+F12	Display the Open dialog box.
Ctrl+P	Print the current document.
Ctrl+S	Save the current document.

B

Press	To
Working with Documents	
Ctrl+F2	Switch between the current view and Print Preview.
Ctrl+F4	Close the current document.
Ctrl+F6	Switch to the next open window.
Ctrl+Shift+F6	Switch to the previous open window.
Ctrl+F10	Maximize the current document window; restore a maximized document window.
F12	Display the Save As dialog box.
General	
F1	Get context-sensitive Help.
F6	Move the focus forward through the available window sections: the current document, the status bar, the Ribbon, open task panes, non-modal dialog boxes (such as Find and Replace), and so on.
Shift+F6	Move the focus backward through the available window sections: the current document, the status bar, the Ribbon, open task panes, non-modal dialog boxes, and so on.
F7	Run the spelling checker.
Alt+F4	Exit the application.
Alt+F8	Display the Macros dialog box.
Alt+Shift+F10	Display the menu associated with a smart tag.
Alt+F11	Switch between the Visual Basic Editor and the application.

Word 2007 Keyboard Shortcuts

Press	To
Navigating a Document	
Ctrl+Right arrow	Move to the next word.
Ctrl+Left arrow	Move to the previous word.
End	Move to the end of the current line.
Home	Move to the start of the current line.
Ctrl+Down arrow	Move to the start of the next paragraph.
Ctrl+Up arrow	Move to the start of the previous paragraph.

continues

Press	To
Navigating a Document	
Ctrl+Alt+Page Down	Move to the end of the window.
Ctrl+Alt+Page Up	Move to the start of the window.
Ctrl+End	Move to the end of the document.
Ctrl+Home	Move to the start of the document.
Ctrl+Alt+Home	Display the Browse by Object window.
Ctrl+Page Down	Move to the next object (based on your selection in the Browse by Object window).
Ctrl+Page Up	Move to the previous object (based on your selection in the Browse by Object window).
Shift+F5 or Ctrl+Alt+Z	Cycle through the four most recently edited locations in the current document.
Ctrl+Shift+F5	Open the Bookmark dialog box.
Selecting Text	
Shift+*navigation key*	Move the cursor as dictated by the *navigation key* (see "Navigating a Document," above) and also extend the current selection to that point.
Ctrl+A	Select the entire document.
F8	Expand the selection to the current word, sentence, paragraph, and then document.
Shift+F8	Collapse the selection to the current paragraph, sentence, and then word.
F8, *character*	Expand the selection from the current cursor position to the next instance of *character* (this is case-sensitive).
Esc	Exit Extend mode (which is activated by pressing F8 or Shift+F8).
Editing Text	
Ctrl+Backspace	Delete from the current cursor position to the beginning of the word.
Ctrl+Delete	Delete from the current cursor position to the end of the word.
Shift+Home, Delete	Delete from the current cursor position to the beginning of the line.
Shift+End, Delete	Delete from the current cursor position to the end of the line.
Ctrl+Shift+Down arrow, Delete	Delete from the current cursor position to the end of the paragraph.

Press	To
Editing Text	
Ctrl+Shift+Up arrow, Delete	Delete from the current cursor position to the beginning of the paragraph.
Alt+Shift+Down arrow	Move the current paragraph down by one paragraph.
Alt+Shift+Up arrow	Move the current paragraph up by one paragraph.
F2	Move the selected text (place the cursor in the new position, and then press Enter).
Shift+F2	Copy the selected text (place the cursor in the new position, and then press Enter).
Ctrl+Alt+Y	Repeat the most recent Find.
Ctrl+G or F5	Open the Find and Replace dialog box with the Go To tab displayed.
Alt+F3	Open the Create New Building Block dialog box.
Ctrl+F3	Cut the selected text to the Spike.
Ctrl+Shift+F3	Paste the text that has been cut to the Spike.
Ctrl+Alt+M	Insert a comment.
Ctrl+Shift+E	Toggle Track Changes on and off.
Alt+Shift+C	Close the Reviewing Pane.
Alt+Shift+I	Mark the selected text as a citation.
Alt+Shift+O	Mark the selected text as a table of contents entry.
Alt+Shift+X	Mark the selected text as an index entry.
Alt+Ctrl+F	Insert a footnote for the selected text.
Alt+Ctrl+D	Insert an endnote for the selected text.
Ctrl+Shift+G	Open the Word Count dialog box.
Formatting Text	
Shift+F1	Display the Reveal Formatting pane.
Shift+F3	Cycle the case of the current word or selection through UPPERCASE, lowercase, and Title Case.
Ctrl+Shift+A	Apply uppercase to the selected text.
Ctrl+Shift+D	Apply double underline to the selected text.
Ctrl+Shift+H	Apply Hidden formatting to the selected text.
Ctrl+Shift+K	Apply small caps to the selected text.

B

continues

Press	To
Formatting Text	
Ctrl+Shift+W	Underline each word in the selected text.
Ctrl+=	Apply subscript to the selected text.
Ctrl++	Apply superscript to the selected text.
Ctrl+Shift+Q	Apply the Symbol font to the selected text.
Ctrl+>	Apply the next highest font size to the selected text.
Ctrl+]	Grow the font size of the selected text by one point.
Ctrl+<	Apply the next lowest font size to the selected text.
Ctrl+[	Shrink the font size of the selected text by one point.
Ctrl+D or Ctrl+Shift+F	Display the Font dialog box with Font selected.
Ctrl+Shift+P	Display the Font dialog box with Size selected.
Ctrl+Shift+N	Apply the Normal style to the selected text.
Alt+Ctrl+1	Apply the Heading 1 style to the selected text.
Alt+Ctrl+2	Apply the Heading 2 style to the selected text.
Alt+Ctrl+3	Apply the Heading 3 style to the selected text.
Ctrl+Shift+S	Display the Apply Styles task pane.
Ctrl+Alt+Shift+S	Display the Styles task pane.
Ctrl+L	Apply Align Left to the selected text.
Ctrl+E	Apply Center to the selected text.
Ctrl+R	Apply Align Right to the selected text.
Ctrl+J	Apply Justify to the selected text.
Ctrl+T	Increase the hanging indent of the selected text.
Ctrl+Shift+T	Decrease the hanging indent of the selected text.
Ctrl+M	Increase the indent of the selected text.
Ctrl+Shift+M	Decrease the indent of the selected text.
Ctrl+Shift+L	Apply bullets to the selected text.
Ctrl+0	Add or remove one line space prior to the current paragraph.
Ctrl+1	Set the paragraph line spacing to 1 for the selected text.
Ctrl+5	Set the paragraph line spacing to 1.5 for the selected text.
Ctrl+2	Set the paragraph line spacing to 2 for the selected text.
Ctrl+*	Show/Hide ¶ (formatting symbols).
Ctrl+Space or Ctrl+Shift+Z	Clear the character formatting of the selected text.
Ctrl+Q	Clear the paragraph formatting of the selected text.

B

Press	To
Creating Borders	
---+Enter	Create a thin border.
___+Enter	Create a thick border.
===+Enter	Create a double border.
###+Enter	Create a triple border (two thin, one thick).
~~+Enter	Create a wavy border.
***+Enter	Create a dotted border.
Inserting Symbols	
Shift+Enter	Insert a line break.
Ctrl+Enter	Insert a page break.
Ctrl+Shift+Enter	Insert a column break.
Ctrl+Alt+- (numeric keypad)	Insert an em dash (—).
Ctrl+- (numeric keypad)	Insert an en dash (–).
Ctrl+-	Insert an optional hyphen.
Ctrl+Shift+-	Insert a nonbreaking hyphen.
Ctrl+Shift+Spacebar	Insert a nonbreaking space.
Ctrl+Alt+C	Insert a copyright symbol (©).
Ctrl+Alt+E	Insert a euro symbol ( ).
Ctrl+Alt+R	Insert a registered trademark symbol (®).
Ctrl+Alt+T	Insert a trademark symbol (™).
Ctrl+Alt+. (period)	Insert an ellipsis (…).
Ctrl+Alt+Shift+?	Insert an inverted question mark (¿).
Ctrl+Alt+Shift+!	Insert an inverted exclamation point (¡).
Ctrl+`,`	Insert a single opening quotation mark.
Ctrl+','	Insert a single closing quotation mark.
Ctrl+`,Shift+`	Insert a double opening quotation mark.
Ctrl+', Shift+'	Insert a double closing quotation mark.
Ctrl+/, C	Insert a cents sign (¢).
Ctrl+@, Spacebar	Insert a degrees symbol (°).

continues

B

Press	To
Changing the View	
Ctrl+Alt+N	Switch to Draft view.
Ctrl+Alt+O	Switch to Outline view.
Ctrl+Alt+P	Switch to Print Layout view.
Ctrl+Alt+I	Switch between the current view and Print Preview.
Ctrl+Alt+S	Display the split bar for the current document window (use the up and down arrow keys to position the split bar and then press Enter).
Alt+Shift+C	Remove the split bar from the current document.
Working in Outline View	
Alt+Shift+Left arrow	Promote the current paragraph.
Alt+Shift+Right arrow	Demote the current paragraph.
Ctrl+Shift+N	Demote the current paragraph to body text.
Alt+Shift+Up arrow	Move the selected text up.
Alt+Shift+Down arrow	Move the selected text down.
Alt+Shift+Plus sign	Expand the text under a heading.
Alt+Shift+Minus sign	Collapse the text under a heading.
Alt+Shift+A	Expand or collapse all text or headings.
/ (numeric keypad)	Hide or display character formatting.
Alt+Shift+L	Show the first line of body text or all body text.
Alt+Shift+1	Show all headings with the Heading 1 style.
Alt+Shift+n	Show all headings up to Heading n.
Ctrl+Tab	Insert a tab character.
Working with Fields	
Alt+Shift+D	Insert a DATE field.
Alt+Shift+P	Insert a PAGE field.
Alt+Shift+T	Insert a TIME field.
Ctrl+Alt+L	Insert a LISTNUM field.
F9	Update the selected field or fields.
Ctrl+F9	Begin a new field.
Shift+F9	Display the code for the selected field.
Alt+F9	Display the codes for all the document's fields.

Press	To
Working with Fields	
Alt+Shift+F9	Activate a GOTOBUTTON or MACROBUTTON field.
F11	Go to the next field.
Shift+F11	Go to the previous field.
Ctrl+F11	Lock the selected field to prevent it from being updated.
Ctrl+Shift+F11	Unlock the selected field.
Ctrl+Shift+F9	Convert the selected field's result to text.

Excel 2007 Keyboard Shortcuts

Press	To
Navigating a Worksheet	
Arrow keys	Move left, right, up, or down one cell.
Home	Move to the beginning of the row.
Page Down	Move down one screen.
Page Up	Move up one screen.
Alt+Page Down	Move one screen to the right.
Alt+Page Up	Move one screen to the left.
Ctrl+Home	Move to the beginning of the worksheet.
Ctrl+End	Move to the bottom, right corner of the used portion of the worksheet.
Ctrl+arrow keys	Move in the direction of the arrow to the next nonblank cell if the current cell is blank or to the last nonblank cell if the current cell is nonblank.
Ctrl+Backspace	Scroll the worksheet to bring the active cell of the current selection into view.
F5 or Ctrl+G	Open the Go To dialog box.
Ctrl+Page Up	Move to the previous worksheet.
Ctrl+Page Down	Move to the next worksheet.
Selecting Data	
Shift+*navigation key*	Move the active cell as dictated by the *navigation key* (see "Navigating a Worksheet") and also extend the current selection to that point.
Ctrl+*	Select the rectangular area that includes every cell adjacent to the current cell.

continues

B

Press	To
Selecting Data	
Ctrl+Spacebar	Select the entire column (or columns) that contains the active cell (or cells).
Shift+Spacebar	Select the entire row (or rows) that contains the active cell (or cells).
F8	Toggle extend mode on and off. (When extend mode is on, use the navigation keys to extend the selection.)
Shift+F8	Toggle add mode on and off. (When add mode is on, select a cell or range to add it to the current selection.)
Ctrl+Shift+O	Select all the cells in the current worksheet that contain comments.
Ctrl+/	Select the array containing the active cell.
Ctrl+\	Select the cells that don't match the active cell in the current horizontal selection.
Ctrl+I	Select the cells that don't match the active cell in the current vertical selection.
Ctrl+[	Select the cells directly referenced by the formula in the active cell.
Ctrl+{	Select the cells directly or indirectly referenced by the formula in the active cell.
Ctrl+]	Select the cells with formulas that directly reference the active cell.
Ctrl+}	Select the cells with formulas that directly or indirectly reference the active cell.
Ctrl+A	Select the rectangular area that includes every cell adjacent to the active cell. Press Ctrl+A again to select the entire worksheet.
Moving the Active Cell in a Selection	
Enter	Move the active cell down rows and left-to-right across columns.
Shift+Enter	Move the active cell up rows and right-to-left across columns.
Tab	Move the active cell left-to-right across columns and down rows.
Shift+Tab	Move the active cell right-to-left across columns and up rows.
Ctrl+.	Move the active cell clockwise from corner to corner.
Ctrl+Alt+right arrow	Move the active cell to the next noncontiguous selection to the right.
Ctrl+Alt+left arrow	Move the active cell to the next noncontiguous selection to the left.
Editing a Worksheet	
F2	Edit the active cell.
Shift+F2	Insert or edit a comment in the active cell.
Alt+=	Enter an AutoSum formula into the current cell.

B

Press	To
Editing a Worksheet	
Alt+Enter	Insert a carriage return in a cell formatted with wrapped text.
Ctrl+Enter	Fill the selected cells with the contents of the Formula Bar.
Ctrl+Shift+Enter	Enter the contents of the Formula Bar into the current cell as an array formula.
Ctrl+Shift+U	Toggle the expanded version of the Formula Bar on and off.
Ctrl+`	Toggle the worksheet between showing formulas and cell values.
Ctrl++	Insert an entire row or column before the currently selected row or column.
Ctrl+−	Delete the currently selected row or column.
Ctrl+;	Insert the current date.
Ctrl+:	Insert the current time.
Ctrl+'	Copy the contents from the cell directly above the current cell.
Ctrl+"	Copy the value of the cell directly above the current cell.
Ctrl+<	Copy the contents from the cell directly above the current cell and adjust cell references.
Ctrl+>	Copy the contents from the cell directly to the left of the current cell and adjust cell references.
Ctrl+A	Open the Function Arguments for the current function (place the cursor to the right of the function name before pressing Ctrl+A).
Ctrl+Shift+A	Insert a function's arguments into the current cell (place the cursor to the right of the function name before pressing Ctrl+Shift+A).
Ctrl+D	Fill the contents and formatting of the topmost cell in the current vertical selection down to the rest of the cells in the selection.
Ctrl+R	Fill the contents and formatting of the leftmost cell in the current horizontal selection right to the rest of the cells in the selection.
Ctrl+T	Open the Create Table dialog box.
F3	Open the Paste Names dialog box.
Shift+F3	Open the Insert Function dialog box.
Ctrl+Shift+F3	Open the Create Names from Selection dialog box.
Shift+F11	Insert a new worksheet.
F11	Insert a new chart sheet and create a chart from the current selection.

B

continues

Press	To
Formatting Text	
Ctrl+1	Open the Format Cells dialog box with the most recently used tab displayed.
Ctrl+5	Apply strikethrough to the current selection.
Ctrl+6	Toggle objects on and off.
Ctrl+8	Toggle outlining symbols on and off.
Ctrl+9	Hide the row or rows containing the current selection.
Ctrl+(	Unhide any rows that lie in the current selection.
Ctrl+0	Hide the column or columns containing the current selection.
Ctrl+)	Unhide any columns that lie within the current selection.
Ctrl+&	Apply an outline border to the selection.
Ctrl+_	Remove an outline border from the selection.
Alt+'	Open the Style dialog box.
Alt+Shift+right arrow	Group the selected rows or columns for an outline.
Alt+Shift+left arrow	Ungroup the selected rows or columns for an outline.
Ctrl+Shift+F	Open the Format Cells dialog box with the Font tab displayed.
Ctrl+Shift+D	Apply double underline to the current selection.
Ctrl+5	Apply strikethrough to the current selection.
Ctrl+~	Apply the General format to the current selection.
Ctrl+!	Apply the Number format (two decimal places; using thousands separator) to the current selection.
Ctrl+$	Apply the Currency format (two decimal places; using dollar sign; negative numbers surrounded by parentheses) to the current selection.
Ctrl+%	Apply the Percentage format (zero decimal places) to the current selection.
Ctrl+^	Apply the Scientific format (two decimal places) to the current selection.
Ctrl+#	Apply the Date format (d-mmm-yy) to the current selection.
Ctrl+@	Apply the Time format (h:mm AM/PM) to the current selection.
Working with Workbooks and Windows	
F9	Recalculate all open workbooks.
Shift+F9	Recalculate the active worksheet.

Press	To
Working with Workbooks and Windows	
Ctrl+Alt+Shift+F9	Recalculate all open workbooks, even formulas that are unchanged since the previous calculation.
Ctrl+F9	Minimize the current window.
Ctrl+F5	Restore the current window.

PowerPoint 2007 Keyboard Shortcuts

Press	To
Navigating a Slide	
Ctrl+Right arrow	Move to the next word.
Ctrl+Left arrow	Move to the previous word.
End	Move to the end of the current line.
Home	Move to the start of the current line.
Ctrl+Down arrow	Move to the start of the next paragraph.
Ctrl+Up arrow	Move to the start of the previous paragraph.
Ctrl+End	Move to the end of the current placeholder.
Ctrl+Home	Move to the start of the current placeholder.
Ctrl+Enter	Move to the next placeholder. If the cursor is in the current slide's last placeholder, pressing Ctrl+Enter inserts a new slide with the same layout as the current slide.
Selecting Data	
Shift+*navigation key*	Move the cursor as dictated by the *navigation key* (see "Navigating a Slide") and also extends the current selection to that point.
Tab	Select the next slide placeholder (another object on the slide must first be selected).
Shift+Tab	Select the previous slide placeholder (another object on the slide must first be selected).
Enter	Select all the text in a placeholder when the placeholder is selected.
Esc	Select a placeholder when the cursor is inside the placeholder.
Ctrl+A (placeholder)	Select all the text in a placeholder when the cursor is inside that placeholder.
Ctrl+A (Slides tab)	Select all the objects in the presentation.

continues

Press	To
Selecting Data	
Ctrl+A (Outline tab)	Select all the text in the presentation.
Ctrl+A (Slide Sorter)	Select all the slides in the presentation.
Formatting Text	
Shift+F3	Cycle the case of the current word or selection through UPPERCASE, lowercase, and Title Case.
Ctrl+=	Apply subscript to the selected text.
Ctrl++	Apply superscript to the selected text.
Ctrl+>	Apply the next highest font size to the selected text.
Ctrl+]	Grow the font size of the selected text by one point.
Ctrl+<	Apply the next lowest font size to the selected text.
Ctrl+[	Shrink the font size of the selected text by one point.
Ctrl+Shift+F	Display the Font dialog box with Font selected.
Ctrl+L	Apply Align Left to the selected text.
Ctrl+E	Apply Center to the selected text.
Ctrl+R	Apply Align Right to the selected text.
Ctrl+J	Apply Justify to the selected text.
Ctrl+Space or Ctrl+Shift+Z	Clear the character formatting of the selected text.
Editing a Presentation	
Tab	Demote the current paragraph.
Shift+Tab	Promote the current paragraph.
Alt+Shift+up arrow	Move the current paragraph up.
Alt+Shift+down arrow	Move the current paragraph down.
Ctrl+D	Duplicate the current object.
Ctrl+M	Insert a new slide using the default layout.
Ctrl+Shift+M	Insert a new slide using the same layout as the most recently inserted slide.
Controlling the Outline	
Alt+Shift+1	Show only the slide titles.
Alt+Shift+A	Show all outline text.
Alt+Shift++	Expand the current outline item.
Alt+Shift+–	Collapse the current outline item.

B

Press	To
Changing the View	
Alt+F9	Toggle the drawing guides on and off.
Shift+F9	Toggle the grid on and off.
F5	Switch to Slide Show view and start the current presentation from the first slide.
Controlling a Slide Show	
N	Advance to the next slide or run the next animation. PowerPoint also supports the following keys for this task: Spacebar, Enter, right arrow, down arrow, or Page Down.
P	Return to the previous slide or reverse the most recent animation. PowerPoint also supports the following keys for this task: Backspace, left arrow, up arrow, or Page Up.
n, Enter	Jump to slide number *n*.
S or +	Pause or resume an automatic slide show.
B or .	Toggle the black screen on and off.
W or ,	Toggle the white screen on and off.
A	Toggle the mouse pointer and slide show navigation tools on and off.
Ctrl+A	Change the mouse pointer to an arrow if the mouse is currently displayed as a pen or eraser.
Ctrl+P	Change the mouse pointer to a pen.
E	Erase ink annotations.
H	Display the next slide, if that slide is hidden.
Ctrl+T	Display the Windows taskbar.
Esc	End the slide show. PowerPoint also ends the slide show if you press hyphen [-] or Ctrl+Break.

Outlook 2007 Keyboard Shortcuts

Press	To
Switching Folders	
Ctrl+1	Switch to the Mail folder.
Ctrl+Shift+I	Switch to the Inbox in the Mail folder.
Ctrl+Shift+O	Switch to the Outbox in the Mail folder.

continues

Press	To
Switching Folders	
Ctrl+2	Switch to the Calendar folder.
Ctrl+3	Switch to the Contacts folder.
Ctrl+4	Switch to the Tasks folder.
Ctrl+5	Switch to the Notes folder.
Ctrl+6	Switch to the Folder List.
Ctrl+7	Switch to the Shortcuts folder.
Ctrl+8	Switch to the Journal folder.
Ctrl+Y	Open the Go to Folder dialog box.
Creating New Items	
Ctrl+N	Create a new item in the current folder.
Ctrl+Shift+A	Create a new appointment.
Ctrl+Shift+C	Create a new contact.
Ctrl+Shift+E	Create a new folder.
Ctrl+Shift+J	Create a new journal entry.
Ctrl+Shift+K	Create a new task.
Ctrl+Shift+L	Create a new distribution list.
Ctrl+Shift+M	Create a new e-mail message.
Ctrl+Shift+N	Create a new note
Ctrl+Shift+P	Create a new search folder.
Ctrl+Shift+Q	Create a new meeting request.
Ctrl+Shift+S	Create a new post in the current mail folder.
Ctrl+Shift+T	Display the Choose InfoPath Form dialog box.
Ctrl+Shift+U	Create a new task request.
Ctrl+Shift+X	Create a new Internet fax.
Working with E-mail Messages	
Enter	Open the current message.
Alt+down arrow	Display the next message (in the mail folder).
Alt+up arrow	Display the previous message (in the mail folder).
Ctrl+> or Ctrl+.	Display the next message (with the current message open in a window).
Ctrl+< or Ctrl+,	Display the previous message (with the current message open in a window).
Ctrl+< or Ctrl+,	Display the previous message (with the current message open in a window).

B

Press	To
Working with E-mail Messages	
Spacebar	Display the next screen of message text in the Reading pane.
Shift+Spacebar	Display the previous screen of message text in the Reading pane.
Ctrl+D	Delete the current message.
Ctrl+F	Forward the current message.
Ctrl+Alt+F	Forward the current message as an attachment.
Ctrl+R	Reply to the sender of the current message.
Ctrl+Shift+R	Reply to the sender and all recipients of the current message.
Ctrl+Alt+J	Mark a message as not junk (in the Junk E-mail folder).
Ctrl+Q	Mark the current message as read.
Ctrl+U	Mark the current message as unread.
Ctrl+Shift+G	Flag the current message for follow-up.
Insert	Apply a Quick Flag to the current message.
Ctrl+Shift+V	Move the current message to another folder.
Ctrl+Shift+W	Select the Information bar and display its list of commands.
Ctrl+A	Select all the messages in the current folder.
F9	Send and receive messages on all e-mail accounts.
Ctrl+Alt+S	Open the Send/Receive Groups dialog box.
Ctrl+Alt+M	Mark the current message header for downloading.
Ctrl+Alt+U	Unmark all message headers selected for downloading.
Ctrl+K	Check the validity of addresses (when composing a new mail message).
Alt+S	Send the message (when composing a new mail message).
Working with Appointments	
Ctrl+<	Move to the previous appointment.
Ctrl+>	Move to the next appointment.
Ctrl+Alt+1	Switch to Day view.
Ctrl+Alt+2	Switch to Work Week view.
Ctrl+Alt+3	Switch to Week view.
Ctrl+Alt+4	Switch to Month view.
Ctrl+G	Open the Go To Date dialog box.
Ctrl+G	Set the appointment recurrence (when an appointment window is open)

continues

Press	To
Working with Appointments	
Ctrl+*n*	Display *n* days in the calendar (where *n* is a number between 0 and 9; use 0 to display 10 days).
Ctrl+right arrow	Move to the next day.
Ctrl+left arrow	Move to the previous day.
Alt+down arrow	Move to the same day in the next week.
Alt+up arrow	Move to the same day in the previous week.
Alt+Page Down	Move to the same day in the next month.
Alt+Page Up	Move to the same day in the previous month.
Alt+Home	Move to the start of the current week.
Alt+End	Move to the end of the current week.
Working with Contacts	
Shift+*character*	Move to the first contact with a name that begins with *character* (you must be in a table or list view).
Ctrl+F	Send the current contact in Outlook format via e-mail.
Ctrl+Shift+D	Open the New Call dialog box.
Ctrl+Shift+X	Display the current contact's Web site.
F11	Activate the Search Address Books text box.
Alt+D	Open the Check Address dialog box (in a contact window).
Alt+Shift+1	Display the contact's main e-mail address (in a contact window).
Alt+Shift+2	Display the contact's second e-mail address (in a contact window).
Alt+Shift+3	Display the contact's third e-mail address (in a contact window).
Searching	
Ctrl+E or F3	Activate the Instant Search box.
Ctrl+Alt+A	Search all items in the current folder.
Ctrl+Alt+K	Run a Windows desktop search.
Ctrl+Alt+W	Toggle the Query Builder on and off.
Ctrl+Shift+F	Open the Advanced Find dialog box.
Esc	Clear the search results.

Press	To
Miscellaneous	
Alt+F1	Cycle the Navigation pane between on, minimized, and off.
Alt+F2	Cycle the To-Do Bar between on, minimized, and off.
Ctrl+Shift+F8	Display the Address Book window.
Ctrl+Shift+Y	Copy the current item to another folder.

Access 2007 Keyboard Shortcuts

Press	To
Using the Navigation Pane	
Down arrow	Move to the next object.
Up arrow	Move the previous object.
End	Move to the last object.
Home	Move to the first object.
Enter	Open the selected object.
Ctrl+Enter	Open the selected object in Design view.
F2	Rename the selected object.
F11	Hide or show the Navigation pane.
Navigating in Datasheet View	
Tab or right arrow	Move to the next field to the right, or to the first field of the next record if you're in the last field of a record.
Shift+Tab or left arrow	Move to the previous field to the left, or to the last field (the Add New Field column) of the previous record if you're in the first field of a record.
Ctrl+Right arrow	Move to the next word in the current field if the cursor is in the field.
Ctrl+Left arrow	Move to the previous word in the current field if the cursor is in the field.
Home	Move to the first field or move to the beginning of the current field if the cursor is in the field.
End	Move to the last field (Add New Field) or move to the end of the current field if the cursor is in the field.
Up arrow	Move to the current field in the previous record.
Down arrow	Move to the current field in the next record.

continues

Press	To

Navigating in Datasheet View

Press	To
Ctrl+Up arrow	Move to the current field in the first record.
Ctrl+Down arrow	Move to the current field in the last record.
Ctrl+Home	Move to the first field of the first record.
Ctrl+End	Move to the last field of the last record.
Alt+F5	Activate the Record Number box. To navigate to a specific record, type the record number and press Enter.
Ctrl+Shift+Down arrow	Display the subdatasheet associated with the current record.
Ctrl+Shift+Up arrow	Hide the subdatasheet associated with the current record.

Selecting Data in Datasheet View

Press	To
F8	Extend the selection to the current word, all the text in the current field, the current field, the current record, and then all records.
Shift+F8	Collapse the selection to the current record, the text in the current records, and then the current word.
Shift+arrow keys	Extend the current selection in the arrow key direction.
Shift+Spacebar	Select the current record. (Press Shift+Spacebar again to select the first field in the current record.)
Ctrl+Spacebar	Select the current field. (Press Ctrl+Spacebar again to select the first item in the current field.)
Ctrl+Shift+F8	Enter Move mode, which enables you to move the selected column left or right by pressing left arrow or right arrow. Press Esc to exit Move mode.
Ctrl+A	Select all records.

Editing Data in Datasheet View

Press	To
F2	Edit the current cell.
Shift+F2	Display the contents of the current field in the Zoom dialog box.
F9	Refresh the contents of a lookup field.
Ctrl+Alt+Spacebar	Insert the default value for the field.
Ctrl+;	Insert the current date.
Ctrl+:	Insert the current time.
Ctrl+'	Copy the contents from the field directly above the current field.
Ctrl++	Add a new record.
Ctrl+−	Delete the current record.
Ctrl+Enter	Start a new line in a multiline field.

B

Press	To
Editing Data in Datasheet View	
Shift+Enter	Save changes to the current record.
Esc	Undo the changes in the current field. Press Esc again to undo all changes to the current record.
Navigating in Form View	
Tab or right arrow	Move to the next field to the right or to the first field of the next record if you're in the last field of a record.
Shift+Tab or left arrow	Move to the previous field to the left or to the last field of the previous record if you're in the first field of a record.
Ctrl+Right arrow	Move to the next word in the current field if the cursor is in the field.
Ctrl+Left arrow	Move to the previous word in the current field if the cursor is in the field.
Home	Move to the first field or move to the beginning of the current field if the cursor is in the field.
End	Move to the last field or move to the end of the current field if the cursor is in the field.
Ctrl+Up arrow	Move to the current field in the first record.
Ctrl+Down arrow	Move to the current field in the last record.
Ctrl+Page Up	Move to the current field in the previous record.
Ctrl+Page Down	Move to the current field in the next record.
Ctrl+Home	Move to the first field of the first record.
Ctrl+End	Move to the last field of the last record.
Alt+F5	Activate the Record Number box. To navigate to a specific record, type the record number and press Enter.
Working in Design View	
F4 or Alt+Enter	Toggle the Property Sheet pane for the current object on and off.
F5	Switch to Form view (from the form Design view).
F7	Display the Choose Builder dialog box. If the object already has code associated with it, pressing F7 displays the code.
Alt+F8	Toggle the Field List pane on and off.
Arrow keys	Move the selected control in the arrow key direction.
Ctrl+arrow keys	Move the selected control one pixel in the arrow key direction.
Shift+right arrow	Increase the width of the selected control.

continues

Press	To
Working in Design View	
Shift+down arrow	Increase the height of the selected control.
Shift+left arrow	Decrease the width of the selected control.
Shift+up arrow	Decrease the height of the selected control.

B

INDEX